KV-251-593

MULTILATERALISM IN THE 21ST CENTURY

This volume focuses on multilateralism in the twenty-first century and examines how, and how effectively, the European Union delivers on its commitment to effective multilateralism. Presenting results generated by MERCURY, an EU research programme into multilateralism, this book addresses a central research question: does Europe deliver on its commitment to effective multilateralism?

Globalisation has created powerful new incentives for states to cooperate and generated renewed interest in multilateralism. While a large body of work exists on multilateralism as a concept, it continues to be ill defined and poorly understood. This book sheds new light on twenty-first-century multilateralism by exploring conceptual approaches as well as generating innovative, empirical knowledge on its practice.

Research on EU external relations has increasingly focused on the concept of 'effective multilateralism'. Yet, the application of this concept as a guiding principle of EU foreign policy in non-security policy areas has rarely been examined. This book explores whether the EU is pursuing effective multilateralism in specific issue areas, including trade, climate change and conflict resolution, and distinct geographical and institutional settings, both internal to the EU and in specified regions, international organisations (IOs) and bilateral partnerships. Our contributors offer evidence-based, actionable policy lessons from Europe's experience in promoting multilateralism.

Multilateralism in the 21st Century will be of interest to students and scholars of international relations, international organisations, and European Union politics and foreign policy.

Caroline Bouchard's research focuses on the EU at the United Nations and international human rights negotiations. She has held Research and Teaching Fellowships at the University of Edinburgh, UK.

John Peterson is Professor of International Politics at the University of Edinburgh, UK.

Nathalie Tocci is D

University of Edinburgh

30150   027008595

MULTILATERALISM IN THE 21ST CENTURY

Europe's quest for effectiveness

Edited by Caroline Bouchard, John Peterson and Nathalie Tocci

Routledge
Taylor & Francis Group

LONDON AND NEW YORK

EDINBURGH UNIVERSITY LIBRARY
WITHDRAWN
EX BIBL UNIV. EDINBURGENSI

First published 2014
by Routledge
2 Park Square Milton Park Abingdon Oxon OX14 4RN

Simultaneously published in the USA and Canada
by Routledge
711 Third Avenue, New York, NY 10017

Routledge is an imprint of the Taylor & Francis Group, an informa business

© 2013 Caroline Bouchard, John Peterson and Nathalie Tocci for selection and editorial matter;
individual contributors their contribution.

Trademark notice: Product or corporate names may be trademarks or registered trademarks, and are used
only for identification and explanation without intent to infringe.

The right of the editors to be identified as the authors of the editorial material, and of the authors for
their individual chapters, has been asserted in accordance with sections 77 and 78 of the Copyright,
Designs and Patents Act 1988.

All rights reserved. No part of this book may be reprinted or reproduced or utilised in any form or by
any electronic, mechanical, or other means, now known or hereafter invented, including photocopying
and recording, or in any information storage or retrieval system, without permission in writing from
the publishers.

British Library Cataloguing in Publication Data

A catalogue record for this book is available from the British Library

Library of Congress Cataloging in Publication Data
Multilateralism in the 21st century : Europe's quest for effectiveness / edited by Caroline Bouchard,
John Peterson and Nathalie Tocci.
    pages cm
    Includes bibliographical references and index.
    1. European cooperation. 2. Europe–Foreign relations. 3. European Union countries–Foreign
    relations. 4. International relations. 5. Security, International. I. Bouchard, Caroline.
    JZ1570.M85 2013
    341.242'2–dc23

                                                        2013003209

ISBN: 978-0-415-52003-4 (hbk)
ISBN: 978-0-415-52004-1 (pbk)
ISBN: 978-0-203-71949-7 (ebk)

Printed and bound in Great Britain by
CPI Group (UK) Ltd, Croydon, CR0 4YY

CONTENTS

FIGURES AND TABLES

Figures

Tables

CONTRIBUTORS

Nur Abdelkhaliq Politics and International Relations, School of Social and Political Science, University of Edinburgh, UK

Bo Yan School of International Relations and Public Affairs, Fudan University, Shanghai, China

Caroline Bouchard Politics and International Relations, School of Social and Political Science, University of Edinburgh, UK

Chen Zhimin School of International Relations and Public Affairs, Fudan University, Shanghai, China

Silvia Colombo IAI Istituto Affari Internazionali, Rome, Italy

Chad Damro Politics and International Relations, School of Social and Political Science, University of Edinburgh, UK

Geoffrey Edwards The Department of Politics and International Studies (POLIS), University of Cambridge, UK

Lorenzo Fioramonti Department of Political Sciences, University of Pretoria, South Africa

Christopher Hill The Department of Politics and International Studies (POLIS), University of Cambridge, UK

Hubertus Jüergenliemk The Department of Politics and International Studies (POLIS), University of Cambridge, UK

Nadia Klein University of Cologne, Germany

Tobias Kunstein University of Cologne, Germany

Elena Lazarou Center for International Relations – CPDOC, Fundação Getúlio Vargas, Rio de Janeiro, Brazil

Nona Mikhelidze IAI Istituto Affari Internazionali, Rome, Italy

John Peterson Politics and International Relations, School of Social and Political Science, University of Edinburgh, UK

Nicoletta Pirozzi IAI Istituto Affari Internazionali, Rome, Italy

Wulf Reiners University of Cologne, Germany

Giulia C. Romano Sciences Po, Centre for International Studies and Research (CERI), Paris, France

Charlotte Rommerskirchen Politics and International Relations, School of Social and Political Science, University of Edinburgh, UK

Ivo Šlosarčík Institute of International Studies, Faculty of Social Sciences, Charles University in Prague, Czech Republic

Julie Smith The Department of Politics and International Studies (POLIS), University of Cambridge, UK

Yolanda Spies Department of Political Sciences, University of Pretoria, South Africa

Nathalie Tocci IAI Istituto Affari Internazionali, Rome, Italy

Tomáš Weiss Institute of International Studies, Faculty of Social Sciences, Charles University in Prague, Czech Republic

ABBREVIATIONS

ACP	African, Caribbean and Pacific group of states
AMA	Agreement on Movement and Access
APEC	Asia-Pacific Economic Cooperation forum
APF	African Peace Facility
ASEAN	Association of Southeast Asian Nations
ASEM	Asia-Europe Meeting
AU	African Union
BASIC	China, India, South Africa and Brazil
BiH	Bosnia and Herzegovina
BRICS	Brazil, Russia, India, China, South Africa
CAN	Climate Action Network
CARICOM	Caribbean Community and Common Market
CARIFORUM	Caribbean Forum
CCP	EU's Common Commercial Policy
CEEP	EU's Common External Energy Policy
CEPS	Centre for European Policy Studies
CFSP	EU's Common Foreign and Security Policy
COP	Conference of the Parties
COREPER	Committee of Permanent Representatives in the European Union
CSDP	Common Security and Defence Policy
DAC	Development Assistance Committee
DC	Development Committee
EaP	Eastern Partnership
EBA	Everything But Arms
EC	European Commission
ECB	European Central Bank

ECSC	European Coal and Steel Community
EDF	European Development Fund
EDP	Excessive Deficit Procedure
EEAS	European External Action Service
EEB	European Environmental Bureau
EEC	European Economic Community
EEG	Eastern European Group
EERP	European Economic Recovery Plan
EMHRM	Euro-Mediterranean Human Rights Network
EMP	Euro-Mediterranean Partnership
ENP	European Neighbourhood Policy
ENPI	European Neighbourhood Policy Instrument
EP	European Parliament
EPAs	Economic Partnership Agreements
EPC	European Policy Centre
ESS	European Security Strategy
EU	European Union
EUBAM	EU Border Assistance Mission
EUFOR	EU Force
EUPM	EU Police Mission
EUPOL-COPPS	European Union Co-ordinating Office for Palestinian Police Support
EUR-Lex	EU's Central Online Database on EU Law
EUSR	EU Special Representative
FRONTEX	Frontières Extérieures (EU)
FTAs	Free Trade Agreements
GATT	General Agreement on Tariffs and Trade
GDP	Gross Domestic Product
GHG	Greenhouse Gas
GNI	Gross National Income
GSM	Global System of Mobile Communications
GSP	Generalized System of Preferences
GSP+	EU Incentive Arrangement for Sustainable Development and Good Governance
HoMs	Heads of Missions
HR	High Representative
IASB	International Accounting Standards Board
IEA	International Energy Agency
iEPA	Interim Economic Partnership Agreement
ICA	International Consultation Analysis
ICC	International Criminal Court
ICG	International Crisis Group
ICI	Istanbul Cooperation Initiative
IFRS	International Financial Reporting Standards

IISD	International Institute for Sustainable Development
ILO	International Labour Organization
IMF	International Monetary Fund
IMFC	International Monetary and Financial Committee
IMO	International Maritime Organization
IOM	International Organization for Migration
IOs	International Organizations
IOSCO	International Organization of Securities Commissions
IPCC	Intergovernmental Panel on Climate Change
IPTF	UN International Police Force
IR	International Relations
JAI	*Justice et Affaires Intérieures* (Justice Internal Affairs)
JCC	Joint Control Commission
JHA	Justice Home Affairs
LDCs	Least-Developed Countries
LSE	London School of Economics
MAP	Mutual Assessment Process
MD	Mediterranean Dialogue
MDGs	Millennium Development Goals
MPCs	Mediterranean Partner Countries
MPE	Market Power Europe
MRV	Measurement, Report and Verification
MTAs	Mutual Trade Agreements
NAFTA	North American Free Trade Agreement
NATO	North Atlantic Treaty Organization
NDRC	National Development and Reform Commission
NGOs	Non-Governmental Organizations
NPE	Normative Power Europe
NSS	(US) National Security Strategy
NUG	National Unity Government
OCT	Overseas Countries and Territories
ODA	Official Development Assistance
OECD	Organisation for Economic Co-operation and Development
OEEC	Organisation for European Economic Co-operation
OHR for BiH	Office of the High Representative for Bosnia and Herzegovina
OPT	Occupied Palestinian Territories
OSCE	Organization for Security and Co-operation in Europe
P2	France and the UK
P5	Five Permanent Members in the UN Security Council
PA	Palestinian Authority

PDF	Partnership Dialogue Facility
PIC	Peace Implementation Council
PLO	Palestine Liberation Organization
PRC	People's Republic of China
PSC	Political and Security Committee of the European Union
PTAs	Preferential Trade Agreements
RECs	Regional Economic Communities
SADC	Southern African Development Community
SCO	Shanghai Cooperation Organization
SEA	Single European Act
SMR	Single Market Review
START	Strategic Arms Reduction Treaty
TDCA	Trade, Development and Cooperation Agreement
TEC	Treaty of the European Communities
TEU	Treaty on European Union
TEU-Nice	Treaty of Nice on European Union
TFEU	Treaty on the Functioning of the European Union
TIM	Temporary International Mechanism
UfC	Uniting for Consensus
UfM	Union for the Mediterranean
UK	United Kingdom
UN	United Nations
UNCTAD	United Nations Conference on Trade and Development
UNFCCC	United Nations Framework Convention on Climate Change
UNGA	United Nations General Assembly
UNSC	United Nations Security Council
US	United States
VAT	Value Added Tax
WEOG	Western Europe and Others Group
WHO	World Health Organization
WTO	World Trade Organization

1

INTRODUCTION

Multilateralism in the twenty-first century

Caroline Bouchard, John Peterson and Nathalie Tocci[1]

The grand narrative of twenty-first-century international relations (IR) has become notably clearer in the first years of the century's second decade. It has two fundamental features. First, much about globalisation is clearly irreversible. States face powerful new incentives to cooperate with trade, capital, ideas, people, technology, information, weapons, diseases and crime all flowing more freely than in any previous era. Moreover, transnational issues over which individual states have very limited control have become sources of conflict: global warming, migration and resource scarcity have created profound collective action problems.

A second fundamental feature of the international order is that power – especially economic power – is shifting. The rise of the so-called BRICS (Brazil, Russia, India, China and South Africa) lends a new and unsettling fluidity to the international order. Historically, eras marked by the rise and fall of great powers have experienced considerable turmoil that often has culminated in armed conflict, especially in Europe (see Gilpin 1981; Layne 2006). To avoid such a return to the future, tectonic shifts in international power have, somehow, to be managed.

Naturally, one effect of these two primordial shifts in IR, and a place where their pressures converge, is in the generation of heightened and renewed interest in multilateralism. While a large body of research exists on multilateralism as a concept, it continues to be ill defined and poorly understood. The essential features and dimensions of multilateralism remain contested and ambiguous. Arguably, it does not qualify as a core concept in the study of IR as (say) anarchy or interdependence do (see Chapter 2). This book aims to make it one, or at least to consider whether it deserves such status. It does so by analysing the evolution of the concept and practice of multilateralism, examining forms, models and cases of multilateralism, and confronting debates about how it can be made durable and effective in the twenty-first century. It also focuses on Europe's contribution – especially that of the European Union (EU) – to multilateralism: past, present and future. In particular, it seeks to explore whether and how the European Union delivers on its stated goal of promoting effective multilateralism in its external action.

Scholars have increasingly bracketed multilateralism as a European-specific approach towards international security. This move is not surprising. The member states of the EU repeatedly have agreed that the logical response to new global challenges created by globalisation is more extensive and intensive multilateralism, even if they are waking up late (if at all) to the need to try to 'govern' shifts in power through multilateral means. In any case, European consensus on the virtues of multilateralism was clearly stated in both the European Security Strategy and the Lisbon Treaty.

> in a world of global threats, global markets and global media, our security and prosperity increasingly depend on an *effective multilateral system* (emphasis added)
>
> *(ESS 2003: 10)*

> The EU shall … promote an international system based on stronger multilateral cooperation and good global governance
>
> *(Treaty of Lisbon: Article 10A, 2(h))*

Multilateralism, and more specifically 'effective multilateralism', have become focal points for analysing the EU's Common Foreign and Security Policy (CFSP). Effective multilateralism, according to the European Security Strategy, refers to 'development of a stronger international society, well functioning international institutions and a rule-based international order' (European Council 2003: 10). Arguably, the EU has done more than most of its partners to address old and new global challenges through the pursuit of effective multilateralism. Nonetheless, the EU has conflicting strategies and priorities. Alongside multilateralism, it often promotes regionalism and embraces inter-regional dialogue. It increasingly seeks bilateral strategic partnerships with old and emerging great powers.

Beyond multilateralism, it also vigorously defends European interests within international organisations such as the World Trade Organization (WTO), at times in line with the broader goals of the multilateral grouping in question, at times not. These conflicting strategies and priorities raise two crucial issues. First, despite the general commitment to effective multilateralism, there is little clarity about what precisely is meant by it, and thus whether and to what extent effective multilateralism is compatible with other foreign policy goals. Second, in view of conflicting strategies, matching supply to demand for effective multilateralism is a significant challenge for the European Union, not least because it has other priorities that conflict with this objective.

This book is fundamentally about multilateralism in the twenty-first century and the European Union's contribution to making it effective. It presents findings generated within MERCURY (an acronym that admittedly stretches to abbreviate *Multilateralism and the EU in the Contemporary Global Order*), a three-year, €2 million EU-funded research programme. It develops and investigates specific theses about multilateralism, the EU, the quest for effectiveness, and what effectiveness means. Its central research question – addressed in all chapters – is: does the EU deliver on its commitment to effective multilateralism?

The volume has two main objectives. First, to shed new light on twenty-first-century multilateralism by developing and operationalising a new, enhanced, refined, modern definition of multilateralism, while generating innovative, empirical knowledge on the practice of multilateralism. Second, to pinpoint the effects of the EU's external relations by gauging whether, how and how much Europe contributes to the building of effective multilateralism.

The chapters in this volume grapple with five main areas of inquiry:

1. How should we understand multilateralism, both historically and in contemporary terms? Is there a 'European way' of multilateralism that is culturally specific?
2. By what criteria can multilateralism be deemed 'effective'? Should effectiveness be interpreted exclusively in procedural terms – i.e. focusing on the functioning of multilateral action – or does it also or primarily regard the substantive policy objective that multilateralism sets out to pursue?
3. Is the European Union – in its constitutional and institutional setup as well as its policy instruments – well tailored to promote effective multilateralism?
4. Does the EU live up to its ambitions to contribute to effective multilateralism, both in its neighbourhood and globally, and in a variety of policy areas ranging from trade, fiscal coordination and climate change to conflict resolution?
5. What policy lessons can be drawn from Europe's experience of promoting multilateralism?

Ultimately, we and our authors confront a question that no single academic work has so far explicitly answered: that is, whether, how, and how effectively, does the EU deliver on its commitment to effective multilateralism? We do so by exploring different conceptual approaches to multilateralism, as well as by testing and comparing the EU's experience in different policy areas, and distinct geographical and institutional settings, including those that are internal to the Union and in specified regions, international organisations (IOs) and bilateral partnerships. We begin by mapping how this volume seeks to achieve its aims.

The EU's quest for effective multilateralism

The first part of this book – *Mapping modes of multilateralism* – reviews competing approaches to multilateralism. Subsequent sections of the book – *Multilateralism in EU policies, Multilateralism in practice: Key regions and partners,* and *The European*

Union in multilateral fora – explore empirically EU institutional and policy dynamics, regional and strategic (bilateral) partnerships, and the Union's practice of multilateralism within formal and informal international organisations.

Multilateralism may be understood as a system of interaction combining rules, institutionalised cooperation and inclusiveness. It is recognised as a distinct form of cooperation in international relations, rooted in voluntary decisions taken by the participants, involving a plurality of actors, and based upon the recognition of norms and/or standards rather than ad hoc or asymmetrical arrangements. Beyond this definition, a number of features and dimensions of multilateralism remain contested and ambiguous. The three chapters in Part I of this book – *Mapping modes of multilateralism* – directly plunge into debates about conceptualising multilateralism.

In Chapter 2, Peterson and Bouchard argue that conceptual and definitional confusion about what multilateralism means co-exists, paradoxically, with the EU's clear commitment to effective multilateralism. They propose a new, twenty-first-century, modernised definition of multilateralism that takes account of developments in global governance in the (now) multiple decades since seminal works on multilateralism were published. But they also look retrospectively at ebbs and flows in the development of multilateralism historically, with a view to specifying Europe's contribution to its specific advances and retreats. The authors confront squarely claims that a 'European way' of multilateralism is culturally specific and clashes with views about the purpose and practice of multilateralism beyond European shores.

Elena Lazarou, Geoffrey Edwards, Christopher Hill and Julie Smith examine the idea of multilateralism as doctrine and trace its development throughout the twenty-first century in Chapter 3. The EU is the principal actor that has implemented and operationalised the doctrine of multilateralism, particularly since designating 'effective multilateralism' a clear foreign policy priority. They argue that conceptualising a *doctrine* of multilateralism enriches current debates about global governance in an era of emerging multipolarity, and that developing a consensus on the basic rules and principles that guide multilateral policy-making is a prerequisite for effective action. Hence, effectiveness is applied to the actual pursuit of a given foreign policy *goal*, rather than simply to the functioning of multilateral *means* of action.

Whereas effectiveness can thus be applied to both goals and means, multilateralism itself, according to Peterson and Hill in Chapter 4, is by nature messy, disorderly and unwieldy. It also may be deemed to be effective in multiple different and incompatible ways. The authors argue that it is usually *defective* insofar as it rarely produces quick solutions to international problems or applies the same rules to all. But to judge multilateralism by these criteria is, they suggest, to take an inflexible, naïve and even dogmatic view about what the purpose and practice of multilateralism should be. Its purpose usually is to find some kind of compromise between affected actors with conflicting interests, which in practice often requires a bending of rules. The authors offer a historical account of Europe's experience of multilateralism, challenge accepted wisdoms about the EU's commitment to multilateralism and its international persona more generally, and consider external trade policy as a case study of the Union's external action. They argue that the EU's experience of multilateralism is not typical but also not unique in IR.

Part II of the book – *Multilateralism in EU policies* – explores systematically how the Union's institutional machinery and policy externalisation equip it to contribute to a multilateral order. It examines the structural framework of EU external relations, including constitutional (treaty), institutional and policy change at the European level. This part of the book is concerned with evolving interactions between the Union and its member states. It also considers the causes and dynamics of the externalisation of EU policy. The two chapters in this part of the book aim to elaborate how the institutional machinery works to produce external policy, and how well equipped the EU is to act externally in multilateral frameworks.

Drawing on research on the Union's performance as an international actor, Nadia Klein, Tobias Kunstein and Wulf Reiners in Chapter 5 provide a framework for assessing the varying levels of multilateral action in EU external policies. The analysis takes into account both the legal and the living framework – the actual use of the provisions – of EU trade policy and the CFSP. The chapter's findings demonstrate that the EU is stronger in supporting international law (multilateral legal basis) than in pooling resources with other international actors (multilateral implementation).

While the European Union's identity may have normative and/or other characteristics, it is fundamentally a large single market with significant and distinct institutional features and competing interest groups. Or so argues Chad Damro in Chapter 6. Given these central characteristics, Damro suggests that the EU may be best understood as 'Market Power Europe' that exercises its power through the externalisation of economic and social market-related policies and regulatory measures, including in multilateral settings. The chapter provides an analytical framework for understanding what kind of power the European Union is, what the EU says as a power and what the Union does as a power.

Multilateralism in practice: Key regions and partners – Part III of this book – explores the external dimension, and in particular addresses the EU's interactions with external regions and strategic partners in the southern and eastern neighbourhoods, as well as in Africa and Asia. All are critically important regions and partners both in terms of global order and in terms of specific EU interests. A focus on key regions and partners complements the study of internal institutional and policy dynamics, providing an additional cut or perspective on EU external action. There is at least the possibility that, by focusing its efforts on regions and strategic partners, the EU undermines its own objectives of contributing to effective multilateralism.

Silvia Colombo and Nur Abdelkhaliq in Chapter 7 explore the practice of EU multilateralism vis-à-vis the Mediterranean – a key region for the European Union – by examining energy and migration policies. These two issue areas are crucial in the Union's strategy of incorporating internal policy objectives related to energy security and the management of migration flows into its external multilateral frameworks with the Mediterranean. The chapter assesses the extent to which the EU can be defined as a multilateral actor in the Mediterranean by exploring the internal and external dimensions of EU energy and migration policies as related both to the actors and to the policy frameworks involved. Hence, the chapter gauges the extent of multilateralism that results by addressing the actions pursued by different stakeholders engaged in these policies – the European Commission and the External Action Service, member states, partner countries and international organisations. It addresses the extent to which multilateralism can be considered 'effective', by taking effectiveness to mean the actual policy outcomes of the different actors' engagement with these policy areas.

In Chapter 8 Tomáš Weiss, Nona Mikhelidze and Ivo Šlosarčík focus on the European Union's practice of conflict resolution in the Balkans and the eastern neighbourhood. It considers the extent to which the EU lives up to its declarations and works multilaterally in cooperation with other international actors. Two case studies are presented – on Georgia and Bosnia – where concrete EU behaviour on the ground is studied. The chapter examines various types of engagement that are used by the EU in conflict situations: inaction, unilateralism, bilateralism and multilateralism. The chapter concludes that the EU is much more effective in supporting multilateral activities driven primarily by other international actors than in triggering and leading them.

Turning to regions further afield, for several decades Europe entertained a preferential relationship with its former colonies in Africa, which translated into a set of trade and development preferences. With the progressive diffusion of market liberalisation, this preferential relationship came to be called into question. Lorenzo Fioramonti in Chapter 9 analyses how the 'multilateralization' of development policy has influenced the EU approach, culminating with the adoption of the Economic Partnership Agreements (EPAs) with sub-Saharan African countries. Here too, effectiveness is applied primarily to the actual policy outputs which multilateral action produces, raising a number of questions about the actual nature of multilateral processes by focusing on the intended and unintended effects of political, economic and technical asymmetries between rich and poor countries.

The last chapter in this part on the EU's interactions with external regions and strategic partners focuses on the EU and China as two significant players in the global governance of climate change. Bo Yan, Giulia Romano and Chen Zhimin in Chapter 10 argue that EU–China relations on climate change have important implications, both for the governance of global warming and for bilateral EU–China relations beyond climate change. The two players' striking cooperation at the bilateral level has not always led to successful cooperation at the multilateral level, especially in the quest for a post-Kyoto agreement. Examining the 2009 Copenhagen Climate Change Conference, the authors argue that the two sides' different expectations and negotiation strategies led to conflicting relations in (and after) the conference. However, the EU and China's assessments and reflections on the conference and the ensuing adoption of new strategies eventually led to changes in their negotiating behaviour on the way to the successive Cancun and Durban summits, producing more cooperative relations.

The EU's quest for effective multilateralism in its external action has also taken the form of seeking membership and influence in formal and informal international organisations. The EU has indeed become an important actor in some international organisations, despite the fact that enlargement to an EU of 27 has often made it more difficult to act coherently or strategically within these multilateral settings. The three chapters in Part IV of the book – *The European Union in multilateral fora* – explore the EU's performance in institutionalised and non-institutionalised multilateral contexts. The chapters examine whether and how the Union contributes to effective multilateralism through the strengthening of international law, the building of international institutions as well as the promotion of multilateral principles in peace and security matters. This part of the volume complements the empirical study of policies, institutions and external partners by focusing directly on the EU's role within international fora.

The first chapter focuses on the EU's role in the United Nations, the organisation considered by the EU to be standing 'at the apex of the international system' (European Council 2003:10). Nicoletta Pirozzi with Hubertus Jürgenliemk and Yolanda Spies in Chapter 11 assesses the likely impact of the Lisbon Treaty on the EU's contribution to the reform of the UN Security Council. They outline the prospects for future developments under three main dimensions: coordination (among EU member states and institutions); representation (of the EU as a single actor); and outreach (measured in terms of what the EU and its member states collectively achieve). They argue that the representation of the EU at the UN, notably within the General Assembly, could offer a model both for its future representation at the Security Council, and, more broadly, for the representation of regional organisations and the evolution of regionalism within the UN system.

The two other chapters in this part of the book consider the role of the EU in informal or unconventional forms of multilateralism. They aim to determine what role the EU plays in developing the emerging rules of two multilateral groupings in which international cooperation is not fully institutionalised: the G20 and the Middle East Quartet.

In sharp contrast to the Great Depression, the Great Recession of 2008–10 saw unprecedented attempts to coordinate macroeconomic policies internationally. As the financial crisis turned into a deeper macroeconomic crisis in the autumn of 2008, the political dilemma posed by the post-Bretton Woods system – financial integration without fiscal coordination – became apparent, thus highlighting the 'fiscal realities of financial integration'. In the light of increased international policy interdependence, the need for international policy coordination was brought into bolder relief. Charlotte Rommerskirchen in Chapter 12 investigates the state of fiscal multilateralism and the European Union's contribution in the G20 during and in the aftermath of the economic and financial crisis.

In Chapter 13, Tocci examines the role of the EU in the Middle East Quartet. In the past, mediation of the protracted Arab–Israeli conflict was exclusively unilateral in character and dominated by the United States. With the outbreak of the second intifada in 2000, the time appeared to be ripe for a substantial reshuffle of

Middle East mediation. In 2002, what became known as the Middle East Quartet came into being, constituted by the EU, Russia, the UN and the US. The chapter explores the Quartet as an informal multilateral mediation forum focusing on two questions. First, can the Quartet be regarded as a case of 'effective multilateralism'? Second and relatedly, in view of the EU's declared goal of promoting effective multilateralism, how can we assess the Union's performance as an actor in the Middle East Quartet? The conclusions are sobering, pointing to the fact that, while the EU has been the principal driver behind the Quartet, the latter has neither become a genuinely multilateral forum nor has it been effective in pursuing the goal of a two-state solution in the Middle East.

A final chapter (14) – by Bouchard, Klein, Peterson and Reiners – revisits the question: does the EU deliver on its commitment to effective multilateralism? It reviews the main findings of the volume and considers how a comprehensive research programme into multilateralism and the European Union's contribution to it has elaborated and clarified forms of multilateralism. It collects together specific theses that have been developed within these pages about how and when the EU embraces multilateralism – or not. It also reflects on how the Union has used multilateral instruments to pursue its interests and strategic objectives, and explores the effects on the multilateral system of the EU's engagement with other regions and strategic partners. Finally, it examines the consequences of European external relations for the functioning and legitimacy of institutionalised and non-institutionalised multilateral contexts.

We hope – and are even cautiously optimistic – that this volume sheds considerable new light on the grand narrative of twenty-first-century IR. The EU clearly has faced enormous difficulties in seeking to live up to its distinctive commitment to effective multilateralism, especially in an era when, by most accounts, it is losing power relative to other, emerging states. The Union continues to pursue a diverse mix of strategies in its external relations because – as Olsen (2003: 50) has argued in the case of EU institutional reform – European leaders 'want many, different and not necessarily compatible things'. But so, too, do the leaders of other major powers. They might well find that Europe's experience of multilateralism holds lessons for them.

Note

1 The authors wish to thank Andrea Dessì for all his support in putting this manuscript together.

References

European Council (2003) *A Secure Europe in a Better World. European Security Strategy*, Brussels, 12 December. Online. Available: http://ue.eu.int/pressdata/EN/reports/78367.pdf (accessed 25 November 2012).

Gilpin, R. (1981) *War and Change in World Politics*, Cambridge and New York: Cambridge University Press.

Layne, C. (2006) 'The Unipolar Illusion Revisited: The Coming End of the United States' Unipolar Moment', *International Security* 31(2): 7–41.

Olsen, J. (2003) 'Reforming European Institutions of Governance', in J.H.H. Weiler, I. Begg and J. Peterson (eds) *Integration in an Expanding European Union: Reassessing the Fundamentals*, Oxford and Malden MA: Blackwell.

Official Journal of the European Union (2007) 'Treaty of Lisbon amending the Treaty on European Union and the Treaty establishing the European Community, signed at Lisbon', 13 December, C306, Vol.50. Online. Available: http://eur-lex.europa.eu/LexUriServ/LexUriServ.do?uri=OJ:C:2007:306:FULL:EN:PDF (accessed 25 November 2012).

PART I
Mapping modes of multilateralism

2

MAKING MULTILATERALISM EFFECTIVE

Modernising global governance

John Peterson and Caroline Bouchard

Introduction

We, along with all contributors both to this volume and to research on European Union (EU) external policy, must face up to a fundamental incongruity, which borders on a contradiction. Multilateralism is an under-specified concept in the study of international relations (IR). Yet, it is also a core goal of the EU's external action. As we have suggested elsewhere, multilateralism is arguably not a core concept in IR or in the same league with anarchy, sovereignty or interdependence (Bouchard and Peterson 2011: 1). Part of the problem is that seminal works on multilateralism are now decades old (see Keohane 1990; Caporaso 1992; Ruggie 1992, 1993). The end of the Cold War seemed to trigger interest in multilateralism among both scholars and practitioners as a device to usher in a new era of international cooperation. Then, the line seemed to go cold, perhaps because most attempts to build or extend multilateralism – outside of the World Trade Organization (WTO) – yielded disappointing results. Meanwhile, the focus of IR scholarship shifted towards 'unipolar politics' in an era of American hegemony (see Kapstein and Mastanduno 1999; Ikenberry 2002), which – according to much accepted wisdom about IR – hardly constituted a favourable set of international conditions for building multilateralism.

Another part of the problem remains definitional. Caporaso (1992) was an early advocate of developing a clear set of criteria to define multilateralism so that scholars would stop using it to describe a variety of different forms of international cooperation. Debatably, nothing has really changed since then. What is clear is that research on multilateralism has recently expanded, and even exploded. New work has emerged on 'global governance'[1] (Alexandroff 2008; Muldoon *et al.* 2011), regional cooperation (particularly in Asia; see Calder and Fukuyama 2008; Frost 2008; Green and Gill 2009), and how multilateral incentives can advance democratisation (Keohane *et al.* 2009; Ikenberry *et al.* 2009). In particular, John Ikenberry (2003, 2006, 2011) has insisted that, even during the darkest days of post-9/11 American unilateralism, a 'new multilateralism' had arrived: more demanding of states, and with breaches of more binding international rules more obvious and costly than in previous eras.

More recently, Van Langenhove (2010) has suggested that multilateralism in the twenty-first century has morphed into a more open form of international system, a 'multilateralism 2.0'. It is characterised by a diversification of multilateral organisations, the growing importance of non-state actors, increased inter-linkages between policy domains, and growing space for citizen involvement. An alternative view has suggested three distinct, ideal types of multilateralism that now co-exist: institutionalised, crystallised and aspirant. Rules-based organisations such as the WTO reflect institutionalised multilateralism. New international norms, rules and organisations – such as the International Criminal Court (ICC), more active international judicial intervention, or efforts to tackle climate change – are examples of crystallising multilateralism: they are 'becoming' as opposed to 'being' and are still not fully established. The emergence of more inchoate norms on child labour or foreign investment reflects aspirant multilateralism: 'norms inform foreign policy behaviour in the absence of codified rules or even the prospect of establishing them' (Peterson *et al.* 2008: 8–9).

Multilateralism still means different things to different scholars. Sometimes, it is portrayed as merely an 'extended policy' of cooperation (Touval and Zartman 2010: 227). Other times, it is presented as a 'recent strand...of international relations theory' (Øhrgaard 2004: 35). Even though (as we will show) all definitions of multilateralism stress the importance of rules, which apply (more or less) to all, hard-nosed realists continue to insist that the only multilateralism worth having is 'a concert of Great Powers' (Rosecrance 2008: 86). In short, we do not seem much closer than we were in the early 1990s to a clear conception of when international cooperation deserves to be called multilateralism, and when it does not.

Definitional confusion has not deterred the EU from committing itself doctrinally to promoting 'effective multilateralism'. The 2003 European Security Strategy presents a 'stronger international society' as one of the EU's primary objectives:

> Our security and prosperity increasingly depend on an effective multilateral system. We are committed to upholding and developing International Law. The fundamental framework for international relations is the United Nations Charter.
>
> *(EU 2003: 14)*

One effect is to fuel the fire of scholars – particularly American ones – who insist that multilateralism is a 'weapon of the weak' (Kagan 2002: 4). In other words, the strong do what they can. The weak – including European states – do what they must, which is to try to bind other, stronger states into dense webs of multilateral rules. The 'fundamental framework' for such an effort is the UN Charter. But the

UN remains toothless, as evidenced by (*inter alia*) the failure of Security Council reform, the war in Iraq, and the UN's inability to halt the bloodshed in Syria.

Clearly, it is difficult to measure 'demand' for multilateralism. However, there is plenty of evidence to suggest that it is on the rise and that much of it remains unmet (see Bouchard and Peterson 2011). Even the most powerful states – including those widely reputed to be rising powers – find themselves under pressure from forces over which they, acting alone, cannot control. Europe's own experience of the sovereign debt crisis was illustrative not just of the vulnerability of Eurozone states to developments beyond their borders. Non-Eurozone members such as the United Kingdom (UK), Sweden and even the United States (US) found themselves at risk of contagion from the crisis, with their own rates of economic growth depressed by the austerity that sent weaker Eurozone members into recession. The US Treasury Secretary, Timothy Geithner, anxiously urged EU leaders to find a way out of the crisis when he visited an EU summit in Poland in September 2011. Afterwards, a joke made the rounds in Brussels that was not without substance: 'Who's the only candidate who can defeat Barack Obama in the 2012 election? Answer: Angela Merkel', the German Chancellor, who was widely viewed as primarily responsible for decisions that could solve the crisis, and thus help revive the global – including the US – economy.[2]

The EU's mission to promote multilateralism is frequently discredited by claims that Europe's own experience of cooperation cannot be replicated elsewhere. Moreover, the EU's pursuit of bilateral 'strategic partnerships' with emerging powers – as well as established ones – is often viewed as contrary to any effort to build multilateralism globally. Still, other regions of the world, including Asia, increasingly appear to look to the EU for lessons that can be learned about how cooperation can solve transnational problems (see Katzenstein 2005; Kang 2007; Calder and Fukuyama 2008; Frost 2008; Green and Gill 2009). European policymakers argue that the EU seeks privileged bilateral relationships with the BRICS countries (Brazil, Russia, India, China and South Africa) because it wants to maximise opportunities to convince them to embrace the goal of building multilateralism (Grevi and de Vasconcelos 2008).

Our purpose in this chapter is fourfold. First, despite its inevitable ambiguity, we seek to define multilateralism in a way that takes account of its evolution since seminal works on the subject were written. Second, we review the historical record of multilateralism to pinpoint Europe's role in establishing it. Third, we compare how multilateralism is viewed in political capitals beyond the European continent. Finally, we grapple with the question of what makes multilateralism 'effective', and what objectives might be pursued by building or extending it. Our conclusion summarises our argument and offers reflections on:

- what a modern definition of multilateralism should comprise;
- what Europe's contribution to modern multilateralism has been;
- whether the European 'way' of multilateralism is echoed or eschewed in other parts of the world;
- what 'effective multilateralism' means and how it might be achieved.

Defining multilateralism[3]

As the Cold War ended, Keohane (1990) – along with many Europeans – insisted that multilateralism had developed a momentum of its own. A device for ensuring stability in the midst of geopolitical earthquakes, it had increasingly become both an objective and an ordering device in IR, especially as new, post-Communist states in Europe made clear their desire to join what became (in 1993) the European Union. Yet, multilateralism at this point still 'served as a label more than as a concept defining a research program' (Keohane 1990: 731).

Keohane (1990: 731) defined multilateralism as 'the practice of coordinating national policies in groups of three or more states, through *ad hoc* arrangements or by means of institutions'. It thus involved (exclusively) states and sometimes (not always) institutions.[4] Multilateralism became institutionalised when enduring rules emerged. Institutions thus could 'be distinguished from other forms of multilateralism, such as *ad hoc* meetings and short-term arrangements to solve particular problems' (Keohane 1990: 733). Multilateral institutions, by implication, took the form of international regimes or bureaucratic organisations.

Keohane's opus did not meet with universal enthusiasm. Ruggie (1992: 564) even critiqued it as 'nominal' and neglectful of the '*qualitative* dimension of the phenomenon' (emphasis in original). With this dimension in mind, multilateralism meant 'coordinating relations among three or more states…in accordance with certain principles' that ordered relations between them. It thus represented a 'generic institutional form'. Multilateralism entailed institutional arrangements designed to 'define and stabilize property rights of states, manage coordination problems and resolve collaboration problems'. But it often took place in the absence of international organisations (IOs), which were a 'relatively recent arrival and still of only modest importance' (Ruggie 1992: 567–8).

Two decades on, the question of how much leading IOs have developed and gained in importance remains debatable.[5] In any case, Ruggie's treatment has proven timeless insofar as it identified three basic foundations that distinguishes multilateralism from other forms of IR such as bilateralism and imperialism:

- generalised principles of conduct;
- indivisibility; and
- diffuse reciprocity.

First, states engage in multilateral cooperation when relations between three or more of them are based on *principles*. They identify 'appropriate conduct for a class of actions, without regard to particularistic interests of the parties' (Ruggie 1992: 571). To give a concrete illustration, Germany and Bulgaria are both obliged by the rules of the EU's budgetary process to engage in 'appropriate conduct' – that is, to negotiate and seek a settlement – regardless of their divergent interests as a net contributor or recipient.

Second, multilateralism is based on a specific social construct: *indivisibility*. It can take various forms, but in all cases it constitutes 'the scope (both geographic and functional) over which costs and benefits are spread' when actions are taken that affect the collectivity (Caporaso 1992: 602). For instance, peace is usually deemed indivisible in a collective security system. The EU's Charter of Fundamental Rights presents social, civil, political and environmental rights as indivisible: all are 'treated *equally* as fundamental rights' (Chalmers and Tomkins 2007: 255; emphasis added).

Third, multilateralism is constructed on the basis of *diffuse reciprocity*: participants expect 'a rough equivalence of benefits in the aggregate and over time' (Ruggie 1992: 571). Even states that lose out when cooperative deals are struck do not defect if they have the chance to 'win' when the next deal is struck. Diffuse reciprocity also explains why powerful states, while invariably choosing institutions that serve their interests, may find that multilateral arrangements become more attractive to them as they value the future more highly.

For Ruggie (1992), international orders, regimes and organisations could be multilateral in form, but not necessarily. An international regime might not operate on the basis of indivisibility: financial powerhouses such as the United States or UK have 'particularistic interests' within the International Organization of Securities Commissions (IOSCO), which promotes sound regulation of securities markets. These interests make any collectivity that groups them together with (say) Albania, Guatemala or Tanzania in this issue-area a very unrestrictive one. Put simply: to qualify as a case of multilateralism, an international organisation must coordinate relations among states on the basis of organising principles. In theory (if not always in practice), the same rules apply to all.

Here, modern multilateralism differs from earlier versions: the same rules might apply to all *states*, but states are by no means the only actors that partake in multilateralism (see Keck and Sikkink 1998; A. F. Cooper 2002; Kaldor 2003; Jones and Coleman 2005; Van Langenhove 2010). Non-state actors – multinational corporations, non-governmental organisations (NGOs) and the secretariats of IOs (such as the EU's European Commission) – may push states to make multilateral commitments or even agree to such commitments between themselves. To illustrate, consider agreement by airlines within their trade association, the International Air Transport Association, to cut net emissions by 50 per cent from 2005 levels.[6] The increasingly prominent and active 'Group of 20' (G20) brings together 20 leading economies but only 19 states: the EU itself is its twentieth member. Without (probably) even realising it, Hillary Clinton (2010) deployed a concept previously reserved for describing the EU's international mission – that of 'civilian power' (Duchêne 1972) – to connote the need for US foreign policy to focus on ordinary citizens as well as their governments to achieve its goals.

Alternatively, non-state actors may help block new multilateral agreements, such as on climate change, or even scupper existing ones as, for example, on whaling. However they contribute to modern multilateralism, few dispute that non-state actors 'have become progressively more assertive in demanding a voice at the top decision-making tables' (Thakur 2002: 270). What has changed the most about multilateralism since the early 1990s is, almost certainly, the more active participation of non-state actors.

Meanwhile, there is abundant evidence that multilateralism has flourished in the 20 years since Ruggie (1992) weighed in. In the roughly three decades after 1970, the number of international treaties more than tripled, leading to a significant increase (by about two-thirds) in international institutions (Ikenberry 2003: 536). The 2000s have brought the birth of the G20, the Shanghai Cooperation Organisation (SCO) and other regional institutions in Asia, and radical enlargement of the EU. Yet, there still exists no accepted definition of multilateralism, let alone a coherent, conceptually driven research programme to investigate it.

In fact, multilateralism might be most clearly understood when we consider what it is *not*: unilateralism, bilateralism or (arguably) inter-regionalism.[7] It contrasts with imperialism, or cooperation based on coercion. It is not entirely *ad hoc*. It is based on rules that are durable and (at least potentially) affect the behaviour of actors that agree to multilateral cooperation. As such, multilateralism in its modern, twenty-first-century guise may be defined as:

> *Three or more actors engaging in voluntary and (essentially) institutionalised international cooperation governed by norms and principles, with rules that apply (by and large) equally to all states.*

Multilateralism, at minimum, must involve three actors (usually states). Critics might argue that this is to set the bar too low. But there are imaginable cases of multilateralism that could have major impacts on IR involving only a few actors, which need not all be states. Major international agreements – on emissions reductions, regulatory cooperation, labour rights – might involve, even necessarily, non-state actors. Consider what might be accomplished, in terms of industry retrenchment and the embrace of green technologies, by cooperation between just three actors (only one of which is a state): the US, the EU and the automobile industry.[8]

Multilateral cooperation is voluntary. Dependency theorists pose hard questions about whether it is innately coercive for the same rules to apply to all, powerful as well as weak, even leaving aside the concessions frequently made to Great Powers (see Velasco 2002; Amsden 2003). Nonetheless, our definition assumes that most, if not all, international actors have real choices when they decide whether or not to partake in multilateral cooperation.

On institutionalisation, we hedge our bets. By definition, multilateral cooperation is *essentially*[9] institutionalised: it may or may not spawn actual international organisations, with headquarters, staffs and delegated powers. The G20, as one example, employs no permanent staff. But policy cooperation within it has become institutionalised in that it is governed by norms and principles (see Jokela 2011).

We argue that the same rules must apply *by and large* to all: generally and for the most part, all must play by the same rules. When the UN agrees a resolution, it applies equally to all states. But only five states enjoy permanent membership and veto power on the UN Security Council. Moreover, not all participants in multilateral cooperation are states that possess sovereignty under international law, the ability to sign treaties (unless they have legal personality), or a monopoly on the use of force. Thus, by definition, the same rules that apply to states in multilateral cooperation cannot apply to non-state actors.

Plenty of cases of modern multilateralism apply rules differently to different states. As we demonstrate, claims that today's multilateralism is more binding, rules-based and demanding than past versions are not without substance. But the 'old' multilateralism – with its opt-outs, derogations and special privileges for Great Powers – lives on in the UN, the International Monetary Fund (IMF) and elsewhere. Our definition – with its qualifying phrase of 'by and large' – therefore reflects caution about claims of a new, more demanding, twenty-first-century multilateralism. Relatedly, any claim that progressively more multilateralism will always serve the interests of any international actor, let alone lead to a more peaceful or prosperous global order, must be treated with prudence. And that is without even considering the question – which we *do* consider below – of what constitutes *effective* multilateralism. Nevertheless, armed with a definition that reflects the actually existing multilateralism of the twenty-first century, we can consider what Europe has contributed to it, and might contribute in the future.

Europe's contribution thus far

The EU's commitment to effective multilateralism means that Europeans who seek to build it must consider how it has arisen in different contexts, of both time and space. Both the historical evolution of the international order *and* the dimensions of that order – determined by the distribution of power and patterns of interdependence – have determined patterns of multilateralism at any given time. Domestic political space clearly matters, too, since politics at the domestic level of individual states – especially powerful ones – have narrowed or widened the political space for multilateral initiatives in different historical eras. Put simply, the past holds lessons for any effort to deepen or extend the reach of multilateral cooperation.

The Westphalian state as well as the first attempts to organise cross-border cooperation were European in origin (see Chapter 4). One of the distinct contributions of the Renaissance in Europe was the establishment, as early as the 1400s, of the conventions of diplomacy. Yet, multilateral cooperation was relatively rare until the nineteenth century, when a host of cooperative agreements on (especially) trade, river transport and public health were sealed in response to the cross-border implications of the industrial revolution. Again, Europe was in the forefront with the UK as the birthplace of industrialisation which then spread to western Europe and, subsequently, North America and Japan.

Most multilateral agreements did not generate formal organisations. The Concert of Europe was an almost purely informal framework in which the Great Powers of the day – Austria, Great Britain, Prussia, Russia – agreed to consult and negotiate on issues of peace and security, which initially mostly had to do with containing France. The Concert lasted nearly 100 years after the Napoleonic wars ended in 1815. It eventually incorporated France as its fifth member and kept Europe peaceful for nearly four decades. However, the Concert's legitimacy was damaged by the surge in European nationalism after the revolutions of 1848. It collapsed entirely at the outbreak of World War I in 1914. Still, the Concert paved the way for twentieth-century multilateralism by establishing that issues of peace and security could be addressed in multilateral fora, and by recognising the special roles, rights and obligations of Great Powers.

Europe was mostly a bystander or bandwagoner – sometimes a blemish – when the seeds of modern multilateralism were planted in the early twentieth century. For the first time, attempts were made to create formal multilateral organisations with rules that were codified and mechanisms for dispute settlement. The end of the Great War saw the US under Woodrow Wilson take the lead in seeking to construct a new international order in which 'military rivalry and alliances…power and security competition would be decomposed and replaced by a community of nations' (Ikenberry *et al.* 2009: 12). In retrospect, given the forces set in motion by the 1919 Treaty of Versailles, it is sobering to recall that

> those who gathered at Versailles believed that the League of Nations and other international associations not only might help avoid a return to war but also could help civilize nations and bring about progress…International organizations such as the League of Nations were designed not only to more rationally steer the world but also to produce a more liberal world that would be self-regulating in more desirable ways.
>
> *(Barnett and Finnemore 2005: 166)*

Wilson's liberal vision was ostensibly extinguished by the American Congress, which refused to permit US entry (see George and George 1964; J. M. Cooper 2002). Yet, Germany, Italy and Spain also contributed to its demise by withdrawing. In an era of continual crisis, that included a global economic depression and the rise of Hitler's Germany and Mussolini's Italy, the League became moribund and eventually was abandoned in 1946. Diplomatic historians and international lawyers have long debated why the League failed (see Fenwick 1936; Knock 1992; J. M. Cooper 2002). But France's insistence on the punitive terms of Versailles, Germany's lapse into economic chaos, and Italy's military adventurism in Abyssinia (Ethiopia), where its forces used mustard gas and poisoned water supplies, were all central to its failure. Arguably, the League died in Europe as much as it did on Capitol Hill.

Whatever its weaknesses, the League of Nations was an essential precursor to international institution-building after 1945. A major spike in multilateral cooperation occurred over the next ten years when the Bretton Woods institutions and the General Agreement on Tariffs and Trade (GATT), the UN, and NATO were all created. Western European states were party to all and at times individual European states – particularly the UK – were central in designing them. But, with Europe still recovering from the ravages of World War II, it fell to the emergent hegemonic power, the US, and its leaders, particularly Franklin Roosevelt, to be the primary catalysts. For the US, 'multilateralism in its generic sense served as a foundational principle on the basis of which to reconstruct the post-war world' (Ruggie 1992: 586). For weaker states, including several European ones – especially France – multilateralism not only promised benefits but also constrained a hegemon.

It was always clear that the UN would be built as a collective security organisation and follow in the steps of the League. However, past traumas made consensus possible on the need to recognise the privileged role of Great Powers. Offering the US, Soviet Union, France, the UK and China permanent membership on the UN Security Council, and thus effectively a veto, not only marked a return to a balance-of-power. It also acknowledged the necessity of unanimity among major powers as a prerequisite of multilateral cooperation. And, in contrast to the League, the UN's role was extended to economic and social affairs and human rights.

Multilateral cooperation became seen, above all in Washington, as an essential antidote to the protectionism of the 1920s and 30s. New multilateral agreements were thus struck on a range of issues that were past sources of international friction and, often, outright conflict. They included a stable exchange rate system, a reserve unit of account (the gold standard) and the reduction of trade barriers.

Bipartisanship on foreign policy between the two major American political parties, which emerged during the war and persisted after it ended, was an essential element of US support for the new multilateral system. It was nurtured by the White House: Roosevelt took Republicans' reservations about the UN seriously enough to work to incorporate them in the Charter. Two pillars of the foreign policy of his successor, Harry Truman, were that a prosperous and united Europe and a rules-based international economic order were central to US interests. In the end, the creation of the United Nations, the Marshall Plan and GATT enjoyed broad bipartisan support in the US (see Ikenberry 2003; Kupchan and Trubowitz 2007).

So did the creation of the European Coal and Steel Community (ECSC) and then the European Economic Community – the forerunners of today's EU – in the 1950s. In the hagiography that surrounds the origins of European institution-building, it is often forgotten that Europe's 'Great Men' – Monnet, Schuman, Adenauer – who embraced European integration as the path to economic recovery and resolution of the German problem only were able to after vigorous prompting from Washington. The outcome of inter-European negotiations on the use of Marshall Plan aid in 1947, which produced the Organisation for European Economic Co-operation (OEEC, later to become the OECD), frustrated the Truman administration since 'the lack of a customs union and absence of strong, central institutions indicated that the Europeans continued to look at American aid from a national, rather than continental, perspective' (Messenger 2006: 38).

For Washington, the key problem 'was a lack of leadership on the European side' (Lundestad 1998: 30).

In particular, the UK remained allergic to supranational institution-building despite Churchill's rhetoric about the desirability of a United States of Europe. Eventually, implementation of the European Recovery Programme (as the Marshall Plan was officially known) gave the US leverage to demand that recipient states cooperate. Pressure from the Truman administration, especially Secretary of State Dean Acheson, on Paris led France to embrace institution-building and take the lead via the Schuman Plan in creating the ECSC. Europeans thus created their own brand of deep multilateralism. But the US played midwife and was very much present at the creation.[10]

Amidst the early steps towards European integration, the Cold War made 'Franco-American agreement easier to achieve' since European integration promised Paris a sort of 'double containment' of the Soviets and Germans (Messenger 2006: 39). More generally, it ushered in a new and unprecedented international context that led Washington to support the creation of NATO in 1949, with an attack on one member treated as an attack on all. The American commitment to multilateral security cooperation was pragmatic, not doctrinal. It was reluctant in the case of NATO. The 1949 Washington Treaty that created it was 'seen by many American officials as a transitional agreement that would provide encouragement and support' for a mostly European security architecture that would, in the words of the Marshall Plan's first (American) administrator, 'get Europe on its feet and off our backs' (quoted in Ikenberry 2001: 201).

When the Cold War ended, many predicted a shift towards multipolarity, with a more integrated Europe rising in power after the signing (and eventual ratification) of the landmark Maastricht Treaty. Instead, the EU lurched from crisis to crisis, particularly in the Balkans. In the event, '[w]hat the 1990s wrought is a unipolar America... more powerful than any other great state in history' (Ikenberry 2003: 538).

In these circumstances, most IR theory predicts that a hegemon will shun multilateralism and agree nothing that limits its room to manoeuvre or even dominate. Yet, the Clinton administration was a primary architect of new agreements to create the WTO and the Asia-Pacific Economic Cooperation forum (APEC). It also was instrumental in the 'robust multilateralism' that ended the Balkan wars (Talbott 2008: 3). It was permissive, at least, of considerable strengthening of the UN's systems for peacekeeping, peace-building and humanitarian aid (Jones and Forman 2010). The EU threw its full weight behind strengthening UN cooperation and was, in some ways, an equal partner to the US in agreeing the Uruguay Round that gave birth to the WTO. But its capacity for leadership remained strictly limited by its own internal divisions as well as its persistent and habitual instinct to look to Washington to lead.

In other areas – arms control, environmental affairs and some human rights issues – US support for new multilateral initiatives ranged from patchy to non-existent. Bipartisan consensus, a vital lubricant to US support for post-war multilateralism, crumbled (see Kupchan and Trubowitz 2007: 25). In these areas, Europe enjoyed greater scope to lead, particularly on the 1997 Ottawa Treaty to ban landmines, albeit only after much advocacy by a coalition of NGOs, the Canadian Foreign Minister Lloyd Axworthy and the UK's Princess Diana. The EU also was a crucial advocate in the creation of the International Criminal Court and agreement on the Kyoto Protocol to limit global warming. Yet, the opening up of rifts in the transatlantic alliance over new cooperative initiatives stunted the growth of multilateralism and limited its impact. Partisanship in US domestic politics increased markedly during the Clinton administration and became even more entrenched during the administration of George W. Bush. Many of its top officials openly aired their mistrust of international institutions (see Bolton 2007; Feith 2008), and the US reneged on a range of multilateral commitments.

In the background, the early twenty-first century witnessed rapidly advancing interdependence spurred by globalisation. The internationalisation of financial regulation and diseases, the threat of catastrophic terrorism, and the post-2008 Great Recession all created fresh demand for multilateralism. The election of Barack Obama in 2008 raised hopes in European political capitals of a new impetus behind multilateral cooperation on climate change, human rights and arms control. Limited successes – including ratification of a New Strategic Arms Reduction Treaty (START) with Russia, intensified multilateral collaboration with Europe on Iran's nuclear programme, and NATO's successful military intervention in Libya – ensued. But the combination of ever-intensifying partisan conflict in Washington, focus on the drawdown of American troops in Iraq and Afghanistan, and Obama's 'Asian pivot' crowded the US foreign policy agenda. The Obama administration was consumed with 'attempts to reconcile the president's lofty vision with his innate realism and political caution', and his administration's 'efforts to engage competing powers…at times c[a]me at the cost of ignoring traditional allies', including the EU (Indyk *et al.* 2012: 30). There was little political space in Washington for 'building multilateralism', with Europe or anyone else (see Laïdi 2012: 4).

While consistent patterns in the historical development of multilateralism are elusive, there is evidence that rising interdependence – as during the Industrial Revolution or modern era of globalisation – increases demand for multilateralism. As generic comments on multilateralism go, Ikenberry's (2003: 540) comes as close as any to unchallenged veracity: 'as global interdependence grows, so does the need for multilateral coordination of policies'. Yet, as we have seen, such need often remains unmet for long periods of time. Thus far, it is unclear whether the modern era of unprecedented international interdependence will eventually see supply adjusted in response to rising demand. Nor is it at all clear that the EU can effectively exploit the international political space open to new multilateral solutions, particularly not without the active support of Washington, given its record in the twenty-first century thus far.

Moreover, in defiance of systemic IR theory, multilateralism clearly thrives or dies as a consequence of alignments at multiple dimensions of political space. It became a form of cooperation with more legitimacy than other forms in the twentieth century because of systemic changes: it was embraced both because it was inclusive – in the case of the UN – *and* exclusive – in the case of NATO. Yet, multilateralism has thrived or died throughout history because of changes at the sub-systemic level of domestic politics, such as the European revolutions of 1848 or the emergence of bipartisanship in post-war US politics. The effort to make the international system a more multilateral one in the future will have to find ways to cooperate with states with flawed democracies – such as Russia – or even autocracies, including China.

Finally, economic crisis tends to spur multilateralism. Of course, the WTO was created in the absence of any deep economic slump. Whether the post-2008 financial crisis yields a strengthening of multilateral institutions such as the G20 remains an open question. But early evidence from the sovereign debt crisis in the Eurozone suggests that one outcome will be 'more Europe', with a banking union and other stronger multilateral economic institutions to forestall future crises.

To these 'lessons' must be added another: aspirant builders of multilateralism must take account of shifts in power in IR. Today's modern institutions of global governance have been built mostly with the US in the lead, sometimes in tandem with Europe. The resulting institutions usually have privileged their superior power. Yet, the rise of the BRICS and the shift to a more multipolar international order means that building – or even preserving – multilateral cooperation will require satisfying the powerful desire of rising powers to have their new status recognised. If Europe is to show leadership in extending its own habits of cooperation, it will need to learn and accept that doing so is likely to be a more complex and difficult endeavour than was the building of the multilateral order that already exists.

Is your multilateralism the same as mine?

Our historical review of multilateralism has, necessarily, been truncated. We have focused mostly on Europe (and America) and on cooperation that is broader than regional in scope. Yet, recent decades have seen a step-level change in regional cooperation and moves by emerging powers outside the North Atlantic area to create and nurture new regional frameworks. The seeds for MERCOSUR – known in English as the Southern Common Market – were sown in 1985 when Brazil and Argentina agreed an economic cooperation programme, thus paving the way for the 1991 Treaty of Asunción linking them with Uruguay and Paraguay in what is now a full customs union.

In Asia, the 1997–8 financial crisis opened eyes, particularly in Beijing, to how far economic interdependence had progressed in the region. Subsequently, China took active, even selfless steps to help stabilise the region's economies. More recently, it has shifted towards 'enthusiastic embrace of multilateral diplomacy' (Gill and Green 2009: 20). This stance has shaped Chinese foreign policy choices in a regional context in which 'East Asian governmental regionalism has grown dramatically in the past few decades' (Kang 2007: 72).

Together with China, Russia can claim to have advanced multilateralism significantly in both regional and global contexts in recent years. Both gave impetus to the founding of the Shanghai Cooperation Organisation (SCO) in 2001 to bring them together with the former Soviet Asian republics of Kazakhstan, Kyrgyzstan, Tajikistan, and Uzbekistan.[11] Russia also was the main advocate behind making BRICS more than just a shorthand term for emerging powers by hosting the group's first-ever formal summit in 2009. BRICS summits now occur annually at the level of Heads of Government. They have thus far focused on the global economic crisis, plans for a development bank, and raising the profile of the five members in global affairs.

In short, the claim that the twenty-first century has witnessed the emergence of a 'new multilateralism' rests not only on the creation of new, global frameworks – such as the Ottawa Convention or International Criminal Court – that are (mostly) western creations and more binding and formally rules-based. The contention also draws succour from the spread of regional cooperation and the embrace of new experiments, at least, in multilateralism by emerging powers. Yet, claims that the international order is becoming progressively more multilateral inevitably run up against the existence of different and perhaps competing cultural visions of multilateralism. To what extent do different understandings of multilateralism lead states to define differently the problem(s) that cooperation seeks to solve? Is the EU deluding itself that it can lead in building multilateralism because there exists no universal set of values to underpin it?

If there is a European way of multilateralism, it contrasts with the 'sovereignty-based' multilateralism that is favoured by China (Xinbo 2009: 68). Perhaps counter-intuitively, Chinese foreign policy analysts tend to concur that, as its international power increases, 'China will become more proactive in its multilateral diplomacy and increase its influence in global multilateral settings' (Li and Chen 2010: 13). There is already plenty of evidence to sustain the claim. Asia is now home to close to 100 multilateral groupings, and China is a member of most. China is as enthusiastic as any state about the rise of the G20.

Yet, China's embrace of multilateralism is cautious, instrumental and conditional. Official Chinese edicts on foreign policy are Confucian in nature and based on the ideas of *he er bu tong* ('harmonious but different'). Li and Chen (2010: 18) find 'notable euphoria in China regarding the emerging world order', with the global financial crisis seen as a sign of the West's decline. Equally, they highlight instinctual caution arising from the doctrine, associated with Deng Xiaoping, of *tao guang yanghui*, or 'hide brightness, nourish obscurity' (Li and Chen 2010: 23). Multilateralism Chinese style is pragmatic and unenthusiastic about grand visions. A more institutionalised international order is desirable above all because it is a hedge against a unipolar, US-dominated world. Still, the belief remains deep-rooted in China that 'global governance equals Western governance' (Li and Chen 2010: 22) and that the principles or values that many multilateral institutions uphold are western – not universal – ones.

Above all, China's embrace of multilateralism is strictly qualified by its non-negotiable insistence that sovereignty is absolute. Kissinger (2011: 515) contrasts China's — and indeed Asia's — approach with that of the West. Disputes between western states

> even at their most bitter…retain the character of an interfamily dispute. Soft power and multilateral diplomacy are the dominant tools of foreign policy… In Asia, by contrast, the states consider themselves in potential confrontation with their neighbours. It is not that they necessarily plan on war; they simply do not exclude it…Sovereignty, in many cases regained relatively recently after periods of foreign colonization, has an absolute character. The principles of the Westphalian system prevail, more so than on their continent of origin. The concept of sovereignty is considered paramount.

Specifically, issues such as the value of the Chinese yuan, Tibet or China's one child policy are strictly off the table for discussion in multilateral fora. China's rise may well result in a more multilateral world, particularly on a regional scale in Asia. But Asia is still home to powerful nationalism, bitter disputes over territory and water, and far more ethnic, linguistic and cultural diversity than, say, in Europe (see Gill and Green 2009: 13).

It bears reminding that Russia — along with China — is an Asian power and itself a major contributor to the region's diversity. Its attitude towards multilateralism is, in important respects, similar to that of China: it is pragmatic, seen as a means to an end (to curb western dominance) and wholly conditional on the understanding that Russia's Czarist 'sovereign democracy' is not open to criticism or even discussion. Marsh and Mackenstein (2005: 200) contrast 'EU multilateralism [as]…generally a reflection of its own values and embrac[ing] concepts such as humanitarian intervention' with a Russian view that 'remains wedded to state sovereignty and tends to see multilateralism in terms of power-balancing rather than transcending Westphalian structures'. Moscow's outlook could be seen as a product of a symbiosis between Vladimir Putin's iron, oligarchic rule and Russia's (re-)emergence of something approaching a Great Power. Kagan (2008: 55) insists that, 'strength and control at home allow Russia to be strong abroad. Strength abroad justifies strong rule at home. Russia's growing international clout also shields Putin's autocracy from foreign pressures.'

Together with China, Russia has become an enthusiastic backer of the SCO. How capable it is of truly collective action — anti-western or otherwise — is debatable. The SCO has made some progress on low-key issues such as water rights in Asia, but also has been the scene of considerable Chinese–Russian rivalry (Cooley 2009). To illustrate, an attempt by the (then) Russian President, Dmitry Medvedev, to use the June 2009 SCO summit to condemn Georgia collectively after the previous year's war with Russia was stymied primarily by the Chinese, who made clear that they wished the SCO to be a forum for pragmatic cooperation, not geopolitical posturing.

On the other hand, the 2012 Beijing SCO summit raised eyebrows in political capitals globally. India made a strong pitch to upgrade its 'observer' status to full SCO membership and called for the group to take on a greater role in Afghanistan.[12] With Syria on the brink of civil war, an SCO summit declaration insisted on 'dialogues that respect Syria's sovereignty, independence and territorial integrity'. A joint statement by the Russian and Chinese presidents used even stronger language on Syria in warning against 'foreign military intervention as well as promoting "regime change" at the UN Security Council and other venues'.[13] The SCO thus offers a good illustration of the argument that multilateralism is naturally unwieldy (see Chapter 4) and how actions taken – or even declarations made – in one multilateral forum can block actions in another.

Equally, the SCO illustrates that solutions to many international problems can be found – if they can be found at all – only through concerted action by multiple multilateral groupings. Notably, the SCO includes Iran as a full member. As such, it was no surprise that its 2012 summit warned that 'any attempts to solve the Iranian problem' – an interesting choice of words – 'with force are unacceptable and could lead to unpredictable consequences that threaten stability and security in the region and the entire world'. Significantly, the Chinese Premier told the SCO gathering that 'China opposes any nation's push to acquire nuclear weapons'.[14] Resolution of the Iranian nuclear question – if possible at all – appeared to require coordination between the SCO and the so-called P5+1: grouping together the permanent members of the UNSC with Germany to negotiate with the Iranians.

Could Washington – given, for example, Hillary Clinton's insistence that China and Russia had to be part of the solution in both Syria and Iran – act as a go-between? More generally, where does the US now stand on the matter of building 'effective multilateralism'? Clinton (2010: 15) herself has written of the Obama administration's 'commitment to building a new global architecture of cooperation'. For his part, Drezner (2011: 58) argues that a key element of Obama's 'grand strategy' in foreign policy has been 'multilateral retrenchment…designed to curtail the United States' overseas commitments, restore its standing in the world, and shift burdens onto global partners'.

Even realists including Kagan (2002), acknowledge that there exists an 'American way' of multilateralism, but caution that it entails 'a cost-benefit analysis, not a principled commitment to multilateral action as the cornerstone of world order'. Others are more circumspect and insist that US

> presidents have to escape from both the concept and the word 'multilateralism'. It's too tarnished. Too many critics have made that word sound like multilateralism for its own sake or like tying the United States to a hopeless international chain gang.
>
> (Gelb 2009: 117)

It is easy to see false dichotomies in America's approach to multilateralism and miss considerable nuance. It is widely accepted that multilateralism can be very costly for any Great Power, but also that it can be a relatively inexpensive 'premium' to pay if it helps to solve problems that affect very powerful states more than others (see Tierney 2010). As we have seen, the US has historically been the primary architect of today's modern multilateralism, including relatively recent additions such as the WTO. The Obama administration has chosen multilateral diplomacy as its preferred route to trying to cope with many of the most challenging issues on its foreign policy agenda, including Iran, Libya and North Korea.

Yet, Obama has also shown himself to be a consummate pragmatist with no real inclination towards or vision of a more multilateral world. The rise of intense partisanship in American domestic politics inevitably spilled over into foreign policy, as shown by the early and intense opposition to Obama's desire to project a 'new spirit of multilateralism' by joining the UN Human Rights Council and increasing US funding to the IMF.[15] In his assessment of 'America's strategic position' as bequeathed to Obama by Bush, Laïdi (2012: 3–4) includes 'domestic mistrust of most multilateral initiatives, including those to which the United States had committed'. It was difficult to argue that the US was any closer to making binding commitments on climate change or joining the ICC at the end of the Obama's first term than it was at the beginning. Even if the bipartisanship of the early post-war period were somehow (miraculously) to re-emerge, the need to secure a two-thirds vote in the US Senate to ratify any treaty would remain a major hurdle to ensuring that Washington would participate in any new, major multilateral venture (Cowhey 1993; Karns and Mingst 2002).

A revealing window on the America way of multilateralism is Strobe Talbott's (2008: 1) opus *The Great Experiment*, the very first words of which are 'multilat is hell': a phrase used by Talbott's executive assistant as he prepared for his first UN General Assembly meeting as Deputy Secretary of State in the Clinton administration. Talbott (2008: 6) insists that 'effective global governance and successful American foreign policy are closely linked…and they will have to be resuscitated together'. Yet, even he reflects on his experience of government and offers the pragmatic nostrum that 'multilat may sometimes be too much of a good thing, but unilat is often too little. The trick is to find the right combination of the two' (Talbott 2008: 2). The George W. Bush administration may have skewed the balance. But it is illustrative that post-9/11 US security policy featured both aggressive, unilateralist behaviour on arms control, airline passenger data and container security alongside considerable 'substantive cooperation' on counterterrorism with the EU and within APEC (Gill and Green 2009: 7; Baker 2010). If the past is any guide to the future, Europeans must acknowledge that no US administration can be expected to embrace multilateralism for its own sake. American exceptionalism remains alive and well, especially among those on the right of the domestic political spectrum. The American 'way' of multilateralism is shrewd, pragmatic and interest-driven.

Finally, as we have argued elsewhere, the notion that EU states are uniformly loyal to their doctrinal commitment to multilateralism is highly questionable (Bouchard and Peterson 2011: 27–8). The sovereign debt crisis in the Eurozone has been illustrative. Despite the rhetorical commitment of the German Chancellor, Angela Merkel, to a stronger 'political union' with more fiscal coordination to put national economies on a 'solid foundation', Germany often seemed to act out of raw national interest in, say, resisting Eurobonds that would mutualise debt or anti-austerity policies that could stimulate growth in weaker economies.[16] It did not require too much cynicism to conclude that what the EU revealed about itself during the Eurozone crisis was that effective multilateralism was easy to embrace in principle but that it hardly motivated member states with divergent interests – even in the Union's own backyard – as the crisis deepened.

In the circumstances, what makes multilateralism 'effective'? What really motivates the European doctrinal commitment to it? We consider the multiple ways in which it may be understood, as well as different motivations to bring it about, in the section that follows.

What makes multilateralism effective?

When we reflect on the meaning of the phrase, we can identify at least three ways in which multilateralism might be considered to be 'effective'. They are not mutually exclusive and our list is by no means exhaustive. But all three consider multilateralism to be a means to some desired – and different – end. As such, they help us understand what motivates EU states or any other when they embark on multilateral cooperation and shed light on the primary objectives advocates of multilateralism can be expected to pursue in the international order of the twenty-first century.

Building international order

First, effective multilateralism may be viewed as a means of achieving *international order*. More specifically, multilateralism is effective when it brings about a more predictable, rules-based order that is more 'biased' towards the peaceful resolution of conflict. If there is a European way of multilateralism, most EU officials would argue that this kind of order is the end to which it is a means. In this version, multilateralism is cumulative. Its extension – think of Russia's WTO membership – teaches others to learn the European habits of compromise, cooperation and consensus. Multilateralism is effective when it aids the transformation of the international order into a less 'anarchical society' (Bull 1977) and a more genuine society of states.

This definition of effective may seem over-idealistic, quixotic and naïve in a world in which all states must seek advantage, defend their interests, and cope with the rising power of emerging states. Yet, when we sample the research literature, we find frequent claims that '[c]ommitment to multilateralism is at the core of EU external activities' (Bretherton and Vogler 2006: 185). As Smith (2008: 62) notes, the European Commission has adopted the mantra that '[r]egional integration can form part of a general strategy for encouraging sustained economic growth' and that there exists 'no tension between multilateralism and regionalism'. The EU increasingly embraces diplomatic activity that is 'bilateral in procedures but multilateral in its purposes' (Correia 2002: 204). That is how it justifies its Strategic Partnerships with major powers or its championing of Russia's WTO membership.

A version of effective multilateralism that promises, in effect, 'we only want what's best for you: a more peaceful and cooperative world' is easy to dismiss as rhetoric. Yet, even Smith (2008: 8), whose survey of EU foreign policy is not short of trenchant criticism of Europe's performance, acknowledges that the EU sometimes genuinely privileges 'milieu goals' – that 'aim to shape the environment in which the state…operates' – over 'possession goals' that seek to further specific interests (see also Wolfers 1962). If the EU often falls short of success, it may be more because of the enormous difficulty of the task than a lack of commitment.

Pursuing European interests

Just because the EU exhibits 'a distinct preference for multilateralism and…inter-regional cooperation' (Marsh and Mackenstein 2005: 62), that does not necessarily mean that it does so for altruistic reasons. Multilateralism might be considered 'effective' when it *furthers European interests*. In particular, we might expect European policy-makers to consider multilateralism effective when it acts to 'export' the results of European cooperation in the form of binding rules and standards that are first internally agreed and adopted by the EU and then generalised across the international system. This outcome might result from region-to-region or Strategic Partnership-type cooperation that yields bilateral regulatory agreements between the Union and other regional organisations or states. Europeans could then claim to be both leading and building effective multilateralism, particularly in ways that advance labour, consumer and environmental protection standards. But they would find it difficult to deny that the outcome serves the interests of European industries that are already producing goods that meet EU standards that become global ones.

When we examine specific relationships between the EU and other powers or regions, we find multiple examples of cooperation that are difficult to reconcile with the first, 'order-building' definition of effective multilateralism, and may be difficult to consider multilateralism at all. In its reform of the Cotonou Agreement with the African, Caribbean and Pacific (ACP) states, the EU – and particularly the Commission's Directorate for Trade – were accused of privileging trade concessions over development considerations and playing hardball with fundamentally weaker partners. The EU's insistence on negotiating Economic Partnership Agreements (EPAs) with the ACP states divided into six regional groupings not only was the subject of intense criticism from Oxfam and other European NGOs for Brussels for its neo-liberal bias; it also has, thus far, mostly failed to promote regionalism (only one of six 'regions' – the Caribbean – signed a full EPA; see Chapter 4).

The transatlantic relationship also illustrates how interest-driven the EU's pursuit of cooperation can be. Regulatory cooperation with the US in the late 1990s appeared designed to narrow the differences between standards enforced by the two economic giants, and then to export them globally by (effectively) imposing and codifying them in multilateral agreements, even if these efforts never amounted to much (see Steffenson 2005; Pollack and Shaffer 2009). In the security arena, Marsh and Mackenstein (2005: 86) are blunt in asking whether 'multilateralism is the European way of avoiding rightful responsibilities whilst simultaneously free-riding on American commitments to international security and sniping at American leadership'.

Of course, no international actor – including the EU – can ever avoid defining and then pursuing their self-interests in IR. Occasionally, as Meunier and Nicolaïdis (2011: 287) find in trade policy, the Union is exposed as 'asserting its central role in the multilateral system less to uphold the value of multilateralism as a public good than to promote the EU's own interest in the system'. At times, inevitably, successful promotion of those interests will be what really makes multilateralism effective in the minds of European policy-makers, however much it is cloaked in the discourse of multilateralism as a public good that makes the world a better place.

Steering the (changing) balance of power

A third, principal way that multilateralism might be considered effective is as a means to recognise, steer and formalise a *shifting balance of international power*. Broadly, multilateralism might achieve this end in two different ways. First, the EU – with, in all likelihood, the US – might seek generally to lock in rising powers to existing multilateral agreements by extending them. China and Russia's WTO accessions are illustrative. So might moves to make G20 a more robust framework for agreeing binding commitments, perhaps policed by a permanent secretariat and enforced by some kind of legal mechanism or court.

But a second and probably more productive goal for the West might well be to pursue a rebalancing of the representation of the BRICS within new or existing multilateral agreements (see Peterson *et al.* 2012). In particular, the reform of the UN Security Council – with its ossified permanent membership reflecting a balance of power long passed – would mark a significant step with enormous symbolic and practical value in the eyes of the BRICS. Giving up the over-representation of Europe and the US, and their monopoly on the directorships of the World Bank and IMF, could also pay political dividends.

The second goal is both more ambitious but also more likely to ensure that China's 'peaceful rise' continues, Russian power in its neighbourhood is deployed peacefully, India and Brazil become more responsible trade powers, and South Africa's aspirations to lead Africa are respected. In this case, multilateralism would be viewed as effective when it is reconfigured to reflect the rise of *multipolarity*. Hard-headed analysts of European foreign policy tend to agree that the EU seems not to have got the memo about how fundamentally important this objective has become. For example, Howorth (2011: 219) dismisses the 2003 European Security Strategy as 'hardly a statement of the EU's strategic purpose' since 'it did not attempt to analyse the emerging centres of strategic power in the 21st century world, or the probe the shifting dynamics of an embryonic multipolar system'. Smith (2008: 240) finds the EU 'flirting rather dangerously with failure and irrelevance', and she is not alone (see Laqueur 2011). If the EU wishes to avoid its own decline, it must arguably embrace the mission of sharing power more widely with a more diverse array of others, and in a way it has never done before.

Conclusion

Our purpose in this chapter has been fourfold. First, we have offered a modernised definition of multilateralism. We have argued that it is no longer the exclusive preserve of states and that the resources of non-state actors are often crucial to giving multilateral agreements between states functionality and legitimacy. Further, we have insisted that cooperation must be minimally institutionalised to be considered multilateralism. It must be voluntary and based on rules that apply more or less equally to all.

Second, we have reviewed the emergence of multilateralism over time and space. Europe has often been at the forefront in its historical development, albeit as Washington's understudy in the post-war period. It has also been the instigator and scene of its collapse during the earlier, roughly 100-year period after the 1848 revolutions. Admittedly, it is difficult to find any 'iron laws' about when multilateralism advances and when it retreats. But it is clear that domestic political conditions, especially within Great Powers, are key causal factors.

Third, we have considered how multilateralism is viewed by non-European eyes. As we have seen, other major powers tend to eschew the 'European way' insofar as it is characterised by a willingness to pool sovereignty and sign up to binding commitments. Multilateral cooperation that is regional in scale has certainly been advanced considerably, including in regions beyond Europe. But only Brussels and other national European political capitals appear to embrace multilateralism as a value for its own sake, as opposed to one among multiple diplomatic configurations that may be chosen depending on whether it advances specific interests. Questions also arise about whether the EU has been true to its doctrinal commitment to multilateralism in its own internal effort to cope with its crisis in the Eurozone.

Finally, we have proposed three different ways in which multilateralism might be deemed to be effective, each of which is defined by the objectives sought. The view that effective multilateralism means constructing a more cooperative, peaceful society of states is a mostly iconoclastic and specifically European view. Yet, as much as it struggles to be true to this view in practice, it remains part of the EU's *raison d'être* as a global actor and, sometimes, at least, that is clear in its actions. Inevitably, Europe also pursues multilateralism that is effective insofar as it advances its own interests, especially its economic interests, in line with Damro's (Chapter 6) characterisation of Market Power Europe. Finally, and increasingly in the near-term future, multilateralism might be considered effective when it binds rising powers into a more cooperative international order, but one that more accurately represents a more multipolar balance of power. The view that embracing this objective is a strategically sound way for Europe to manage its own decline and shift towards power-sharing with the least undue conflict is a credible one.

If there is one, most compelling conclusion that comes from the evidence we have considered, it is that modernising global governance requires Europeans who realise both that other powers are mostly enthusiastic about extending multilateralism, but that it is rarely seen as a uniformly desirable public good beyond the European continent. Too often, what critics describe as Europe's 'almost cultlike worship of multilateralism' (Marsh and Mackenstein 2005: 86) strikes others as supercilious, sanctimonious and hypocritical given the EU's often muscular pursuit of its own interests. Globally, Europe's own experience of deep multilateralism is widely viewed as *sui generis* and mostly unworkable as a model to be applied elsewhere, and besides open to new questions about its own durability. The EU has the potential, at least, to be a leader in building and modernising multilateralism. But it cannot do so by signalling to non-European others: 'we have lofty values, you have narrow interests'.[17]

Notes

1 While usage varies, global governance in most instances can be considered a synonym for multilateralism.
2 Only around half of all US companies listed in the Standard and Poor's 500-stock index list the portion of their revenue that derives from Europe, so precise figures are illusive. Still, it is estimated that US food and beverage as well as pharmaceutical companies generate 22 per cent of their revenues in Europe. The figure for American auto firms is around 27 per cent and for technology companies no less than one-third. See N. Popper, 'US Companies Warn of Slowing Sales in Europe', *New York Times*, 5 June 2012. Online. Available: http://www.nytimes.com/2012/06/05/business/us-companies-warn-of-slowing-sales-in-europe.html?pagewanted=all (accessed 30 August 2012).
3 This section draws heavily on Bouchard and Peterson 2011: 6–11.
4 Institutions were defined as 'persistent and connected sets of rules, formal and informal, that prescribe behavioural roles, constrain activity, and shape expectations' (Keohane 1990: 733). Implicit in Keohane's work appears to be the assumption that *ad hoc* multilateralism is likely to lead to institutionalised multilateralism, as states find themselves unable to enforce the terms of agreements they make with each other (see Keohane 1998; Keohane and Nye 2000).
5 To illustrate, Naïm (2009) claims that no major, new multilateral agreement has been agreed since the mid-1990s.
6 See IATA (2009), 'A Global Approach to Reducing Airline Emissions'. Online. Available: http://www.iata.org/SiteCollectionDocuments/Documents/Global_Approach_Reducing_Emissions_251109web.pdf (accessed 30 August 2012).
7 Many in EU circles, in particular, would reject the notion that relations between regions cannot be multilateralised since an increasingly prominent goal of EU external action is region-to-region cooperation (see Van Langenhove and Costa 2007; Doidge 2011).
8 In fact, the 'automobile industry' is not a single industry, despite considerable cross-investment by both American and European manufacturers. Any agreement on regulatory cooperation would logically require the consent of two automobile associations: the (American) Alliance of Automobile Association and the European Automobile Manufacturers' Association.
9 By 'essentially', we mean fundamentally, inherently, intrinsically and necessarily institutionalised: rules must exist that are durable and (potentially) affect the behaviour of actors.
10 Acheson's (1969) memoirs of the same name make this point clear.
11 India, Iran, Pakistan and Mongolia have observer status. Sri Lanka and Belarus are 'dialogue partners'.

12 S. M. Krishna, 'India Pitches for Larger Role in Shanghai Cooperation Organisation', *The Times of India*, 7 June 2012, http://articles.timesofindia.indiatimes.com/2012-06-07/india/32100606_1_shanghai-cooperation-organisation-sco-india-pitches (accessed 30 August 2012).

13 Quoted in Jaime A. FlorCruz, 'Russia, China and Partners Call for Non-intervention', *CNN International*, 7 June 2012, http://edition.cnn.com/2012/06/07/world/asia/china-russia-syria/index.html (accessed 30 August 2012).

14 Eliot Elwar, 'Shanghai Cooperation Organization warns West against strike', *Digital Journal*, 8 June 2012, http://www.digitaljournal.com/article/326267 (accessed 30 August 2012).

15 See H. Morris, 'US Takes Human Rights Seat at UN', *Financial Times*, 13 May 2009. Online. Available: http://www.ft.com/intl/cms/s/0/78bc3e8c-3f36-11de-ae4f-00144feabdc0.html (accessed 30 August 2012); S. O'Conner, 'Obama's IMF Boost Exacts Heavy Toll', *Financial Times*, 15 June 2009. Online. Available: http://www.ft.com/intl/cms/s/0/e310540a-590b-11de-80b3-00144feabdc0.html#axzz251hZa6VN (accessed 30 August 2012).

16 Quoted in BBC News, 'Merkel Says Germany Cannot Save Eurozone on its Own', 14 June 2012. Online. Available: http://www.bbc.co.uk/news/business-18438402 (accessed 30 August 2012).

17 Here we paraphrase a comment made by our own Lorenzo Fioramenti of the University of Pretoria at a conference in Brussels on 'Global Europe' on 7 October 2011. Online. Available: http://www.pol.ed.ac.uk/news/2011/mercury_takes_part_in_brussels_conference_on_global_europe (accessed 30 August 2012).

References

Acheson, D. (1969) *Present at the Creation: My Years in the State Department*, New York and London: W.W. Norton.

Alexandroff, A. S. (2008) (ed.) *Can the World be Governed? Possibilities for Effective Multilateralism*, Waterloo Canada: Wilfrid Laurier Press.

Amsden, A. H. (2003) 'Good-Bye Dependency Theory, Hello Dependency Theory', *Studies in Comparative International Development*, 38 (1): 32–8.

Baker, S. (2010) *Skating on Stilts: Why We Aren't Stopping Tomorrow's Terrorists*, Stanford CA: Hoover Institution Press.

Barnett, M. and Finnemore, M. (2005) 'The Power of Liberal International Organizations' in M. Barnett and R. Duvall (eds) *Power in Global Governance*, Cambridge and New York: Cambridge University Press.

Bolton, J. (2007) *Surrender is Not an Option: Defending America at the United Nations and Abroad*, London and New York: Pocket Books.

Bouchard, C. and Peterson, J. (2011) *Conceptualising Multilateralism: Can We All Just Get Along?*, MERCURY E-paper series, no.1, MERCURY, available from http://www.europa.ed.ac.uk/global_europa/external_relations/mercury/publications

Bretherton, C. and Vogler, J. (2006) *The European Union as a Global Actor*, London and New York: Routledge, 2nd edition.

Bull, H. (1977) *The Anarchical Society: A Study of Order in World Politics*, London: Macmillan.

Calder, K. E. and Fukuyama, F. (2008) (eds) *East Asian Multilateralism: Prospects for Regional Stability*, Baltimore: Johns Hopkins University Press.

Caporaso, J. (1992) 'International Relations Theory and Multilateralism: the Search for Foundations', *International Organization*, 46 (3): 599–632.

Chalmers, D. and Tomkins, A. (2007) *European Union Public Law: Text and Materials*, Cambridge and New York: Cambridge University Press.

Clinton, H. (2010) 'Leading Through Civilian Power', *Foreign Affairs*, 89 (6) November/December: 13–24.

Cooley, A. (2009) 'Cooperation Gets Shanghaied: China, Russia and the SCO', *Foreign Affairs*, 14 December, available from http://www.foreignaffairs.com/articles/65724/alexander-cooley/cooperation-gets-shanghaied (accessed 2 November 2010).

Cooper, A. F. (2002) 'Like-minded Nations, NGOs, and the Changing Pattern of Diplomacy Within the UN System: An Introductory Perspective' in A.F. Cooper, J. English and R. Thakur (eds) *Enhancing Global Governance: Towards a New Diplomacy*, New York and Paris: United Nations University Press.

Cooper, J. M. (2002) *Breaking the Heart of the World: Woodrow Wilson and the Fight for the League of Nations*, Cambridge and New York: Cambridge University Press.

Correia, J. M. M. (2002) 'Portugal' in B. Hocking and D. Spence (eds) *Foreign Ministers in the European Union*, Basingstoke and New York: Palgrave.

Cowhey, P. F. (1993) 'Domestic Institutions and the Credibility of International Commitments: Japan and the United States', *International Organization*, 47 (2): 299–326.

Doidge, M. (2011) *The European Union and Interregionalism: Patterns of Engagement*, Franham and Burlington VT: Ashgate.

Drezner, D. (2011) 'Does Obama Have a Grand Strategy?', *Foreign Affairs*, 90 (4) July/August: 57–68.

Duchêne, F. (1972) 'Europe's Role in World Peace' in R. Mayne (ed.) *Europe Tomorrow: Sixteen Europeans Look Ahead*, London: Fontana.

EU (2003) *A Secure Europe in a Better World: European Security Strategy*, Paris: EU Institute for Security Studies.

Feith, D. J. (2008) *War and Decision: Inside the Pentagon at the Dawn of the War on Terrorism*, New York and London: Harper.

Fenwick, C. G. (1936) 'The "Failure" of the League of Nations', *The American Journal of International Law*, 30 (3): 506–9.

Frost, E. (2008) *Asia's New Regionalism*, Boulder CO and London: Lynne Rienner.

Gelb, L. (2009) *Power Rules: How Common Sense can Rescue American Foreign Policy*, New York and London: Harper Perrenial.

George, A. L. and George, J. L. (1964) *Woodrow Wilson and Colonel House: A Personality Study*, New York: Courier Dover Publications.

Gill, B. and Green, M. J. (2009) 'Unbundling Asia's New Multilateralism' in M. J. Green and B. Gill (eds) *Asia's New Multilateralism: Cooperation, Competition and the Search for Community*, New York: Columbia University Press.

Green, M. J. and Gill, B. (2009) (eds) *Asia's New Multilateralism: Cooperation, Competition, and the Search for Community*, New York: Columbia University Press.

Grevi, G. and de Vasconcelos, A. (2008) (eds) *Partnerships for Effective Multilateralism: EU Relations with Brazil, China, India and Russia*, Paris: EU Institute for Security Studies, Chaillot Paper 109, June.

Howorth, J. (2011) 'The EU's Security and Defence Policy: Towards a Strategic Approach' in C. Hill and M. Smith (eds) *International Relations and the European Union*, Oxford and New York: Oxford University Press.

Ikenberry, G. J. (2001) *After Victory: Institutions, Strategic Restraint and the Rebuilding of Order After Major Wars*, Princeton NJ: Princeton University Press.

Ikenberry, G. J. (2002) (ed.) *America Unrivaled: the Future of the Balance of Power*, Ithaca NY and London: Cornell University Press.

Ikenberry, G. J. (2003) 'Is American Multilateralism in Decline?', *Perspectives on Politics*, 1 (3): 533–50.

Ikenberry, G. J. (2006) *Liberal Order and Imperial Ambition: Essays on American Power and World Politics*, Cambridge and Malden MA: Polity.

Ikenberry, G. J. (2011) *Liberal Leviathin: the Origins, Crisis and Transformation of the American World Order*, Princeton NJ: Princeton University Press.

Ikenberry, G. J., Knock, T. J., Slaughter, A-M and Smith, T. (2009) *The Crisis of American Foreign Policy: Wilsonianism in the Twenty-First Century*, Princeton NJ: Princeton University Press.

Indyk, M. S., Lieberthal, K. G. and O'Hanlon, M. E. (2012) 'Scoring Obama's Foreign Policy: a Progressive Pragmatist Tries to Bend History', *Foreign Affairs*, 91 (3), May–June: 29–43.

Jokela, J. (2011) *The G-20: a Pathway to Effective Multilateralism?*, Paris: European Union Institute for Strategic Studies, Chaillot Paper 125, April.

Jones, B. D. and Forman, S. (2010) 'Introduction: "Two Worlds" of International Security' in B. D. Jones, S. Forman, and R. Gowan (eds) *Cooperating for Peace and Security: Evolving Institutions and Arrangements in a Context of Changing US Security Policy*, Cambridge and New York: Cambridge University Press.

Jones, D. and Coleman, P. (2005) *The United Nations and Education: Multilateralism, Development and Globalization*, London and New York: Routledge.

Kagan, R. (2002) 'Power and Weakness', *Policy Review*, 113, available from www.policyreview.org (accessed 6 January 2011).

Kagan, R. (2008) *The Return of History and the End of Dreams*, London and New York: Atlantic Books and Knopf.

Kaldor, M. (2003) *Global Civil Society: an Answer to War*, Oxford and Malden MA: Polity.

Kang, D. C. (2007) *China Rising: Peace, Power and Order in East Asia*, New York and Chichester: Columbia University Press.

Kapstein, E. B. and Mastanduno, M. (1999) (eds) *Unipolar Politics: Realism and State Strategies after the Cold War*, New York and Chichester: Columbia University Press.

Karns M. P. and Mingst K. A. (2002) 'The United States as "Deadbeat"? U.S. Policy and the UN Financial Crisis' in S. Patrick and S. Forman (eds) *Multilateralism and U.S. Foreign Policy: Ambivalent Engagement*, Boulder: Lynne Rienner.

Katzenstein, P. J. (2005) *A World of Regions: Asia and Europe in the American Imperium*, Ithaca and London: Cornell University Press.

Keck, M. E. and Sikkink, K. (1998) *Activists beyond Borders*, Ithaca and London: Cornell University Press.

Keohane, R. O. (1990) 'Multilateralism: an Agenda for Research', *International Journal*, 45: 731–64.

Keohane, R. O. (1998) 'International Institutions: Can Interdependence Work?', *Foreign Policy*, 110 (Spring): 82–96.

Keohane, R. O. and Nye, J. S. (2000) *Power and Interdependence,* 2nd edition, New York: Addison-Wesley Longman.

Keohane, R. O., Macedo, S. and Moravcsik, A. (2009) 'Democracy-enhancing Multilateralism', *International Organization*, 63 (1): 1–31.

Kissinger, H. (2011) *On China*, Penguin and Allen Lane: New York and London.

Knock, T. J. (1992) *To End All Wars: Woodrow Wilson and the Quest for a New World Order*, Princeton NJ: Princeton University Press.

Kupchan, C. A. and Trubowitz, P. L. (2007) 'Dead Center. The Demise of Liberal Internationalism in the United States', *International Security*, 32 (2): 7–44.

Laïdi, Z. (2012) *Limited Achievements: Obama's Foreign Policy*, Basingstoke and New York: Palgrave.

Laqueur, W. (2011) *After the Fall: the End of the European Dream and the Decline of a Continent*, New York: Thomas Dunne Books/St. Martin's Press.

Li, M. and Chen, G. (2010) 'China's Search for a Multilateral World: Dilemmas and Desires', *International Spectator*, 45 (4): 13–25.

Lundestad, G. (1998) *"Empire" by Integration: the United States and European Integration, 1945–1997*, Oxford and New York: Oxford University Press.

Marsh, S. and Mackenstein, H. (2005) *The International Relations of the European Union*, Harlow: Pearson Education.

Messenger, D. A. (2006) 'Dividing Europe: the Cold War and European Integration' in D. Dinan (ed.) *Origins and Evolution of the European Union*, Oxford and New York: Oxford University Press.

Meunier, S. and Nicolaïdis, K. (2011) 'The European Union as a Trade Power' in C. Hill and M. Smith (eds) *International Relations and the European Union*, Oxford and New York: Oxford University Press.

Muldoon Jr., J. P., Fagot Aviel, J., Reitano, R. and Sullivan, E. (2011) (eds) *The New Dynamics of Multilateralism: Diplomacy, International Organizations, and Global Governance*, Boulder CO: Westview Press.

Naïm, M. (2009) 'Minilateralism: the Magic Number to Get Real International Action', *Foreign Policy*, 173, July/Aug: 135–6.

Øhrgaard, J. C. (2004) 'International Relations or European Integration: Is the CFSP *Sui Generis*?' in B. Tonra and T. Christiansen (eds) *Rethinking European Union Foreign Policy*, Manchester and New York: Manchester University Press.

Peterson, J., Tocci, N. and Alcaro, R. (2012) *Multipolarity and Transatlantic Relations*, TRANSWORLD Working Paper 1, September; http://www.transworld-fp7.eu/wp-content/uploads/2012/10/TW_WP_01.pdf

Peterson, J., Aspinwall, M., Damro, C. and Boswell, C. (2008) *The Consequences of Europe: Multilateralism and the New Security Agenda*, Europa Institute Mitchell Working Paper, Edinburgh: University of Edinburgh- Europa Institute, 3/08, http://www.law.ed.ac.uk/mitchellworkingpapers/papers.aspx

Pollack, M. and Shaffer, G. C. (2009) *When Cooperation Fails: the International Law and Politics of Genetically Modified Foods*, Oxford and New York: Oxford University Press.

Rosecrance, R. (2008) 'A Grand Coalition and International Governance' in A. S. Alexandroff (ed.) *Can the World Be Governed? Possibilities for Effective Multilateralism*, Toronto: Wilfrid Laurier University Press.

Ruggie J. G. (1992) 'Multilateralism: the Anatomy of an Institution', *International Organization*, 46 (3): 561–98.

Ruggie, J. G. (1993) *Multilateralism Matters: the Theory and Praxis of an Institutional Form*, New York, NY: Columbia University Press.

Smith, K. E. (2008) *European Union Foreign Policy in a Changing World*, 2nd edition, Oxford and New York: Polity.

Steffenson, R. (2005) *Managing US–EU Relations: Actors, Institutions and the New Transatlantic Agenda*, Manchester and New York: Manchester University Press.

Talbott, S. (2008) *The Great Experiment: the Story of Ancient Empires, Modern States, and the Quest for a Global Nation*, New York and London: Simon and Schuster.

Thakur, R. (2002) 'Security in the New Millennium' in A. F. Cooper, J. English and R. Thakur (eds) *Enhancing Global Governance: Towards a New Diplomacy?*, Tokyo: United Nations University Press.

Tierney, D. (2010) 'Multilateralism: America's Insurance Policy Against Loss', *European Journal of International Relations*, first published online on October 7 2010, http://ejt.sagepub.com/content/early/2010/09/28/1354066110372433.full.pdf+html (accessed 6 January 2011).

Touval, S. and Zartman, I. W. (2010) 'Conclusion: Improving Knowledge of Cooperation' in I. W. Zartman and S. Touval (eds) *International Cooperation: the Extent and Limits of Multilateralism*, Cambridge and New York: Cambridge University Press.

Van Langenhove, L. (2010) 'The Transformation of Multilateralism Mode 1.0 to Mode 2.0', *Global Policy*, 1 (3): 263–70.

Van Langenhove, L. and Costa, A.-C. (2007) 'The EU as a Global Actor and "Third Generation" Regionalism' in P. Foradori, P. Rosa and R. Cartezzini (eds) *Managing a Multilevel Foreign Policy*, Plymouth and Lexington MD: Lexington Books.

Velasco, A. (2002) 'Dependency Theory', *Foreign Policy*, 133 (November–December): 44–5.

Wolfers, A. (1962) *Discord and Collaboration: Essays on International Politics*, Baltimore: Johns Hopkins University Press.

Xinbo, W. (2009) 'Chinese Perspectives on Building an East Asian Community in the 21st Century' in M. J. Green and B. Gill (eds) *Asia's New Multilateralism: Cooperation, Competition and the Search for Community*, New York: Columbia University Press.

3

THE EVOLVING 'DOCTRINE' OF MULTILATERALISM IN THE TWENTY-FIRST CENTURY

Elena Lazarou, Geoffrey Edwards, Christopher Hill and Julie Smith[1]

Introduction

In an increasingly interdependent world, multilateralism becomes ever more important across a plethora of policy sectors traditionally deemed to fall within the purview of the nation-state. Issues such as trade through the World Trade Organization (WTO), security via the Organization for Security and Cooperation in Europe (OSCE), or defence via the North Atlantic Treaty Organization (NATO), have been joined by others such as climate change (Kyoto) or, less formally, internal security, through bodies such as the Club of Berne. The EU made 'effective multilateralism' the priority in its Security Strategy of 2003. Yet, however necessary multilateralism has become, the question remains: is there consensus within the EU on the foundations, rules and principles that should guide policy and the construction of multilateral solutions? Put simply, is there a European *doctrine* of multilateralism?

This chapter suggests that the question can be answered by tracing the development of multilateralism in the twenty-first century, which we argue *has* evolved towards a doctrine. We conceptualise doctrine in this instance as a set of principles that guides the behaviour of states and international actors in formulating and negotiating multilateral solutions to global or regional issues. This conceptualisation of a doctrine of multilateralism aims to enrich current debates in an era of emerging multipolarity, focusing on the aims and motives of those promoting multilateralism, the principles that have guided them, and the observable changes in these principles and their operationalisation in the twenty-first century.

The chapter begins with a theoretical discussion of the role of doctrine in the formulation and legitimisation of policy choices, and proceeds by exploring the sources, codification and practice of a doctrine of multilateralism as advocated primarily by the EU in the twenty-first century. In particular, it looks at the cases of trade and security as manifest in the WTO on the one hand and the European

Union's Common Foreign, Security and Defence policies on the other. Drawing on these cases, it addresses the following research questions:

(1) Is there a single doctrine of multilateralism governing different policy areas?
(2) How has the EU contributed to the evolution of the doctrine of multilateralism?

The concept of multilateralism

In 1992, James Caporaso criticised international relations (IR) theory for having neglected multilateralism and its study as a basic concept in IR. Explanations for the lack of theorising vary from the argument that IR remains an American-dominated discipline (Hoffmann 1977), and thus tends to follow US foreign policy, which has rarely embraced the practice of multilateralism, to the simple explanation that there is actually not much multilateralism in practice. In any case, multilateralism has not preoccupied scholars very substantially (Caporaso 1992: 600). Perhaps it comes as no surprise since Ruggie (1992: 572) notes that multilateralism is, by its very nature, a highly demanding institutional form and that its historical incidence is likely to be less frequent than that of alternatives such as bilateralism.

However, the twenty-first century has witnessed a notable increase in the study of multilateralism. The emergence of complex global problems and threats and global markets, as well as the empowerment of new actors with a strong belief in the benefits of multilateral cooperation (the EU, Brazil) led to dynamic developments in the practice of multilateralism, which have not gone unnoticed in the scholarly world (see Garcia 2008; Keohane *et al.* 2009). Furthermore, the success of the EU as a unique and long-standing example of multilateralism in practice has given birth to a new sub-discipline: that of EU Studies. Yet, however much has been written about the EU, it has rarely, until recently, been in the context of a wider debate on multilateralism. To correct this is one of the aims of this volume and of the MERCURY project as a whole.[2]

What is distinctive about multilateralism is not merely that it coordinates national policies in groups of three or more states (along with non-state actors), something applicable to other organisational forms such as transgovernmentalism, networks, and alliances, but that 'it does so on the basis of certain principles of ordering relations among its participants' (Ruggie 1992; 567). This chapter therefore seeks to respond to Ruggie's (ibid.: 567) suggestion that we should recover 'the principled meanings of multilateralism from actual and historical practice'. We seek to show how these principles have come to be institutionalised and explore how and why they may perpetuate themselves, even though conditions change. The idea of an evolving doctrine of multilateralism is proposed here as a potential tool for the investigation of these questions.

Doctrine in international relations

In ordinary language the term 'doctrine' usually refers to a principle or a body of principles that is taught or advocated. Such advocacy or instruction has been particularly significant in the development of the traditions, institutions and practices of religion, which is usually the primary connotation of doctrine. In this context, principles have been taught or advocated as a necessary basis for action and practice, because of a specific need or moral responsibility and as a means to a better end.

In the realm of foreign policy, the use of doctrine has been most strongly associated with the defining approaches taken by various US Presidents, from the early nineteenth century onwards. In this context, the term has been used to refer to a statement of very broad principle(s) designed to shape, justify and communicate policy at the strategic level. Historically, American foreign policy doctrines, such as the Monroe Doctrine or the Truman Doctrine have, for the most part, sought to address moments of crisis and have been grounded equally in ideology and in the concern and language of national security (Selverstone 2001). Thus the Monroe doctrine (1823), perhaps the most famous example, aspired to establish the United States (US) as a global power. It has since remained

> the most recognizable and perhaps most venerated of diplomatic principles, [whose] hold on the popular imagination has been so strong that it has defined the limits of acceptable policy options, shaping the range of choices open to presidents for the better part of two centuries.
>
> *(Selverstone 2001: 521)*

Beyond specific approaches to foreign policy articulated by state leaders to inspire their own citizens and give warning to others, doctrine in the wider area of international relations has often been used almost interchangeably with the term 'practice' or 'strategy' as in the doctrine of prevention, the Responsibility to Protect doctrine, the 'doctrine' of humanitarian intervention, or the doctrine of democratic interventionism (Hodges 1915; Mortier 2004). These doctrines have been named mostly on the basis of the means they propose (for instance, prevention or intervention), and as the most effective and morally justified instruments for the achievement of greater goals, such as the prevention of conflict and the promotion of democracy. Doctrines thus differ from concepts in that they not only provide a mental construction, an idea, of how foreign policy should be carried out, they also attribute an element of ethics and morality to the proposed method. The same applies to the proposed doctrine of multilateralism; although, as discussed below, here the means versus ends question is more convoluted.

Perhaps the most frequent incidence of the use of doctrine in international relations is to be found in the study of military strategy, where reference is often made to 'military doctrine'. In this case, too, the articulation of doctrine serves to justify a course of action as consonant with certain principles deriving from a higher objective. Barry Posen (1984) defines military doctrine as a component of national security policy or 'grand strategy', the latter referring to a state's theory of how it can best bring about security for itself. According to Posen (1984: 13), a grand strategy is a means–end chain that identifies specific threats to security and devises political, economic and military remedies in response to those threats. Military doctrine, in turn, is the component of grand strategy that deals explicitly with the military means to be employed and how they will be used in response to threats and opportunities.

If the articulation and analysis of military doctrine was particularly relevant during the Cold War, specifically in terms of the containment of the Soviet Union (see Monks 1964; Krause and Mallory 1992), the post-1989 shift to unipolarity led to a reconfiguration of power relationships. This included Europe's rejection of power politics, its relative devaluing of military force as a tool of international engagement and its promotion of other aspects of soft or 'civilian' power. The emergence of other kinds of threats, particularly terrorism and international crime, the proliferation of nuclear weapons, and the fragility of a large number of states thus paradoxically further promoted an understanding of doctrine as a component of strategy that went well beyond the military. New, broader, strategic doctrines were needed to address other means that might be appropriate to respond to these different threats and challenges.

Nonetheless, the definition of military doctrine remains a useful starting point for conceptual rethinking. According to Posen, if grand strategy is a key component of any foreign policy, it is 'ultimately about fighting' with all the implications that has in terms of military doctrine. Here, we move beyond this tradition and propose that doctrine is the component of grand strategy that deals with economic and political as well as military means, and specifies how they may be employed to respond to current challenges and opportunities. Thus, for example, a true doctrine of multilateralism generally proposes it as the best means of combating new types of transnational problems and specifically outlines the conditions and rules governing the specific types of cooperation best suited to the particular challenge(s) in view. Keeping in mind the initial definition of doctrine as a set of principles taught or advocated as a means to a better end, a doctrine of multilateralism offers not only a *right* approach to international affairs, inclusive of guidelines that lead to a *better world*, but also specifies how the types of cooperation undertaken will conform with and expedite those normative outcomes.

There is an inevitably close inter-relationship between strategy and doctrine. Biscop (2009: 9) has described the former as 'defining the long term foreign policy objectives to be achieved and the basic categories of instruments to be applied to this end' – thus suggesting a means–end chain.[3] On the basis of this distinction, Biscop claims that, in the field of security, the EU lacks a grand strategy: analysis of key strategic documents produced by the Union suggests that, while the principles and possible instruments are clearly defined, the objectives are too broad and the priorities, at times, unclear. Sometimes what should be done is clearer than how to do it – and sometimes the reverse. Indeed, ends and means are often not easy to distinguish. Thus, to the extent that the EU does have a doctrine, it needs to be translated into strategy – but that in itself is easier to say than to do.

How doctrine can or should be interpreted and used then also becomes problematic. Conceptualisations of military doctrine offer some useful initial insights insofar as they introduce the questions of discretion and flexibility in any application of a doctrine. NATO offers a working definition of military doctrine, describing it as the set of 'fundamental principles by which the military forces guide their actions in support of objectives', adding the key proviso that doctrine is 'authoritative but requires judgment in application'.[4] In other words, the exact circumstances and mode of operation in which doctrine is employed is subject to interpretation. Biscop (2005: viii) suggests the same in relation to the European Security Strategy: namely that, 'like holy scriptures, it is liable to interpretation', and its prospects for successful implementation lie in the interpretation of the document's content by the Union's member states.

Despite these qualifications, doctrine does serve at least two essential functions in the creation of collective and coherent policy: those of coordination and legitimation. If accepted as an authoritative guide, it can provide aspirational focus and serve as a powerful coordinating device. In the case of an EU-wide foreign policy doctrine, all of this presupposes a high degree of consensus on a relatively consistent interpretation of the doctrinal texts. Doctrine thus provides a benchmark, even a rallying point for policy-makers who are likely to refer back to and seek justification in – or at least conformity with – it, leading in principle to greater consistency and coherence in EU policies. In Biscop's (2005: 133) account, this outcome would be the ultimate achievement of a grand strategy for the EU.

The coordinating function of doctrine is particularly germane to the promotion of multilateralism, as the latter's 'highly demanding nature as an institutional form' (Ruggie 1992: 572) renders the existence of a strong coordinating device a necessary precondition for sustainability. If a defining feature of multilateralism is that it organises states (and perhaps other actors also), it does so on the basis of a set of principles and – it would be safe to add – certain objectives. It is in the deconstruction and interpretation of these principles and the sources of their codification, but also of the mechanisms for their diffusion and incorporation into actors' preferences, that the 'doctrine' of multilateralism can be found and its evolution followed. This evolution can be observed in the way in which EU member states approach their policy collectively, even if their individual preoccupations diverge quite widely, with Poland concerned about the Ukraine and Belarus, in contrast (say) to the focus on the Maghreb of France and Spain. The need to incorporate this diversity into a multilateral approach has become part of the foreign policy consensus, even if it is not always achieved.

An equally valuable function of doctrine is that it legitimises certain types of action, both domestically and externally. It thereby excludes other actions as either incompatible with the advocated principles, or as employing the wrong means. Consequently, an actor's doctrine also defines the characteristics of its actions. In the debate on 'types of powers' that has engaged the IR community, greater note could be taken of the sources and nature of doctrine. It has been of critical importance, for example, for opinion both within the United States and outside it that the US

National Security Strategy (NSS) sought to legitimise action taken unilaterally, outside the collective security framework of the UN, or that the Bush pre-emption doctrine legitimised taking action against emerging threats before they were necessarily fully formed (see Dannreuther and Peterson 2006). This choice of doctrine defines the US as an essentially different type of power from the EU and its multilateral approach to the confrontation of the same threats. As Vasconcelos (2008: 22) points out, multilateralism is 'an expression of how power should be used and to what ends', issues which are particularly significant and, inevitably, debated in a multipolar system. Thus, the endorsement of a doctrine of multilateralism is a defining feature of a particular approach to power.[5]

The emergence of new types of power, such as the 'normative' or 'ethical' power represented by the EU, has contributed to the evolution of the doctrine of multilateralism in the late twentieth and early twenty-first centuries (Manners 2002; Hill 2010). The next section offers a brief overview of the evolution of this doctrine during this timeframe. It sets a basis for the analysis of the principles currently advocated by the EU as it seeks to build and reinforce multilateralism.

Towards twenty-first-century multilateralism

The EU's explicit focus on promoting 'effective multilateralism' in Europe and beyond designates it as the principal and most powerful advocate of multilateralism in the twenty-first century. Still, it is hardly a doctrine exclusive to the Union. Principles guiding multilateral cooperation, particularly within the framework of multilateral institutions and regimes, have been advocated in one way or another by other actors within various contexts since the nineteenth century.[6]

Historically, multilateralism has been linked to functional considerations but also to power relationships between different actors. Thus, multilateral forms of cooperation have been based on the central principle of collective decision-making for the generic purposes of stabilising the international property rights of states, managing coordination problems and resolving collaboration problems (Ruggie 1992). At the same time, they clearly have acknowledged the relative balance of power of the actors involved. In this context, the development of a doctrine of multilateralism was inextricably linked to the balance of power in the international order and to the foreign policy doctrine of the dominant world power(s) of the time. For example, the idea of collective security evolved as a consequence of the US President Woodrow Wilson's belief in the need for a community of democratic nations to guarantee and enforce international peace, leading to the replacement after World War I of the balance of power system based on the Concert of Europe – itself an early form of multilateralism – with the League of Nations (Krause 2004; Gordenker and Weiss 1993).

The end of World War II spurred an unprecedented increase in the creation of rules and organisations laying down a global framework for international relations. The United Nations, the International Monetary Fund (IMF), the World Bank and the General Agreement on Tariffs and Trade (GATT) were created, largely as a result of the United States' initiative to promote global institutions which would also safeguard its economic and security interests (Keohane and Nye 1985). To a great extent, the rules governing these multilateral organisations in the early days of their operation were defined by the US approach, which viewed multilateralism as a means to the end of establishing a western, liberal international order.

Gradually, however, multilateral institutions took on a life of their own, not least as new international bureaucracies created new, 'gained' power through their function of institutionalising collective state interests. Especially on the economic front, multilateral organisations began to display a tendency towards collectivistic and shared-wealth doctrines, which soon began to raise concerns in Washington regarding the value of these organisations for the promotion of the US's interests. As early as the 1960s, US administrations began to question whether a doctrine of multilateralism was consistent with American foreign policy goals and its perception of its role in the world, arguing that multilateral negotiations often placed limits on the behaviour of large states by introducing principles such as 'one state, one vote', regardless of relative state size or power, or the principle of 'equal redistribution' (Krause 2004: 47). In the 1980s, the Reagan Administration echoed these concerns, as illustrated by its attitude towards the UN which, at one point, was even portrayed by a top ranking State Department official as posing some 'very difficult challenges and dangers to the interests of the United States' (Luck 1999: 59).

The institutionalisation of cooperation and the subsequent emergence of multilateral organisations with a lesser or greater degree of autonomy, notably the EU which included supranational institutions such as the Commission, led to further changes in the initial principles guiding multilateral cooperation, which had been based on a traditional state-centric view of global society. While the earliest, US-advocated, doctrine of multilateralism was based on the principle that no multilateral organisation could impose its will on members, such a strictly state-centric view displayed signs of erosion as institutionalist and neo-institutionalist understandings of multilateral organisation gained ground (Powell and DiMaggio 1991). After all, from the outset governments wishing to receive the benefits deriving from membership had to accept some restraints on their domestic and international behaviour. On the other hand, new states also showed an understandable attachment to the principle of sovereign independence.

Even before the end of the Cold War, the growing pressures of globalisation brought about an additional change in the normative foundation of multilateralism (Hufner and Naumann 1990: 325). As the notion of a modern 'world society' gradually emerged and challenged state-centred views, the concept of multilateralism was widened to encompass actors other than states, and interests beyond those deriving from the state. The principles and ends which formed the basis of multilateral cooperation were no longer only those endorsed and advocated by states, and specifically states with power and influence, but were redefined through the institutions themselves, mostly in the direction of addressing greater needs. This new phase of multilateralism was captured by Javier Perez de Cuellar in 1987 when he declared:

> By multilateralism I mean a common effort by the international community, based on the principles of the United Nations Charter, to address in a pragmatic manner the world's many needs and problems, so that the entire human family can realise its full potential.
>
> *(Hufner and Naumann 1990: 323)*

In this new phase, the idea of a 'human family', a modern world society, and the discourse of 'one world' transcending national societies began to influence the ideational premises of multilateralism, as the doctrine behind multilateral cooperation found its articulation not only in the strategies of leading states, but in the collectively agreed upon declarations of the UN. The advocates of those collective agreements, the international organisations themselves, especially through their secretariats, began to expand their own role in the international system.

The concern for 'global society' and the provision of benefits for all actors participating in multilateral regimes, aspirations that were voiced by international organisations based on their new claims as actors in their own right, gradually led to a convergence on principles such as the indivisibility of welfare; non-discrimination; and diffuse reciprocity, whereby participants in multilateral cooperation perceive and expect reciprocal balancing to occur in the aggregate and over time (Keohane 1990; Ruggie 1993, 1998). The multilateral approach towards sustainability captured in the Rio Declaration on Environment and Development, which resulted from the meeting of the UN Conference on Environment and Development in June 1992, was indicative of the UN's promotion of these principles. The Declaration emphasised that 'all States and all people shall cooperate in the essential task of eradicating poverty as an indispensable requirement for sustainable development' (Principle 5) and that 'Peace, development and environmental protection are interdependent and indivisible' (Principle 25). To an important extent these principles were deliberately constructed to create perceptions and expectations of indivisibility, non-discrimination and diffuse reciprocity, rather than actually putting them into practice (Wilkinson 2000: 41–2). That is, they functioned as the basis for the creation of a certain set of 'rules of conduct' within one of the post-Cold War multilateral institutions. The principle of a rules-based international order became seen as inherent in the practice of multilateralism.

Enthusiasm and idealism were short-lived, however. The only superpower that remained in the new unipolar, post-Cold War order was reluctant to embrace the multilateral wave wholeheartedly or unconditionally. This reluctance was epitomised by the George W. Bush Administration, which endorsed the position of 'à la carte multilateralism' (Haass 2008), and steered the US away from the principles of indivisibility and non-discrimination in their initial form.

But as early as the end of the 1990s, attitudes towards multilateralism had become more sceptical. The new scepticism was largely a consequence of a crisis in the provision of security goods by the international community, a central cause of which was the failure of the United Nations, the 'intended centrepiece of multilateralism'

(Krause 2004: 43) to deal with the festering conflicts that had emerged from the shadow of the Cold War. Combined with the US's withdrawal from or abrogation of a number of multilateral treaties (including the International Criminal Court, Kyoto protocol and Anti-Ballistic Missile Treaty) under the George W. Bush Administration, the effectiveness of multilateralism, including but not limited to cooperation on security issues, became subject to profound doubts. As Krause (2004: 43) argued: 'As long as the crisis of collective security is not directly addressed, the reputation of other forms of multilateral foreign policy will suffer collateral damage, with potentially disastrous consequences for international order'.[7]

In spite of the disillusion it provoked outside the US, where the neo-conservative attitude was regarded as an aberration,[8] a new 'crisis of multilateralism' in the wake of the invasion of Iraq highlighted the need for a more coherent and detailed definition of the aims and principles guiding multilateralism and the best means of promoting it. From the perspective of doctrine, the crisis had raised many of the critical issues relating to differences in the interpretation of both guiding principles and acceptable action, and the degree of flexibility allowed (for example, on the issue of intervention). In other words, Iraq highlighted the necessity of a clearly articulated and widely accepted doctrine of multilateralism, which would enable the international community to take effective multilateral action and to avoid the deep split that emerged, not least in the EU, where the need was seen particularly clearly and as a matter of urgency.

The principal actors engaged in the process of doctrine formulation, whether within the EU or the UN itself, acknowledged the need to take account of new circumstances to gear multilateralism towards confronting new types of threats, including terrorism, the proliferation of nuclear, biological and chemical weapons, illegal immigration, infectious disease, global warming, environmental degradation, extreme poverty and financial turmoil.[9] The role of non-state actors with global reach in fields as diverse as international health, environmental management, security, peace-building, human rights and trade had to be recognised across the range of multilateral fora. States and their leaders were obliged to acknowledge that in an era of accelerated globalisation, where new modes of information sharing, communications and transaction had become widespread, there was an indisputable need for collective action to address problems that transcended national and regional boundaries. According to this logic, action should also expand beyond the developed world to include as many partners as possible on the basis of the principle of fair representation (Macedo 2008). In re-establishing the principled basis for multilateralism, actors should take note that globalisation could strengthen threats to peace, and that a combination of instruments might be needed to combat these threats effectively. Hence, cooperation with and support for *ad hoc*/hybrid interstate and institutional arrangements and decision-making forums (regional, bilateral, national and with participation by non-state and private actors) would be necessary to combat transnational threats and problems. A change in the nature of multilateralism, in terms of a readiness to experiment with various types of interstate cooperation to complement existing multilateralism, seemed to be taking place (Forman and Segaar 2006; Macedo 2008).

Preoccupation with the reform of the UN was indicative of the recognition of those new circumstances and of efforts to reinvigorate multilateralism. In the words of Kofi Annan while Secretary-General of the UN:

> We have come to a fork in the road…It is not enough to denounce uni-lateralism, unless we also face up squarely to the concerns that make some states feel uniquely vulnerable, since it is those concerns that drive them to take unilateral action. We must show that those concerns can and will be addressed effectively through collective action.[10]

The EU in 2003 made 'strengthening the United Nations, equipping it to fulfil its responsibilities and to act effectively' a European priority (European Council 2003: 9), while placing the advocacy of 'effective multilateralism' at the centre of its Security Strategy. The Strategy embraced a broad concept of security that went beyond confronting military threats to incorporate policy areas such as trade, development, justice and home affairs, environment and health. In setting these priorities, the EU made multilateralism a focal point of its foreign policy.

The EU and the doctrine of multilateralism

As the leading advocate of multilateralism as a basis for global governance and international cooperation, the EU has held a central role in the formulation of the doctrine of multilateralism. Since the Treaty on European Union in 1993, conformity with the principles of the United Nations Charter has been at the core of the EU's external action.[11] EU member states contribute around 50 per cent of all national contributions to UN funds and programmes (Wouters 2007). There is no explicit reference to the existence of a doctrine of multilateralism in EU texts. Thus, we examine here whether the treatment of multilateralism in key EU documents that formulate its foreign policy on issues of security, trade and beyond, as well as in the statements and practices of high-level European officials and national leaders, justifies the argument that the Union is in the process of formulating an evolving doctrine of multilateralism. The EU has continuously advocated the need for and benefits of multilateralism both internally, towards its own public, and externally, towards existing and potential partners.

What is often not made clear in documents such as the European Security Strategy or the 2008 'Global Europe' strategy for trade is whether multilateralism is to be treated as a means to an end (an instrument) or as an end in itself (a multilateral global order) for the achievement of which other instruments (such as bilateral partnerships) can be used. Scholars, including Sven Biscop, also use the concept in both ways. Understanding better the difference between the two and thereby being clearer as to the function of multilateralism in European discourse would be a significant step towards clarifying the conceptualisation of an EU-wide doctrine of multilateralism and, encouraging a consensus on its interpretation. This, in turn, could provide the basis for the definition of doctrine and of its functions, coordination and legitimacy. A commonly accepted doctrine of multilateralism by EU member states would arguably increase Europe's effectiveness in its external relations, at least insofar as it brought about coherent, consistent and coordinated action in support of its principles.

Sources of the developing doctrine of multilateralism

Any analysis of the 'doctrine of multilateralism' inevitably touches on the delicate issue of differences between doctrine and other concepts that refer to the norms, rules and principles guiding multilateral/international organisation, particularly that of the 'regime'. A regime is defined as representing a set of principles, norms, rules and procedures around which participants' expectations converge with reference to a more or less distinct issue area (Keohane and Nye 1977; Puchala and Hopkins 1982; Krasner 1983). Multilateral regimes 'roughly reflect the appropriate general-ized principles of conduct' (Ruggie 1992: 573). Drawing on this definition, it can be argued that doctrines are the manifestation and the expression of the rules and procedures that define the limit of acceptable behaviour on various issues and in the 'recognized patterns of practice that define the rules of the game' (Keohane and Nye 1985: 151). Since the critical feature of doctrine is that it is advocated, the focus is necessarily on the sources of these principles and the articulation of these patterns.

The sources of doctrine codification in national foreign policy are found primarily in strategy papers (such as the National Security Strategy) and in the major statements of leaders and policy-makers (consider Truman's speech to Congress on 12 March 1947; see Freeland 1970). Such statements can reaffirm and strengthen the doctrine (Mortier 2004) by, for example, emphasising the moral responsibility behind a spe-cific type of action. The tenets of any doctrine are more likely to be operationalised if they are strengthened by supportive statements at the policy level.[12] Policy-makers are, after all, the intermediaries between the codification and operationalisation of doctrine. Their reiteration of principles and their concomitant actions to implement them can both legitimise doctrines and bind future actors to them.[13]

When considering actors beyond and above the state, such as the EU and NATO, where decision-making is collective and leadership shared, the identifica-tion of doctrinal sources becomes a more complex issue. While the declarations and founding treaties that outline goals and principles can perhaps be viewed as the equivalent of strategy documents, the lack of a specific spokesperson suggests that it is the policy-makers within the organisation, as well as the leaders of its member states, who articulate the doctrine. In the case of the EU, with its unique institu-tional makeup, this matter becomes tied to the complex issue of representation and the famous question of 'Who speaks for the EU?' Agreement on who such a figure should be, whatever the provisions of the treaties say, remains limited.

The EU's attitude to multilateralism thus may be gleaned from the speeches, discourses and actions of the High Representative for the CFSP and the President of the European Council as under the Lisbon Treaty, but also from those of the President of the Commission, and the various EU Heads of Government or Ministers of Foreign Affairs, all of whom may lay claim to speaking on the EU's behalf – or, perhaps more problematically, are assumed to be doing so by others.[14]

Such a medley of voices inevitably reflects the nature of the EU itself and its identity as an actor in international affairs. It creates difficulties, however, if it is assumed that the EU is a normative power, seeking to act as 'a changer of norms in the international system' (Manners 2002: 252). Any text or speech through which the Union – and its member states – seeks to promote or 'export' multilateral cooperation on the basis of the principles embedded in the EU's own approach towards multilateralism can be considered as an expression of the doctrine of multilateralism.

It follows that the sources and expressions of the doctrine of multilateralism put forward by the EU abound in the form of declarations, recommendations, speeches and policy documents. What is missing, and is critical if the aim is *effective* multilateralism, is a continuous and consistent common interpretation and clarification of the doctrine, the identification of one or more texts or speeches which stand out as the 'guiding light' of the EU's approach to multilateralism, and which legitimise and coordinate member states' approaches to multilateralism across foreign policy areas. The following sections look at the areas of security and trade, and, in particular, at the statements and instruments that constitute the EU's approach to multilateralism in these areas. The aim is to tease out the underlying principles that ultimately form the evolving European doctrine of multilateralism.[15]

The doctrine of multilateralism in the European Security Strategy

Perhaps the most clearly articulated commitment of the EU to multilateralism is found in its EU's security policy. While perhaps not originally conceived to profess a doctrine as such, the 2003 European Security Strategy (ESS) encompasses a set of principles, a structure of guidance/instruction, and the clear suggestion of the Union's need and moral obligation to pursue multilateral cooperation in particular areas. Drawn up in the aftermath of European divisions over the invasion of Iraq, the ESS repeatedly emphasises the need for multilateralism as a consequence of the complex nature of today's problems which 'no single country is able to tackle on its own' (European Council 2003: 1). At the same time, engagement and cooperation with other actors is viewed as a moral duty of the EU as part of its effort to build a better world and to share responsibility for global security. The 'credo of effective multilateralism' (Wouters 2007: 2) enshrined in the section entitled 'An International Order Based on Effective Multilateralism' is presented as a necessary precondition for security and prosperity, suggesting that any alternative jeopardises the future of global society. In this sense, multilateralism is framed as a doctrine, as a moral responsibility of the EU and, beyond that, of every global actor.

The ESS presents a number of the characteristics of doctrine. First, the document clearly identifies the current challenges and opportunities that demand action.[16] It then proceeds to enumerate the means needed to address these challenges, emphasising that 'in contrast to the massive visible threat in the Cold War, none of the new threats is purely military; nor can any be tackled by purely military means. Each requires a mixture of instruments' (European Council 2003: 7). With this phrase the ESS recognises the need for a foreign policy doctrine including all three elements of grand strategy in Posen's definition: economic, political and military means, towards the greater end of a 'secure Europe in a better world'.

Within this context, multilateralism is treated in the ESS both as an instrument and as a goal in a quest for the best means and concrete ends. This is demonstrated by the statement that 'the development of a stronger international society, well-functioning international institutions and a rule based international order is our objective' (European Council 2003: 9). The tools for the attainment of a multilateral world order are presented in the document as:

1. promoting the principles of good governance and democracy in the rest of the world in order to be able to enjoy close and cooperative relations;
2. ending the cycle of conflict, insecurity and poverty by promoting development;
3. enhancing the legitimacy of the UN as the fundamental framework for an effective rules-based international order with 'international organisations, regimes and treaties…ready to act when the rules are broken' (European Council 2003: 9);
4. widening the membership of multilateral institutions such as the WTO and the IMF 'while maintaining their high standards' (Ibid.: 2003: 9);
5. displaying flexibility towards other forms of cooperation as mechanisms that hold the potential to reinforce multilateralism by achieving greater efficiency and coordination depending on the nature of particular issues, which may be regional or issue-specific (partnerships or instruments such as the Quartet) (see Musu 2007). The ESS explicitly states that 'we need to pursue our objectives both through multilateral cooperation in international organisations and through partnerships with key actors' (European Council 2003: 13);
6. advocating multilateralism beyond the EU and providing incentives for other actors to endorse the EU's doctrine of multilateralism through the use of diplomatic sanctions: 'Those who are unwilling to [rejoin the international community] should understand that there is a price to be paid, including in their relationship with the European Union' (Ibid.: 10);
7. acknowledging the links between policy areas and promoting a coherent agenda of multilateralism not only in security, but also development, trade and environmental policies (Ibid.: 13).

To a certain extent, the basic principles that underlie these clearly articulated guidelines remain those of *indivisibility, non-discrimination* and *reciprocity* as outlined by

EDINBURGH UNIVERSITY LIBRARY

WITHDRAWN

Ruggie (1992), and the ensuing principle of rule-abiding as noted by Wilkinson (2000). Strong echoes of a principle of *responsibility* towards less developed regions or those parts of the world stricken by conflict, poverty, disease, natural disasters and illegal regimes also resound in the doctrine, as do the principles of peace and democracy and their simultaneous promotion, in accordance with the theory of democratic peace (see Russett 1993). Finally, legitimacy, cooperation and respect for international law become a part of the doctrine almost automatically. Nonetheless, in the face of complex and global threats, flexibility and effectiveness are treated as paramount. Thus, the ESS proposes a less rigid, more malleable doctrine of multilateralism, where responsibility and the need for effective outcomes at times overrides the priority of, for example, non-discrimination, allowing for the bilateral and the regional to co-exist with the wider multilateral setting.[17]

Multilateralism in trade policy: the EU and the World Trade Organization (WTO)

Since its inception in 1995, the WTO has been at the heart of the multilateral trading system. Consequently, it is a core focus for EU trade policy, based on the belief that 'a system of global rules is the best way to ensure that trade between countries is open and fair'.[18] While the EU's policy of trade liberalisation is pursued through bilateral and regional as well as multilateral initiatives, the sum total of the Union's actions in relation to the development of the WTO suggests that the EU is also becoming a stronger advocate of a doctrine of multilateralism in the field of external trade. Here we find much that is similar to the fundamental principles of its approach to collective security. In the words of Pascal Lamy (while European Commissioner for Trade; he later became Secretary-General of the WTO), the EU has had a 'multilateralism first' policy since 1995 (Lamy 2002: 1401), even while being open to other trade policy instruments such as inter-regional and bilateral free trade agreements (FTAs).

But the EU's promotion of the WTO, and its expansion and empowerment, was perhaps the strongest indication of its embrace of multilateralism in the area of trade. During the late 1990s, the EU was one of the leading proponents of a new round of comprehensive negotiations to broaden the agenda that had been built in to the Uruguay Round.[19] It later promoted the Doha Development Agenda as a top priority. Indicatively, following the suspension of the Doha Round negotiations in 2008, the European Parliament adopted a resolution calling on India and the US, as well as the G20, to 'assume their responsibilities and make every effort to reach a deal as rapidly as possible'.[20] The EU has also been a strong supporter of the extension of WTO membership, notably to include China and Russia, on the basis that widening membership was linked to the promotion of further multilateralisation. The Union has also been a leading user of the WTO dispute settlement procedures, convinced (at least most of the time) that its own compliance to the agreements can set an example to other WTO trading partners (WTO Secretariat 2009: paragraph 36). It follows that the emphasis on multilateralism in the EU's trade policy is inextricably linked to upholding the rules that underpin the WTO and to advocating the need for the WTO's expansion and extension.[21]

The values and goals that underlie the WTO, according to the Agreement Establishing the World Trade Organization are reciprocity, non-discrimination and collective actions, both in dispute-settlement and in consensual decision-making, based on the strict 'one state, one vote' mechanism (specified in the Agreement's Article IX). These rules set the framework for the achievement of the greater aims of the organisation, captured in the Preamble of the Agreement, whereby the signatories commit themselves to the 'elimination of discriminatory treatment in international trade relations', to ensuring 'that developing countries, and especially the least developed among them, secure a share in the growth in international trade commensurate with the needs of their economic development', and to both the development of a 'more viable and durable multilateral trading system' and the preservation of the principles underlying this system in the future. The Agreement very clearly envisages these commitments as leading to a more prosperous future for global society, with higher standards of living, optimal use of world resources, sustainable development and environmental protection. At a functional level, the Agreement creates a binding type of multilateralism, as it specifies that Multilateral Trade Agreements (MTAs) bind all their members (Article II, paragraph 2). In addition, it establishes impartial international adjudication by providing for a mutually accepted dispute settlement mechanism guided by specific rules and procedures (via an Appellate Body).[22]

The principles of equality and non-discrimination are thus firmly embedded in the WTO. It is open to 'any state or separate customs territory possessing full autonomy in the conduct of its external commercial relations' (Article xii, paragraph 1). The WTO also allows any member to withdraw from the Agreement (Article XV). The binding nature of the multilateral trading system presupposes that states and other actors will voluntarily adhere to the Agreement, convinced of its benefits and willing to uphold its principles. On this basis, the WTO also allows room for flexibility through, for example, plurilateral agreements which give member countries the choice to agree to new rules on a voluntary basis (without all members necessarily being members of the particular agreement), or by allowing its members to engage in regional and bilateral Free Trade Agreements (FTAs).

Flexibility is strongly endorsed by the EU and is also reminiscent of the Union's doctrine of multilateralism in the field of security. In trade as in security, multilateralism is viewed as an end, allowing for other instruments, such as partnerships, to be used provided that they act as mechanisms that can support multilateralism.[23] Thus, as Lamy points out, regionalism and multilateralism are not necessarily mutually exclusive. Rather, the 'WTO rules constitute a floor in two senses: in the sense of a basic minimum, but also in the sense of underpinning additional commitments at the regional level' (Lamy 2002: 1408). Deeper regional integration, for example, is favoured by the EU as a mechanism that can support multilateralism by underpinning market liberalisation with new and stronger rules for the region. At the same time, the primacy of multilateralism is maintained by giving the multilateral system the power to police such agreements (Lamy 2002: 1411). Thus, the WTO Trade

Policy Board reviews WTO members and, *inter alia*, evaluates the complementarity of its members' various FTAs with the principles that govern the organisation. However, the balance does seem to have swung back towards an assertive bilateralism on the part of the EU (and other major trade powers), to some extent in reaction to the United States strategies. This shift was evident in the EU's 2009 Free Trade Agreement with South Korea, which suggested that the EU had come to look beyond the WTO and universal multilateralism to protect its competitive advantage.

Beyond the debate about the compatibility of regionalism with multilateralism, the EU's promotion of the WTO as part of its doctrine of multilateralism still depends on the belief that multilateral trade liberalisation remains the better way of generating and maximising welfare gains. It is also the preferred strategy for ensuring equal treatment for collective benefit and promoting best practices, while ensuring that they are upheld by developing a collectively accepted, principled system of dispute resolution. The EU's perspective on trade and multilateralism can be found in numerous documents including Council Conclusions, submissions to the WTO, speeches and policy documents. In its entirety, however, this collection of documents reiterates the same main points, namely:

1. that trade policy must build on the premise that Europe's economic prosperity is inextricably linked to that of other regions of the world, and thus the EU should adopt a policy of openness;
2. that barriers to trade, activity and investment should be addressed;
3. that the completion of the internal market is linked to external considerations and thus the EU must play a leading role in sharing best practice and developing high-quality global rules and standards (European Commission 2006);
4. that the EU should remain the cornerstone of a strong and rules-based multilateral trading system, while also engaging in the development of complementary mechanisms towards the same ends;
5. that the EU should engage in the development of the WTO – compatible FTAs with the aim of further liberalising trade, and taking into consideration economic and political considerations in terms of its geographical priorities (European Commission 2006);
6. that the goals of poverty reduction, sustainable and economic development, and the improvement of social and environmental standards, as well as the impact of any policy on developing countries, should be taken into consideration in the formulation of multilateral trade policy.

The striking resemblance between these goals and those of the WTO founding agreement suggest that a strong element of the EU doctrine of trade multilateralism is the practice and promotion of the principles embedded in the WTO. Somewhat unsurprisingly, therefore, in its review of the EU's trade policy in 2009, the WTO praised the EU's stance on multilateral trade and support for developing countries. The report acknowledged that the EU had been a major driving force for the promotion of the WTO's aims in the period since 2006, supporting the Doha negotiations and actively engaging in the integration of developing countries into the multilateral trading system. Among the EU's efforts, the report commended the negotiations for Economic Partnership Agreements with the ACP countries, the implementation of the reformed Generalized System of Preferences (GSP) for developing countries, and the fact that the Union has become the major sponsor of trade-related technical assistance within the Aid for Trade framework (WTO Secretariat 2009). The EU's 'Everything but Arms' regulation of 2001 is also note-worthy, as it gave the world's 50 poorest countries duty-free access for virtually all their exports. At the same time, it must be acknowledged that practice does not always live up to principle – the EU's record of agricultural protectionism, and export subsidies, has often impeded the achievement of a level playing field for developing countries in world trade (as discussed by Fioramonti in Chapter 9).

As in the area of security policy, the principles of *responsibility*, *non-discrimination*, *legitimacy* – deriving from a rules-based cooperation and adjudication system – are evident in the EU's approach to trade. Together with *diffuse reciprocity*, on the basis of increased participation in the multilateral trading system, these principles under-lie the EU's strong advocacy of trade multilateralism. Thus, an initial overview of the two cases justifies an attempt at conceptualising a more generalised doctrine of multilateralism promoted by the EU as an international actor.

Why the EU needs a doctrine of multilateralism

Our comparison of the EU's approaches towards multilateralism in the areas of security and trade suggest a wider question: does a doctrine of multilateralism span the entirety of EU external policy? Despite significant differences in the content of these policy areas and variation in their multilateral arrangements and institu-tions, there are indeed striking resemblances in the principles advocated by the EU as the basis for multilateralism in both. More importantly – particularly if one accepts the validity of the idea of 'rhetorical entrapment' – to use Schimmelfennig's term (2001) – the language used in addressing the goal of 'multilateralising' in the two fields is very similar.

In the ESS, engagement in multilateral cooperation is viewed as the duty of the EU as part of its effort to build a better world on the basis of shared responsibility. Similarly, in the Preamble of the Agreement establishing the WTO, the signatory states resolve to develop an integrated, more viable and durable multilateral trading system, which is viewed as the way to promote growth and sustainable develop-ment. In both trade and security, the Union's approach to multilateralism has been based on ideas of durability, stability and enduring peace, to which arbitration, peaceful dispute resolution and cooperation are central. At the same time, con-flict in all its manifestations is viewed as a root cause of instability and a threat to global society. The promotion of multilateralism as the means of resolving conflict therefore fits with the EU's declared aims and ambitions. A (critical) summary put forward by Robert Kagan (2002: 3) claims that:

Europe is turning away from power, or to put it a little differently, it is moving beyond power into a self-contained world of laws and rules and transnational negotiation and cooperation. It is entering a post-historical paradise of peace and relative prosperity, the realization of Kant's 'Perpetual Peace'.

Beyond the centrality of peace and cooperation, observations from developments in both security and trade policy suggest that: while indivisibility, non-discrimination and reciprocity are the central principles of the EU's doctrine of multilateralism, efficiency and effectiveness may require a degree of flexibility and allowances that go beyond rigidly homogeneous arrangements. Flexibility and discretion are needed to ensure the doctrine's constructive application. The potential for a greater number of partners, with their own differing ideas on the world order of the twenty-first century (such as China), to participate in multilateral cooperation is welcomed. Thus, in pursuit of greater inclusion, the doctrine of multilateralism as it has evolved goes beyond past attempts at moral universalism.[24] On the other hand, the potential democracy-inducing effects of multilateralism (Keohane *et al.* 2009) may be seen as counterbalancing these more lenient criteria on inclusion.

While trade and collective security constitute relatively long-standing multilateral-ised policies, multilateral cooperation in other policy areas has yet to be institutionalised or even collectively agreed upon. The quest for suitable multilateral arrangements in policy areas such as climate change, disease prevention and illegal migration, to name a few, is ongoing and at times hindered by a lack of consensus and competing approaches among partners. In this challenging process, a common point of reference, an over-arching doctrine of multilateralism, would significantly improve the EU's capacity to advocate its positions on the type of multilateralism that is most suitable and effective in confronting these threats. This is consistent with Biscop's (2005: 133) argument on the need for an EU Grand Strategy, reference to which 'should come intuitively to all policy-makers involved in the design, implementation and evaluation of EU exter-nal action' in order for 'greater consistency and coherence of EU policies to follow automatically'. Doctrine could, in such circumstances, have impact both as a useful coordinating device and as a means for garnering support and legitimising subsequent policy. It can only be effective, though, when it is clearly articulated and when its interpretation is not disputed.

Being identified as a significant and consistent promoter of norms and values has both a domestic and external dimension. Domestically, through the Europeanisation of its member states' foreign policies (Wong 2005) and processes of socialisation (Smith 2000), the EU may contribute to the creation of an identity that both extends and subsumes that of the individual member state – though that itself may create tensions among EU states, especially as they seek to respond to crises (Edwards 2011). Externally, such advocacy may have impact by means of the EU's normative power (Manners 2002) or through the power of 'the superpowerless' (Nicolaïdis 2004). Moral suasion, especially when backed by consistent diplomatic action (and perhaps more importantly, economic weight; see Chapter 6 by Damro), makes the EU a potentially significant exporter of norms and values. In the particular case of multilateralism, the degree of persuasion is even stronger as the EU leads by example, insofar as it has attained such an extensive, developed and complex form of multilateralism internally.

It is exactly this complexity of its inter- and intra-relationships that renders the need for an explicit doctrine more urgent for the EU than for other international powers. In spite of the changes introduced by the Lisbon Treaty, it is still not clear who speaks for the EU in global affairs. In the absence of a single actor, able to articulate without challenge the aims and means of the EU in global affairs and define its nature as an international actor, developing a European doctrine of multilateralism could function as a powerful tool in the Europeanisation of national foreign policies. It might embed a more universalist moral discourse, endorsed by the institutions and actors involved in EU foreign policy, within national ministries and agencies. In short, it could make clear as never before precisely what the European Union stands for in international relations.

Conclusion

To what extent and in what ways does the endorsement of multilateralism guide the EU's behaviour in international affairs? This chapter has proposed that an emerging doctrine of multilateralism may provide some answers to this question. Drawing on various definitions and uses of doctrine, we have suggested that doctrine can be defined as an explicit set of principles that justify the pursuit of defined ends, using specific means for action. The triangle of principles–means–ends outlined within the doctrine aims to guide action in an effective and morally authoritative manner. Furthermore, we have argued that in the field of foreign policy, doctrine can function as an accepted guide that serves as a powerful coordinating device for actors involved in the creation and execution of a given foreign policy, and provides legitimacy to the decisions made.

Based on our analysis, the use of multilateralism as a focal point in EU foreign policy may be perceived as constituting an evolving doctrine. The cases of security and trade show that, within the EU's foreign policy discourse and across a number of areas, multilateralism is presented as a means towards the effective accomplishment of specific goals and, ultimately, towards the construction of a 'better world'. At the same time, the 'effective multilateralism' advocated by the EU is principle-based and constitutes part of the Union's moral responsibility to work towards this objective. As such, the European Union can be argued to have adopted the pursuit of effective mutilateralism as a doctrine.

Nevertheless, not least due to the complex nature of the EU itself, questions arise about the interpretation and implementation of the doctrine among EU members. The quest for effectiveness, which lies at the core of the EU's approach to multilateralism, is designed to minimise and bound disagreement among the member states. The lack of a consistent consensus on principles and practice inevitably questions – if not actually undermining – the effectiveness of multilateralism and therefore its usefulness. And yet, multilateralism remains the key element of the EU's approach to all areas of external activity, including security, trade, climate change, immigration and development. The continuous effort to formulate and reformulate collectively agreed-upon texts that reiterate the principles and aims of the EU's approach to multilateralism would seem to suggest a recognition on the part not just of the Union's institutions, but also its of member states, of the value of both multilateralism and the EU's advocacy of it.

Notes

1 We take collective responsibility for this chapter, but Elena Lazarou deserves the major credit for its drafting.
2 The MERCURY programme of research is only one of several EU-funded projects aimed not only at promoting the study of multilateralism, but also at locating it within the EU's wider approach towards global governance, comparing it to other actors' approaches towards international organisation, and shedding light on its various forms and manifestations.
3 Biscop's statement is based on the definition of 'grand strategy' by John Gaddis as 'the calculated relationship between means and large ends' (Gaddis 2005: viii).
4 *NATO Glossary of Terms and Definitions*, 2000: 2-D-6.
5 This does not assume that the concepts of multipolarity and multilateralism are necessarily connected: multipolarity refers to the way power is distributed at world level, and to the emergence of a plurality of global actors, which seek to create some form of concert of powers, while multilateralism is an expression of how that reality should be acted upon (Vasconcelos 2008: 22).
6 The departure from the system of states nominally established in 1648 by the Treaty of Westphalia evolved in the nineteenth century with the establishment of the world's first standing interstate organisations, such as the Danube River Commission, International Postal Union, representing a nascent multilateralism (Schuller and Grant 2003).
7 Collective security here is meant not in the sense of the formal aspiration of the United Nations to overturn any act of aggression, but the ability in a wider sense to resolve conflicts and to combat the non-military threats to 'human security' newly recognised in the 1990s.
8 It also created much disillusion within the US, as illustrated by the election of Barack Obama in 2008.
9 For a detailed analysis of threats which need to be confronted on a multilateral basis see, for example, the 2004 report of the SG High-Level Panel on Threats, Challenges and Change entitled 'A more secure world: Our shared responsibility?'. Also the European Security Strategy (2003) and the 'Report on the Implementation of the European Security Strategy' (2008).
10 Kofi Annan at the opening of the 58th plenary session of the General Assembly of the UN, 23 September 2003.
11 See Article 11(1), Treaty on European Union, Consolidated version of the Treaty on European Union, O.J. (24 December 2002), C-325/5.
12 See, for example, CIA Document on the Evolution of Soviet Doctrine on Limited War (SR-IM 67-9, 10/1/1967) where the author explains: 'these observations in the doctrinal literature were strengthened on the policy-level statement of Minister of Defense Malinovsky'.
13 Beyond the policy-maker level, it could be argued that the operationalisation of doctrine would also require a wider social acceptance of the principles embedded therein, although this applies in certain kind of societies and on the European level would also presuppose the existence of an EU-wide public opinion.

14 See, for example, Lord Mandelson's 'The larger trend: China, Britain and Europe in a multilateral world' speech, Party School Beijing, 8 September 2009; Benita Ferrero-Waldner's speech 'Effective Multilateralism: Building for a Better Tomorrow', to the United Nations Association of Spain, Barcelona 14 April 2009; Angela Merkel's address to the US Congress urging multilateral solutions in the area of climate change http://www.reuters.com/article/GCA-GreenBusiness/idUSTRE5A20NR20091103 (accessed 13 August 2012).

15 Security and trade are also the two areas used as cases by Ruggie to detect the general principles which govern the practice of multilateralism.

16 The ESS identifies terrorism, the proliferation of WMDs, Regional Conflicts, State Failure and Organised crime as the key threats confronting the EU (ESS 2003: 2–5)

17 The urgency of the moment and the emphasis on responsibility and security is also expressed in the 2004 Report 'A more secure world: Our shared responsibility?' produced by the SG High-Level Panel on Threats, Challenges and Change. The resemblance of the two documents in terms of the threats identified and the advocacy of multilateralism as the means to confront them, points towards Wouters' (2007) assumption of bidirectional interaction between the EU and the UN as two levels of governance represented by two actors which are partners in multilateralism.

18 European Commission, DG Trade Website, http://ec.europa.eu/trade/creating-opportunities/eu-and-wto/ (accessed 13 August 2012).

19 'European Union: July 2000' WTO Trade Policy Review, Press/TPRB/137, http://www.wto.org/english/tratop_e/tpr_e/tp137_e.htm (accessed 13 August 2012).

20 'EU Parliament adopts resolution on WTO Doha Round', EU@UN, 9 October 2008, http://www.eu-un.europa.eu/articles/en/article_8207_en.htm (accessed 13 August 2012).

21 It is noteworthy that in spite of the fervently pro-WTO and trade liberalisation rhetoric, in practice the EU finds it difficult to make sacrifices which would highlight the priority of 'multilateralising' trade (for example, at the cost of intra-European trade).

22 The WTO Appellate Body is authorised to rule that national measures are in violation of trade treaties. It is composed of members chosen by member governments (see Steinberg 2004; Narlikar 2005). It is also noteworthy that for some authors (see Macedo 2008: 11) impartial international adjudication is a prerequisite for effective multilateralism.

23 See European Commission (2006) in which the Commission clarifies the 'Global Europe Strategy' and emphasises its commitment to multilateralism, and explains that 'The EU's priority is to ensure that any new FTAs, including our own, serve as a stepping stone, not a stumbling block for multilateral liberalisation' (p.2).

24 On the concept of universalism see Puchala (2003: 164–89).

References

Biscop, S. (2005) *The European Security Strategy: A Global Agenda For Positive Power.* Aldershot: Ashgate.

Biscop, S. (2009) 'The Value of Power, the Power of Values: a Call for an EU Grand Strategy'. Royal Institute for International Relations: *Egmont Paper*, n. 33.

Caporaso, J.A. (1992) 'International Relations Theory and Multilateralism: the Search for Foundations'. *International Organization* 46(3), 599–632.

Dannreuther, R. and Peterson, J. (2006) *Security Strategy and Transatlantic Relations.* London and New York: Routledge.

Edwards, G. (2011) 'The Pattern of the EU's Global Activity' in Hill, C. and Smith, M. (eds) *International Relations and the European Union.* New York: Oxford University Press.

European Commission (2006) 'Global Europe: Competing in the World', COM(2006) 567 final, Brussels: European Commission.

European Council (2003) *A secure Europe in a better world.* European Security Strategy [ESS]: Brussels, 12 December.

Forman, S. and Segaar, D. (2006) 'New Coalitions for Global Governance: The Changing Dynamics of Multilateralism'. *Global Governance* 12 (2), 205–25.

Freeland, Richard M. (1970) *The Truman Doctrine and the Origins of McCarthyism: Foreign Policy, Domestic Policy, and Internal Security, 1946–48.* New York: Alfred A. Knopf.

Gaddis, J.L. (2005) *Strategies of Containment : A Critical Appraisal of American National Security Policy During the Cold War.* Oxford: Oxford University Press.

Garcia, M.A. (2008) 'The Strategic Partnership between Brazil and the European Union' in Vasconcellos, A. (ed.) *Partnerships for Effective Multilateralism: EU Relations with Brazil, China, India and Russia.* Chaillot Paper 109. Paris: European Union Institute for Security Studies, 49–57.

Gordenker, L. and Weiss, T.G. (1993) 'The Collective Security Idea and Changing World Politics' in Weiss, T.G. (ed.) *Collective Security in a Changing World.* Boulder: Lynne Rienner, 3–18.

Haass, R.N. (2008) 'The Age of Nonpolarity: What Will Follow U.S. Dominance'. *Foreign Affairs* 87, 44–56.

Hill, C.J. (2010) 'European Union and Soft Power' in Michael Cox and Inderjeet Parmar (eds) *Soft Power and Hegemony in US Foreign Affairs: Theoretical, Historical and Contemporary Perspectives.* London and New York: Routledge, 182–98.

Hodges, H.G. (1915) *The Doctrine of Intervention.* Princeton: The Banner Press.

Hoffmann, S. (1977) 'An American Social Science: International Relations'. *Daedalus* 106 (3), 41–60

Hufner, K. and Naumann, J. (1990). 'Are the Moral and Value Foundations of Multilateralism Changing?' *International Political Science Review* 22(3), 323–34.

Kagan, R. (2002) '*Power and Weakness*'. *Policy Review* No. 113 (June–July), 3–28.

Keohane, R. (1990) 'Multilateralism: an Agenda for Research'. *International Journal*, 45(4), 731–64.

Keohane, R. and Nye, J. (1977) *Power and Interdependence.* Boston: Little Brown.

Keohane, R and Nye, J. (1985) 'Two Cheers for Multilateralism'. *Foreign Policy* 60, 148–67.

Keohane, R.O., Macedo, S. and Pettit, P. (2009) 'Democracy-Enhancing Multilateralism'. *International Organization* 63, 1–31.

Krasner, S.D. (ed.) (1983) *International Regimes.* Ithaca: Cornell, 372.

Krause, J. (2004) 'Multilateralism: Behind European Views'. *The Washington Quarterly*, Spring 2004, 43–59.

Krause, J. and Mallory, C.K. (1992) *Chemical Weapons in Soviet Military Doctrine: Military and Historical Experience, 1915–1991.* Boulder: Westview Press.

Lamy, P. (2002) 'Stepping Stones or Stumbling Blocks: The EU's Approach Towards the Problem of Multilateralism vs. Regionalism in Trade Policy'. *World Economy* 25(10).

Luck, E.C. (1999) *Mixed Messages: American Politics and International Organization, 1919–1999.* Virginia: Brookings Institution Press.

Macedo, S. (2008) 'Representation-Reinforcing Multilateralism: How International Institutions can Promote Fairer Representation and (Non-Electoral) Democracy'. Draft paper presented at the Representation Workshop, Princeton University Centre for Human Values, 5–6 December.

Manners, I. (2002) 'Normative Power Europe: A Contradiction in Terms?' *Journal of Common Market Studies* vol. 40, 235–58.

Monks, A.L (1964) *Soviet Military Doctrine, 1960 to the present.* New York: Irvington.

Mortier, J. (2004) 'The Doctrine of Intervention in the Twenty-first Century'. *The Henry Jackson Society.* Based on a speech given to the 21st Century Trust 'Global Governance: Scenarios for the Future' Conference at Madingley Hall, Cambridge, 26 October 2004.

Musu, C. (2007) 'The Middle East Quartet: An Effective Instrument of Multilateralism?' Paper presented at the annual meeting of the International Studies Association 48th Annual Convention, Chicago, 28 February.

Narlikar, A. (2005) *The World Trade Organization: A Very Short Introduction*. Oxford: Oxford University Press.

Nicolaïdis, K. (2004) 'The Power of the Superpowerless' in T. Lindberg (ed.) *Beyond Paradise and Power: Europeans, Americans and the Future of a Troubled Partnership*. London: Routledge.

Posen, Barry R. (1984). *The Sources of Military Doctrine: France, Britain and Germany between the World Wars*. Ithaca: Cornell University Press.

Powell, W.W. and DiMaggio, P.J. (eds) (1991) *The New Institutionalism in Organizational Analysis*. Chicago: University of Chicago Press.

Puchala, D.J. (2003) *Theory and History in International Relations*. New York: Routledge.

Puchala, D.J. and Hopkins, R.F. (1982) 'International Regimes: Lessons from Inductive Analysis'. *International Organization* 36(2), 245–75.

Ruggie, J.G. (1992) 'Multilateralism: The Anatomy of an Institution'. *International Organization* 46(3), 562–98.

Ruggie, J. (ed.) (1993) *Multilateralism Matters*. New York: Columbia University Press.

Ruggie, J. (1998) *Constructing World Polity*. London/New York: Routledge.

Russett, B. (1993) *Grasping the Democratic Peace: Principles for a Post-Cold War World*. New York: Princeton University Press.

Schimmelfennig, F. (2001) 'The Community Trap: Liberal Norms, Rhetorical Action, and the Eastern Enlargement of the European Union'. *International Organization* 55 (1), 47–80

Schuller, F.C. and Grant, T.D. (2003) 'Executive Diplomacy: Multilateralism, Unilateralism and Managing American Power'. *International Affairs* 79(1), 37–51.

Selverstone, M.J. (2001) 'Doctrines' in *Encyclopedia of American Foreign Policy vol. 1* (2nd edition), Burns, R.D., DeConde, A. and Logevall, F. (eds). New York: Scribner's, 521–41.

Smith, M.E. (2000) 'Conforming to Europe: The Domestic Impact of European Foreign Policy Cooperation'. *Journal of European Public Policy* 7(4), 613–31.

Steinberg, R.H. (2004) 'Judicial Law-Making at the WTO: Discursive, Constitutional and Political Constraints'. *American Journal of International Law*, 98, 247–75.

Vasconcelos, A. (2008) '"Multilateralising" multipolarity' in Vasconcellos, A. (ed.) *Partnerships for Effective Multilateralism: EU Relations with Brazil, China, India and Russia*. Chaillot Paper 109. Paris: European Union Institute for Security Studies, 11–32.

Wilkinson, R. (2000) *Multilateralism and the World Trade Organisation: the Architecture and Extension of International Trade Regulation*. Oxford: Routledge.

Wong, R. (2005) 'The Europeanisation of Foreign Policy' in Christopher Hill and Michael Smith (eds) *International Relations and the European Union*. Oxford: Oxford University Press, 134–53.

Wouters, J. (2007). 'The United Nations and the European Union: Partners in Multilateralism'. Working Paper No.1. Leuven: Leuven Centre for Global Governance.

WTO Secretariat (2009) 'Trade Policy Review/Report by the Secretariat: European Communities'. World Trade Organisation, WT/TPR/S/214, 2 March.

Further reading material

Agreement Establishing the World Trade Organization. Available online at: http://www.wto.org/english/docs_e/legal_e/04-wto.pdf

'A More Secure World: Our Shared Responsibility? Report of the SG High-Level Panel on Threats, Challenges and Change, United Nations Department of Public Information. December 2004.

'A Secure Europe in a Better World'. European Security Strategy, Brussels, 12 December 2003. Available online at: http://www.consilium.europa.eu/uedocs/cmsUpload/78367. pdf

Barry, B.R (2008) 'A Grand Strategy of Restraint' in Michele A Flourney and Shawn Brimley (eds.) *Finding Our Way: Debating American Grand Strategy*. Washington, DC: Center for a New American Security, 83–102.

Bush, G.W. (2002) 'The National Security Strategy of The United States of America'. Washington, DC: The White House.

Central Intelligence Agency Directorate of Intelligence, Intelligence Memorandum, 9 October 1967, Subject: The Evolution of Soviet Doctrine on Limited War. CIA FOIA Electronic Reading Room. Available online at http://www.foia.cia.gov/browse_docs. asp?doc_no=0000309808

'Effective Multilateralism: Building for a Better Tomorrow'. Speech by Benita Ferrero-Waldner to the United Nations Association of Spain, Barcelona 14 April 2009.

'EU and WTO'. European Commission, DG Trade Website: http://ec.europa.eu/trade/creating-opportunities/eu-and-wto

'EU Parliament Adopts Resolution on WTO Doha Round'. Europan Union@United Nations, Brussels, 9 October 2008. Available online at: http://www.europa-eu-un.org/articles/en/article_8207_en.htm

European Commission 'Global Europe: Some Questions and Answers'. Press Release, Brussels, 4 October 2006. Available online at: http://trade.ec.europa.eu/doclib/docs/2006/october/tradoc_130367.pdf

'European Union: July 2000'. WTO Trade Policy Review, Press Release PRESS/TPRB/137, 4 July 2000.

International Commission on Intervention and State Sovereignty (2001) 'The Responsibility to Protect: Report of the International Commission on Intervention and State Sovereignty'. Available online at: http://www.iciss.ca/pdf/Commission-Report.pdf

'Merkel Makes Historic US Address'. BBC News Online, 3 November 2009.

NATO Glossary of Terms and Definitions, NATO Military Agency for Standardization, 7 August 2000. Available online at: http://www.dtic.mil/doctrine/jel/other_pubs/aap_6v.pdf

'Reform, Revitalization of United Nations to Face New Global Threats Stressed'. 58th General Assembly Highlights, United Nations Press Release GA/10226, 24 December 2003. Available online at: http://www.un.org/News/Press/docs/2003/ga10226.doc.htm

'Report on the Implementation of the European Security Strategy – Providing Security in a Changing World'. Brussels, 11 December 2008, S407/08. Available online at: http://www.consillium.europa.eu/ueDocs/cms_Data/docs/pressData/en/reports/104630.pdf

'Rio Declaration on Environment and Development'. The United Nations Conference on Environment and Development, Rio de Janeiro 14 June 1992. Available online at: http://www.un-documents.net/rio-dec.htm

Study Group on Europe's Security Capabilities (2006) 'A Human Security Doctrine for Europe: The Barcelona Report of the Study Group on Europe's Security Capabilities'. Centre for the Study of Global Governance, LSE.

'The Larger Trend: China, Britain and Europe in a Multilateral World'. Speech by Lord Mandelson, Party School Beijing, 8 September 2009.

Treaty on European Union, Consolidated version of the Treaty on European Union, O.J. (24 December 2002), C-325/5.

4

EFFECTIVE OR DEFECTIVE?

Europe's experience of multilateralism[1]

Christopher Hill and John Peterson

The European Union (EU) is commonly portrayed as a distinct and even unique foreign policy actor. After all, no other regional organisation has ever aspired to a Common Foreign and Security Policy (CFSP). None has ever sought to define a doctrine to guide its external action as the EU did with its European Security Strategy (ESS) (European Council 2003). The ESS deemed 'effective multilateralism' to be one of Europe's strategic objectives. Subsequently, numerous declarations at the EU's highest political level – the European Council, or summits of Heads of State and Government – have reiterated the Union's commitment to building multilateralism as an existential foreign policy objective. Arguably, one upshot is to lay to rest the argument that the ESS – agreed at the end of the year in which the invasion of Iraq seemed to deal multilateralism a fatal blow – was merely a European *cri du coeur* with no lasting resonance.

What is less arguable is that post-war Europe marks an apogee of multilateralism in itself. Nowhere else do we find a treaty-based regional organisation with its own binding system of law and international legal personality. In foreign policy, the EU is far more active than its equivalents in other regions of the world. To illustrate, by mid-2012 it was running around 20 active military or civilian missions on three continents under the guise of its Common Security and Defence Policy (CSDP[2]). All of these missions were developmental or peace-building in nature and true to the idea of the EU as a 'civilian power': that is, a benign force that favours non-military instruments and engagement over the use of force, seeks 'milieu goals' (not possession goals) in IR, and prioritises the pursuit of international peace, human rights and development over its own material interests (see Wolfers 1962; Duchêne 1972; Hill 2003: 121–2; Hill and Smith 2011: 469). In short, the EU may be viewed as unique, not least because of its commitment to building multilateralism, which itself is privileged in EU external action ahead of its own, European interests.

What is more, the EU's European External Action service (EEAS) could be viewed as finding its feet after its creation in the 2009 Lisbon Treaty. Its supporters claim (or at least hope) that it is beginning to work as the equivalent of an EU Foreign Ministry. Combining officials from EU institutions and member states, the EEAS now staffs 136 EU delegations globally. For the first time, the Union has something like real embassies with expertise, resources and clout in major political capitals. The head of the EEAS, Catherine Ashton, combines the (previously separate) positions of Vice-President of the European Commission and High Representative for the CFSP. Despite early criticism of her performance, which often revealed her previous lack of foreign policy experience, it can be argued that Ashton gives the EU one authoritative face for its foreign policy to an extent previously unseen. No other international organisation has such a figurehead or anything like a 'foreign ministry'.

Meanwhile, the EU is in the process of fleshing out 'strategic partnerships' with ten of the world's most powerful states (see Peterson *et al.* 2012: 302). One view is that these agreements reflect an acceptance in Brussels and national EU capitals that other regions lag behind Europe in developing their own regional multilateralism or committing themselves to building multilateralism more generally. Despite the Union's region-to-region dialogues such as ASEM (the Asia-Europe meeting) or the Cotonou Agreement with former European colonies, coaxing other powers to embrace multilateralism requires direct, bilateral engagement. Russia's accession to the World Trade Organization (WTO) in 2012 is a case in point. In short, the reasons for considering Europe to be a unique player in IR, not least because its commitment to multilateralism is pure and unparalleled, are numerous.

We seek to challenge much of this accepted wisdom. We have argued elsewhere that multilateralism is increasingly unwieldy, involving more non-state actors, international organisations (IOs) whose missions often clash, and region-to-region dialogues (see Hill *et al.* 2012). The universal aspirations of United Nations-style multilateralism – featuring membership by all states, one common set of rules and clear jurisdictions – are increasingly sacrificed in the interest of pragmatism and problem-solving. Even the EU itself features various contact groups, sub-set memberships in distinct policy areas, and – of course – distinctive national foreign policies that persist and have by no means been melded into one. We thus argue that three assumptions featured prominently in the research literature on EU external policy – that the EU is unique, that it is uniquely committed to universal multilateralism, and that it eschews its own interests to 'build multilateralism' – are flawed.

We have seen (in Chapter 2) that there is no one plausible criterion by which multilateralism can be held to be 'effective'. Still, by many measures, modern multilateralism is messy, disorderly and *defective* insofar as it is rarely universal and often cannot produce quick solutions to international problems. It frequently does not apply the same rules to all.

But to judge multilateralism by these criteria is to take an inflexible, naïve and even dogmatic view about what the purpose and practice of multilateralism should be. The EU's own pragmatism, in terms of how it organises itself and engages with the non-European world, is indicative of its gradual coming to terms with how IR actually works, not how it might work in the best of all possible worlds. The real world of IR rarely features universal multilateralism, in which the same rules apply equally to all, and the EU itself reflects this reality. As such, its own experience is hardly unique. Nor is its commitment to multilateralism unadulterated. Accordingly, we shall argue that it is less distinctive, singular and *sui generis* as a foreign policy actor than is often claimed.

We proceed in four sections. First, we examine how multilateralism evolved from its earliest origins as a device for managing the emerging European state system to the present day. Second, we mine the research literature on EU foreign policy to demonstrate how the academy has coalesced around a consensus about the Union as an external actor. Third, we scrutinise the EU's practice of external action – specifically in trade policy – to show how it is both primarily motivated, as are other trading powers, to defend its own economic interests and that it adds to the unwieldiness of modern multilateralism in the way it engages with its trading partners. Finally, we offer an assessment of the current state of regionalism in modern IR to demonstrate that claims of or hopes for 'third generation' regionalism – featuring strong relationships between regional organisations – are premature. Our conclusion restates our central argument: that pragmatism is mostly what drives EU foreign policy and that Europe's experience of multilateralism is far less distinctive than often is claimed.

The spread of multilateralism: an historical perspective[3]

One of the true classics in the study of international relations (IR), E. H. Carr's *The Twenty Years' Crisis*, offers frequent and sobering reminders of the need to qualify any notion that a harmony of interests may be found in IR with the stark reality that power rules. Any investigation of the prospects for multilateralism in the twenty-first century is wise to consider Carr's (1939 [2001]: 100) injunction that a 'failure to recognize that power is an essential element of politics has hitherto vitiated all attempts to establish international forms of government…To internationalize government in any real sense means to internationalize power.'

By all accounts, Europe was where the first attempts were made to 'internationalize government' because it is where the modern system of states was born. Even before that historical moment, we can trace congresses of various sorts back to the Olympic games of ancient Greece, and to the medieval church councils, which were inherently international and sometimes overtly political (Barber 1979: 36). Still, multilateralism as we know it today traces its roots to 'Renaissance diplomacy' (Mattingly 1955). As Europe emerged from the medieval period, it began to develop a class of professional diplomats, with an increasing permanence of residence abroad. The results were negotiations leading to treaties such as those agreed at Augsburg (1555), Cateau-Cambrésis (1559) and ultimately Westphalia (1648). At Augsburg, after a convocation of the Imperial Diet lasting seven months, the principle of *cuis regio, eius religio* – literally, 'whose realm, his religion' – was introduced, thus establishing that the religion of whoever ruled determined the religion of those ruled. The first attempt to establish a sort of multilateral rule of law was a product of the perceived need to try to settle religious disputes peacefully within the Holy Roman Empire.

At Cateau-Cambrésis, high-ranking representatives of France and Spain were present together with a more modest English delegation at what is now a commune in the Nord *département* of northern France. In 1559, however, it was neutral ground belonging to the Spanish Netherlands (which became Belgium). The Treaty of Cateau-Cambrésis settled matters mostly relating to the Italian peninsula but also determined the fate of Calais. The seven-week discussions took place in the hastily refurbished surroundings of a ruined chateau, and featured translation problems of the kind subsequently to plague the EU (Elton 1968: 11–17).

Westphalia, of course, is far better known because it established the principle of state sovereignty and a predisposition against interference in the internal affairs of other states. In fact, the Peace of Westphalia – something of a myth in itself since France and Spain remained at war for another 11 years – actually involved two treaties, those of Münster and Osnabrück, emerging from multilateral discussions in the two cities over four years (Osiander 1994). This was what is usually thought of as the first modern diplomatic congress, with an accompanying *peinture de famille* – the precursor to the 'family photo' taken at each EU summit – to prove it.[4]

Whatever the arguments over the significance of Westphalia, there can be little doubt that it represents the beginning of the series of major multilateral gatherings associated with a self-conscious valuing of the ability to stop war and make peace. Articulated in the seventeenth-century writings of Samuel Pufendorf – a multi-talented German jurist, philosopher, economist and statesman (Boucher 1998: 223–5, 240–7) – this approach was on display in Dutch cities during the Congresses of Nijmegen (1676–9), Rijswijk (1696–7) and Utrecht (1712–13) (Barber 1979: 37–9). Diplomacy did not prevent war. But over time it increasingly came to grips with its consequences and allowed diplomats at least to ventilate the causes of disputes that were endemic to the early and very fragile European states-system. The foundations for the more familiar exhibitions of multilateral diplomacy that we know from the nineteenth century were thus laid during the period of the very emergence of the modern sovereign state.

Accepting the principle of independence also meant accepting the need to communicate, negotiate and ultimately agree on means of mediating separateness (Der Derian 1987). This process gathered pace only very slowly. But the great war of 1792–1815 not only produced a great peace, at the Congress of Vienna, but also a faltering 'Congress system', followed by the 'Concert of Europe'. Even if it did not lead to regular summits of the kind that are now a familiar feature of life in the EU, the Concert did at least establish the expectation that Great Powers would need to engage in a semi-permanent process of discussion if war was to be avoided. The 1815 Congress was remarkable for its scale, pulling in leaders (at foreign minister level or above) from all over Europe, while most activity took place in what we would now call the margins of formal meetings. For its part, the Concert of Europe 'served to reduce uncertainty by generating expectations of behaviour' and 'membership in the Concert and the status that went along with it became a prize in itself' (Richardson

1999: 76), thus foreshadowing today's EU and especially its radical enlargement after 2004. Both the Congress and Concert thus may be viewed as models for modern multilateralism (Hurd 2010: 32–43).

The Congresses of Paris (1856) and Berlin (1878) confirmed the intention of the major powers to use the immediate reason for a meeting to widen the agenda towards the maintenance of both the overall balance of power and international commerce. Subsequently, the Hague Conferences of 1899 and 1907 attempted to take things further in the direction of substantive international law. They thus set the stage for the creation of the League of Nations in 1919, which marked an ambitious – even audacious – attempt to bring together the various strands of multilateralism in existence before World War I. The League explicitly sought to create a working peace system that integrated diplomacy, law and even public opinion.[5] Unfortunately, recalling Carr's admonition, it failed to take an even more important element into proper consideration: that of power (Hinsley 1967).

One of the great ironies of IR scholarship is that Carr's *The Twenty Years' Crisis* was published just as the storm clouds gathering over Europe began to unleash what became World War II. The end of that conflict finally concentrated minds on the need for an effective architecture of multilateralism in which state rivalries could operate, and with luck be contained, by international organisations open to all states but whose rules reflected the reality of power differentials. As such, the Wilsonian notion of an international architecture in which all states were equal was sacrificed at the altar of pragmatism. It is often forgotten by committed Wilsonians that universalism was never even a possibility until after World War II, while even now not every *de facto* state is a member of the United Nations (UN) system. Moreover, much multilateral cooperation is not conducted at the global level. If, in retrospect, the immediate post-war period seems like a golden age of building multilateralism, it is only because so much subsequent multilateral cooperation has been *ad hoc*, imperfect and less than universal. And those 'present at the creation' of the UN, the Bretton Woods institutions, NATO and what is now the EU were at least subconsciously responsive to Carr's warning that 'internationalizing power' required building in mechanisms that reflected disparities of power: weighted voting, opt-outs, escape clauses and rights of veto.

Ikenberry's (2006: 245–82) claim that the twenty-first century has brought a 'new multilateralism', in which such mechanisms are often absent, is examined elsewhere in this volume (see Chapter 2). Here we note that he specifically insists that '[p]ower does not disappear from this multilateral order, but it operates in a bargaining system in which rules and institutions – and power – play an interactive role' (Ikenberry 2006: 253). It is possible to accept that IR is now more governed by rules and institutions than ever before in the past, and yet still view the multilateral order as unwieldy and far from optimal if that means absent of power politics.

In particular, two new multilateral institutions have appeared over the past two decades that fit the characterisation of a new multilateralism. One is the International Criminal Court (ICC), which subjects all of its member states – powerful, weak or in between – to the same standards of justice on grievous violations of human rights.

The other is the World Trade Organization (WTO) which – unlike its predecessor, the General Agreement on Tariffs and Trade – works according to a binding set of rules that apply equally to all. Yet, upon close inspection, both fall short of their Wilsonian aspirations. As of 2012, 121 states were members of the ICC. But leading powers including China, India, Russia and – of course – the United States (US) were not. In the WTO dispute panel rulings are binding on the litigants. But they are often so legally vague as to leave both sides in a dispute – frequently, the EU and US – claiming victory (Hoekman and Kostecki 2009: 84–130).

Moreover, it is an empirical fact that considerably more multilateral cooperation now operates on a regional than universal, international level.[6] The EU has certainly been a major contributor to the advance of regionalism as it has taken steps towards further and/or deeper integration with each successive revision of its treaties. It also has sought, if often in words more than deeds, to promote and convert other regions to its own habits of cooperation (see Smith 2008: 76–110). Yet, as we demonstrate in our next section, it is portrayed most often in the academy as a unique international actor. We consider both ways in which it deserves this designation, and ways that it does not.

EU foreign policy and the research literature: getting to grips?

Research on EU foreign policy – broadly defined – has expanded exponentially in recent decades. This expansion has been in response to two developments:

1. the end of the Cold War and the myriad geopolitical changes that ensued, not least on the European continent and its environs;
2. the progressive expansion of the EU's international ambitions and its new external policy instruments, especially – by no means exclusively – the creation of the CFSP via the 1991 Maastricht Treaty, the emergence of what is now the CSDP in 1999, and the entry into force of the Lisbon Treaty, with its various institutional innovations in external policy, a decade later.

The literature now features a very broad array of substantive preoccupations (often specific policies) and a diversity of perspectives about the EU's potential as a foreign policy actor, if perhaps somewhat less variety in theoretical approaches.[7] Despite its eclecticism, existing research tends to start with three assumptions about the nature of the EU as a global player:

1. it is a unique, *sui generis*, foreign policy actor;
2. it is committed – in a primordial, almost genetic way – to the goal of 'effective multilateralism';
3. it is a normative actor, which prioritises values over interests.

In a sense, all three assumptions are intertwined. For example, the argument is often made that it is precisely the Union's commitment to multilateralism and normative bent that make it unique. Its primordial mission to build multilateralism makes it a normative actor, which often sacrifices its own interests to build multilateralism. The prominence of these assumptions in the research literature is striking.

The EU as 'n of 1'

On the first point, we have already rehearsed the basic case for the EU's uniqueness. No other IO (even NATO) has the audacity to claim for itself a 'common foreign policy', let alone a common security policy. None has sought to create for itself a nascent foreign ministry nor assigned one individual to be its foreign policy face to the world. But the basic case often leads to a sort of singularity in EU foreign policy scholarship: the Union is an 'n of 1' which cannot be compared to any other international power. Thus, traditional IR scholarship cannot explain its impact on IR.

Consider the logic of the argument that '[s]ince the EU is a unique, non-traditional and relatively new contender' for global power, an approach 'to actors and actorness' is required 'that enables us to treat the EU as unique' (Bretherton and Vogler 2006: 13). Here, the point may be conceded that the Union's 'actorness' – its ability to act purposively and effectively – is clearly distinct from its 'presence' – or its geopolitical magnetism, particularly for states on its borders. No one who studies EU foreign policy could argue that this distinction does not matter (see Hill 1994; Hill and Smith 2011). The European Union is clearly far more powerful for what it *is* than for what it *does* (see Cooper 2003). But whether that means it requires its own, distinct theoretical approach – and whether using one gets us any closer to understanding it – is very debatable.

What seems less debatable is that there exists near-unanimity in the research literature that the EU is an 'n of 1' in IR. In practical terms, 'the *sui generis* nature of the EU means that international organisations and other fora vary in their willingness to recognise it as an actor in its own right' (Marsh and Mackenstein 2005: 56). Its uniqueness also causes other problems: as a '*sui generis* entity it possesses none of the traditional advantages accorded to states, such as popular support based around national identity' (Marsh and Mackenstein 2005: 247).

At times, the EU's uniqueness is presented as aspirational. For example, Gnesotto (2004: 1) argues that debate about 'Europe as a civil or a military power definitely seems to be a thing of the past…[because] what the Union intends to become is a *sui generis* power'. Usually, however, it is taken for granted and implicitly cited as excusing its decidedly modest record in foreign policy. Ginsberg (2001: 274) insists that scholars have been too critical and focused overmuch on the Union's lack of foreign policy successes; it is enough to show that it has *impact*: 'the EU is a complex, partially constructed, *sui generis*, and evolving international actor that has political impact – across a range of degrees – on non-members' foreign policy interests and on many issues of international politics'.

Yet, the main problem seems analytical: 'CFSP remains a *sui generis* problem for both international relations theory and integration theory' (Øhrgaard 2004: 36).

In particular, '[t]he assumption that this actor is unique poses particular problems for foreign policy analysts who have been traditionally wedded to a comparative cross-country methodology' (White 2004b: 29). Starting with this assumption, then, seems to lead members of multiple theoretical schools to analytical dead ends. One of the few scholars to avoid this fate, by actually testing the *sui generis* assumption, is Karen Smith (2008: 234), who finds that 'the EU may not be so unique in its choice of foreign policy objectives, but the way it pursues them does distinguish it from other international actors...What it does is less unique than how it does it.' In other words, the EU is distinctive in that it seeks to combine so many different policy instruments and resources, sourced at the national and regional levels, in the pursuit of its objectives (see also Bretherton and Vogler 2006: 223). It is thus little wonder that it often struggles to succeed. But the wider point is that our basic understanding of the EU's global role seems severely limited by assuming that it is an 'n of 1'.

The EU's existential commitment to multilateralism

A second assumption feeds the first: namely, the EU's commitment to multilateralism is, perhaps above all, what most makes it unique. Not only is Europe's commitment to multilateralism unassailable, according to Jørgensen (2004: 35), EU foreign policy *is* multilateralism, thus making most of the analytical tools of IR useless: '[t]he assumption here is that the emergence of a European (multilateral) foreign policy implies that our analysis should be based on conceptualisations that *differ* from those applied in the traditional foreign policy of states'.

Taking the assumption about as far as it can go, McCormick (2007: 12) claims a 'European superpower' has emerged that offers an entirely 'new model of international relations': in contrast to the 'US preference for coercion and unilateralism we now have the European preference for diplomacy, economic development, *multilateral cooperation*, and the politics of influence' (emphasis added).[8] Similarly, Bretherton and Vogler (2006: 185) concur that '[c]ommitment to multilateralism is at the core of EU external activities...it expresses both the Union's preferred approach to international affairs and a desire to emphasize its distinctiveness from the unilateralism of the USA'. Yet, careful investigation of claims of 'unilateral America, multilateral Europe' yields considerable evidence to suggest that the contrast between the two is far less stark in practice than rhetoric (see Pollack 2003).

However, as European foreign policy evolves, '[o]ne thing that is not likely to change is EU attachment to multilateralism, international law, engagement and coalition building as preferred mechanisms through which to pursue its objectives' (Marsh and Mackenstein 2005: 259). It comes as little surprise that European policy-makers buy into this assumption. Witness the European Commission's (2003: 5) extolling of 'the EU's ability to act as a "front-runner" in developing and implementing multilateral instruments and commitments' and its committed support for enhancing 'the capacity of other countries to implement their multilateral commitments effectively'.

The EU as a normative power

A final, heroic assumption guiding much scholarship on EU foreign policy is that the Union is unique insofar as it ranks values above interests when it makes foreign policy choices. In other words, the EU is different from other international powers: it is a *normative power*. One implication is that it often, even routinely, prioritises its vision of how the international order should look in the long term over any short-term gain that the Union might achieve.

The primary exponent of this view is Ian Manners (2002, 2006, 2008a, 2008b, 2010). In a variety of works, he has refined the concept – first introduced in 2002 – of Europe as a normative power: 'an attempt to suggest that not only is the EU constructed on a normative basis, but importantly that this predisposes it to act in a normative way in world politics' (Manners 2002: 252). The argument puts Manners (2002: 252) in the camp of those who claim that 'the most important factor shaping the international role of the EU is not what it does or what it says, but what it is', specifically: 'a changer of norms'. Yet, when it acts it often does so in 'the absence of obvious material gain from its interventions' (Manners 2002: 253) and on the basis of 'international principles, particularly those advocated by transnational civil society and originating from within the UN system such as sustainable peace, sustainable development or good governance' (Manners 2010: 76–7; see also Manners 2008a, 2008b). Far from being a weak, inconsequential player in IR, the Union is powerful because 'the ability to define what passes for "normal" in world politics is, ultimately, the greatest power of all' (Manners 2002: 253).

Manners' perspective has been widely – albeit not universally – embraced by EU scholars. For Marsh and Mackenstein (2005: 250–1), what guides EU foreign policy is 'the principles of peace and reconciliation that underpinned post-war integration', which 'lead to it appearing more ethically driven and less suspect than do states, including, ironically, its own member states'.[9] For their part, Bretherton and Vogler (2006: 60) dutifully survey the literature to show how the EU's identity is contested and a 'hybrid' one: it is both 'a model and promoter of values' *and* a 'fortress'. Ultimately, however, they veer towards accepting the Union as a relatively benign power whose methods contrast sharply with the US. Similarly, McCormick (2007: 12) claims 'a resurgence of European global influence, which has had the effect of replacing the Cold War bipolar system with a post-modern bipolar system':

> In this new system, the European Union is a superpower that relies upon soft power to express itself and to achieve its objectives, and that finds itself at a moral advantage in an international environment where violence as a means of achieving influence is increasingly detested and rejected, and at a strategic advantage because its methods and priorities fit more closely with the needs and consequences of globalization.
>
> *(McCormick 2007: 6)*

Surely, few IR scholars would recognise the contemporary international order as one in which the US and Europe constitute separate poles in a 'post-modern bipolar system', despite the claim – made by Toje (2008) and others – that one outcome of the 2003 Iraq War was a bipolar West. Few besides committed constructivists and post-modernists would take the EU's rhetoric about its international mission at face value, as Toje (2010: 152) – a thoughtful realist – clearly does not: '[t]he EU is expected to safeguard the national interests of its members and make the world a better place. Emphasis is on the latter'. Two of the top EU trade specialists rather bluntly conclude that the Union has asserted 'its central role in the multilateral system less to uphold the value of multilateralism as a public good than to promote the EU's own interest in this system' (Meunier and Nicolaïdis 2011: 287).

Again, the research literature does not present any *pensée unique* on EU foreign policy. It features lively debate, and for good reason: the European Union is no doubt a *distinctive* international actor that, in important respects and as we have acknowledged, is unique. However, we take issue with the assumptions that the Union is entirely *sui generis*, committed to multilateralism purely as a public good, or matchlessly willing to sacrifice its interests for its values. We find evidence in the EU's actually existing external action – reviewed in the section that follows – for portraying the Union as an international actor that has more in common with other powers than is often assumed.

EU external action in practice: the case of trade policy

In turning to how the EU *acts* – what it actually does – in its external action, we must offer several caveats. First, we cannot pretend that our overview comes remotely close to being comprehensive. It would require at least a book-length study devoted entirely to the subject to survey the full range of foreign policy choices the Union makes. For our analytical purposes, and in contrast to Ginsberg's (2001) mission to show the EU has 'impact', such a survey would need specifically to test the assumptions that the Union is unique, that its commitment to multilateralism is hard-wired, and that it is a fundamentally normative actor.

Second, any such survey would need to be preceded by careful reflection about the parameters that define 'external action'. For a start, decisions about the EU's own internal policies and institutional make-up (what might be termed its 'internal multilateralism') can have powerful external effects. Moreover, any surveyor would be wise to remind themselves that, in its classic definition, public policies are what governments – or, in this case, the EU's institutions or member states – decide to do or decide *not* to do. Relatedly, there is the power of 'non-decisions' (Bachrach and Baratz 1963): not to choose is, in a sense, to choose. To illustrate, the decisions *not* to punish pre-Arab Spring states in north Africa for human rights abuses by imposing economic sanctions showed how the EU's reluctance to pull strings attached to market privileges constitutes non-action with powerful consequences. In this case it prioritised stability above human rights.

Third and finally, while querying the accepted wisdom that the EU is *sui generis*, we have acknowledged that the Union may be unique in that it wields more policy instruments, and a more diverse set of them, than any other international power. This status has consequences, especially given that powers are shared far more than they are separated between the EU's institutions (see Peterson and Shackleton 2012), or – particularly in external policy – and between the Union and its member states (see Hill and Smith 2011). One important consequence is that the EU is almost ideally engineered for turf wars both between its institutions and between them and its member states, as illustrated by the tortured creation of the European External Action Service (Vanhoonacker and Reslow 2010) or the ungainliness of European aid and development policies (Carbone 2011). The upshot is that the Union adds to the unwieldiness of modern multilateralism because different external institutions, member states and policies can easily work at cross-purposes, since authority between them is so finely divided, or simply because the EU itself is so unwieldy.

With these admonitions made, we focus specifically on the EU's record in a prime area of external action – trade policy.[10] Arguably, trade policy is a hard case with which to test EU distinctiveness since it is where the Union is most state-like. To argue that the EU is not very distinctive in trade policy says nothing about other aspects of the Union's external policy, and does not refute the contention that it is distinctive amongst major powers for what it does *not* do: that is, to wage war. But we focus here on the Common Commercial Policy because it is where the Union is best equipped to speak and act as one, to do so decisively, and to engage in 'strategic action' (see Smith 1998).

The EU could claim to have played an essential part in the successful negotiation of the Uruguay Round that created the WTO, which itself is often viewed as the apogee of 'effective multilateralism'. It then gave crucial backing to China's and (especially) Russia's WTO accession. Arguably, it tried to make the best of a (somewhat harsh) WTO decision that led it to alter its Lomé Convention system of trade preferences with African, Caribbean and Pacific states (ACP, former European colonies). Its response – enshrined in the 2000 Cotonou Agreement – was to encourage ACP states to adopt European-style multilateralism and conclude regional free trade agreements between themselves. Then, they could (and should) conclude bilateral Economic Partnership Agreements (EPAs) with the EU.[11]

Yet, there is ample evidence to suggest that the EU usually acts as a major economic power would be expected to do: by privileging its own economic interests above all else and defending those interests, at times aggressively. As we have seen (in Chapter 2), one possible definition of 'effective' multilateralism is global governance that effectively advances the EU's interests. Still, however much its framers might claim that it was designed to build multilateralism, in the sense of creating a more just and equitable international order, scholarly analysis of the Cotonou Agreement – the successor to the Lomé Convention – has ranged from critical to outright scathing (see Hurt 2003; Babarinde and Faber 2004, 2005).

Cotonou's timetable for the liberalisation of ACP markets was presented as effectively non-negotiable by the EU. It was widely viewed as far out of sync with its promises of aid specifically to help ACP states adjust to trade liberalisation and achieve better access to European markets. By late 2006, only 28 per cent of such aid committed for 2000–5 via the European Development Fund had actually been spent. It was telling that reform of the EU's sugar regime, which cut prices paid to 18 ACP exporters by around one-third, was sweetened by an aid package of around €1.4 billion to help European producers adjust by the end of a transition period in 2013. Meanwhile, European sugar beet producers were offered no less than €6 billion in compensation.[12] It was perhaps even more telling that, however much the EU was committed to 'exporting' European-style multilateralism to the ACP states, it had successfully concluded only one EPA with a regional grouping of ACP states by late 2012: with the CARIFORUM (formerly CARICOM) group of Caribbean states.

The EU's highly contentious Trade, Development and Cooperation Agreement (TDCA) with South Africa is another case in point. The deal was agreed in 1999 after nearly four years and 22 rounds of extremely hard-nosed negotiations. The original offer by the EU of a trade agreement had been much trumpeted as a European gesture of support for the 'new South Africa' after Nelson Mandela had successfully led the country to embrace multi-party democracy. The TDCA would, according to the official Brussels line, be asymmetrical – with the Union offering more liberalisation than it demanded – and thus would symbolise a post-Lomé model for the EU's development policy towards the rest of the world.

In practice, the EU's approach in the negotiations was, in the words of a leading commentator, 'consistently devious, destructive and, above all, shamefully protectionist'.[13] Negotiations dragged on over four years primarily because the European side proposed to turn upside down asymmetry on the deal's agricultural element, demanding access to around 80 per cent of the South African market in exchange for opening only 62 per cent of the EU's market. Many of the items on a long list of European exclusions – such as potatoes and cut flowers – posed little or no threat to European producers because of South Africa's entirely opposite growing season. Adding insult to injury, Spain and Portugal demanded that South African fortified wines be relabelled despite the fact that some amongst them had been sold as port or sherry for as many as 200 years. It became a final sticking point that, according to multiple participants, prolonged negotiations for more than a year.[14]

In the end, only 61 per cent of South Africa's farm products gained unrestricted access to EU markets (trade barriers on another 13 per cent were partially liberalised). Meanwhile, South Africa was obliged to scrap tariffs on 95 per cent of agricultural imports from the EU. The Union's notorious Common Agricultural Policy heavily subsidised products, such as processed fruits and vegetables, for which South African producers were certain to suffer heavy losses as a result of the deal.[15] As is often the case when free trade agreements are agreed, innocent bystanders were also hurt: Botswana, Namibia, Lesotho and Swaziland stood to lose around 15 per cent of fiscal revenue from tariffs scrapped under the pact because of their economic links to South Africa through the Southern African Customs Union.

Effectively, all four were forced to accept a *de facto* free trade area with the EU which they played no role in negotiating.

Two years later, the EU's 'Everything But Arms' (EBA) initiative was agreed. It offered ostensibly unrestricted access to the EU's market for all products except arms to the world's 49 least developed countries. EBA was agreed over the objections of France[16] with a French Trade Commissioner, Pascal Lamy, piloting the deal to conclusion. On the surface, it appeared to be a result of truly strategic action in the use of trade policy.

Yet, it was always clear that EBA would likely divert as much trade as it created. An early analysis actually predicted that EBA would work at cross-purposes with the EU's stated goals of promoting regional cooperation and ensuring reciprocity in its trade relations since it unilaterally abrogated existing agreements (see Page and Hewitt 2002). By most accounts, the Commission's Directorate-General for Agriculture fought successfully to water down EBA's liberalisation of several important product sectors, even if EU agricultural interest were forced to fight 'a defensive battle' and EBA generally marked 'a defeat for the agricultural community' (Pilegaard 2006: 237). A 2005 study suggested that EBA had had an impact in only a few economic sectors (such as sugar) and that its benefits for the world's poorest countries were likely to be eroded over time (see Gallezot and Bureau 2006). More generally, since they represented 'less than 0.5% of world trade, the LDCs [least-developed countries did]...not have the capacity to significantly increase their production capacity (at least not in the short run)' (Pilegaard 2006: 249).

Multiple analyses of EBA have broadly concurred that it was driven by 'essentially political, not developmental, motives' (Page and Hewitt 2002: 91). Generally, EBA seemed an act of symbolic politics designed to counter the dissatisfaction of the world's poorest countries with the multilateral system as well as, possibly, a deliberate spur to an overdue effort to overhaul Europe's own (internal) sugar regime. More specifically, Pilegaard (2006: 237) argues that EBA 'reflected the relative decline of development policy in the EU political system...[It] was not primarily an instance of development policy influencing the trade agenda, but rather an instance of the trade agenda encroaching on the development agenda'. To be clear, there are serious academic analyses of EBA that view it more benignly (see Orbie 2007; Young and Peterson 2012). But if EBA is a case of strategic action, it is one with apparently mixed motives and ambiguous results, besides those of marking the new ascendance of the Directorate-General for Trade in the Commission's internecine policy battles and a more general effort to offer poorer countries trade instead of aid.

Since EBA was agreed, DG Trade has become – if anything – more assertive and, partly as a consequence, the EU has become progressively more self-regarding in its trade policy. By way of illustration, the 2007 'Global Europe' market access strategy marked a major statement of intent. The most distinctive aspect of Global Europe was its emphasis on pursuing market access through bilateral rather than multilateral agreements. The Commission (2007: 4) presented this shift as a necessary policy correction in response to demands from European firms:

As a result of the priority the EU has given to multilateral efforts to reduce trade barriers, the Commission's focus has to some extent shifted away from specific barrier removal. There is a strong need to correct this, both because of the growing importance and complexity of non-tariff barriers and because of the demands of stakeholders.

Global Europe's focus on economically significant markets represented a departure from the EU's existing preferential trading agreements. Most had been concluded primarily for political reasons with former European colonies or countries of the EU's 'near abroad' (Messerlin 2001). According to Heron and Siles-Brügge (2012: 2), Global Europe 'presaged a shift in the EU's external commercial strategy from *multilateralism first* to *competitive liberalization*',[17] specifically with the EU competing with the US to secure access to valuable third markets (see also Dür 2010). Subsequently, bilateral negotiations on free trade agreements were launched with the Association of South East Asian Nations (ASEAN), India and South Korea starting in 2007 and Canada in 2009. However, by 2012 negotiations had been concluded only with South Korea.[18]

In the interim, the Commission announced a 'renewed' strategy as trade policy's contribution to the EU's more general 2020 growth strategy. As Trade Commissioner in the second Barroso Commission, Karel De Gucht reaffirmed that the Global Europe agenda of pursuing bilateral trade agreements was 'the right course for Europe to follow' (European Commission 2010a: 9). Nevertheless, EU trade policy underwent significant changes in emphasis under De Gucht. In substantive terms, the Commission stressed the 'depth and quality' of its trade relationships (De Gucht 2010: 2–3), and thus became more focused on regulatory barriers to goods and services and the promotion of the EU's environmental and social values. The EU's largest trading partners and emerging economies were singled out as never before as priorities: the US, China, Russia, Japan, India, Brazil.

In stylistic terms, De Gucht explicitly signalled that the EU would 'defend its interests and its values with greater self-confidence' (European Commission 2010b: 17). Similarly, the EU's European Council (2010: 1) stressed the need for 'the EU to promote its interests and values more assertively and in a spirit of reciprocity and mutual benefit'. The emphasis in bilateral trade negotiations, therefore, would be on 'achieving reciprocity and a true level playing field for our operators. Where there is asymmetry of openness, we must redress that balance.' (De Gucht 2010: 3).

Further evidence of a more assertive EU was the new 'enforcement agenda' unveiled by De Gucht. It sought to ensure that others abided by the letter of their agreements and ostensibly threatened that the Union would use trade defence instruments to combat 'unfair' trade practices. As De Gucht (2010: 6) put it, 'Our motto is: we should be open, but not naïve'. Put another way, 'The EU should remain an open economy, not a disarmed economy' (European Commission 2010c: 29).[19]

Global Europe had envisaged reform of the EU's anti-dumping practices to make them more liberal. In stark contrast, as part of the enforcement agenda, the Commission (2010b: 2) rejected any reform of anti-dumping policy until after the conclusion of the Doha Round of global trade talks, in order to 'avoid [its] efforts being portrayed as unilateral disarmament'. Of course, it was widely perceived that the Doha Round fell apart not least because the EU – together with the US – was unwilling to open its agricultural markets to developing states.[20] More generally, the Commission justified its greater emphasis on enforcement in general and trade defence instruments in particular as based on the need to persuade the European public to support the EU's trade policy (De Gucht 2010: 6).

Despite shifts in emphasis, the EU's trade strategy has been remarkably consistent since it first began to articulate one in the mid-1990s. It has repeatedly emphasised a commitment to domestic liberalisation and opening foreign markets. But in a dismal climate of economic recession and repeated crises in the Eurozone, the EU appeared to back away from its commitment to domestic liberalisation, in its rhetoric at least. More generally, EU trade strategy appeared to differ over time in terms of the tactics used to try to open foreign markets – dispute settlement, trade defences, bilateral agreements or multilateral trade rounds – but it has effectively pursued all of them throughout. Where it has been most consistent has been in trying to secure real benefits for European firms.

Of course, our evidence is far more selective than comprehensive. Even in trade policy, cases could be cited when trade preferences were withdrawn, as from Belarus (2007) for violating core labour rights or from Sri Lanka (2010) for human rights violations. Such cases could be presented as validating the EU as a normative actor paradigm. More recent economic sanctions imposed on Iran – which, by all accounts, have put severe economic pressure on its regime – in support of the so-called 'P5+1' negotiations (chaired by the EU) could be viewed as the Union showing its commitment to a multilateral effort to curb Iran's nuclear ambitions.[21] Beyond trade policy, to give but one example, the EU's rhetorical support for and financial contribution to a wide array of organisations and regimes dedicated to the non-proliferation of weapons of mass destruction (Van Ham 2011) could be taken to symbolise its unique status as both a normative power and one that instinctively seeks to build multilateralism.

Yet, the case of trade policy still puts into serious question the accepted wisdom about what kind of global actor the EU actually is. We have considered a core area of EU external policy and found that when there are tangible European economic interests at stake, the Union acts as would any other trading power by defending its interests. Our evidence suggests, as a hypothesis worth testing, that the Union becomes a normative actor that prioritises the building of multilateralism only when that goal does not conflict with defence of its own interests. It clearly engages with other states and regions both bilaterally and multilaterally. Moreover, the EU's recent forays into region-to-region dialogues, as we argue in the section that follows, adds to the unwieldiness of modern multilateralism.

'Third generation' regionalism: effective or defective?

Yet another area where we can investigate the nature of the EU as an external actor is in its attempts to engage in so-called 'third generation' regionalism, a phenomenon whose meaning is perhaps best understood by considering what preceded it. 'First generation' regionalism is viewed as strictly economic integration: combining national economies into larger regional economic units via free trade areas or customs unions. What is now the EU could be seen as a pioneer for other regions – such as Mercosur in Latin America or NAFTA in North America – that later followed (albeit more modestly) in its footsteps.

'Second generation' regionalism – or what for a time in the 1990s was termed the 'new' regionalism – was defined as a 'multidimensional form of integration which includes economic, political, social, and cultural aspects and thus goes far beyond the goal of creating region-based free trade regimes or security alliances' (Hettne 1999: xvi). In other words, a second generation of regional organisations was foreseen that would become more politically determined and develop ambitions that went beyond economics.

For a time, the 'new regionalism' became a focus for many IR scholars (see Fawcett and Hurrell 1995; Gamble and Payne 1996; Hveem 1999), including some whose primary focus was the EU (Telò 2001). What was never entirely clear in this scholarship was whether the rise of regional multilateralism was a normative position or a prediction about the future, or both. The alleged 'resurgence of regionalism in world politics' (Fawcett and Hurrell 1995: 1) was perhaps an understandable preoccupation arising from both the EU's emergence as a considerably more ambitious political project – with a single currency and 'common' foreign policy – and the rise of NAFTA, Mercosur and other regional projects. The question of whether the formation of regional economic blocs might be a recipe for fragmentation rather than globalisation and trade wars in economic terms became a salient one (see Friedberg 1993–4).

More recently, a new literature has emerged on 'third generation' regionalism to which a leading contributor – together with a variety of co-authors – is Luk Van Langenhove.[22] This work seeks to move forward debates about whether regional organisations are building blocks or 'stumbling blocks' in attempts to advance multilateralism globally. A frequently cited contributor to such debates is one of the most talented and able European Commissioners of recent years, Pascal Lamy (2001: 1), who as EU Trade Commissioner was determined in arguing that

> regionalism and multilateralism are not mutually exclusive but complementary: regional arrangements are governed by the multilateral rules and disciplines of the WTO…this is the framework that gives the EU the best means to influence global governance and to negotiate balanced arrangements…Our bilateral or bi-regional relations with third countries are a reflection of our priority to multilateralism and our commitment to regional integration.

Such claims are given academic ballast by Woolcock (2005; 2012), who generally finds that second generation regionalism did not act to undermine multilateral trade and investment regimes. In fact, it may have given them added credibility by respecting (most of) their rules. As a caveat, complex rules of origins, which discriminate between sources of supply and fine-tuned preferential liberalisation at the product level, were frequent features of regional or region-to-region trade agreements. As a standard work on twenty-first-century political economy put it, '[f]irst principles would suggest that preferential and nonpreferential rules should be the same and that rules of origin should be simple to administer and transparent. Currently, this remains far from being the case' (Hoekman and Kostecki 2009: 214).[23] That aside, however, the feared trade wars between integrated regions never materialised. Different levels of rule-making generally co-existed, leading Woolcock memorably to suggest the result was 'more like Lasagne than spaghetti' (quoted in Van Langenhove and Costea 2007: 69).

A next logical step in normative terms is to build on this platform and seize on what Mark Leonard (2005) calls 'the regional domino effect'. In his audacious and media-friendly tract predicting a 'New European Century', he argues that the EU should lead in creating 'a community of interdependent regional clubs' or a 'Union of Unions' by promoting regional integration elsewhere and seeking region-to-region cooperative agreements (Leonard 2005: 140–2). Third generation regionalism entails nothing less than 'the rise of a new world order based on the gradual transition from multilateralism to multiregionalism' (Van Langenhove and Costea 2007: 80). Anticipating scepticism about such breathless predictions, advocates of third generation regionalism insist that 'realizing a multiregional world order is not utopian, and it starts from today's reality that, next to nations, world regions are becoming increasingly important tools for global governance' (Van Langenhove and Costea 2007: 81).

Here, it seems appropriate to take several steps back to get a rounded perspective on such claims and prescriptions. First, perhaps inevitably, they emerged out of a specific international political context: specifically, one in which an overweening hyper-power – the United States – was perceived as trampling on multilateralism and seeking a unipolar global order, as manifested in the invasion of Iraq. For example, Leonard (2005: 141) is clear that his recipe for multiregionalism as a path to a 'European Century' 'is an attempt to get beyond the "unipolar world"'.

Second, EU activism in seeking both to promote regional integration beyond Europe and agree economic cooperation agreements with other regional blocs gives some empirical foundation to work on third generation regionalism. As we have seen, the Union has sought – albeit with very modest results – to pick up the pieces of its relationship with ACP states by agreeing region-to-region economic agreements with them. It continues to seek a 'comprehensive FTA' (free trade agreement) with Mercosur and is 'assessing the level of ambition at bilateral level' with ASEAN.[24] Outside the realm of trade, the EU continues – to cite two examples – to engage bilaterally with Asia through the annual ASEM summits and the African Union, with whom it has established the African Peace Facility (APF) and to which it has channelled €740 million since 2004 in pursuit of conflict prevention and post-conflict stabilisation. Tangible results from the latter case of region-to-region cooperation have been visible in counter-piracy operations near the Horn of Africa and actions against the Islamist militant group al-Shabaab in Somalia in 2012. These actions might plausibly be viewed as ones designed to advance effective multilateralism.

Third, and revealingly, Van Langenhove and Costea (2007: 81) argue that '[t]he essence of third-generation regionalism is…that a region sees itself as a fully fledged actor in the theatre of international relations. This implies that the region claims a position similar to that of a state in multilateral organizations.' Visions of a multiregional world order seem rather utopian if they rely on the notion that regional institutions – including the EU – claim a position equivalent to states in multilateralism and are *assigned* a position equivalent to their member states in multilateral diplomacy. The EU has, of course, learned hard lessons about the difficulties of seeking this position in its post-Lisbon attempts to speak with a single voice in the UN (see Smith 2006).[25]

The best evidence we thus far have about the EU's attempts at interregionalism is probably work by Doidge (2011). His essential argument is clear: what determines outcomes of attempts by regional institutions to foster cooperation between one another is their capacity for *actorness*, or 'the ability to behave actively and deliberately in relation to other actors in the international system' (Sjöstedt 1977: 16). Doidge (2011) concludes that the EU's actorness remains strictly limited by the constraints imposed on it by its member states, while other regional organisations – Mercosur, NAFTA, ASEAN and so on – act with even stricter limitations.

The point is not that third generation multiregionalism is a pipedream or that advocates of this route to a 'New European Century' are naïve. Nor is it to suggest that the EU's pursuit of region-to-region cooperation undermines multilateralism. It is merely to note that the results that have been generated by this strategy – if it deserves that moniker – have been very limited. It is also to observe that the EU has played the cards that it has been dealt pragmatically. That is, it has tried to seize upon the trend towards regional integration elsewhere by promoting such cooperation – with its own, internal multilateralism always an exemplar – and then seeking to push forward international cooperation through region-to-region cooperation. The results have been modest. Ironically, if advocates of third generation regionalism are right, the EU would be cast as a considerably less *sui generis* regional institution, because others would model themselves on the Union's example. However, thus far, there is little evidence that other regional institutions have, or are likely to anytime soon, lived up to this hope.

Conclusion

We have considered Europe's experience of multilateralism from a variety of different perspectives. Our first section considered its historical experience of multilateralism. As we saw, European states were innovators and even 'inventors' of what has evolved to become modern multilateralism. Without European antecedents – particularly, of course, the Concert of Europe – it is difficult to imagine that

American leaders from Wilson and the League of Nations to Clinton and the WTO would have chosen to invest so much of themselves politically in international cooperation with teeth in the form of binding rules, or been able to find enough cooperative partners.

We also have considered whether the twenty-first century has witnessed the emergence of a 'new multilateralism' that more strictly binds states in an unprecedentedly wide range of policy realms, including trade and human rights. Here, we observed that today's multilateralism is, upon investigation, more unwieldy than it first appears, with major powers remaining aloof from recent, major international agreements. Rules that look binding in fact can often be bent.

We then considered how the research literature on European foreign policy portrays the EU as a participant in and promoter of modern multilateralism. We found overwhelming consensus amongst scholars that the Union is unique as an institution and an actor, that commitment to 'effective multilateralism' is part of its DNA, and that the EU is more a normative than self-interested international player. On the first point, it must be conceded that the Union is *sui generis* insofar as it wields more policy instruments, sourced in more and different places, than any other major power. Yet, as one of us has argued (with a co-author):

> Even if the EU is deemed *sui generis*, the definition still depends on comparison with other kinds of actors. Comparative analysis, as generated in IR principally by foreign policy analysis, is indispensable in identifying those aspects of the political and decision-making processes which are to be found in the EU as well as in states, and those that can only be understood from the inside out.
>
> *(Hill and Smith 2011: 479)*

In other words, if we start with the assumption that the EU is an 'n of 1', we can easily end up contributing to a body of work on the EU's international role that Jørgensen (2006: 508) describes as 'heavily compartmentalized' and having 'come to resemble an archipelago' in scholarship on IR. There is merit in the injunction that '[t]he EU should fit distinctively, but without excessive strain, in the general categories of [IR] scholarship' (Hill and Smith 2011: 479).

One vein of scholarship that another of us – again, with a co-author – has begun to mine productively is work on international political economy (see Young and Peterson 2013; see also Damro's chapter in this volume). As a headline finding, the EU generally lives up to its aspirational status as a relatively open economic power that seeks to strengthen and extend the multilateral trade order where and when it can. But it also does what all economic powers do: it defends its own interests and, by some yardsticks, ever more forcefully over time. It has also responded to the stalling of the multilateral trade agenda by seeking FTAs or other cooperative economic agreements with states and regions that offer European firms growing market opportunities. If the international trade order that has resulted is more like lasagne than a spaghetti bowl, with multilateral and bilateral rules co-existing in layers, it could be claimed it is in large part because the EU is both committed to multilateralism and is true to its self-image as a normative or civilian power. Equally, however, evidence to sustain the claim of Messerlin (2001) and others that the EU uses trade policy as *foreign* policy – and as a tool to promote its values or substitute for its lack of cohesion or muscle in foreign policy traditionally defined – is thin.

We then considered how the European experience of regionalism has encouraged work on various 'generations' of multilateralism on a regional scale. Our survey reviewed work that either predicts or prescribes – sometimes both – a multiregional world order, with the EU often viewed as in the vanguard of its creation. This work seems to highlight two disconnects in the literature on global Europe. First, interregionalism of the kind envisaged by students of its 'third generation' would require other regions to embrace European-style, regional multilateralism. The result would be an EU that loses its distinctiveness and *sui generis* nature.

Second, third generation regionalism appears to assume a European Union that is endowed with considerably more actorness, or independence from its member states, than it actually possesses. An even more formidable obstacle is the (thus far) very minimal actorness that member states of other regional organisations such as NAFTA, Mercosur or ASEAN have allowed them to develop. About the most that can be said about the EU's attempted forays into region-to-region cooperation is that they illustrate its pragmatism in external policy: where it makes sense to pursue European interests by encouraging others to achieve economies of scale in international cooperation and negotiating agreements with other regions, it does so. But any doctrinal commitment to 'export' European multilateralism to other regions appears, at most, skin deep, while the EU is inevitably limited in its ability to follow through.

As a final point, connecting research on the EU to wider IR scholarship – or moving it off its archipelago and into the heartland of IR research – might well benefit from more scholarship that compares the internal processes of EU governance to those found in other multilateral organisations, or even federal states. One benefit would be to highlight the many internal anomalies of the EU that have counterparts either in other IOs or in highly decentralised states. Scholarship on EU external action frequently portrays the Union as a far more single-minded entity whose member states all 'sail at one speed', when the reality is very different.

On the one hand, the emergence of the EU since the early 1990s as a far more politically ambitious institution with a vastly expanded policy agenda has given sustenance both to claims of a new and more demanding twenty-first-century multilateralism and those of a new generation of more ambitious regional institutions between which relationships become deep and codified. On the other hand, the EU has had to grant all manner of opt-outs, derogations and multi-speed arrangements to come as far as it has. One of its most distinguished and experienced former officials (Piris 2012) now argues tirelessly that European integration will stagnate unless the EU finds ways to allow an inner core to move towards much closer political and economic union regardless of the consequences for those states not in the vanguard. Piris (2012: 62) is at least on strong ground in observing that 'the reality is that the EU is already working at two speeds in some fields, in particular, in the two important fields of border controls…and monetary policy…and at several speeds in other fields'. Talk of a more integrated Eurozone, a banking union, and even an EU budget that is split in two according to whether spending occurs in or outside of 'core' states, increasingly portends a new multi-speed political settlement as a recipe for recovery from the post-2008 economic crisis. The recipe can be defended as effective or attacked as defective. But what it shows, above all, is that even Europe's own internal experience adds to the unwieldiness of multilateralism more generally, just as externally it pursues pragmatism more than doctrine. On both fronts the EU behaves in ways which are surprisingly recognisable to students of other major powers in IR and the dilemmas that they face.

Notes

1 We are grateful to Elizabeth Bomberg and Alasdair Young for helpful comments on earlier drafts.
2 The EU keeps an updated tally of such missions online. Available at: http://www.consilium.europa.eu/eeas/security-defence/eu-operations?amp;lang=en
3 This section draws considerably on section 2 of Hill *et al.* (2012)
4 The painting by Gerard ter Borch II is of the gathering at the signing of the Treaty of Münster. It is on display at the Rijksmuseum, Amsterdam. See: http://www.rijksmuseum.nl/aria/aria_assets/SK-A-405?lang=en
5 Hoffmann (2006: 15) has said that by 1919 'the habit of treating entire populations like cattle' had 'lost its legitimacy'.
6 We explore regional multilateralism below (see final section).
7 To illustrate, the literature now features prominent book-length works by institutionalists (see Smith 2004), normative realists (see Morgan 2005) and foreign policy analysts (see White 2001; see also White 2004a; 2004b). Yet, as one of us has previously argued, the study of EU foreign policy has come to be dominated by constructivists of various kinds (see Peterson 2012).
8 McCormick (2007: 111) can hardly be blamed for failing to foresee the post-2008 global financial crisis or the (related) subsequent economic crises in the Eurozone, but his claim that 'Europe today has a new confidence' is sobering in retrospect.
9 At the same time, they show a degree of scepticism in claiming that what they repeatedly refer to as the Union's 'Mr Nice Guy' image 'serves the *realpolitik* calculations of its member states' (Marsh and Mackenstein 2005: 251).
10 This section draws on material that will appear in Young and Peterson (2013), especially chapters 3 and 8.
11 The official EU line is that new EPAs needed to be agreed because during the 30 years when ACP countries enjoyed the most preferential access possible to the Union's market, the proportion of all EU imports that came from the ACP fell from 7 to 3 per cent. See: http://ec.europa.eu/trade/wider-agenda/development/economic-partnerships/
12 A. Beattie and A. Bounds, 'EU struggles to improve reputation of "aid for trade"', *Financial Times* (UK edition), 20 October 2006, p. 9.
13 Philip Stephens, 'Shame on them', *Financial Times* (UK edition), 9 November 1998, p. 15.
14 See Michael Smith, 'Brussels urges push for S Africa trade deal', *Financial Times* (UK edition), 14 December 1998, p. 4.
15 South Africa Foundation, 'South Africa and the EU: the Free Trade Agreement and Related Developments', Johannesburg, April 1999.
16 This point was stressed by French officials and representatives of the 2000 French EU Council Presidency at a colloquium on the Treaty of Nice held at Chatham House (the Royal Institute of International Affairs) in London on 4 December 2002.

17 Emphasis in original.
18 The EU-ASEAN free trade area negotiations have been 'pause[d]' since March 2009, although the EU is pursuing individual FTAs with Malaysia and Singapore. Negotiations with the Andean Community and Mercosur were initiated in 1999. See DG Trade, 'Overview of FTA and Other Trade Negotiations', updated 13 September 2012. Online. Available at: http://trade.ec.europa.eu/doclib/docs/2006/december/tradoc_118238.pdf (accessed 19 November 2012).
19 It should be noted that embracing the 'enforcement agenda' has not translated to an obvious increase in the imposition of anti-dumping duties. To illustrate, the EU imposed a total of 11 anti-dumping duties in 2011. While this total was more than were imposed in 2009 or 2010, it fell below the numbers imposed annually between 2005 and 2008 and below the annual average of 17 imposed during 1995–2010. Data on anti-dumping measures imposed by WTO members can be accessed from: http://www.wto.org/english/tratop_e/adp_e/adp_e.htm (accessed 19 November 2012). We are grateful to Alasdair Young for compiling and sharing this data with us.
20 This view is actually simplistic: the EU tabled considerable reductions in agricultural support and tariffs in the Doha Round, and essentially accepted the elimination of export subsidies. For its part, Washington seemed to accept that these concessions were sufficient. But the EU offer became irrelevant after 2008: it was 'pocketed' and, in any case, held limited interest for key participants, including India and China.
21 This example highlights the difference between multilateralism as an end in itself, as opposed to a means of achieving other, more particular goals. In the case of Iran, the EU imposed sanctions less for the sake of multilateralism *per se* than because of strong belief in the non-proliferation regime, as a particular milieu goal.
22 See Farrell *et al.* 2005; Söderbaum and Van Langenhove 2005; Söderbaum *et al.* 2005; Söderbaum and Van Langenhove 2006; Thakur and Van Langenhove 2006/7; Van Langenhove and Costea 2007.
23 It should be noted that the WTO has no rules on rules of origin (see Hoekman and Kostecki 2009: 211).
24 DG Trade, 'Overview' (see note 7).
25 See also, Euractiv, 'Ashton to obtain speaking rights at the UN', 26 August 2010. Online. Available at: http://www.euractiv.com/future-eu/ashton-obtain-speaking-rights-un-news-497162 (accessed 19 November 2012).

References

Babarinde, O. and Faber, G. (2004) 'From Lomé to Cotonou: Business as Usual?', *European Foreign Affairs Review*, 9 (1): 27–47.
_____ (2005) (eds) *The European Union and Developing Countries: the Cotonou Agreement* (Leiden: Bull).
Bachrach, P. and Baratz, M. S. (1963) 'Decisions and Nondecisions: an Analytical Framework', *American Political Science Review*, 57 (4): 639–57.
Barber, P. (1979) *Diplomacy: the World of the Honest Spy* (London: the British Library).
Boucher, D. (1998) *Political Theories of International Relations* (Oxford: Oxford University Press).
Bretherton, C. and Vogler, J. (2006) *The European Union as a Global Actor* (London and New York: Routledge), 2nd edition.
Carbone, M. (2011) 'The EU and the Developing World: Partnership, Poverty, Politicization' in C. Hill and M. Smith (eds) *International Relations and the European Union* (Oxford and New York: Oxford University Press).
Carr, E. H. (2001 [1939]) *The Twenty Years' Crisis 1919–1939* (Basingstoke and New York: Palgrave Macmillan).

Cooper, R. (2003) *The Breaking of Nations: Order and Chaos in the Twenty-First Century* (London: Atlantic Books).

De Gucht, K. (2010) 'Speaking Points: INTA', Committee for International Trade, European Parliament, Brussels, 12 April; http://trade.ec.europa.eu/doclib/docs/2011/april/tradoc_147815.pdf

Der Derian, J. (1987) *On Diplomacy: A Genealogy of Western Estrangement* (Oxford: Basil Blackwell).

Doidge, M. (2011) *The European Union and Interregionalism: Patterns of Engagement* (Franham and Burlington VT: Ashgate).

Duchêne, F. (1972) 'Europe's Role in World Peace' in R. Mayne (ed.) *Europe Tomorrow: Sixteen Europeans Look Ahead* (London: Fontana)

Dür, A. (2010) *Protection for Exporters: Power and Discrimination in Transatlantic Trade Relations, 1930–2010* (Ithaca, NY: Cornell University Press).

Elton, G. (1968), *Europe Divided, 1559–1598* (London: Fontana).

European Commission (2003) 'The European Union and the United Nations: the Choice of Multilateralism', communication from the Commission to the Council and to the European Parliament, COM (2003) 526, final, Brussels, 9 September.

____ (2007) *Global Europe: a Stronger Partnership to Deliver Market Access for European Exporters*, Brussels, DG Trade; http://trade.ec.europa.eu/doclib/docs/2007/april/tradoc_134591.pdf

____ (2010a) 'Towards a Single Market Act: For a Highly Competitive, Social Market Economy: 50 Proposals for Improving our Work, Business and Exchanges with One Another', COM(2010) 608, 11 November.

____ (2010b) 'Trade as a Driver for Prosperity,' SEC (2010) 1269, November.

____ (2010c) 'Trade, Growth and World Affairs: Trade Policy as a Core Component of the EU's 2020 Strategy,' COM(2010) 612, 9 November.

European Council (2003) *A Secure Europe in a Better World: European Security Strategy*, Brussels, 12 December: http://www.consilium.europa.eu/uedocs/cmsUpload/78367.pdf

____ (2010) 'Conclusions', Brussels: General Secretariat of the Council, 12 October, http://www.consilium.europa.eu/uedocs/cms_data/docs/pressdata/en/ec/116547.pdf

Farrell, M., Hettne, B. and Van Langenhove, L. (2005) (eds) *Global Politics of Regionalism: Theory and Practice* (London: Pluto).

Fawcett, L. and Hurrell, A. (1995) (eds) *Regionalism in World Politics: Regional Organization and International Order* (Oxford and New York: Oxford University Press).

Friedberg, A. L. (1993–4) 'Ripe for Rivalry: Prospects for Peace in a Multipolar Asia', *International Security*, 18 (3): 5–33.

Gallezot, J. and Bureau, J. C. (2006) *The Trade Effects of the EU's Everything But Arms Initiative* (Paris, CEPII, INRA, and Brussels, Commission of the European Union, Directorate-General for Trade, preceded by a comment from the European Commission), available from: http://trade.ec.europa.eu/doclib/docs/2006/november/tradoc_131254. pdf

Gamble, A. and Payne, A. (1996) *Regionalism and World Order* (Basingstoke and New York: Palgrave Macmillan).

Ginsberg, R. H. (2001) *The European Union in International Politics: Baptism by Fire* (Lanham MD and Oxford: Rowman and Littlefield).

Gnessoto, N. (2004) 'European Strategy as a Model', *ISS Newsletter*, 9 January: 1–4.

Heron, T. and Siles-Brügge, G. (2012) 'Competitive Liberalization and the "Global Europe" Services and Investment Agenda: Locating the Commercial Drivers in the EU-ACP Economic Partnership Agreements', *Journal of Common Market Studies*, 50 (2): 250–66.

Hettne, B. (1999) 'The New Regionalism: a Prologue' in B. Hettne, A. Inotai and O. Sunkel (eds) *Globalism and the New Regionalism* (Basingstoke and New York: Palgrave Macmillan).

Hill, C. (1994) 'The Capability-Expectations Gap, or Conceptualizing Europe's International Role' in S. Bulmer and A. Scott (eds) *Economic and Political Integration in Europe: Internal Dynamics and Global Context* (Oxford and Cambridge MA: Blackwell).

—— (2003) *The Changing Politics of Foreign Policy* (Basingstoke and New York: Palgrave Macmillan).

Hill, C. and Smith, M. (2011) 'Acting for Europe: Reassessing the European Union's Place in International Relations' in C. Hill and M. Smith (eds) *International Relations and the European Union* (Oxford and New York: Oxford University Press), 2nd edition.

Hill, C., Peterson, J. and Wessels, W. (2012) 'Unwieldly Multilateralism: Socialized Anarchy and the Case of Europe', manuscript.

Hinsley, F. H. (1967) *Power and the Pursuit of Peace: Theory and Practice in the History of Relations Between States* (Cambridge and New York: Cambridge University Press).

Hoekman, B. M. and Kostecki, M. M. (2009) *The Political Economy of the World Trading System: the WTO and Beyond* (Oxford and New York: Oxford University Press).

Hoffmann, S. (2006), 'Peace and Justice: A Prologue' in P. Allan and A. Keller (eds) *What is a Just Peace?* (Oxford and New York: Oxford University Press).

Hurd, D. (2010), *Choose Your Weapons: The British Foreign Secretary- Two Years of Argument, Success and Failure* (London: Weidenfeld & Nicolson).

Hurt, S. (2003) 'Co-operation and Coercion? The Cotonou Agreement Between the European Union and ACP States and the End of the Lomé Convention', *Third World Quarterly*, 31 (2): 159–68.

Hveem, H. (1999) 'Explaining the Regional Phenomenon in an Era of Globalization' in R. Stubbs and G. Underhill (eds) *Political Economy and the Changing International Order* (Oxford and New York: Oxford University Press), 2nd edition.

Ikenberry, G. J. (2006) *Liberal Order and Imperial Ambition* (Oxford and Malden MA: Polity).

Jørgensen, K. E. (2004) 'European Foreign Policy: Conceptualising the Domain' in W. Carlsnaes, H. Sjursen and B. White (eds) *Contemporary European Foreign Policy* (London and Thousand Oaks CA: Sage).

—— (2006) 'Overview: the European Union and the World' in K. E. Jørgensen, M. A. Pollack and B. Rosamond (eds) *Handbook of European Union Politics* (London and Thousand Oaks CA: Sage).

Lamy, P. (2001) 'Opening Speech', 5th EC/Candidate Countries Ministerial Conference on Trade, Malta, 31 May–1 June.

Leonard, M. (2005) *Why Europe Will Run the 21st Century* (London and New York: 4th Estate).

McCormick, J. (2007) *The European Superpower* (Basingstoke and New York: Palgrave).

Manners, I. (2002) 'Normative Power Europe: a Contradiction in Terms?', *Journal of Common Market Studies*, 40 (2): 235–58.

—— (2006) 'Normative Power Europe Reconsidered: Beyond the Crossroads', *Journal of European Public Policy*, 13 (2): 182–99.

—— (2008a) 'The Normative Ethics of the European Union', *International Affairs*, 84 (1): 65–80.

—— (2008b) 'The Normative Power of the European Union in a Globalized World' in Z. Laïdi (ed.) *European Union Foreign Policy in a Globalized World: Normative Power and Social Preferences* (London and New York: Routledge).

_____ (2010) 'Global Europa: Mythology of the European Union in World Politics', *Journal of Common Market Studies*, 48 (1): 67–87.

Marsh, S. and Mackenstein, H. (2005) *The International Relations of the European Union* (Harlow: Pearson Longman).

Mattingly, G. (1955) *Renaissance Diplomacy* (London: Jonathan Cape).

Messerlin, P. (2001) *Measuring the Costs of Economic Protection in Europe* (Washington DC: Institute for International Economics).

Meunier, S. and Nicolaïdis, K. (2011) 'The European Union as a Trade Power' in C. Hill and M. Smith (eds) *International Relations and the European Union* (Oxford and New York: Oxford University Press).

Morgan, G. (2005) *The Idea of a European Superstate: Public Justification and European Integration* (Princeton NJ and Oxford: Princeton University Press).

Øhrgaard, J. C. (2004) 'International Relations or European Integration: is the CFSP *Sui Generis?*' in B. Tonra and T. Christiansen (eds) *Rethinking European Union Foreign Policy* (Manchester and New York: Manchester University Press).

Orbie, J. (2007) 'The Development of EBA' in G. Faber and J. Orbie (eds) *European Union Trade Politics and Development: 'Everything But Arms' Unravelled* (London and New York: Routledge).

Osiander, A. (1994) *States System of Europe 1640–1990: Peacemaking and the Conditions of International Stability* (Oxford: the Clarendon Press).

Page, S. and Hewitt, A. (2002) 'The New European Trade Preferences: Does "Everything But Arms" (EBA) Help the Poor', *Development Policy Review*, 20 (1): 91–102.

Peterson, J. (2012) 'Europe as a Global Actor' in E. Bomberg, J. Peterson and R. Corbett (eds) *The European Union: How Does it Work?* (Oxford and New York: Oxford University Press).

Peterson, J. and Shackleton, M. (2012) *The Institutions of the European Union* (Oxford and New York: Oxford University Press), 3rd edition.

Peterson, J., Byrne, A. and Helwig, N. (2012) 'International Interests: the Common Foreign and Security Policy' in J. Peterson and M. Shackleton (eds) *The Institutions of the European Union* (Oxford and New York: Oxford University Press), 3rd edition.

Pilegaard, J. (2006) *Between Coherence and Fragmentation: the EU's Everything But Arms Initiative* (Copenhagen: University of Copenhagen Department of Political Science), PhD dissertation.

Piris, J.-C. (2012) *The Future of Europe: Towards a Two-Speed EU?* (Cambridge and New York: Cambridge University Press).

Pollack, M. A. (2003) 'Unilateral America, Multilateral Europe?' in J. Peterson and M. A. Pollack (eds) *Europe, America, Bush: Transatlantic Relations in the 21st Century* (London and New York: Routledge).

Richardson, L. (1999) 'The Concert of Europe and security management in the 19th century' in H. Haftendorn, R. O. Keohane and C. A. Wallander (eds) *Imperfect Unions: Security Institutions over Time and Space* (Oxford and New York: Oxford University Press).

Sjöstedt, G. (1977) 'The Exercise of International Civil Power: A Framework for Analysis', *Cooperation and Conflict*, 12 (1): 21–39.

Smith, K. E. (2006) 'Speaking with One Voice? European Union Co-ordination on Human Rights Issues at the United Nations', *Journal of Common Market Studies*, 44 (1): 113–37.

_____ (2008) *European Union Foreign Policy in a Changing World* (Oxford and Malden MA: Polity).

Smith, M. (1998) 'Does the Flag Follow Trade? "Politicisation" and the Emergence of a European Foreign Policy' in J. Peterson and H. Sjursen (eds) *A Common Foreign Policy for Europe? Competing Visions of the CFSP* (London and New York: Routledge).

Smith, M. E. (2004) *Europe's Foreign and Security Policy: the Institutionalization of Cooperation* (Cambridge and New York: Cambridge University Press).

Söderbaum, F., Stalgren, P. and Van Langenhove, L. (2005) 'The EU as a Global Actor and the Dynamics of Interregionalism: a Comparative Analysis', *European Integration*, 27 (3): 365–80.

Söderbaum, F. and Van Langenhove, L. (2005) 'The EU as a Global Actor and the Rise of Interregionalism', *Journal of European Integration*, 27 (3): 249–62.

_____ (2006) (eds) *The EU as a Global Player: the Politics of Interregionalism* (London and New York: Routledge).

Telò, M. (2001) (ed) *European Union and New Regionalism: Regional Actors and Global Governance in the Post-Hegemonic Era* (Aldershot and Burlington VT: Ashgate).

Thakur, R. and Van Langenhove, L. (2006/7) 'Enhancing Global Governance through Regional Integration', *Global Governance*, 12 (3): 233–40.

Toje, A. (2008) *America, the EU and Strategic Culture: Renegotiating the Transatlantic Bargain* (London and New York: Routledge).

_____ (2010) *The European Union as a Small Power: After the Post-Cold War* (Basingstoke and New York: Palgrave Macmillan).

Van Ham, P. (2011) 'The European Union's WMD strategy and the CFSP: a critical analysis', *EU Non-Proliferation Consortium Non-Proliferation Papers*, no.2, September; http://www.sipri.org/research/disarmament/eu-consortium/publications/publications/EUNPC_no%202.pdf

Van Langenhove, L. and Costea, A.-C. (2007) 'The EU as a Global Actor and "Third Generation" Regionalism' in P. Foradori, P. Rosa and R. Cartezzini (eds) *Managing a Multilevel Foreign Policy* (Plymouth and Lexington MD: Lexington Books).

Vanhoonacker, S. and Reslow, N. (2010) 'The European External Action Service: Living Forwards by Understanding Backwardness', *European Foreign Affairs Review*, 15 (1): 1–23.

White, B. (2001) *Understanding European Foreign Policy* (Basingstoke and New York: Palgrave).

_____ (2004a) 'Foreign policy analysis and European foreign policy' in B. Tonra and T. Christiansen (eds) *Rethinking European Union Foreign Policy* (Manchester and New York: Manchester University Press).

_____ (2004b) 'Foreign policy analysis and the new Europe' in W. Carlsnaes, H. Sjursen and B. White (eds) *Contemporary European Foreign Policy* (London and Thousand Oaks CA: Sage).

Wolfers, A. (1962) *Discord and Collaboration: Essays on International Politics* (Baltimore: Johns Hopkins University Press).

Woolcock, S. (2005) 'Conclusions' in G. P. Sampson and S. Woolcock (eds) *The Interaction Between the Regional and Other Levels of Governance in the International Trading System* (Tokyo: UNU Press).

Young, A. and Peterson, J. (2012) *European Union Economic Diplomacy* (Farnham, Surrey and Burlington, VT: Ashgate).

_____ (2013) 'We Care About You, But…: the Politics of EU Trade Policy and Development', *Cambridge Review of International Affairs*, 26 (2): forthcoming.

_____ (2013) *Parochial Global Europe: the Politics of EU Trade Policy* (Oxford and New York: Oxford University Press), forthcoming.

PART II

Multilateralism in EU policies

5

ASSESSING EU MULTILATERAL ACTION

Trade and foreign and security policy within a legal and living framework

Nadia Klein, Tobias Kunstein and Wulf Reiners

Introduction [1]

During a conference at the European University Institute in June 2010, European Commission President José Barroso (2010: 2) claimed that '[m]ultilateralism is the right mechanism to build order and governance in a multipolar world, and the European Union is well-placed to make a decisive contribution'. Over the past decade, the European Union (EU) has indeed frequently underlined its commitment to institutionalised multilateral policy-making – as opposed to *ad hoc* unilateralism. For example, the European Security Strategy of 2003 embraced 'effective multilateralism' (European Council 2003: 9) as one of the EU's three strategic goals in order to define and implement common solutions to international political problems. With the coming into force of the Lisbon Treaty on 1 December 2009, this general commitment to multilateral co-operation has also been enshrined in the Union's primary law (see Art. 21(2,h) TEU).[2] Moreover, previous EU Treaties contained a variety of references to multilateral organisations such as the United Nations (UN) or the Organization for Security and Co-operation in Europe. Thus, from the EU perspective, co-operation with and support of multilateral organisations represents a key contribution to prosperous international relations. Given the EU's own multilateral foundation, that is its 'multilateral genes' (Jørgensen 2009b: 189), it has been described as a 'champion of multilateralism' (Lucarelli 2007: 12). Some scholars, however, have pointed to the fact that the EU's actual influence on multilateral policy-making – including its influence on the set-up of multilateral arrangements – varies significantly across different policy fields (see Laatikainen and Smith 2006b: 16–19).

This study contrasts the multilateral aspirations enshrined so prominently in the Lisbon Treaty with the institutional basis for the EU's (inter)action (with)in multilateral forums and organisations. It explores questions about whether and how far its institutional architecture enables the Union to live up to the ambition to contribute to (effective) multilateralism. Moreover, by using the process-oriented term 'multilateralisation', the study captures trends in EU external action, in view of a (potentially) changing share of multilateral policy-making.[3] The next section sets the stage for the analysis by defining the concepts of 'multilateralism' and 'effectiveness' in view of the EU's external action. In the third and fourth sections, the chapter systematically takes stock of the recent development of the EU's legal framework (*de jure*) from the Nice Treaty (2003) to the Lisbon Treaty (2009). This analysis of the underlying legal architecture is subsequently complemented by an analysis of the (*de facto*) 'living architecture' or 'living constitution' (Wessels 2001: 200). The latter notion refers to all EU action based on its Treaties, comprising the legal output in the form of various treaty-defined legal instruments (secondary law) as well as the formal rules of procedure of EU institutions and, at the most informal level, established practices of EU policy-making.

The analysis is carried out from a rational institutionalist perspective, starting from the basic assumption that institutional factors play a central role for the assessment of EU multilateral action. Although domestic and international factors might also account for policy choice at EU level, we focus on the specific nexus of the Union's legal and living framework, assuming that the institutional set-up is a formative factor when it comes to the formulation of EU legislation. Furthermore, we build on the basic idea that changes in the EU's legal architecture result from a consensus among its member states, namely the shared conviction that a modified institutional set-up will allow them to pursue foreign policy goals in the EU framework more effectively. The effectiveness of the EU's external action, in turn, is seen as a function of the ability of the involved institutions to shape a common policy and to represent the European position vis-à-vis third actors (see Delcourt and Remacle 2009: 235–6).

Empirically, the study focuses on two different cases: the EU's common commercial policy (CCP) and its common foreign and security policy (CFSP). Trade and CFSP represent two core policy fields in the area of external action. At the same time, the two cases are very distinct in terms of actors, competences and procedures – as illustrated also by their belonging to two different pillars in the pre-Lisbon set-up (trade: pillar I; CFSP: pillar II). While the post-Lisbon institutional architecture of the EU's trade policy (see Balan 2008; Dimopoulos 2010; Kleimann 2011) and its foreign and security policy (see Centre for European Policy Studies (CEPS) *et al.* 2010; Regelsberger 2008; Wessels and Bopp 2008; Whitman and Juncos 2009; Vanhoonacker 2011) has been examined intensively, the implications of the new treaty for *multilateral* EU action in particular has mostly remained untouched (one exception is Emerson *et al.* 2011). The choice of cases – despite the limited number – allows analysis of variation in the effectiveness of EU multilateralism in relation to the different institutional characteristics. Thus, in the conclusion, the paper tentatively assesses the implications of the Union's institutional architecture for its *ability* to perform in multilateral settings.

Conceptualising the EU as an (effective) actor in multilateral frameworks

Notwithstanding different conceptions of the EU as a foreign policy actor,[4] we start from the assumption that the Union does act in its own right at the international level and within multilateral settings. Like state actors, it 'has developed a dense web of relations with states, regions and international organizations' (Jørgensen 2006: 509; see also Keukeleire and MacNaughtan 2008; Marsh and Mackenstein 2005). For the purpose of this chapter, the definition of 'multilateralism' proposed in this book (see Chapter 2) is used.

Some elements of this definition, namely the capacity of (voluntary) decision-making and the interaction with other, more 'unified' (state) actors, point at structural difficulties the EU has to cope with when acting multilaterally. In order to gauge the EU's actorness in multilateral frameworks – understood as its capacity to pursue policy objectives in its own right – scholars have recently focused on the question of how to assess the EU's actual 'performance' (Jørgensen 2009a) or its 'effectiveness' (Laatikainen and Smith 2006a).

In this context, Jørgensen (2009a: 6; 2009b: 194–5) focuses on five analytical dimensions regarding the EU's performance in international institutions, ranging from the form of representation, domestic characteristics of the EU's negotiation style, its actual impact on multilateral negotiation processes, and its influence on institutional reform of contemporary multilateral institutions. In turn, Laatikainen and Smith propose a concept of effectiveness (see Laatikainen and Smith 2006b: 9–10). In the context of EU–UN relations they distinguish the EU's *internal* effectiveness from its *external* effectiveness in multilateral settings, arguing that the willingness and ability of EU member states to act collectively (internal effectiveness) represent necessary conditions for the actual achievement of objectives within a given organisation (external effectiveness). Furthermore, the EU's *contribution to* the effectiveness of a given multilateral setting – a criterion closely related to Jørgensen's dimension on institutional reform – is differentiated from the effectiveness of a given multilateral setting *as such*.

In their contributions, both Jørgensen, and Laatikainen and Smith highlight the relevance of institutional factors for explaining EU multilateral action. Against this background, we decided to analyse in depth two main elements of the institutional architecture that are central to both analytical frameworks outlined above: *(1) the structural set-up for the internal co-ordination of a given EU position* and *(2) the EU's external representation*. The first element mainly builds on rules and procedures defining when and how an EU position is formulated and related decisions are taken. In other words, the capacity of decision-making depends on the EU's capacity to reach an internal agreement on what it will do within (and for) the respective multilateral organisation to muster the necessary resources to carry out an agreement, and then to carry through with the implementation. As Jørgensen has underlined, 'the world of multilateral institutions is generally […] far from an ideal environment for the EU, the prime reason being that multilateral diplomacy is strongly state-centric, invites [...] frequent tactical manoeuvring and requires profound co-ordination among EU member states' (Jørgensen 2009a: 2). Thus, compared to nation states, the EU faces specific co-ordination challenges when it pursues a multilateral approach because of its internal set-up.

As for the second element, various scholars have analysed how the fragmented external representation of the EU – in many policy areas split at least between the EU Presidency and the European Commission – has interfered with the perception of the EU as a unitary actor (see White 2001; Ginsberg 2001; Peterson 1995). The inherent increase of transaction costs for third parties when dealing with a fragmented EU potentially circumscribes the effectiveness of the Union as a multilateral partner. Crucially, the external representation of the EU also functions as a linchpin between the EU-internal co-ordination and communication with external actors.

To sum up, we argue that the question of whether the EU can effectively act within, have influence on, and maybe lead in larger multilateral settings crucially depends on its institutional set-up, or the way in which the Union has been equipped by the EU member states during treaty reform negotiations. Notwithstanding the relevance of other factors – such as the political will of the EU member states to take the initiative in a given situation and the polarity structure of the international system – we claim that an effective institutional set-up is a necessary condition for the EU to make its voice heard in multilateral settings (see also Orbie 2008a: 20). We aim at providing a thorough, data-based analysis on the specific relevance of the institutional set-up, which can be related to the relevance of other factors in future research.

Assessing the legal and the living framework: methodological considerations

Arguably, a comprehensive assessment of the EU's external effectiveness includes analysing how the treaty provisions for EU external action are actually used. For example, the Nice Treaty extended the possibility of enhanced co-operation to the field of CFSP (Art. 27a,b TEU-Nice). However, this much-debated provision was never used and has therefore had *de facto* no impact on the Union's external action. Given the fact that the Lisbon Treaty entered into force only in December 2009, there is little empirical data on the use of its new provisions. While our basic approach to such a longer-term analysis of the living framework – that is the legal output – can be applied for a comprehensive comparative assessment as soon as sufficient empirical data is available, here we present an analysis of the legal output for the years leading up to the Lisbon Treaty. We have analysed samples of legal acts in the fields of trade policy and the CFSP with a view to pinpoint their relevance for multilateral policy-making. In order to assess their impact on multilateralism, we focus on two main indicators: first, the legal basis of a given act (Indicator I) and second, the measures foreseen for its implementation (Indicator II). In investigating the *legal basis*, we have, for example, checked if a given act explicitly refers to specific international agreements such as UN Security Council Resolutions, international conventions or internationally brokered peace agreements.

The methodological approach can be best illustrated by an example. For instance, the first EU military operation in the Former Yugoslav Republic of Macedonia in 2003 was launched by a joint action (Council of the European Union 2003). This joint action refers to the internationally brokered Ohrid Framework Agreement (Ohrid Framework Agreement 2001), which spelt out post-conflict measures to mitigate the political and interethnic tensions in the country. For the purpose of our analysis, the multilateral Ohrid Agreement is considered as the *legal basis* of the above-mentioned joint action. Given its explicit reference to the Ohrid Agreement, the joint action is therefore characterised as 'multilateral'. Likewise, an example of a 'multilateral' EU legal act in the area of CCP would be a Commission decision imposing anti-dumping duties that makes reference to a World Trade Organization Anti-Dumping Agreement.

As an indicator of multilateral *implementation*, we have examined whether and how far the legal act stipulates co-operation with other international actors or international organisations. Crucially, we only considered an act to be multilateral in terms of its implementation if there was some kind of pre-defined division of labour between the EU and other (at least two) non-EU actors. In the above-mentioned case of the Ohrid Framework Agreement, its Annex C foresees specific tasks and confidence-building measures to be carried out, among others, by the EU, the Council of Europe, the Organization for Security and Co-operation in Europe, the Office of the United Nations High Commissioner for Refugees, and the World Bank. Consequently, the implementation of this legal act can be considered as 'multilateral' as well. In contrast to the CFSP, this pattern is rare in the field of CCP where implementation measures are usually not specified in the respective legal act.[5]

For the time being, in view of its explorative character, the study focuses on core legal instruments for the respective policy field. In situations where the EU envisages operational CFSP action, the instrument of 'joint action'[6] represents such a core legal instrument. In the CCP, no single type of legal act stands out as prominently. Therefore, our sample of legal acts in the field of trade includes all binding instruments: regulations, directives and decisions. What is crucial in both cases is to differentiate between *substantial* legal acts on the one hand, for example final decisions, and second-order legal acts such as proposals or limited amendments on the other hand. The selection of substantial legal acts helps avoid distortion of our findings as it excludes the misleading comparison of legal acts that are not of the same nature and relevance.[7] Overall, while comprehensive lists of legal acts can be drawn from the EU's online search engine EUR-Lex,[8] the categorisation and assessment of legal acts in view of the level of multilateralism is a qualitative exercise. On this empirical basis, the Union's basic legal capacity can be compared with its actual performance in the pursuit of foreign policy goals over time.

Common commercial policy: from Nice to Lisbon

CCP is the classic area of supranational external action, introduced as early as 1957 in the Treaty establishing the European Economic Community (Art. 110ff.). The decisive factor behind the choice of a dominant role for the supranational level in external trade relations is the internal process of integration towards a single market. As a result member states have largely relinquished their authority to conduct individual commercial policies vis-à-vis non-EU countries. While the exclusive community competence in trade is more or less uncontested, the scope of trade policy is not. Consequently, while the EU (supposedly) acts as a bloc to further its trade agenda, both the definition and subsequent implementation of this agenda are subject to disagreement and complex internal co-ordination processes.

Overall, there seems to be agreement in the literature that the EU evolved from a protectionist and regionalist actor to a proponent of international free trade (see Baldwin *et al.* 2003: 36; Meunier and Nicolaïdis 2005: 259–61). While many different explanations for this posture are brought to the fore,[9] for the purpose of this chapter it is sufficient to underline that liberalisation is at the ideological core of Europe's CCP. Furthermore, the CCP also provides 'a unique tool for forwarding policy priorities that extended beyond pure trade considerations' (Dimopoulos 2010: 153) such as development. Scholars have even argued that trade 'serves partly as a substitute for a "real" EU foreign policy' (Orbie 2008b: 54).

Traditionally, external trade policy is about negotiating levels of market access (see Orbie 2008b: 36). Assessing the context of today's CCP, and in particular its multilateral dimension, many scholars highlight the debate on regulatory issues and the 'deep' trade agenda in the framework of the WTO (Young and Peterson 2006: 795–6; Conconi 2009: 156). Thus, over the past decade, the multilateral trade agenda has begun to address regulatory differences hampering international trade. Essentially, the focus has shifted from 'at-the-border' to 'behind-the-border' issues – a development which has been described as a core element of the 'new trade politics' (see Young and Peterson 2006: 795–6). Based on its own experience with deep (regional) economic integration, the EU has championed the establishment of multilateral guidelines for domestic rules in areas such as competition and investment.

Yet, two examples illustrate that a multilateral approach is by no means the standard option for EU trade policy. The first example refers to preferential trade agreements. Conconi (2009: 163) has stressed that '[the Union] has developed the most extensive network of preferential trade agreements (PTAs) of any GATT/WTO member'. These agreements, many of which are concluded bilaterally, by nature contradict the World Trade Organization (WTO)'s ultimate goal of eliminating preferential treatment in international trade. The second example is the EU incentive arrangement for sustainable development and good governance (GSP+), which offers preferential access to EU markets for imports from developing countries that have ratified specific agreements on environmental protection, human rights and good governance. GSP+ can be characterised as a unilateral EU policy – developed after the failure to push through EU positions in WTO negotiation rounds. In the context of this study, it is noteworthy that despite its unilateral character, GSP+ nevertheless refers to multilaterally agreed principles (see Young and Peterson 2006: 807; Orbie 2008b: 60). This standardised integration of multilateral references even in unilateral European measures illustrates the strength of the EU's commitment to multilateralism, at least at the conceptual level.

The debate on whether *non*-trade policy objectives should also be pursued through trade is equally relevant for understanding the CCP and its multilateral dimension. Since the mid-1990s, the EU has increasingly canvassed the inclusion of normative objectives such as environmental protection and workers' rights on the international trade agenda (see Conconi 2009: 172; Orbie 2008b: 47). The EU has argued that in cases of violation of environmental or labour standards, trade sanctions should be applied. As such, the EU has tried to upload its own trade policy practice, which is characterised by more or less comprehensive good governance clauses in trade and co-operation agreements,[10] to the multilateral level. Most developing countries, though, remain sceptical about these EU initiatives, 'considering them as hidden forms of protectionism' (Conconi 2009: 172). Here, it is important to keep in mind that the EU has proactively pursued certain initiatives and objectives in the field of trade policy even against the will of other actors. We thus are brought back to our initial question: which institutional characteristics enable the Union to act multilaterally in its own right?

Internal co-ordination

The European Commission has traditionally played a pivotal role in the formulation and implementation of the CCP, the scope of which member states have reluctantly agreed to extend over time (see Woolcock 2008: 2ff.). In line with the assignment of competences to the supranational level, the Commission disposes of an exclusive right of initiative in this policy field. Moreover, where agreements with third states or international organisations have to be negotiated, the Commission makes recommendations to the Council, which in turn authorises the Commission to open and conduct the necessary negotiations. During the negotiations, the Commission is controlled via a special committee composed of EU member state representatives (Art. 133(2-3) TEC-Nice; Art. 207(2-3) TFEU). EU member state positions thus have to be co-ordinated and taken into account by the Commission after having received the initial negotiation mandate. In sum, though, 'the Commission disposes of unique advantages in terms of expertise and information. For example, the Commission may confront the Council members with a *fait accompli* and present a take-it-or-leave-it package deal' (Orbie 2008b: 40). Given the dominant rule of majority voting (instead of unanimity) in the Council, internal policy-making in the CCP has been relatively smooth and bureaucratic – in a sense that decisions are not blocked by excessive political manoeuvring.[11] As a result, the Union can act rather easily as a unified (trade) actor at the international level. The minor involvement of the European Parliament which, until the coming into force of the Lisbon

Treaty, was limited to information and consultation rights also underpinned this unified appearance.

In sum, the division of competences between the European level and the member states together with a strong role for the Commission and qualified majority voting in the Council indicate a high degree of internal effectiveness. Consequently, the EU is well equipped to pursue its CCP in a multilateral setting. Its legal framework has helped the EU to become 'the most outspoken proponent of an ambitious round of multilateral trade negotiations from 1995 onwards' (Orbie 2008b: 49).

How far is this multilateral agenda reflected in the EU's day-to-day trade policy? Before turning to the analysis of the institutional innovations of the Lisbon Treaty, we will have a closer look at the living framework under the Nice Treaty. As outlined before, the actual use of legal instruments in a given policy field can be taken as a general indicator for assessing the level of multilateralisation. In the field of trade, we specifically analyse references to a multilateral legal basis (Indicator I – see above).

External trade is the sector with the highest level of legal output in external relations (on average 130 binding legal acts per year over the past decade, not counting agreements). Our analysis therefore had to resort to sampling. The years 2000, 2003, 2006 and 2009 were selected for closer analysis in order to cover the most recent decade. Following our methodological approach, in order to avoid distortions from second-order legal acts such as proposals or limited amendments, legal acts classified as non-substantial have been excluded from the analysis.

When looking at legal acts with a direct and/or indirect reference to multilateral institutions (Indicator I), we note that these 'multilateral' legal acts constitute a relatively high overall share of all substantial legal acts, but with marked differences between single years (see Table 5.1 and Figure 5.1). In 2006, 91 per cent of substantial acts include a multilateral reference. In 2003, this is the case for only 57 per cent, which is the lowest ratio observed in our sample.[12]

TABLE 5.1 The level of multilateralisation in the CCP: Analysing substantial[13] secondary legislation[14] in the years 2000, 2003, 2006 and 2009[15]

Year	Total number of legal acts	Total number of substantial legal acts	Indicator I: number of substantial acts with multilateral legal basis[16]	Indicator I: acts with multilateral legal basis as share of substantial legal acts
2000	189	121	87	72%
2003	161	94	53	57%
2006	117	57	52	91%
2009	89	49	41	84%

Source: Own calculation, based on EUR-Lex (January 2010).

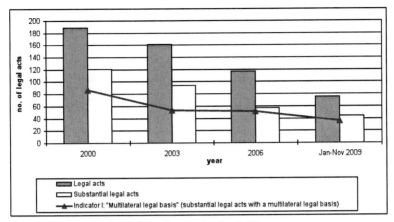

FIGURE 5.1   The level of multilateralisation in the CCP

Legal acts with *direct* references to multilateral institutions (in the legal act itself) are relatively scarce. They appear in 7 per cent to 23 per cent of all substantial legal acts in the four-year sample (see Table 5.2). The topics of these legal acts vary considerably and concern many aspects of trade: procedures such as anti-dumping or anti-subsidy measures, but also trade in dangerous chemicals, textiles, agricultural products or fish. A similar variety can be observed in terms of which multilateral institution is referred to: WTO agreements, the General Agreement on Tariffs and Trade (GATT), conventions of the International Labour Organization as well as the International Commission for the Conservation of Atlantic Tunas, to name only a few. *Indirect* references – that is when a legal act does not directly refer to multilateral institutions but to another underlying legal act which, in turn, refers to multilateral institutions – can be found in 50 per cent to 70 per cent of all substantial acts (see Table 5.2). Most indirect references materialise on the basis of three main legal acts, covering certain procedures in international trade:[17]

TABLE 5.2 Indicator I subtypes: Direct and indirect references to a multilateral legal[18]

Year	Total number of substantial legal acts	Direct references	Direct / substantial	Indirect references	Indirect / substantial
2000	121	18	15%	77	64%
2003	94	7	7%	47	50%
2006	57	12	21%	40	70%
2009	44	10	23%	29	66%

Source: Own calculation, based on EUR-Lex (January 2010).

1. Council Regulation (EC) No 384/96 (anti-dumping) is by far the most common indirect reference and refers to GATT (cited 132 times in the four years under observation).
2. In 2000 and 2003, Council Regulation (EEC) No 3030/93 (textile quotas) is the second-most cited underlying act but does not appear in subsequent years. Its text refers to the GATT Textiles Committee and is cited 21 times in 2000 and 2003.
3. Council Regulation 2026/1997 (anti-subsidy) is the last underlying act which has been referred to regularly (cited 19 times). Its text refers to the GATT Uruguay round and the framework of the WTO.

Interestingly, protectionist anti-dumping duties (see Conconi 2009: 160) are the most frequently cited instrument with an (indirect) reference to a multilateral framework (GATT in this case). This finding seems to indicate that multilateralism in the common commercial policy is largely reflected in measures contradicting the notion of free trade.

The Lisbon Treaty introduced a number of changes in the field of EU trade policy. For the first time, it has explicitly embedded the CCP within the broader context of 'The Union's External Action' (Part V TFEU). Article 21 TEU, stipulating general provisions of the Union's external action, includes multilateralism as an objective. The link to general aims of EU external action is also strengthened in Art. 207(1) TFEU: 'The common commercial policy shall be conducted in the context of the principles and objectives of the Union's external action.'

Most importantly, the new treaty extended the exclusive Union competence to all areas covered by the CCP (Art. 3(1,e) TFEU). With 'mixed agreements' in these areas now abolished, national parliaments no longer play an active role in ratifying trade agreements (see Woolcock 2008: 5). In turn, the Lisbon Treaty has significantly enhanced the competences of the European Parliament by introducing the ordinary legislative procedure – formerly known as the co-decision procedure – in the context of the CCP (Art. 207(2) TFEU). The increased involvement of the European Parliament has led to a further politicisation. This trend has persisted since the 1990s and is also characterised by the involvement of non-governmental actors such as human rights activists, trade unions and industrial lobby groups (see Orbie 2008b: 42). Yet it is in particular the inclusion of the European Parliament which increases demands for co-ordination and makes it more difficult to reach agreement on common EU positions.

While the Lisbon Treaty has extended the scope of action of the CCP, many of the new trade-related competences remain subject to unanimous decision-making (see Art. 207(4) TFEU).

> the issue of control over trade negotiations is much more contentious than the competence issue [...]. Even when the Community competences remain unquestioned, considerable disagreements between (and within) the

Commission and the Council may emerge, weakening Europe's international negotiating power.

(Orbie 2008b: 39)

Thus, on one hand, the inclusion of new issues in the CCP has increased the EU's relevance as a trade actor as such. On the other hand, the new legal framework has not necessarily enhanced its internal co-ordination capacity.

External representation

In its external representation generally, the EU has repeatedly underlined its commitment to multilateralism. As far as the CCP is concerned, the most important example is the WTO. The Union (formerly the European Communities) is itself a member since 1995, with the European Commission representing the EU member states. Because the EU speaks with one voice in the WTO framework, external effectiveness vis-à-vis third parties is facilitated. The dispute settlement mechanism in the WTO context represents a particularly interesting case of unified EU external representation in international trade policy.

> The Union, through the Commission, will stand always on behalf of Member States both as complainant or defendant, even when only one Member State is directly affected by a measure of a third country [...] or when the challenged measure is a law of only one Member State.
>
> *(Balan 2008: 9–10)*

In general, EU relations with rules-based international organisations such as the WTO can be considered, in the terminology of Peterson and Bouchard as the strengthening of 'institutionalised multilateralism' (see Chapter 2).

The Lisbon Treaty's impact on the external representation of the EU in international trade relations is rather limited. From the perspective of third countries, introducing the European Parliament to the decision-making procedure (Art. 207 TFEU) may blur horizontal responsibilities. At the same time, a new source of legitimacy is introduced in EU trade relations. Yet, the Commission alone speaks for the EU and its members (Art. 207 and 218 TFEU), so it is doubtful that parliamentary involvement in internal decision-making will impact on the EU's external representation in trade.

The lasting role of the Commission in EU trade policy, including representational tasks, was also underlined when the Council decided upon the set-up of the European External Action Service (EEAS) in July 2010. The Lisbon Treaty foresees that 'Union delegations in third countries and at international organisations shall represent the Union' (Art. 221 TFEU). While the EEAS and the upgraded Union delegations are placed under the general authority of the High Representative of the Union for Foreign Affairs and Security Policy (Art. 1(3), Council of the

European Union 2010), some areas of external action remain exempt from her strategic oversight. Thus, the Commission has been allowed to give directions to the Union delegations '[i]n areas where the Commission exercises the powers conferred upon it by the Treaties' (Art. 5(3), Council of the European Union 2010). Given the fact that the CCP represents one of the core areas of Commission action through-out the European integration process, the Commission clearly retains control of the external representation of the policy also at the level of Union delegations.

Overall, the Union's external representation in trade will remain relatively uni-fied. As speaking with a single voice facilitates interaction with third parties in multilateral contexts, the second precondition for effective multilateralism – the capacity to represent an EU position externally – is largely met.

Common foreign and security policy: from Nice to Lisbon

Since its creation in 1993 by the Maastricht Treaty, the CFSP has served as a prime example of the difficulties of co-ordinating and representing a common EU posi-tion at the international level. This intergovernmental field is characterised by a constant interplay between the EU and the member state level – both at the planning and at the implementation stage – and especially strong member state reservations. At the same time, observers have witnessed various efforts on the part of the EU member states to mitigate institutionally the basic dilemma between coherence and effectiveness on the one hand, and the preservation of member state sovereignty on the other.

Internal co-ordination

Despite various examples of non-co-ordination throughout the history of EC/EU foreign policy (see Hill 2004), scholars have stressed that '[b]y the time of the [...] Maastricht Treaty [in 1993], there was virtually an injunction to co-operate within international organizations, especially with respect to issues that the member states had already agreed on within CFSP' (see Farrell 2006: 31–2). Until the Lisbon Treaty, the internal co-ordination of EU member state positions was a major task of the rotating Council Presidency, held by an EU member state during the period of six months. The Presidency was assisted by the Permanent Representatives Committee (COREPER; Art. 207 TEC), the Political and Security Committee (PSC) (Art. 25 TEU-Nice) and the High Representative for CFSP (Art. 26 TEU-Nice). In par-ticular the PSC, the 'linchpin' (Duke 2005) of the CFSP, has always played a central role for the drafting of decision-making proposals for the Council. Created as a permanent body in 2001, and composed of ambassadors from the permanent EU member state representations in Brussels, it meets at least twice a week to discuss current and looming foreign policy crises and related EU action. According to the institutionalist literature, these 'Brusselised' foreign policy structures, and especially the high frequency of the meetings of the PSC, have induced a significantly higher level of co-ordination among the member states compared to the times of the *ad hoc* arrangements of the European Political Cooperation in the 1970s and 1980s (see Allen 1998; Howorth 2001; Klein 2010; Wallace 2005).

Yet, as outlined above, the EU's internal capacity to co-ordinate its external action not only depends on the possibility to formulate common positions, but also on the ability to take (binding) decisions. In the CFSP context, unanimity has always represented the general decision-making rule. Exceptions are limited to few issues and procedures, which can be characterised as subordinate or second-order decisions (see Art. 31 TEU).

Before turning to the analysis of the institutional innovations of the Lisbon Treaty, we will have a closer look at the *living* framework under the Nice Treaty. The joint action[19] represented a core legal instrument in the CFSP, used in situations where the Union envisaged operational action. Against this background the year 2003 can be seen as a milestone for the EU's foreign and security policy, when the European Security and Defence Policy finally became operational, four years after its establishment. As regards the level of multilateralisation, our analysis of EUR-Lex data reveals for the period from 2003 to 2009 that more than half of all substantial joint actions for a given year (only exception: 2005) contained references to a multilateral legal basis (Indicator I). Since 2006, no less than two-thirds of all substantial joint actions contained respective references. Moreover, for roughly half of the substantial joint actions, a multilateral implementation (Indicator II) was foreseen.

TABLE 5.3 The level of multilateralisation in the CFSP: Analysing substantial[20] joint actions[21]

Year	Total number of joint actions	Total number of substantial joint actions	Indicator I: number of substantial joint actions with multilateral legal basis[22]	Indicator I: acts with multilateral legal basis as share of substantial legal acts	Indicator II: number of substantial joint actions with multilateral implementation[23]	Indicator II: acts with multilateral implementation as share of substantial legal acts
2003	26	12	7	58%	6	50%
2004	28	13	8	62%	6	46%
2005	40	16	7	44%	6	38%
2006	37	10	8	80%	8	80%
2007	46	21	16	76%	13	62%
2008	47	28	21	75%	14	50%
2009	32	14	10	71%	7	50%
Total	256	114	77	68%	60	53%

Source: Own calculation, multiple entries for Indicator I and II, based on EUR-Lex (January 2010).

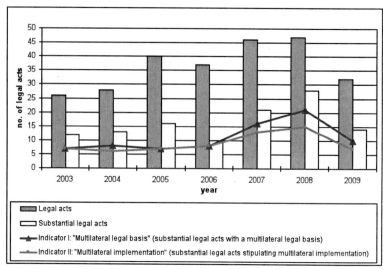

FIGURE 5.2 The level of multilateralisation in the CFSP

These findings suggest, overall, that the Union's foreign policy has been characterised by a significant multilateral approach. At the same time, the number of
substantial joint actions with a multilateral legal basis has always been higher (except
for 2006 where the numbers are equal) than the number of substantial joint actions
for which a multilateral implementation was foreseen (see Figure 5.2). From these
findings, we can conclude that the EU seems to be relatively stronger in taking into
account and thereby strengthening international law than in pooling resources with
other international actors. 'Effective' multilateralism, though, would ideally be based
on both dimensions – a multilateral legal basis and implementation.

In 2009, the Lisbon Treaty introduced important institutional innovations in the
field of EU foreign and security policy, which have a major impact on the Union's
ability to perform in multilateral contexts. For both the internal co-ordination
process and the external representation of the Union, two areas of reform are most
relevant: (i) the High Representative of the Union for Foreign Affairs and Security
Policy, head of the European External Action Service and (ii) the permanent
President of the European Council. Most of the relevant provisions are contained
in Title V 'General provisions on the Union's external action and specific provisions
on the Common Foreign and Security Policy' of the TEU. Given that there are still
'specific provisions' on the CFSP, one might argue that despite the official abolish-
ment of the former pillar structure – illustrated by the introduction of the single
legal personality of the Union (Art. 47 TEU) – *de facto*, there is still some kind of a
second pillar in terms of institutions and procedures (see also Piris 2010: 260).

In December 2009, Catherine Ashton became the first High Representative
of the Union for Foreign Affairs and Security Policy. She is required to 'conduct
the Union's common foreign and security policy' (Art. 18(2) TEU), including the

Common Security and Defence Policy, and to chair the Foreign Affairs Council, replacing the rotating Presidency. Moreover, she has obtained a right of initiative – shared with the member states – for the CFSP (Art. 30(1) and 42(4) TEU). Arguably, these new competences further enhance the agenda-setting power of the High Representative. However, given her parallel position as a Vice-President of the Commission, Ashton has to promote a consensus, which takes into account not only the different political interests of the EU member states, but also the different departments of the Commission and the respective networks they form (Wessels and Bopp 2008: 21). Structurally, compared to other policy fields where the Commission is provided with a sole right of initiative, particularly in accordance with the ordinary legislative procedure (Art. 294 TFEU), foreign and security policy is less centralised, making it harder to formulate and represent a coherent position on behalf of the EU in multilateral settings.

Furthermore, the High Representative shall ensure the implementation of the decisions taken in the field of CFSP (Art. 27(1) TEU). In this context, there is a certain overlapping of competences with the intergovernmental PSC, which shall 'monitor the implementation of agreed policies, without prejudice to the powers of the High Representative' (Art. 38 TEU). The position of the High Representative vis-à-vis this pivotal committee for CFSP has been strengthened, though, by the appointment of a representative of the High Representative as chairperson of the PSC (Art. 4(4), Council of the European Union 2010; see also Morillas 2011: 254).

The intense discussions on how to link the PSC with the new EEAS led by Ashton illustrate the salience of the co-ordination issue in this policy field. As the European Parliament has to give a vote of consent to the entire Commission (Art. 17(7) TEU) and since the President of the Commission can request the withdrawal of single Commissioners, the High Representative is responsible to three bodies at the same time: the Commission, the Council and (to a lesser extent) the Parliament. This mix of loyalties has been expected early on to be difficult to balance, leading analysts to the conclusion that the High Representative needs the characteristics of a 'superhuman gymnast' (European Policy Centre (EPC) 2007: 20). After the first one and a half years under the Lisbon Treaty, Ashton was heavily criticised for not being able to forge a common EU position in view of important political crises such as the uprisings in North Africa in 2011.[24] Regardless of the discussion of her personal skills in terms of leadership and delegation, the set-up of the new post – and last but not least the mere workload – hardly allows for quick and firm reactions in foreign affairs on behalf of the Union as a whole.

The co-ordination tasks of the High Representative for EU action within multilateral arrangements appear likewise challenging. She is responsible for the organisation of the co-ordination of the action of the member states in international organisations and at international conferences (Art. 34(1) TEU) as well as for the implementation of the co-operation of the EU with other international organisations such as the UN and the Council of Europe (Art. 220 TFEU). Moreover, the High Representative is also responsible for the Union delegations in third countries and at international organisations (Art. 221 TFEU), which have been integrated into the EEAS.

The EEAS, which is expected to co-operate closely with the national diplomatic services, is crucial for the functioning of the internal co-ordination processes for CFSP. Yet, in July 2010, the Council decided to leave the strategic oversight over core areas of EU external relations such as the European Neighbourhood Policy and development policy with the responsible Commissioners (Art. 9(4), Council of the European Union 2010). Thus, while the new EEAS does provide the High Representative with new resources in terms of staff and competences, it has also introduced new co-ordination demands between the various areas of EU external action which in turn might weaken the capacity to co-ordinate EU positions in the CFSP.

The position of a full-time President of the European Council represents the second major institutional innovation in view of the internal co-ordination processes in the CFSP framework. As the Lisbon Treaty specifies, the President shall 'ensure the preparation and continuity of the work of the European Council in co-operation with the President of the Commission, and on the basis of the work of the General Affairs Council' (Art. 15(6) TEU). Thus, his main task is to promote consensus among the heads of state and government and to ensure member states' compliance. In 2009, Herman Van Rompuy was elected as the first President of the European Council. Having been just as unknown (and inexperienced) in the field of foreign and security policy as Catherine Ashton, the expectation was that, at least at the beginning, both would rather moderate than steer EU internal discussion and co-ordination processes. Some observers, however, have stressed that in the case of Van Rompuy, he 'has tried to articulate an autonomous and original analysis of the new international environment in which the Union operates' (Missiroli 2010: 4–5). As for the discussion and the formulation of EU foreign policy positions at the working level, Van Rompuy – whose cabinet is composed of fourteen political advisors, four of them focusing on external relations[25] – essentially relies on the support of the EEAS.[26] Thus, the creation of an additional high-level post in EU foreign policy does not seem to hamper the internal co-ordination process.

As for decision-making procedures, the Lisbon Treaty did not mark a breakthrough in terms of establishing more efficient decision-making procedures in the CFSP context: unanimity remains the standard for decision-making in this policy field (Art. 24(1), 31(1) TEU), including the possibility of constructive abstention. As it is up to the Council to 'frame' the CFSP and to 'take the decisions necessary for defining and implementing it' (Art. 26(2) TEU), the Council needs to take decisions unanimously on operational action by the Union 'where the international situation requires' (Art. 28(1) TEU). In turn, member states 'shall commit' to these decisions 'in the positions they adopt and in the conduct of their activity' (Art. 28(2) TEU). In the daily decision-making practice in the first year under the Lisbon Treaty, some member states emphasised and used their veto right in EU foreign policy as a way to counter far-reaching interpretations of the new structures, which according to them must not undermine the intergovernmental character of CFSP (Morillas 2011: 249; 253–4). Thus, at least in the beginning, the increase of co-ordination capacity by the introduction of the double-hatted High Representative and the

European External Action Service has been partly counterbalanced by the member states being on alert to defend their sovereignty in EU foreign policy.

External representation

As far as the EU (and not the former European Community) is concerned, the Nice Treaty did not provide for a single institution to represent the Union. In this context, the composition of the so-called 'Troika', representing the EU in the CFSP,[27] can serve as an illustrative example. While typically various actors have been involved with the external representation of the CFSP, the treaty nevertheless foresaw a leading role for the rotating Presidency: it could speak on behalf of the Union in international organisations and international conferences (see Art. 18 TEU-Nice).

The question of 'who speaks for the EU' is closely linked to the question of 'who signs for the EU' as well as to the issue of the EU's membership in international organisations. Under the Nice Treaty, the European *Union* had no explicit legal personality. Yet, as Govaere *et al.* have pointed out, article 24 TEU-Nice could be interpreted as 'an implicit confirmation of the EU's functional legal personality' (Govaere *et al.* 2004: 161). This article provided for the Council the competence to conclude an agreement with one or more states or international organisations on CFSP-related issues such as crisis management missions. Crucially, international agreements concluded on the basis of article 24 TEU-Nice did not have to be ratified by the EU member states (see Govaere *et al.* 2004: 160–1). Thus, while the supranational Commission played only a marginal role (as part of the Troika) in the external representation of EU foreign policy issues, it was nevertheless a European institution, the Council, which functioned as a single contact body for external partners.

The Lisbon Treaty has changed substantially the external representation in the field of EU foreign and security policy by upgrading the High Representative, by creating a permanent President of the European Council and by introducing for the first time a legal personality for the European Union as a whole (see above). Crucially, the new double-hatted High Representative is supposed to improve the coherence of the Union's external action by providing the Union with a 'single voice' and 'face' (Wessels and Bopp 2008: 19). Thus, the Lisbon Treaty states that 'the High Representative shall represent the Union for matters relating to the common foreign and security policy. [She] shall conduct political dialogue with third parties on the Union's behalf and shall express the Union's position in international organisations and at international conferences' (Art. 27 (2) TEU). Additionally, she is granted the right to represent the Union's position on a specific topic in the UN Security Council given that the Union has defined a position on one of the topics on the agenda and that she is requested to do so by the member states represented in the UN Security Council (Art. 34 (2) TEU). This legal innovat̃ -̃ current *de facto* practice (see Regelsberger 2008: 272).

As mentioned above, the EEAS and the related Union delegat̃.
EU's external representation to a large extent. Legally, the Head of D̃

a special role: he/she 'shall have the power to represent the Union in the country where the delegation is accredited, in particular for the conclusion of contracts, and as a party to legal proceedings' (Art. 5(8), Council of the European Union 2010). Politically, the new composition of the staff of the delegations – including Council officials and national diplomats in addition to Commission officials – leads to the expectation that the EU might pursue a more strategic approach on the ground, in contrast to the previous, mostly technical implementation work of the Community delegations. Yet, the fact that Commission officials typically administer significant amounts of the EU budget – in contrast to Council officials and national diplomats – has already created tensions within the new EU delegations.[28] Thus, the new set-up might also give rise to a rather inward-looking attitude.

As for the external representation role of the European Council President, conflict with the High Representative is institutionally inherent. The new treaty states that 'at his level and in that capacity, [the President of the European Council shall] ensure the external representation of the Union on issues concerning its common foreign and security policy, without prejudice to the powers of the High Representative' (Art. 15(6) TEU). The formulation 'without prejudice to' indicates that potential role conflicts are being recognised but their resolution has been shifted to daily practice. An incident in February 2010, when Ashton missed an informal meeting of the EU defence ministers in Mallorca partly because Van Rompuy had sent her to Kiev to attend the investiture ceremony of the new Ukrainian President Yanukovych, indicates that in the case of conflicting institutional interests, the President's powers outweigh those of the High Representative.

From a longer-term perspective, it remains to be seen how far the Union's external representation will be shared between these two institutions in day-to-day policy-making – it seems that the EU might have at least two telephone numbers. In this context, it is interesting to note the recent diplomatic success of the EU at the UN. Following a resolution of the UN General Assembly of 3 May 2011, the EU has no longer to be represented in this body by the UN ambassador of the EU member state holding the rotating Presidency, but, alternatively, the Head of the EU delegation at the UN, the High Representative or the President of the European Council can speak on behalf of the EU (Kenna 2011). On the one hand, this advanced status at the UN reinforces the EU's character as an international actor in its own right. On the other hand, though, a (new) split in the representation of EU foreign and security issues would arguably reduce the EU's capacity to pursue its objectives in multilateral settings such as the UN.

Conclusion and outlook

This chapter has explored the question of how far its institutional architecture enables the Union to live up to the ambition to contribute to (effective) multilateralism. It started from the assumption that the EU acts in its own right at the international level and within multilateral settings. In this context, an effective institutional set-up was considered as a necessary condition for the EU to influence multilateral policy-making according to its interests. Drawing on the literature on the EU's performance in international organisations, institutional effectiveness was investigated along two dimensions: (i) the structural set-up for the internal co-ordination of the EU position and (ii) the EU's external representation.

The analysis of two different cases – the CCP and the CFSP – has generated varying results. In the area of trade, the structural set-up has facilitated the internal co-ordination of a common EU position within multilateral forums such as the WTO. Most importantly, the exclusive right of initiative of the European Commission, its expertise and its leading role during the negotiation process with third actors account for a centralised policy-making. The dominant majority voting further enhances the possibility of forging a common EU position; even if this position is not supported by all EU member states.

The innovations introduced by the Lisbon Treaty have partly contradictory effects on the Union as a multilateral actor in the field of trade. On one hand, the scope of EU trade policy has been extended considerably. This extension of EU competences accounts for a *general* increase of the EU's weight as a trade actor in multilateral forums, at the expense of its member states' competences. On the other hand, the legal provisions of the Lisbon Treaty introduce new obstacles in terms of an effective internal co-ordination process, such as the inclusion of the European Parliament as a full actor, unanimity voting for many of the new trade related competences, as well as the fact that the common commercial policy is now placed within the broader context of the Union's external action, constraining the EU as a multilateral trade actor.

As for the external representation of the Union in the field of trade, however, the institutional set-up has remained highly effective due to the central role of the European Commission. The fact that the European Commission is also responsible for carrying out dispute settlement actions on behalf of single EU member states in the framework of the WTO underlines the extraordinary level of coherence.

Overall, comparing the legal provisions of EU trade policy with its foreign and security policy, trade represents a policy field where the EU is institutionally much better equipped to act multilaterally compared to the CFSP. The CFSP has only complemented, but not substituted for the national foreign policies of the EU member states. Thus, this policy field has been characterised by a particularly pressing need for co-ordination between the EU institutions on the one hand and EU member state positions and actions on the other. Since 2001, 'Brusselised' foreign policy structures have induced a significantly higher level of co-ordination. Yet, given the dominant mode of unanimous decision-making – before and after the Lisbon Treaty – the internal co-ordination capacity can be described as severely restricted.

Within these structural limits, two institutional innovations of the Lisbon Treaty might nevertheless have a major impact. First, the High Representative of the Union for Foreign Affairs and Security Policy, supported by the European External Action Service, not only brings together the formerly separated Council and Commission structures ('double hat'), but also chairs the Foreign Affairs Council. By abolishing the chair of the rotating EU Presidency in the field of foreign affairs, the set-up for a continuous and smooth co-ordination of EU member state positions has been improved. How far this improvement can be translated into effective multilateral policy-making depends not least on the second main institutional innovation of the Lisbon Treaty, the permanent President of the European Council. However, institutionally, the mere existence of two major spokespersons for the CFSP argu-ably leaves much room for internal power struggles and causes confusion among third actors.

Our study aimed not only at the analysis of the legal framework for EU multi-lateral action, but also at an assessment of its living framework that is the actual use of the legal provisions. While it is still too early to refer to the use of the Lisbon provisions over time, empirical data on the use of the Nice provisions from 2003 onwards revealed a strong EU commitment to multilateralism in its legal output. The samples of legal acts in the fields of trade and foreign and security policy have shown that in more than half of the cases – most of the time even in more than two-thirds of the cases – at least one reference to a multilateral legal basis (Indicator I) such as UN resolutions or international conventions was included. Comparing the two policy fields, from 2006 onwards, CCP appears to be slightly stronger mul-tilateralised than CFSP: while more than 80 per cent of substantial legal acts in the area of CCP in the years 2006 and 2009 refer to a multilateral legal basis, the respec-tive share for CFSP substantial legal acts ranges between 71 per cent (2009) and 80 per cent (2006) (see Tables 5.1 and 5.3). These findings basically confirm the rel-evance of the institutional factor for EU multilateralism: under the Nice Treaty, the legal framework of the EU's trade policy, compared to the CFSP, provided a higher capacity to act multilaterally. Consequently, this capacity was also illustrated by a higher level of actual multilateral output or a more multilateralised *living* framework in the area of trade policy.

Our methodological approach allows for further differentiation, namely between the reference to a multilateral *legal basis* (Indicator I) and a multilateral *implementa-tion* (Indicator II). In the framework of the CFSP, our findings indicate that the EU is relatively stronger in supporting international law by referring explicitly to it than in pooling resources with other international actors such as the North Atlantic Treaty Organization. Thus, from 2003 to 2009, multilateral implementation is foreseen in only half of the substantial joint actions (with some slight deviations from this average, see Table 5.3). In the context of scarce resources to be deployed for example in international crisis management missions, 'effective' multilateralism, would ideally be based on both dimensions – a multilateral legal basis and imple-mentation. In the area of trade, where Indicator II did not produce viable results, it is interesting to note that protectionist anti-dumping duties are the most frequently used instrument including a reference to a multilateral framework, which is the GATT in this case. Thus, paradoxically, multilateralism in EU trade policy has been primarily reflected in measures contradicting the notion of free trade – the notion that lies at the heart of the GATT framework.

Overall, the qualitative analysis of legal output of the EU proves to be a promis-ing tool to assess the multilateralisation of the EU. However, the varying levels of multilateralisation across foreign policies can only be explained if seen in the light of the differing living and legal frameworks. Together the manifold and comprehensive external relations of the EU and its complex and ever-evolving institutional set-up make research over time a demanding exercise. Still, this approach constitutes a promising path to better understand how far and under which circumstances the EU can live up to its ambition as an (effective) multilateral player.

Notes

1   The authors wish to thank Mark Aspinwall, Geoffrey Edwards, Christopher Hill and John Peterson for most valuable comments on earlier drafts of this paper. The views expressed in this chapter reflect only those of the authors. It is based on Reiners, Wulf and Klein, Nadia (2010): 'Acting multilaterally at home and abroad: The EU's institutional set-up in the cases of health and the Common Foreign and Security Policy', paper for the 'The EU in International Affairs II' Conference, Brussels, 22–24 April 2010.

2   In the following, references to the Treaty on European Union (TEU) and the Treaty on the Functioning of the European Union (TFEU) are based on consolidated versions of the Treaty on European Union and the Treaty on the Functioning of European Union, OJ C 83. 30.03.2010. References to the former Treaty of Nice are marked explicitly: Treaty on European Union (TEU-Nice) and Treaty of the European Communities (TEC).

3   In this context the multilateralisation of an EU policy is understood as an increasing share of EU legal acts with multilateral legal basis and/or multilateral policy implementation in comparison to legal acts of uni- or bilateral nature. Likewise, a certain policy can be considered as stronger multilateralised than another, if the share of legal acts with multilateral legal basis and/or implementation is higher than in the case of the other policy.

4   On the discussion of the EU's actorness in the field of foreign policy, see for example Allen and Smith 1990; Tonra and Christiansen 2004; Bretherton and Vogler 2006.

5   The share of legal acts where the indicator multilateral implementation applies is in the low single-digit range, or 2–4 legal acts per year in absolute numbers, which allows no inferences to be made. See also description of the DATEX database at http://www. europa.ed.ac.uk/global_europa/external_relations/mercury

6   'Joint actions' were adopted by the Council of the EU. They addressed 'specific situations where operational action by the Union is deemed to be required', laying down 'their objectives, scope, the means to be made available to the Union, if necessary their duration, and the conditions for their implementation' (Art. 14 TEU-Nice). In the Lisbon Treaty, 'joint actions' have been replaced by the instrument of 'decision'(Art.28 TEU).

7   In the EU, any given legal procedure typically includes a series of decision proposals until the Council of the EU, sometimes together with the European Parliament, takes a *final* decision which enters into force when published in the *Official Journal of the European Union*. Sometimes, final decisions are amended by subsequent decisions. For example, financial resources for the implementation can be increased. For the purpose of our study, this kind of limited amendments is classified as *second-order legal acts* and sorted out from the analysis because they are of a technical nature only and neither amend the multilateral content of a specific legal act, nor do they represent new political acts that stand on their own.

8   EUR-Lex is the EU's central online database on EU law. It offers a search engine providing direct access to and background information on all types of binding and non-binding EU legislation. The EUR-Lex web address is: http://eur-lex.europa.eu/en/index.htm

9   See, for example, Scharpf's analysis of positive and negative integration (Scharpf 2008).

10 For example, since 1992 all EU trade and co-operation agreements have contained a clause on human rights; since 1995, trade preferences under Europe's Generalized System of Preferences have included labour conditionality (see Orbie 2008b: 54).

11 However, many new areas of EU competence introduced by the Nice and Lisbon Treaties remain subject to unanimity.
12 It should be noted that in a few cases, a legal act contained both a direct and an indirect reference. For this reason, the number of direct and indirect references do not always exactly sum up to the number of legal acts with (in)direct reference.
13 Excludes limited amendments such as the prolongation of an existing legal act or amendments of selected articles regarding an existing legal act.
14 Regulations, Directives, Decisions.
15 Until 30 November 2009, before the Lisbon Treaty entered into force on 1 December 2009.
16 Includes references to specific UN Resolutions, WTO/GATT or other international conventions.
17 Additionally, 14 other underlying legal acts with multilateral references were cited in our sample, but at most once or twice per year.
18 Until 30 November 2009, before the Lisbon Treaty entered into force on 1 December 2009.
19 Renamed 'decision' in the Lisbon Treaty.
20 Excludes limited amendments such as the prolongation of an existing joint action or amendments of selected articles regarding an existing joint action.
21 Until 30 November 2009, before the Lisbon Treaty entered into force on 1 December 2009.
22 Includes references to specific UN Resolutions, international conventions or internationally brokered peace agreements.
23 Includes a pre-defined division of labour with other international actors and the participation of third states.
24 See *Süddeutsche Zeitung*, 17 June 2011
25 See the website of the European Council: http://www.european-council.europa.eu/the-president/cabinet.aspx?lang=en
26 Telephone interview with EU official, 2 June 2011.
27 The 'Troika' was composed of the foreign affairs minister of the member state holding the Presidency of the Council of the European Union, the High Representative for the Common Foreign and Security Policy, the European Commissioner in charge of external relations and European Neighbourhood Policy and, where necessary, the representatives of the future Presidency (see Art. 18 TEU-Nice).
28 Telephone interview with EU official, 2 June 2011.

References

Allen, D. (1998) 'Who Speaks for Europe? The Search for an Effective and Coherent External Policy', in J. Peterson and H. Sjursen (eds) *A Common Foreign Policy for Europe? Competing Visions of the CFSP*, London: Routledge, pp. 41–58.

Allen, D. and Smith, M. (1990) 'Western Europe's Presence in the Contemporary International Arena', *Review of International Studies* 16 (1): 19–37.

Balan, G.-D. (2008) 'The Common Commercial Policy under the Lisbon Treaty'. Jean Monnet Seminar 'Advanced Issues of European Law', 6th session, Re-thinking the European Constitution in an Enlarged European Union, 20–27 April 2008, Dubrovnik. Online. Available HTTP: <http://www.pravo.hr/_download/repository/GDB_JM_CCP.pdf> (accessed 22 June 2010).

Baldwin, M., Peterson, J. and Stokes, B. (2003) 'Trade and Economic Relations', in J. Peterson and M. A. Pollack (eds) *Europe, America, Bush. Transatlantic Relations in the Twenty-first Century*, London: Routledge, pp. 29–46.

Barroso, J. M. D. (2010) 'The European Union and Multilateral Global Governance'. Inaugural Lecture of the Global Governance Programme at the European University Institute, Florence, 18 June 2010. Online. Available HTTP: <http://europa.eu/rapid/pressReleasesAction.do?reference=SPEECH/10/322&format=TML&aged=0&language=EN&guiLanguage=en> (accessed 22 June 2010).

Bretherton, C. and Vogler, J. (2006) *The European Union as a Global Actor,* 2nd edition, London/New York: Routledge.

Centre for European Policy Studies (CEPS), Royal Institute for International Relations EGMONT and European Policy Centre (EPC) (2010) 'The Treaty of Lisbon: A Second Look at the Institutional Innovations. Joint Study', Brussels. Online. Available HTTP: <http://www.epc.eu/documents/uploads/pub_1150_epc_egmont_ceps__treaty_of_lisb on.pdf> (accessed 13 October 2010).

Conconi, P. (2009) 'The EU's Common Commercial Policy and Regional/Global Regulation', in M. Telò (ed.) *The European Union and Global Governance,* Abingdon: Routledge, pp. 156–75.

Council of the European Union (2003) Council Joint Action 2003/92/CFSP of 27 January 2003 on the European Union military operation in the Former Yugoslav Republic of Macedonia. Doc, 2003/92/CFSP, in *Official Journal* L 34, 11.2.2003, pp. 26–9.

Council of the European Union (2010) Council Decision of 26 July 2010 establishing the organisation and functioning of the European External Action Service, Doc. 2010/427/EU, in *Official Journal* L 201, 3.8.2010, pp. 30–40.

Delcourt, B. and Remacle, E. (2009) 'Global Governance. A Challenge for Common Foreign and Security Policy and European Security and Defence Policy', in M. Telò (ed.) *The European Union and Global Governance,* Abingdon: Routledge, pp. 233–57.

Dimopoulos, A. (2010) 'The Effects of the Lisbon Treaty on the Principles and Objectives of the Common Commercial Policy', *European Foreign Affairs Review* 15: 153–70.

Duke, S. (2005) 'The Linchpin COPS. Assessing the Workings and Institutional Relations of the Political and Security Committee', No. W/05, Maastricht: European Institute of Public Administration. Online. Available HTTP: <http://www.eipa.nl> (accessed 21 January 2008).

Emerson, M., Balfour, R., Corthaut, T., Wouters, J., Kaczyński, P. M. and Renard, T. (2011) 'Upgrading the EU's Role as Global Actor: Institutions, Law and the Restructuring of European Diplomacy'. Brussels: Centre for European Policy Studies. Online. Available HTTP: <http://www.ceps.eu/ceps/download/4135> (accessed 22 August 2011).

European Council (2003) European Security Strategy, Brussels, 12 December 2003.

European Policy Centre (EPC) (2007) 'The People's Project? The New EU Treaty and the Prospects for Future Integration'. Challenge Europe Issue No. 19, Brussels: European Policy Centre (EPC). Brussels. Online. Available HTTP: <http://www.epc.eu/PDF/CE17.pdf> (accessed 26 March 2010).

Farrell, M. (2006) 'EU Representation and Coordination within the United Nations', in K. V. Laatikainen and K. E. Smith (eds) *The European Union at the United Nations. Intersecting Multilateralisms,* Houndmills: Palgrave Macmillan, pp. 27–46.

Ginsberg, R. H. (2001) *The European Union in World Politics: Baptism by Fire,* Lanham, MD: Rowman and Littlefield.

Govaere, I., Capiau, J. and Vermeersch, A. (2004) 'In-Between Seats: the Participation of the European Union in International Organizations', *European Foreign Affairs Review* 9: 155–87.

Hill, C. (2004) 'Renationalizing or Regrouping? EU Foreign Policy Since 11 September 2001, *Journal of Common Market Studies* 42 (1): 143–63.

Howorth, J. (2001) 'European Defence and the Changing Politics of the European Union: Hanging Together or Hanging Separately?', *Journal of Common Market Studies* 39 (4): 765–89.

Jørgensen, K. E. (2006) 'Overview: The European Union and the World', in K. E. Jørgensen, M. A. Pollack and B. Rosamond (eds) *Handbook of European Union Politics*, London/ Thousand Oaks/New Delhi: SAGE, pp. 507–25.

Jørgensen, K. E. (2009a) 'Analyzing the European Union's Performance in International Institutions'. Paper presented at the ISA Convention 2009, New York, 15–18 February 2009.

Jørgensen, K. E. (2009b) 'The European Union in Multilateral Diplomacy', *The Hague Journal of Diplomacy* 4 (2): 189–209.

Kenna, M. (2011) 'The European External Action Service and the United Nations: a Missed Opportunity for Self-Promotion'. Commentary, European Policy Centre, 16.05.2011. Online. Available HTTP: <www.epc.eu> (accessed 17 August 2011).

Keukeleire, S. and MacNaughtan, J. (2008) *The Foreign Policy of the European Union*, Houndmills/New York: Palgrave Macmillan.

Kleimann, D. (2011) 'Taking Stock: EU Common Commercial Policy in the Lisbon Era', Centre for European Policy Studies Working Paper No. 346, 04.5.2011. Online. Available HTTP: <http://ssrn.com/abstract=1831636> (accessed 22 August 2011).

Klein, N. (2010) *European Agents out of Control? Delegation and Agency in the Civil Military Crisis Management of the European Union*, Baden-Baden: Nomos.

Laatikainen, K. V. and Smith, K. E. (eds) (2006a) *The European Union at the United Nations. Intersecting Multilateralisms*, Houndmills: Palgrave Macmillan.

Laatikainen, K. V. and Smith, K. E. (2006b) 'Introduction – The European Union at the United Nations: Leader, Partner or Failure?', in K. V. Laatikainen and K. E. Smith (eds) *The European Union at the United Nations. Intersecting Multilateralisms*, Houndmills: Palgrave Macmillan, pp. 1–23.

Lucarelli, S. (2007) 'European Political Identity and Others' Images of the EU: Reflections on an Underexplored Relationship', *CFSP Forum* 5 (6): 11–15.

Marsh, S. and Mackenstein, H. (2005) *The International Relations of the European Union*. Harlow: Pearson Longman.

Meunier, S. and Nicolaïdis, K. (2005) 'The European Union as a Trade Power', in C. Hill and M. Smith (eds) *International Relations and the European Union*, Oxford: Oxford University Press, pp. 247–69.

Missiroli, A. (2010) 'Implementing the Lisbon Treaty: The External Policy Dimension'. Bruges Political Research Papers No. 14/2010, Bruges: College of Europe.

Morillas, P. (2011) 'Institutionalization or Intergovernmental Decision-Taking', *European Foreign Affairs Review* 2 (16): 243–57.

Ohrid Framework Agreement. 2001. Online. Available HTTP: <http://siteresources.world-bank.org/INTMACEDONIA/Resources/SolutionofPoliticalandSecurityCrisis.doc> (accessed 20 December 2011).

Orbie, J. (2008a) 'A Civilian Power in the World? Instruments and Objectives in European Union External Policies', in J. Orbie (ed.) *Europe's Global Role: External Policies of the European Union*, Aldershot: Ashgate, pp. 1–33.

Orbie, J. (2008b) 'The European Union's Role in World Trade: Harnessing Globalisation?', in J. Orbie (ed.) *Europe's Global Role: External Policies of the European Union*, Aldershot: Ashgate, pp. 35–66.

Peterson, J. (1995) 'Decision-making in the European Union: Towards a Framework for Analysis', *Journal of European Public Policy* 2 (1): 69–93.

Piris, J.-C. (2010) *The Lisbon Treaty: a Legal and Political Analysis*, Cambridge: Cambridge University Press.

Regelsberger, E. (2008) 'Von Nizza nach Lissabon – das neue konstitutionelle Angebot für die Gemeinsame Außen- und Sicherheitspolitik', *Integration* 31 (3): 266–80.

Scharpf, F. W. (2008) 'Negative und positive Integration', in M. Höpner and A. Schäfer (eds) *Die Politische Ökonomie der europäischen Integration*, Frankfurt am Main: Campus. 49–87.

Süddeutsche Zeitung, 17 June 2011.

Tonra, B. and Christiansen, T. (eds) (2004) *Rethinking European Foreign Policy*. Manchester/New York: Manchester University Press.

Vanhoonacker, S. (2011) 'The Institutional Framework', in C. Hill and M. Smith (eds) *International Relations and the European Union*, Oxford: Oxford University Press, pp.75–100.

Wallace, H. (2005) 'An Institutional Anatomy and Five Policy Modes', in H. Wallace, W. Wallace and M. A. Pollack (eds) *Policy-Making in the European Union,* 5th edition, Oxford: Oxford University Press, pp. 49–90.

Wessels, W. (2001) 'Nice Results: The Millennium IGC in the EU's Evolution', *Journal of Common Market Studies* 39 (2): 197–219.

Wessels, W. and Bopp, F. (2008) 'The CFSP after the Lisbon Treaty: Constitutional Breakthrough or Challenges Ahead?'. Challenge Research Paper No. 10. Online. Available HTTP: <http://www.libertysecurity.org>.

White, B. (2001) *Understanding European Foreign Policy*, Houndmills/New York: Palgrave.

Whitman, R. G. and Juncos, A. (2009) 'The Lisbon Treaty and the Foreign, Security and Defence Policy: Reforms, Implementation and the Consequences of (non)Ratification', *European Foreign Affairs Review* 14 (1): 25–40.

Woolcock, S. (2008) 'The Potential Impact of the Lisbon Treaty on European Union External Trade Policy'. *European Policy Analysis* No. 8, Stockholm: Swedish Institute for European Policy Studies.

Young, A. R. and Peterson, J. (2006) 'The EU and new trade politics', *Journal of European Public Policy* 13 (6): 795–814.

6

MARKET POWER EUROPE

Externalization and multilateralism

Chad Damro

Introduction[1]

The role of the European Union (EU) in the multilateral system and the extent to which it engages in effective multilateralism can be understood and analysed as a function of its power. Since the 1970s, much scholarly attention has focused on what kind of power the EU is, what it says as a power, and what the Union does as a power. These 'EU as a power' debates have been challenging and contentious because of the unique nature of the EU as an actor in the international system. This uniqueness has led scholars to generate various competing labels for the Union as a power. For example, in his discussion of civilian power, Orbie provides a list that includes gentle power, superpower, quiet superpower and middle power (2008, 2).[2] Perhaps the liveliest debate in this rich literature revolves around Normative Power Europe (NPE), which moved the conceptual understanding of the EU as a power beyond the dichotomy of military power and civilian power. According to NPE, 'the most important factor shaping the international role of the EU is not what it does or what it says, but what it is' (Manners 2002, 252). What the EU is – a particular identity with a normative basis – makes it different from other actors in the international system. This influential formulation has led to a number of scholars to agree that 'we may best conceive of the EU as a "normative power Europe"' (Manners 2002, 235).

While this is an attractive premise, other important factors may contribute to what the EU is, meaning the Union's identity may follow from a different basis. This chapter asserts that the EU need not necessarily be preconceived – at least not for analytical purposes – as a particular or different normative identity in order to understand it as a power. Rather, because the EU is, at its core, a market, it may be best to conceive of the EU as a Market Power Europe (MPE). It is worth clarifying at the outset that conceptualizing the EU as MPE is not intended to portray it as an exclusively neo-liberal and capitalist actor. Although MPE may seem to highlight such pro-market aspects of the EU's identity, it also emphasizes the importance of interventions in the market via economic and social regulation. The conceptualization, therefore, sits comfortably with the co-existent economic and social agendas of the EU. By covering both of these agendas, the conceptualization is not intended to promote any particular normative claims about what the EU should be or how it should act as MPE.

Conceptualizing the EU as MPE requires a degree of analytical reductionism to ascertain the fundamental basis of the EU's identity. The EU's identity, both historically and presently, is crucially linked to its experience with market integration. The single market provides the material existence of the EU as an MPE that externalizes its economic and social market-related policies and regulatory measures in the multilateral system. The single market has institutional features that help to determine the roles and interactions of various actors and provide the EU with considerable regulatory capacity for externalizing policies and regulatory measures. If the Union is an MPE, its efforts at externalization become an important way in which to engage in effective multilateralism. The single market also operates as an arena in which interest contestation helps to determine the likelihood of the EU intentionally and unintentionally exercising its power in multilateral settings.

While such an approach may be provocative, this chapter develops the concept with the intent of being empirically accurate and theoretically productive. Empirically, the notion of MPE contributes to the contemporary debates over the EU-as-a-power by focusing on the context within which the Union is already often and readily recognized by other actors in the multilateral system. The approach incorporates the exercise of power vis-à-vis public *and* private actors and draws attention to the role of coercion in the exercise of power. Theoretically, the conceptualization reveals the most important factors and actors that account for the EU as a power and identifies avenues for generating testable hypotheses and new research. While the Union as a power debates stand as a distinct contribution to our understanding of the EU in pursuit of effective multilateralism, a growing body of comparative and international political economy literature – which is used below to develop the characteristics of MPE – is typically reticent to problematize explicitly the EU-as-a-power. This project is, therefore, inspired by a belief that various strands of research have not yet fruitfully communicated with each other. The conceptualization advanced herein also reflects and encourages a broader understanding of what is meant by foreign policy. Beyond traditional security and defence policy, the EU's other policy areas have considerable external aspects and effects. Insofar as these policies are linked to efforts at externalization (e.g. foreign economic policy, foreign environmental policy), they contribute in decisive ways to the EU's foreign policy and its exercise of power in multilateral settings.

The chapter proceeds in the following manner. The next section elaborates different bases of identity (what the EU is) upon which the conceptualizations of NPE and MPE rest. The third section develops the three characteristics of the EU's identity that provide the foundations for MPE. The fourth section discusses the variables, subjects, targets and tools related to MPE. The fifth section explores the empirical record of MPE, focusing on EU strategies (what it says) for externalization and identifying initial evidence (what it does) deserving of further investigation. The final section summarizes the argument and encourages further theoretical and empirical research on the EU as MPE in the multilateral system.

Bases of EU as a power

The EU is a power that can and does use its market and regulatory strengths to externalize internal policies in a variety of multilateral settings. Central to this argument is an assertion that the EU's identity provides an important basis for its power. To specify the assertion, this section begins by focusing on NPE as a prominent scholarly contribution to the relationship between what the EU is and its power.

Basis of Normative Power Europe

The conceptualization of NPE emerged from the debates associated with civilian power Europe (Duchêne 1972) and has generated a decade's worth of contributions to our understanding of the EU as a power. Manners argues that the EU, due to 'its particular historical evolution, its hybrid polity, and its constitutional configuration', has a 'normatively *different* basis' for its external relations (2002, 252). This different normative basis or identity of the Union – not what it does or says – is the most important factor for determining the EU's role in international affairs.

According to the initial formulation of NPE, the EU's identity includes five core and four minor norms that have developed through a 'series of declarations, treaties, policies, criteria and conditions' (Manners 2002, 242). By projecting these collective norms in various ways, the EU is able to shape the identities of non-members and change their perceptions of what is 'normal' in international relations. The various ways through which NPE projects its norms include contagion, informational diffusion, procedural diffusion, transference, overt diffusion, and the cultural filter. These projection mechanisms, which may include both intentional and unintentional exercises of power, are notable for their 'relative absence of physical force' (Manners 2006, 184).

While the projection mechanisms do not exclude coercion or a role for material incentives, NPE tends to emphasize the need for persuasion and other non-coercive actions. The emphasis arises because the projection of norms needs to be normatively justified and 'if normative justification is to be convincing or attractive then the actions taken must involve persuasion, argumentation, and the conferral of prestige or shame' (Manners 2011, 235).[3] The projection of norms is also likely to be more 'normatively sustainable' if it involves these three types of actions 'rather than coercion or solely material motivations' (Manners 2009, 792).

This chapter accepts that particular core and minor norms may contribute to the EU's identity. But if the EU's identity has an important alternative basis – as the result of its consistent historical experience and current presence – it may be best to conceive of the EU as a different type of power that exercises its power in different ways.

An alternative basis of power

The EU has always been an experiment at market integration. Even if it may have been initiated as cooperation for confidence building, it has consistently been a market-integration undertaking, with limited forays into defence integration. The focus of integration in 1951 was the coal and steel sectors, while the 1957 Treaty of Rome expanded the experiment to market integration more broadly. As an economic bloc with a common external tariff, the EU's market also necessarily had an external dimension. Thus, the common market and the common commercial policy served as original and essential building blocks of European integration and EU identity. Even during the 1970s 'Eurosclerosis', the EU was still first and foremost an experiment in market integration, as witnessed by important legal decisions like *Cassis de Dijon*.

The 1986 Single European Act (SEA) propelled the market integration experiment forward and helped to reaffirm and bolster this identity. According to Young, 'The success of the single market programme has been such that many authors see it as a defining feature of the EU' (2006, 376). While the EU has always been a prominent experiment at market integration, it makes even more sense following the SEA to think of the EU's identity as linked to its large regulated market. Indeed, the Union now considers itself an important international actor and shaper of globalization due to the collective economic weight of its single market (Commission 2010, 2007a, 2006, 2001). According to Sapir, 'This way of considering the EU is new. As recently as twenty years ago, [the EU] was primarily envisaged as a regional integration experiment among a relatively small number of participating countries' and not necessarily an important international actor and shaper of globalization (2007, vii–viii). The EU, therefore, has evolved from being a regional market integration experiment into the comprehensive and capable international market power that it is today. The EU's own collective awareness of this evolution helps to underline and reinforce its identity as MPE.

Emphasizing the market basis of the EU's identity and its external implications is not entirely dissimilar from earlier conceptualizations of a capitalist superpower (Galtung 1973) or a trading state (Rosecrance 1986), which prioritized the economic orientation of powerful actors. Likewise, such an emphasis may resemble NPE's core norm of liberty (Manners 2002, 242), which may be interpreted to include market freedom. However, unlike these previous formulations, MPE includes a prominent role for market *interventions* via economic and social regulation. Such market interventions act as constraints on the capitalist superpower or trading state as well as NPE's market freedom. In addition, the alternative basis for the EU's identity as MPE is explicitly linked to three important characteristics, which are introduced in the next section.

The characteristics of Market Power Europe

The alternative basis for the EU's identity as MPE informs three interrelated and mutually reinforcing characteristics: material existence, institutional features and interest contestation. Focusing on these characteristics advances our understanding of the Union as a power by considering the EU's position in its international environment and identifying the institutions and actors (and relationships among them) that contribute to its power. Likewise, the characteristics provide an analytical framework for theorizing and empirically testing the EU's externalization of its market-related policies and regulatory measures in the multilateral system.

EU as single market

At a base level, the European single market represents the EU's *material existence* and the most salient aspect of its presence in the international system (Allen and Smith 1990). Comparative economic figures reveal the importance of the EU's market as a characteristic of its identity. The EU today exists as the largest advanced industrialized market in the world. According to the Commission, the EU is 'the world's biggest trading bloc and leading destination for foreign direct investment' (2010, 7). This significant comparative economic power allows Van Rompuy to claim that

> Even with only 7 percent of world population we still generate almost 22 percent of the world's wealth. (This is compared to about 21 percent for the US, 11.5 percent for China and 4.7 percent for India.) Together, we are the first commercial power in the world, bigger than the US, China or Japan.
>
> *(Van Rompuy 2010, 5)*

The size of the EU in the global economy is, therefore, a significant factor that studies of the Union as a power should consider seriously. But how can the EU's size influence the externalization of market-related policies and regulatory measures? As a major economic power with a large single market, the EU is capable of externalizing various internal policies, in particular its regulatory standards (Vogel 1995). It exercises this power specifically through the relative size of its market.[4] This power is felt by all other actors in the international system, although it may have less of an effect on other relatively large economic powers.

As Drezner argues, market size is important for two reasons related to the externalization of internal regulations: 1) market size affects the material incentives facing governments when choosing whether to coordinate regulatory standards and 2) market size affects actor perceptions over outcomes. On the issue of material incentives, 'A sufficiently large internal market drastically reduces a government's incentive to switch its standards, creating a set of expectations that encourages other actors to switch their regulatory standards' (2007, 32). While this effect may occur unintentionally, it may also occur intentionally through economic coercion because market powers 'can use the threat of complete or partial market closure to force recalcitrant states into switching their regulatory standards' (2007, 32). Regarding the effect on others' perceptions, market powers 'by dint of their market size can alter the beliefs of other actors over the likelihood of possible outcomes. Their standards act as an attractor, causing other actors to converge to their preferences' (2007, 32–3). Again, this effect may occur intentionally or unintentionally. The EU, therefore, by being a comparatively large market, is able to exercise its power in multilateral settings by affecting material incentives and others' perceptions over possible outcomes.

EU as regulatory institution

In addition to material existence, the conceptualization of MPE takes into account the *institutional features* of the EU. These features determine which official actors contribute to MPE and the rules under which they operate. Reflecting internal institutional developments, the EU has been referred to as a 'regulatory state' that pursues and prioritizes governance through rules and regulations (Majone 1994, 1997). In this capacity, the EU generates a considerable amount of economic and social regulation, which can either liberalize or restrict market activity, and which can also have important external effects.

If the EU is a regulatory state, MPE must take into consideration the policy-making processes and decision-making rules for issuing regulatory measures, which can vary depending on the market-related policies in question. When scrutinizing these processes, MPE must also consider the possible importance of unity/diversity among EU Member States (Fioretos 2010) and the roles played by its different institutions – e.g. European Commission, European Parliament, Council of Ministers, European Court of Justice – in the rule-making process. Likewise, important roles are played by various networks of national regulators and EU-level regulatory agencies (Coen and Thatcher 2008; Eberlein and Newman 2008; Eberlein and Grande 2005). Given this large number of actors, the MPE conceptualization acknowledges that the EU constitutes itself differently at different times. Analyses of MPE should, therefore, consider the ways in which variation across decision-making rules for issuing and enforcing regulatory measures determine which actors contribute, at any given time, to the external dimension of the regulatory state that is the EU.

As a regulatory state, the EU is a generator of standards to which other actors may converge. As MPE, the EU's identity incorporates its various institutional qualities and also depends importantly on its institutional ability to externalize regulatory measures. To understand this institutional ability, it is useful to look at MPE's regulatory capacity. According to Bach and Newman, high levels of regulatory expertise, coherence and sanctioning authority are preferable for externalizing regulatory measures. *Regulatory expertise* is reflected in a 'staff with sufficient training to identify areas of concern and to make policy demands on third countries. Comprehensive budgetary resources, years of experience, and a high level of professional staffing thus all demonstrate regulatory expertise' (2007, 831). *Regulatory coherence* is reflected in the extent to which 'regulatory authority has been delegated to a specific regulatory body that has authority to shape and enforce market rules' (2007, 831). Without such a delegation – which may vary depending on the institutional rules in different policy areas – and when regulatory authority is dispersed, regulators' commitment to monitoring and enforcement is less credible. Under such conditions, the regulators 'cannot clearly articulate the demanded [externalization] strategy', which gives external actors 'little incentive to adjust their domestic rules' (2007, 831–2). *Sanctioning authority* is the statutory authority to impose costs on third parties for non-compliance. Such authority is typically included in implementing legislation and again may vary across policy areas. Examples of sanctioning authority include banning market entry, imposing fines or exacting reputational costs (2007, 832), all of which may be directed at individual non-state actors (e.g. firms) and imply coercion as an important part of externalization.

Understanding the EU as a regulatory state helps to emphasize the importance of internal rules – including the decision-making rules that determine which official actors are involved – as a central characteristic of MPE. Because the EU has relatively high levels of regulatory expertise, coherence and sanctioning authority, it is able to exercise its power in the multilateral system. The mere existence of these three institutional components of regulatory capacity may provide a foundation for unintentional externalization, but when put into action, they clearly bolster MPE's intentional efforts at externalization.

EU as interest contestation

An understanding of the EU as MPE also takes into account the important role played by competing interest groups in the European single market. Because the EU is a regulatory institution that is open to public consultation and influence, it serves as an arena in which various groups compete for regulation that serves their interests (Coen and Richardson 2009). This *interest contestation* adds a third characteristic to the EU's identity and helps to determine the likelihood of MPE exercising power in multilateral settings.

According to the literature on regulatory politics, regulatory outcomes can vary depending on the type of regulation being developed. One basic variation is between economic regulations, 'which govern entry to and competition within particular sectors', and social regulations, 'which are aimed at addressing negative externalities (such as pollution) and information asymmetries (e.g. consumer protection)' (Young 2006, 377). The EU's different types of economic and social regulation distribute costs and benefits differently throughout society and can result in different sets of incentives for different types of interest groups.

The contestation among these different interest groups helps to determine internal regulatory outcomes but also plays a role in MPE's externalization. As with previous work on environmental and trade policy, MPE's strategy for externalizing regulatory standards may be determined by the relative influence of specific interest groups

(Dür and DeBièvre 2007; Falkner 2007; Vogel 1995). Given the externalizing nature of MPE, the role of foreign interest groups must also be incorporated into analyses of interest group contestation. This interest group contestation interacts with the institutional features noted above insofar as the EU regulatory institutions and actors become targets for domestic and foreign interest group lobbying.

How then does interest contestation influence MPE's externalization of market-related policies and regulatory measures? Such contestation matters for MPE because interest groups may push specifically for the externalization, whether coercive or non-coercive, of internal regulation. As external actors observe the internal contestation and anticipate outcomes, the EU's unintentional MPE may increase. When pro-externalization interest groups begin to influence policymaking and regulatory outcomes, their activity bolsters the EU's intentional MPE. The building of internal coalitions is inherently contested as groups compete with different interests in relation to the internal regulatory measure and its externalization. This process of coalition-building is complicated further by the inclusion of foreign interest groups and private actors which may have considerably different interests in relation to the externalization of specific EU economic and social regulatory measures.

When pro-externalization coalitions form and become more influential than anti-externalization coalitions, this interest-based support may drive forward the EU's externalization strategies more so (and more precisely) than its normative identity and helps to account for MPE's ability to exercise power. The contestation of coalition-building also explicitly incorporates private actors into the understanding and analysis of MPE beyond that typically provided by other conceptualizations of the EU as a power.

The combination of these three important and interactive characteristics – relative market size, institutional features and interest group contestation – provides the EU with the basis for its identity as MPE. Just as Manners argues that the EU has a normative basis that 'predisposes it to act in a normative way' (2002, 252), so too this chapter argues that the existence and interaction of these three characteristics predisposes the EU to act as MPE.

The exercise of Market Power Europe

The three characteristics that help to form what the EU is as MPE can operate as independent variables that influence the externalization of market-related policies and regulatory measures in the multilateral system. As these three independent variables increase – growth in market size, expansion of regulatory capacity and pressure from pro-externalization coalitions – it can be hypothesized that so too the dependent variable of EU externalization will increase. However, the precise relationships remain open to further theorizing and empirical testing as external pressures and certain combinations of institutions and actors may actually reduce the likelihood of externalization. Because these independent variables are interactive, empirical testing will also need to consider the extent to which the various actors and institutions can be analytically separated across different cases and different times.[5]

Central to MPE's exercise of power, 'externalization' can be understood and explored in two stages (DeSombre 2000). The first stage of externalization occurs when the institutions and actors of the EU attempt to get other actors to adhere to a level of regulation similar to that in effect in the European single market or to behave in a way that generally satisfies or conforms to the EU's market-related policies and regulatory measures.[6] The *subjects* of externalization, therefore, are market-related policies and regulatory measures normally generated through an internal process of rule-making. Because the process is politically contested, the resulting policies or measures are often compromises that reflect bargains among numerous public and private actors, which may not be consistent with the collective core and minor norms of the EU. Such subjects facilitate reliable and robust analysis because the tools, standards, guidelines and objectives in these policies and measures are typically specified in legal and technical documents, making them and their externalization empirically identifiable and traceable.

The *targets* of externalization typically include various non-EU public and private actors – such as states, international and regional organizations, and non-state actors – all of which operate in multilateral settings. The second stage of externalization requires these non-EU targets actually to adhere to said level of regulation or to behave in said way. The two-stage process, therefore, requires consideration of both attempts to externalize and actual success in doing so, analysis of which is beyond the scope of this chapter and may require considerably different theoretical and methodological approaches.

The exercise of power through externalization can be understood as primarily intentional behaviour. It is important to reiterate that the EU's efforts at externalization are not merely happenstance; as MPE, the EU has the intention to externalize its market-related polices and regulatory measures. While intentionality is a frequent part of externalization, there may also be an unintentional dimension of MPE's externalization. As noted above, the EU may unintentionally externalize its policies and measures simply because the size of its internal market makes its standards attractive to outsiders. A deeper exploration of the unintentional exercise of MPE, while important, is outside the scope of this study and remains for further research. Therefore, while the remainder of this study focuses on intentional behaviour, it should be noted that such an emphasis only underestimates the actual exercise of MPE.

If the EU is externalizing its market-related policies and regulatory measures, MPE must include an understanding of the means and tools through which this power is exercised in the international system. Regarding *means*, different conceptualizations of the EU as a power identify various mechanisms and distinguish them as either persuasive or coercive. While persuasive and coercive means both imply the intentional exercise of power, coercion is not typically considered part of the soft power that is frequently (but not exclusively) emphasized by other conceptualizations. Although this study shares the common assertion that there is a relative absence of physical force in the EU's exercise of power, it argues that by the very nature of what it is – a relatively large market with significant institutional features and competing interest groups – the Union is likely to exercise intentionally its power via persuasive and often coercive means.

Before continuing the discussion of persuasion and coercion, it is worthwhile considering what is meant by the terms. Smith provides a useful distinction: 'Coercion involves threatening or inflicting "punishment" ... persuasion entails cooperating with third countries to try to induce desired internal or external policy changes' (2003, 22). That said, it is difficult to differentiate between coercion and persuasion because individual actions can often include both coercive and persuasive elements. Likewise, a target may feel coerced even when the action is intended to be persuasive. Given these pitfalls and because the MPE conceptualization does not depend upon the persuasion – coercion distinction, this chapter simplifies the two concepts as positive and negative conditionality and focuses on various *tools* of MPE.

According to Smith, positive conditionality 'entails promising benefit(s) to a state if it fulfils the conditions' while negative conditionality 'involves reducing, suspending, or terminating those benefits if the state in question violates the conditions' (2003, 57). The tools of externalization associated with positive conditionality include reaching trade, cooperation and association agreements; reducing tariffs and quotas; granting preferences; providing aid; and extending loans. The tools of externalization associated with negative conditionality include implementing embargoes and boycotts; delaying, suspending and denouncing agreements; increasing tariffs and quotas; withdrawing preferences; reducing and suspending aid; and delaying successive loans (Smith 2003, 60). These tools of positive and negative conditionality, which can be found in various agreements to which the EU is party, both imply intentionality.

Although a useful starting point, the tools of MPE also cover actions beyond conditionality. Such tools may include offering membership through the enlargement process, using incentives and disincentives to push EU standards in multilateral settings, and threatening and actually bringing states to international dispute settlement mechanisms. In addition, positive and negative conditionality represent primarily formal governmental actions that do not tend to include EU tools directed specifically at non-state actors, such as individual firms. Following from the idea of externalization advanced in this chapter, the EU's intentional actions are not directed exclusively at states. Externalization also includes regulatory standards which foreign firms must follow if they wish to operate in the European single market. Failing to abide by these standards may lead to punishment via the implementing regulations of MPE's sanctioning authority. Here arises another difference from other conceptualizations of the EU as a power, which typically do not make explicit the analysis of EU tools that are based largely in internal regulations and directed at non-state actors. The EU as MPE, therefore, exercises its power of externalization through various tools – such as the use of positive and negative conditionality, international legal instruments and internal regulatory measures – in its relations with both states and non-state actors.

As will be shown in the next section, this externalization frequently takes place in multilateral settings.

The evidence of Market Power Europe

The evidence supporting the conceptualization of MPE is impressive. Given this abundance of data in multilateral and bilateral settings, this study cannot undertake comprehensive and systematic empirical testing of the relationships introduced above. Rather, this chapter focuses on the exercise of power in multilateral settings and employs two ways in which to organize evidence of the EU's efforts to externalize market-related policies and regulatory measures. First, the chapter investigates *what the EU says* – the extent to which the EU itself articulates strategies for acting as MPE. By looking at the strategies presented in official documents, the analysis is most likely to reveal evidence of intentionality and, again, underestimate any unintentional impact of MPE. Second, the chapter investigates *what the EU does* by considering initial evidence from official documents and briefly exploring the EU's exercise of MPE in trade policy in multilateral settings.

What the EU says – strategies for MPE

Scrutinizing EU documents and communications is instructive because they are the result of public consultation, in which not only the official actors of the EU have input, but also various interest groups submit comments. While not legally binding rules, the documents investigated herein are indicative of what the EU says about the exercise of its power because they detail the broad strategies to be pursued. How the EU implements these strategies (what it does) is a separate issue.

In 2001 and 2006, the EU issued strategies that began to reflect an awareness of MPE. The 2001 contribution to establishing the EU's externalization agenda came in the form of a working group report on *Strengthening Europe's Contributions to World Governance* that 'analyses governance beyond the EU's borders with an emphasis primarily on First Pillar themes' (Commission 2001, 3). This report presented the EU as an active advocate of global governance and international policy convergence in the market-related areas associated with MPE. In 2006, the Commission released its communication on *Global Europe: Competing in the World*, which focused heavily on the EU's external trade agenda, especially in relation to the EU's market-related policies. The document contains a section on 'opening markets abroad', which identifies priorities such as non-tariff barriers, access to resources and new areas of growth. Conforming to the logic of MPE, the document asserts that 'We must play a leading role in sharing best practice and developing global rules and standards' (Commission 2006, 7). The first priority laid out in the external action agenda concerns the multilateral World Trade Organization, where the EU argues 'The world needs a strong multilateral trading system. It is the most effective means of expanding and managing trade for the benefit of all and provides a unique framework for dispute settlement' (Commission 2006: 8).

In 2007, the EU more clearly indicated its role as MPE with the release of its Single Market Review (SMR). In the review, the EU argues that it is 'being looked upon as the global standard-setter' (Commission 2007a, 7). The EU's strategy was based upon three objectives, which reflect the general logic of MPE and point to the need to pursue externalization of economic and social regulation: 1) expanding the competitive space for European firms, 2) expanding the regulatory space of the single market, and 3) actively ensuring that European citizens enjoy better safety, health and environmental standards, lower prices, and greater choice.

The SMR was accompanied by a Commission Staff Working Document, which provides further evidence of the EU's capacity and intentional strategy to act as MPE. Regarding the EU's market size, the document notes that 'the rapid expansion of the EU to 27 Member States with a total of almost half a billion consumers has turned Europe into the world's biggest import market' (Commission 2007b, 6). This large import market clearly supports the conceptualization of an MPE that is capable of exercising power in multilateral settings. The document clarifies ways in which its size influences other actors:

> for many companies around the world, complying with EU rules has become both a prerequisite and an asset to access key markets. Many global companies that produce goods for the EU market will also apply the EU's standards elsewhere as they can assume that in many instances their products will then be accepted more easily in view of the resulting high quality.
>
> *(Commission 2007b, 6)*

While an apparently unintentional side-effect of the large market, the EU can use this incentive as an important intentional component of its externalization strategy.

Regarding the EU's regulatory coherence and sanctioning authority, the European single market has led to 'the creation of a modern and innovative regulatory and supervisory framework in many areas' (Commission 2007b, 5). Regarding regulatory expertise, the document asserts that the EU 'has gathered much experience on how to best cope with differing regulations and draw on the best features of different regulatory traditions: this gives European regulators an edge when dealing with international standards' (2007b, 6). Finally, regarding interest contestation, the SMR and the accompanying working document frequently emphasize the need for the European single market to be responsive to and create opportunities for citizens and to empower consumers and small- and medium-sized enterprises. Thus, citizens, consumers and firms all contest their respective interests within this 'responsive' European single market process.

The SMR also identifies a number of ways forward, which reflect its objectives as MPE. For example, the working document highlights the need to 'expand the regulatory space' by 'promoting, globally and with like-minded countries, supervisory and regulatory convergence and equivalence, in line with EU rules' (Commission 2007b, 9). Such efforts to expand the regulatory space help to increase the EU's regulatory expertise and clearly reveal the EU's desire to externalize its regulatory measures. Again, MPE can pursue these efforts in various multilateral settings that deal with standard setting and regulatory issues.

The EU also strongly asserts its desire to continue playing a 'leading role' in international rule-making bodies

> such as in World Intellectual Property Organisation, Basel Committee, International Labour Organisation (ILO) or multilateral environment agreements ... or through private international standard setters like the IASB. This means pushing for the adoption of high quality standards and putting these in place as early movers to provide a competitive edge (such as on IFRS international accounting standards and Basel II implementation).
>
> *(Commission 2007b: 11)*

Such instrumental efforts to push standards as an early mover in order to obtain a competitive edge support the claim that MPE intentionally strives to externalize its regulatory measures.

In 2010, the Commission issued its next significant strategy for the exercise of MPE over the next decade: *Europe 2020*. Demonstrating ambitious intentionality, the strategy argues that 'the EU must assert itself more effectively on the world stage, playing a leading role in shaping the future global economic order through the G20, and pursuing the European interest through the active deployment of all the tools at our disposal' (Commission 2010, 21). The EU also notes the importance of exercising its power both multilaterally and bilaterally: 'Acting within the WTO and bilaterally in order to secure better market access for EU business ... and a level playing field vis-à-vis our external competitors should be a key goal' (2010, 21).

In another section, *Europe 2020* notes the integral role of various interest groups:

> The impact of these challenges will differ from sector to sector, some sectors might have to 'reinvent' themselves but for others these challenges will present new business opportunities. The Commission will work closely with stakeholders in different sectors (business, trade unions, academics, NGOs, consumer organisations).
>
> *(Commission 2010, 15)*

The EU clearly intends to solicit input from a wide variety of groups interested in the implementation of its *Europe 2020* strategy. The extent to which pro-externalization coalitions emerge among these various interests will help to determine the exercise of MPE.

These official documents – especially the SMR and *Europe 2020* – and the externalization strategies therein provide clear evidence of an EU ambition to be MPE. While these externalization strategies can be exercised in bilateral settings, the documents clearly show the EU's desire to undertake such efforts in multilateral settings. In addition to indicating what the EU says as MPE, the documents also demonstrate the important role of all three characteristics that comprise what the EU is as a power.

What the EU does – initial evidence

While the above documents lay out broad strategies for the EU to act as MPE, initial evidence reveals some success at externalizing both economic and social agendas. This evidence, discussed to varying degrees in the official documents, helps to show what the EU does as MPE. For example, the 2007 SMR identifies a number of cases in which the EU has acted as an international standard-setting MPE, including product safety, food safety, environmental protection, public procurement, financial regulation and accounting. According to the Commission, EU rules in carbon emissions trading, aviation safety and chemicals are being 'adopted across the world', and EU competition policy has been used to challenge 'cartels, anti-competitive mergers and abuses of a dominant position affecting European consumers and businesses, regardless of the nationality of the companies concerned' (Commission 2007a, 7). All of these policy efforts can be undertaken in multilateral settings.

In the areas of food safety and tobacco control, EU policies have often been adopted in the work of the Codex Alimentarius, and 'EU single market legislation on tobacco products and cross-border advertising has been the key reference for the World Health Organization's Framework Convention on Tobacco Control' (Commission 2007b: 6). On the regulation of maritime safety, the EU's 'early move towards implementation of double-hull requirements for tankers led to their adoption by the International Maritime Organisation (IMO), with the IMO contracting parties agreeing to follow the calendar adopted by the EU' (Commission 2007b: 7). With regard to financial services, the EU 'switched to International Financial Reporting Standards (IFRS) in financial reporting in 2005. Since then more than 100 jurisdictions around the world have decided to require or allow them. The US, too, has taken significant steps in this direction' (Commission 2007b: 7). The adoption of the GSM standard for mobile telephony is cited as 'one of the best examples of the export of European regulatory approaches, European standards and European technology' (Commission 2007b, 6).

While a great number of other cases and policy areas provide evidence of MPE, a brief look at trade policy illustrates how the EU intentionally attempts to externalize its regulatory measures and operates as MPE. In accordance with the characteristics of MPE's identity, the relative size of the single market provides the EU with considerable leverage to externalize its internal regulatory measures through trade. Internal regulation is the result of interactions among the institutional rules and official actors that give the EU regulatory capacity as well as contestation among competing interest groups. These various actors also help to determine whether and which internal regulatory measures the EU will attempt to externalize through trade.

The externalization of internal regulatory measures can take place if, for example, the EU attempts to include standards in bilateral and multilateral trade agreements (i.e. positive conditionality). Even if the EU employs the tools of positive conditionality with the intent of persuading changes in behaviour, the third parties in question may feel they have been coerced into changing their behaviour because they have no alternative: they must agree to undesirable terms in trade agreements because they need access to the large European single market; and they must abide by the EU's relevant internal regulatory measures or they will be subject to sanctioning under the associated implementing legislation.

Foreign regulation can also create non-tariff barriers to multilateral trade, which the EU is able to identify as a result of its regulatory expertise and information from official and non-state actors via, for example, the Trade Barriers Regulation. Depending on the pressure exerted by these actors, the EU may bring an offending foreign non-tariff barrier before the World Trade Organization's (WTO) Dispute Settlement Mechanism (i.e. negative conditionality). By doing so, the EU undertakes an intentional effort at externalization – an attempt to get the target WTO member(s) to comply with international trade rules in a way that generally satisfies or conforms to the EU's market-related policies and regulatory measures. Bringing a foreign regulatory measure or any perceived violation of international trade rules to the WTO's Dispute Settlement Mechanism is a clear instance of the EU using coercion to adjust the behaviour of other actors in the multilateral trade regime.

While evidence of MPE abounds in trade policy, further analyses should include all of the EU's market-related policies and regulatory measures, as long as they include tools and elements – whether intentional or unintentional, positive or negative – of externalization. The purview of MPE analyses is, therefore, extensive and may cover all areas related to market regulation, including but not limited to investigations of agricultural policy, competition policy, consumer policy, development policy, energy policy, enlargement policy, environment policy, fisheries policy, migration policy, monetary and financial policy, labour and social policy, neighbourhood policy, and trade policy. The extent to which the EU attempts and is successful at externalizing all these policies and associated regulatory measures likely depends on the size of the EU's market, its institutional features and the contestation of interest groups.

Conclusions

This chapter asserts that empirical developments and theoretical advances have brought us to the point where we should reconsider what the EU is and conceptualize it as MPE, a powerful actor that actively engages in multilateral settings through the externalization of its economic and social market-related policies and regulatory measures. While MPE is not limited to working at the multilateral level, the evidence above shows that multilateral settings are important venues for the EU's externalization of market-related policies and regulations. Such a reconsideration does not depend upon an analytical preconception that the EU is a particular, different or even unique actor in the multilateral system.

Empirically, the EU has evolved from its origins as a market integration experiment into the world's foremost economic bloc. Especially since the SEA, the EU itself has increasingly developed strategies (what it says) and undertaken efforts (what it does) to exercise MPE through the externalization of its economic and social agendas. To explore further the propositions of MPE, comprehensive and systematic empirical testing of the EU's intentional and unintentional attempts and success at externalization is needed.

As a conceptualization, MPE is not intended to serve as a full-blown explanatory theory. Rather it offers an understanding of the EU that provides essential assumptions for guiding research on the Union as a power. By introducing insights from the comparative and international political economy literature to the EU as a power debates, the chapter elaborates fundamental characteristics of the EU's identity. The ways in which these characteristics influence MPE deserve further theorizing and empirical work on the expected relationships among them and the likelihood of externalization.

Because the EU is an international actor with competing internal agendas, MPE does not begin with an attempt to elaborate or explain the sum of the EU's official external relations. Rather, MPE is intentionally reductionist and refocuses the debate over the EU as a power squarely on the areas in which the EU happens to be often and readily recognized by other actors: market-related policies and regulatory measures. By focusing on MPE, we may not get an immediate sense of the EU's ability to use physical force via its intergovernmental security and defence policy. However, we do get a more realistic sense of the Union as a power and the ways in which it most actively and consequentially influences today's multilateral system.

As an analytical starting point, MPE assumes that a reconsideration of identity is important when conceptualizing the EU as a power. As with NPE, the EU's identity as MPE is what it is, instead of what it does or says. However, MPE differs from NPE by arguing that the EU's identity is not a particular set of collective norms but rather a comparatively large regulated market with institutional features and interest group contestation. These three primary and explicit characteristics are central to the analysis of the EU as a power because they condition the choices of when, where and how to exercise MPE. They also predispose the EU to act as MPE and help to explain why the EU often exercises power through coercion.

Ultimately, the best way to evaluate NPE versus MPE may be to determine whether the EU is more likely to influence the behaviour of others through the projection of its core and minor norms or the externalization of its market-related policies and regulatory measures. However, the point of MPE is not to inspire analytical intolerance of norms-based and other approaches, but rather to encourage new avenues of research into the EU as a power and the possible compatibility of other conceptualizations with market power insights. For example, in which ways do normative justifications interact with material incentives? Under what conditions might norms contribute to the politically contested formulation of EU regulatory measures and their externalization? To what extent does market power interact with the ability to use physical force? With MPE as a starting point for conceptualizing what the EU is, says and does, we can begin answering these questions while rebuilding our understanding of the EU as a power and concentrating research on the implications of market power for the potential use of force (military power), the projection of norms (normative power) and the scope for effective multilateralism.

Notes

1   For useful comments, the author is grateful to the members of the MERCURY network (http://www.europa.ed.ac.uk/global_europa/external_relations/mercury) – in particular John Armstrong, Mark Aspinwall, David Camroux, Zhimin Chen, Geoffrey Edwards, Christopher Hill, Nadia Klein, John Peterson, Maxi Schoeman, Julie Smith, Nathalie Tocci, Tomas Weiss and Wolfgang Wessels – as well as Ferdie De Ville, David Howarth, Bart Kerremans, Ian Manners, Abraham Newman, Kalypso Nicolaïdis, Ben Rosamond, Simon Schunz, Michael Smith, Helen Wallace and Alasdair Young. The author is also particularly grateful to Caroline Bouchard for editorial guidance on this chapter. This chapter is a revised version of 'Market Power Europe', *Journal of European Public Policy* (19) 5: 682–99 (2012).
2   Among others, the EU has also been labelled an ethical power (Aggestam 2008), fragmented power (Sapir 2007), realist power (Zimmermann 2007), conflicted trade power (Meunier and Nicolaïdis 2006) and transformative power (Leonard 2005).
3   This is not the same as equating normative power with 'force for good', a common problem that Manners seeks to avoid (2011, 243).
4   For more on the importance of and issues related to market/economic power, see Newman and Posner (2011).
5   For recent examples of research that provide evidence and broadly conform with the conceptualization of MPE, see the *Journal of European Public Policy* special issue edited by Jacoby and Meunier (2010) and the *Review of International Political Economy* special issue edited by Farrell and Newman (2010).
6   For a similar definition, see DeSombre (2000, 7).

References

Aggestam, L. (2008) 'Introduction: Ethical Power Europe', *International Affairs* 84(1): 1–11.
Allen, D. and Smith, M. (1990) 'Western Europe's Presence in the Contemporary International Arena', *Review of International Studies* 16(1): 19–37.
Bach, D. and Newman, L. (2007) 'The European Regulatory State and Global Public Policy: Micro-institutions, Macro-influence', *Journal of European Public Policy* 14(6): 827–46.
Coen, D. and Richardson, J. (eds) (2009) *Lobbying the European Union*, Oxford: Oxford University Press.
Coen, D. and Thatcher, M. (2008) 'Network Governance and Multi-level Delegation: European Networks of Regulatory Agencies', *Journal of Public Policy* 28(1): 49–71.
Commission (2001) *Strengthening Europe's Contribution to World Governance*, Report of Working Group 5 on White Paper on Governance, May.

Commission (2006) *Global Europe: Competing in the World, A Contribution to the EU's Growth and Jobs Strategy*, COM(2006) 567 final, 4 October.

Commission (2007a) *A Single Market for 21st Century Europe*, COM(2007) 724 final, 20 November.

Commission (2007b) *The External Dimension of the Single Market Review*, Commission Staff Working Document, SEC(2007) 1519, 20 November.

Commission (2010) *Europe 2020: A European Strategy for Smart, Sustainable and Inclusive Growth*, COM (2010) 2020, 3 March.

DeSombre, E. (2000) *Domestic Sources of International Environmental Policy*, Cambridge, MA: MIT Press.

Drezner, D. (2007) *All Politics is Global: Explaining International Regulatory Regimes*, Princeton: Princeton University Press.

Duchêne, F. (1972) 'Europe's Role in World Peace', in R. Mayne (ed.), *Europe Tomorrow*, London: Fontana, pp. 32–47.

Dür, A. and DeBièvre, D. (2007) 'The Question of Interest Group Influence', *Journal of Public Policy* 27(1): 1–12.

Eberlein, B. and Grande, E. (2005) 'Beyond Delegation: Transnational Regulatory Regimes and the EU Regulatory State', *Journal of European Public Policy* 12(1): 89–112.

Eberlein, B. and Newman, A. (2008) 'Escaping the International Governance Dilemma? Incorporated Transgovernmental Networks in the European Union', *Governance* 21(1): 25–52.

Falkner, R. (2007) 'The Political Economy of "Normative Power" Europe', *Journal of European Public Policy* 14(4): 507–26.

Farrell, H. and Newman, A. (2010) 'Market Regulation', *Review of International Political Economy* 17(4).

Fioretos, O. (2010) 'Europe and the New Global Economic Order: Internal Diversity as Liability and Asset in Managing Globalization', *Journal of European Public Policy* 17(3): 383–99.

Galtung, J. (1973) *The European Community: A Superpower in the Making*, London: Allen & Unwin.

Jacoby, W. and Meunier, S. (2010) 'Europe and the Management of Globalization', *Journal of European Public Policy* 17(3).

Leonard, M. (2005) 'Ascent of Europe', *Prospect* 108: 34–7.

Majone, G. (1994) 'The Rise of the Regulatory State in Europe', *West European Politics* 17(3): 77–101.

Majone, G. (1997) 'From the Positive to the Regulatory State', *Journal of Public Policy* 17(2): 139–67.

Manners, I. (2002) 'Normative Power Europe: A Contradiction in Terms?', *Journal of Common Market Studies* 40(2): 235–58.

Manners, I. (2006) 'Normative Power Europe Reconsidered: Beyond the Crossroads', *Journal of European Public Policy* 13(2): 182–99.

Manners, I. (2009) 'The Social Dimension of EU Trade Policies: Reflections from a Normative Power Perspective', *European Foreign Affairs Review* 14(5): 785–802.

Manners, I. (2011) 'The European Union's Normative Power', in R. Whitman (ed.), *Normative Power Europe: Empirical and Theoretical Perspectives*, Basingstoke: Palgrave, pp. 226–77.

Meunier, S. and Nicolaïdis, K. (2006) 'The European Union as a Conflicted Trade Power', *Journal of European Public Policy* 13(6): 906–25.

Newman, A. and Posner, E. (2011) 'International Interdependence and Regulatory Power: Authority, Mobility, and Markets', *European Journal of International Relations* 17(4).

Orbie, J. (ed.) (2008) *Europe's Global Role*, Farnham: Ashgate.

Rosecrance, R. (1986) *The Rise of the Trading State*, New York, NY: Basic Books.

Sapir, A. (ed.) (2007) *Fragmented Power*, Brussels: Bruegel.

Smith, K. (2003) *European Union Foreign Policy in a Changing World*, Cambridge: Polity Press.

Van Rompuy, H. (2010) 'The Challenges for Europe in a Changing World', EU Diplomacy Papers 3/2010, Bruges: College of Europe.

Vogel, D. (1995) *Trading Up*, Cambridge, MA: Harvard University Press.

Young, A. (2006) 'The Politics of Regulation and the Internal Market', in K. E. Jorgensen, M. A. Pollack, and B. Rosamond (eds), *Handbook of European Union Politics*, London: Sage, pp. 373–94.

Zimmermann, H. (2007) 'Realist Power Europe?', *Journal of Common Market Studies* 45(4): 813–32.

PART III

Multilateralism in practice: Key regions and partners

7

THE ENERGY AND MIGRATION DIMENSIONS OF THE EU'S COOPERATION WITH THE MEDITERRANEAN

Nur Abdelkhaliq and Silvia Colombo[1]

The Mediterranean represents the southern backyard of the European Union (EU). As such, it poses challenges and opportunities in a variety of domains. The recent turmoil that has affected several southern Mediterranean countries confirms the salience of the region for the EU. It has also exposed some of the difficulties in pursuing EU–Mediterranean relations that have accumulated over the decades due to structural and substantial biases; for instance, the privileged focus on bilateral cooperation at the expense of multilateral endeavours, despite the constant effort to establish a multilateral Mediterranean policy. While there has been an abundance of analyses of EU–Mediterranean relations in general, with some focused on recent developments,[2] assessing them in the framework of a discussion of the EU's pursuit of effective multilateralism (or the lack thereof) represents a new and original endeavour.

In this chapter, we explore different patterns of multilateral EU–Mediterranean cooperation, according to the definition adopted in the MERCURY Project: that is, 'three or more actors engaging in voluntary and (essentially) institutionalised international cooperation governed by norms and principles, with rules that apply (by and large) equally to all states' (see Chapter 2). We look specifically at two policy areas: energy and migration cooperation. By reviewing and analysing the content and directions of the actions pursued by key European actors (EU institutions and member states) on specific issues, we address the question of whether the EU, in relation to a range of relevant regional and international actors, works multilaterally.[3] These two policy sectors have been chosen as they represent important areas of cooperation between the EU and the southern Mediterranean region, most notably under the European Neighbourhood Policy (ENP) and Union for the Mediterranean (UfM).

The chapter is structured as follows: the first section conceptualizes multilateralism with reference to EU–Mediterranean relations. The second and third sections delve into EU-Mediterranean energy and migration cooperation respectively, examining the Union's engagement with the aforementioned actors and focusing on the assumptions, values and interests that guide the EU's actions and objectives in these policy domains. The aim is to assess existing forms of EU multilateral cooperation and their effectiveness in the Mediterranean. The picture that emerges is one in which these (potential) forms of multilateralism are often not institutionalized and the room for effective multilateralism is rather limited.

Conceptualizing multilateralism in EU-Mediterranean relations

Europe's policies in the Mediterranean in both the energy and migration domains can be assessed by reviewing the internal vs. external dimension of multilateralism. The former underscores the extent to which the EU's Mediterranean policies regarding energy and migration cooperation are characterized by initiatives mainly at the member state (i.e. bilateral) or EU (i.e. multilateral) level. The latter considers room for cooperation and active engagement between the EU and non-EU governmental and non-governmental actors in the pursuit of policy objectives in the region.

With reference to the level of EU and member states' actions, it is possible to analyse two separate but interrelated policy paths: the internal policy path and the external one. The former relates to the EU's internal legal and institutional mechanisms aimed at creating the conditions for intra-EU action on energy and migration issues. The latter encompasses the strategies that the Union and the member states apply in external energy and migration policies when dealing with the Mediterranean. As far as the external policy path is concerned, the Mediterranean is not the predominant geographical priority of the EU's energy endeavours. By contrast, the Mediterranean is a priority high in the EU's migration agenda due to its status as a region of origin and transit of migrants en route to Europe. Although we mainly assess these policies in relation to the external context, that is, the Mediterranean, the analysis also illuminates the extent to which the internal and external policy paths are interconnected. It is not possible to fully gauge the potential of the external dimension without addressing the shortcomings of the internal one.

By combining these two variables, we build a matrix summarizing the possible directions and outcomes of EU multilateral cooperation (see Table 7.1). Our objective is to use the matrix as a guide for assessing the extent to which the EU acts multilaterally in its relations with the Mediterranean region when dealing with energy and migration matters. Some concluding remarks will be formulated at the end of the chapter about the effectiveness of the EU's multilateral action.

In the vertical columns we have two different sets of actors: in the first, we find EU institutions, in particular the Commission, and the member states; in the second, we have the Union in relation to non-EU governmental and non-governmental actors. The columns conceptualize the distinction between internal and external multilateralism mentioned above. While in the first column we will mainly focus on the internal

TABLE 7.1 The dimensions of effective EU multilateralism in the Mediterranean: Squaring internal–external circles

Actors / Levels	EU Institutions and Member States	EU and non-EU governmental and non-governmental actors
Internal EU policies		
EU policies in the Mediterranean		

dynamics at the EU level between member states and the Union's institutions, in the second column we look at the EU as a unitary actor, thus stressing the degree of cooperation and engagement with other non-EU actors such as third countries, international organizations, civil society groups and private sector companies.

In the horizontal rows we have two different types of EU cooperation depending on the context in which it is pursued. The upper row deals with the articulation of internal EU policy, while the lower one with external policy in the Mediterranean. For example, in the upper row attention will be devoted to the policies concerning the EU's internal energy market, on the one hand, and the debate on internal migration policies on the other. In the lower row the focus will rest on the EU's external energy and migration policies with specific reference to the Mediterranean. The analysis will underscore the extent to which EU internal and external policies are closely connected, in both the energy and migration policy arenas, in particular given the geographical proximity of the Mediterranean region, which means that external dynamics reverberate on the internal arena.

Energy policy: limited multilateralism beyond cooperation

The energy challenge is one of the greatest tests facing Europe in the twenty-first century. Not only does the EU have to integrate its internal energy market, but almost all member states are strongly dependent on energy imports. This is why the EU and its member states pay increasing attention to securing safe, competitive and sustainable energy. Given these constraints and the need for energy diversification, the southern Mediterranean becomes a strategic environment in which the EU can test its external energy policy to try to fulfil its energy needs.

When it comes to the EU's energy policy in the southern Mediterranean, to what extent can such a policy be defined as multilateral and as effective? By delving into a mosaic of issues, ranging from the diversification of sources, respect for environmental protection guidelines and the foreign policy dimension of energy security,[4] we will argue that the EU is capable of working multilaterally internally, achieving a certain degree of coordination among its member states. By contrast, the external dimension of effective multilateralism in the EU's energy policy in the Mediterranean is questionable. The argument is summarized in Table 7.2.

Towards the creation of the EU internal energy market: a case of convergence

Multilateral energy cooperation and bargaining between member states and EU institutions at the internal level is a complex process aimed at defining the rules and principles to ensure a fully functioning, interconnected and integrated internal energy market. This stems from two basic concerns regarding, on the one hand, the improvement and harmonization of energy regulations and, on the other, the need to develop interconnected infrastructures. Energy integration within the EU would help counter a number of problems, such as the difficulties faced by new entrants into the European energy space, the existence of concentrated and vertically integrated energy markets, and the concentration of market power in the hands of a limited number of players. All these factors account for the vulnerability and the non-competitiveness of Europe in terms of energy availability.

In the attempt to address these shortcomings, EU heads of state and government – with no input from the European Commission – have devised a common strategy to strengthen the EU's internal energy market. This strategy involves the linkage of national transmission grids by building a series of interconnections among and between states and their national electricity grids (European Commission 2010b). The driving principle guiding this internal cooperation is the idea that the lack of appropriate connections could jeopardize energy security and that no EU member state should remain isolated from the European gas and electricity networks after 2015. Since this is a fundamental preoccupation of all member states, each having a more or less pronounced dependency on external energy sources, it is easy to understand why this policy goal has been the object of converging interests and coordinated actions by the member states. This convergence has empowered the Commission to devise an appropriate strategy to reach this objective.

In practical terms, the first EU Summit on Energy, held on 4 February 2011, set the target date of 2014 for completing the internal energy market (PCE 026/11). The EU Commission has identified 42 infrastructure projects that are eligible

TABLE 7.2 Cooperation patterns on energy policy

Actors Levels	EU Institutions and Member States	EU and non-EU governmental and non-governmental actors
Internal EU Policies	Convergence	Compliance
EU Policies in the Mediterranean	Bilateralism	Limited Cooperation

for financing with a view to connecting electricity and gas networks throughout Europe. According to the Commission's proposal, the main objective of creating an internal energy market should be accomplished through a two-step effort: first, regional energy markets within the EU shall be established with sufficient inter-connection and possibly similar relations with certain energy suppliers, for example with the Mediterranean region; second, these groupings will then be connected with one another to complete the internal energy market.

All in all, while respecting national competences and procedures, the Commission is pushing member states to operationalize the principle of solidarity. This means that common goals, such as a unified and functioning internal energy market, has to be achieved on the basis of the principle of effort-sharing and common but dif-ferentiated responsibilities (Baumann and Simmerl 2011: 18).

The EU Mediterranean energy policy: the triumph of bilateralism

The EU Mediterranean energy policy aims at addressing the challenges of energy diversification, import dependency and supply security, which were named as global challenges in the European Security Strategy (ESS) of 2003. The Commission and the Council together started to speak of the need to develop a Common External Energy Policy (CEEP) and to integrate energy relations into the EU's foreign policy. In the document outlining the *Partnership for Democracy and Shared Prosperity with the Southern Mediterranean*, launched in March 2011, the EU stressed the strategic importance of the Mediterranean region for its security of gas and oil supplies, but also, more broadly, in terms of energy transit from the region and beyond. It empha-sized the potential for building an EU-Mediterranean partnership in the production and management of renewables, in particular solar and wind energy, and featuring a joined-up approach to ensuring energy security. It declared that:

> it is desirable to open a credible perspective for the integration of the Southern Mediterranean in the EU internal energy market based on a dif-ferentiated and gradual approach. In the mid to long term, this would mean establishing a form of 'EU-Southern Mediterranean Energy Community' starting with the Maghreb countries and possibly expanding progressively to the Mashreq.
>
> *(European Commission 2011b)*

In reality, however, the EU's external energy policy, in particular with regard to the Mediterranean, is characterized by the lack of convergence among the mem-ber states, which leads to the development of strictly bilateral relations with the Mediterranean partners or, more broadly, with energy-rich countries.

Despite shared challenges and strategic objectives, different factors shape the member states' foreign energy policies, making it difficult for them to converge on substantive goals. These energy policies are linked to considerations related to national access to resources, nationally developed facilities, integration into specific systems and connections, and differing or competing national decisions regarding power generation. They are also partly the result of different historic trajectories stemming from national specificities, including domestic resources, geographical location, domestic demand and public opinion. Historically established energy relations with distinctive producing regions or countries narrow the present and future options for external energy policy and lead to conflicting preferences (Baumann and Simmerl 2011: 13).

To take one significant example, it is not surprising that a country like Italy has developed strong relations with energy supplying partners such as Algeria and Libya. A critical factor is the role played by ENI – the leading Italian national energy corporation – in these countries. Years of state intervention and a longstanding presence in these countries – in Libya ENI has been operating since 1959 – have led Italy to protect the interests of its national champion as a means to ensure its energy security, to enhance its negotiating power *vis-à-vis* its partners, and to develop strong bilateral relations. *Mutatis mutandis*, this pattern of action holds true for all EU member states, which may gravitate towards other supplying regions or countries.

According to Baumann and Simmerl (2011: 14–15), it is possible to identify roughly four geographic energy regions within the EU, all of which are constituted by bilateral arrangements between supplying and receiving countries. While the existence of these 'energy regions' could become the bedrock for the integration of the EU's energy policy at the external level, for the time being, member states' efforts to defend their sovereignty and the prevalence of bilateral forums inhibit the creation of the CEEP. Attempts by the Commission to improve the consistency and coherence of the EU's external actions in the field of energy are regularly dampened by the Council due to a lack of consensus, 'while the member states are only able to agree upon very general principles – for example diversification of transit routes and resources – which are just a weak frame of reference for joint action' (Baumann and Simmerl 2011: 3). Finally, it is still unclear who – the Commission, the High Representative for Foreign Affairs and Security Policy or some 'Mr./Mrs. Energy' – should be in charge of representing the EU on energy questions (Ibid.).

Bilateralism in the EU Mediterranean energy policy also has another meaning, which is linked to the 'hub and spoke' approach pursued by the EU in the framework of the European Neighbourhood Policy (ENP). A complementary effort in the development of the CEEP is to reach out to non-member states in a number of regions with which the EU as a whole is interested in building a solid energy relationship. The southern Mediterranean region does not escape from the EU's reach in this respect. The Union is trying to develop beneficial energy partnerships covering a wide range of issues, ranging from energy legislation and regulatory approaches – thereby facilitating foreign investments – to energy security and efficiency.

In this respect, energy cooperation takes place within the context of broader multi-sectoral bilateral agreements, such as the ENP Action Plans with specific partner countries. Both the EU-Morocco and the EU–Egypt Action Plans, dating back to 2005 and 2007 respectively, outline the objectives of cooperation in the field of energy, which include the security of supply, competitiveness and environmental protection.[5] Specific mention is also made in both documents to the need to implement the Memorandum of Understanding (Rome, 2 December 2003) on the gradual integration of electricity markets in the Maghreb countries into the EU's internal electricity market. The EU is, in fact, aware of the necessity for the countries of the Maghreb to pursue regional cooperation and integration, particularly in a fundamental sector such as energy. In this light, while formally remaining bilateral tools, some of the provisions included in the ENP Action Plans contemplate goals to be achieved at the multilateral level. These, however, are for the time being out of reach.

The cases of Algeria and Libya, the two most important energy producers in the region, are distinctive. While these two countries have not yet signed an Action Plan with the EU, they are part of a cooperation programme with the EU Commission under the European Neighbourhood Policy Instrument (ENPI) that refers to their enormous energy potential and crucial contribution to European energy security.[6] Partnering with these two countries, despite difficulties in policy areas such as migration and trade, is a priority for Europe.

A partial deviation from this bilateral trend in the EU's energy relations with the Mediterranean is represented by the Union for the Mediterranean (UfM). Although this form of inter-governmental cooperation (launched in 2008) is, in principle, a mechanism for multilateral cooperation, in practice it has not achieved this goal due to numerous shortcomings. The development of renewable energy, especially solar and wind, is one of the six projects of the UfM. The Mediterranean Solar Plan, not to be mistaken with the Desertec Project launched by a consortium of German and international companies, aims at exploiting the huge solar, and in some cases, wind potential of the Mediterranean Partner Countries (MPC). The development of renewable energy in the MPCs could, according to the authorities in these countries, have significant socio-economic potential in terms of job creation and positive spill-over effects.[7] However, as far as concrete implementation is concerned, the Plan is lagging behind. So far discussions have focused on the development of a Master Plan, which should be submitted by mid-2013 and be made up of five main building blocks: policy and regulatory frameworks, funding and support schemes, physical infrastructures, renewable energy as an industrial policy tool, and know-how transfer and capacity development. Another substantial difficulty concerns the need to mobilize funds for this project. In conclusion, the picture of EU-Mediterranean cooperation on energy issues appears to be rather mixed with a strong prevalence of bilateral initiatives hampering the potential for multilateral cooperation.

A compliant EU policy in terms of environment protection

The EU does not act in a vacuum as far as the articulation of its energy policy is concerned. EU energy policy is permeated by values and objectives that are (partly) developed in compliance with the provisions of other supranational bodies. We refer here to the area of international environment governance that has produced a number of regulations and standards that have percolated in various EU declarations and commitments on the sustainable use of energy.

The emphasis on EU energy sustainability cannot be understood without taking into account the global environment and concerns about climate change. A number of documents by EU institutions outline a clear package of objectives that all member states have 'firmly and independently' agreed on (European Commission 2006d, 2007b). This is the field in which the construction of a comprehensive EU energy policy has undergone the most significant development in the past five years. The EU Commission has in fact been able to drive member states towards agreeing on targets that go beyond the lowest common denominator, thus making the EU a global leader in environmental protection.

The ambitious energy and climate-change objectives for 2020 are the following:

- reduce greenhouse gas emissions by 20 per cent;
- increase the share of renewable energy to 20 per cent – including a minimum of 10 per cent for biofuels subject to availability and second generation technology (Rosner 2009: 163);
- make a 20 per cent improvement in energy efficiency, which requires determined action to tap into the considerable potential for higher energy savings of buildings, transport and production.

These objectives have been incorporated and made even more explicit in the 'Europe 2020 Strategy for smart, sustainable and inclusive growth' as adopted by the European Council in June 2010.[8] These objectives are in line with those set by other non-governmental organizations in which EU member states participate. For example, the Intergovernmental Panel on Climate Change (IPCC) and the United Nations Framework Convention on Climate Change (UNFCCC) have set similar objectives.[9] All in all, the EU has developed internal multilateral guidelines and standards that are also the result of multilateral action in a wider arena made up of governmental and non-governmental supranational institutions. What remains to be assessed is the actual enforcement of these guidelines.

As stressed in the European Council meeting on energy of 4 February 2011, the 2020 sustainable energy targets are presently not on track. As such, the EU is already considering the next step: the elaboration of the low carbon 2050 strategy that should provide the framework for longer-term action in the energy and related sectors. In addition to criticism of the 2020 programme as more of an environmental blueprint than an energy security strategy (Rosner 2009: 164), the major problem relates to the fact that, beyond agreeing on objectives, member states largely retain the right to determine their energy future. All in all, compliance on energy issues at the internal level between the EU and non-EU governmental and non-governmental actors tends to take place more at the rhetorical than practical level.

Mediterranean energy potential in the eyes of external actors

The Mediterranean energy landscape is in constant flux due to the emergence of new actors and international dynamics that add to the complexity of the EU's external energy policy. The degree of energy cooperation between the EU and some of these external state actors, such as Russia and China, in the Mediterranean is very limited. There are no examples of jointly devised or implemented activities. It is, however, possible that their presence may become more significant as a result of the increasing competition over energy resources, thus pushing the EU to develop strategies of engagement towards them.

With regard to NATO and the International Energy Agency (IEA) – two international organizations that deal with energy security in the Mediterranean – the EU has developed only limited cooperation (so far) beyond the rhetorical level. Here the problem is not competition. There is rather a mutually reinforcing attempt to rationalize the Mediterranean energy space in view of its strategic role as energy hub. However, this attempt has not so far translated into effective multilateral cooperation between the EU and IEA. Limited cooperation contacts are ensured by the fact that most EU member states participate in this organization and are thus bound by its institutional framework and objectives. The countries of the Mediterranean, instead, are involved in bilateral cooperation with the IEA as non-OECD recipient countries. This arrangement has not produced institutionalized forms of cooperation between the EU, on the one hand, and IEA, on the other, in the Mediterranean region.

Turning to NATO, the new Strategic Concept adopted at the Summit meeting in November 2010 provides an indication of NATO's new tasks in assuring energy supply. It explicitly refers to 'contribut[ing] to energy security, including protection of critical infrastructure and transit areas and lines, cooperation with partners, and consultations among Allies on the basis of strategic assessments and contingency planning'.[10] The Concept emphasizes the security dimension of energy supply. To achieve these goals, the Alliance is committed to a sustained dialogue with other actors such as the EU and the IEA. The role of NATO in energy security – which extends from promoting consultations, stability, exchange of information and best practices, to the protection of critical energy infrastructures – is perceived as complementary to that of the EU in the Mediterranean. NATO is also actively cooperating, on a multilateral and a bilateral basis, with its partner countries in the Mediterranean through the Mediterranean Dialogue (MD) and the Istanbul Cooperation Initiative (ICI) cooperative frameworks. Despite common interests and shared goals, cooperation between the EU and NATO on Mediterranean energy is extremely limited at the practical level. This is particularly true with reference to a potential triangular convergence among the EU, NATO and the MPCs.

From this analysis, it is clear that the EU's external multilateralism in the Mediterranean has not developed its potential yet. Rather, it is possible to speak of non-institutionalized cooperation among a N-group of actors, which includes the

EU next to other governmental and non–governmental actors, on the grounds of shared energy preoccupations and objectives. A more articulated, comprehensive and institutionalized form of cooperation has not materialized yet.

Europe's migration policy: effective multilateralism or patchy implementation?

Migration is an issue that involves a number of actors, and its effective management involves various parties. But does the EU pursue its migration policy objectives in a multilateral fashion? Is its approach effective? In order to answer these questions it is important to make two distinctions. The first involves the kinds of migration policies involved – whether these are restrictive (related to migration control, surveillance of borders, return and so on), or preventive (linked to developmental goals in countries of origin and/or managing legal migration in a way that benefits all stakeholders involved). The second concerns the level at which multilateralism is being observed: internally (within the EU) or externally, according to the matrix being used in this research. The argument advanced here is that the success of the EU's multilateral aspirations for tackling migration depends on the kinds of policies and the level at which these are pursued. The mismatch in priorities and visions translates into a mixed implementation picture with the Mediterranean.

This section will examine how the member states and the European Commission engage with one another, and with the Mediterranean partners and other relevant organizations in the pursuit of declared common policy objectives. The analysis is summarized in Table 7.3.

Internal multilateralism on migration: a case of selective convergence

Multilateral cooperation between member states and European institutions represents a case of selective convergence on migration issues, which differs from the effective convergence observed in the case of energy policy. Selectiveness is the product of the EU's (and previously the Community's) institutional setting. Prior to the establishment of the EU's three-pillar structure, members of the Communities came together to discuss migration issues and coordinate their national restrictive

TABLE 7.3 Cooperation patterns on migration policy

Actors / Levels	EU Institutions and Member States	EU and non-EU governmental and non-governmental actors
Internal EU Policies	Selective Convergence	Limited Compliance
EU Policies in the Mediterranean	Dominant Bilateralism	Patchy Cooperation

policies (deportations, information exchanges and external frontiers management) mainly under *ad hoc* frameworks (Geddes 2008). The nature of governments' engagement with one another on migration issues was institutionalized under the Maastricht Treaty under the third inter-governmental pillar for cooperation on justice and home affairs (JHA).

European institutions were initially sidelined, until they gained greater say on JHA matters with changes introduced in the 1997 Amsterdam Treaty, when migration and asylum were moved to the Community first pillar (with the exception of legal migration). Then, the 1999 Special Justice and Home Affairs Council held in Tampere advocated a common EU policy on migration and a more comprehensive approach to this issue-area (European Council 1999). Both these developments were reflected in subsequent initiatives and proposals, suggesting that internal multilateralism on migration covers a wide range of specific policies. The Hague Programme exemplifies the scope of internal coordination that the EU and member states envisaged on migration matters.

The Hague Programme, adopted in 2004, sought to coordinate intra-EU concerns in relation to external policies. Measures under the Programme were considered from the angle of establishing an area of freedom and security within the Union. In relation to migration, these included entry and admission of migrants, and their integration into host societies in Europe, effective border controls, as well as external aspects such as return and dealing with the root causes of migration, i.e. the reasons leading people to migrate (European Council 2004). Considering these external aspects, as well as issues of integration, marked a departure from the previous focus on control measures alone. In particular, the presence of legal migration concerns in EU discussions pointed to ways in which migration policy became more comprehensive, in line with the Tampere Conclusions. By the time the last Progress Report of the Hague Programme was published in June 2009, directives had been adopted for setting conditions of entry, employment and residence for certain categories of migrant workers and non-EU residents (European Commission 2009).

The issue of legal migration, however, reveals the extent to which internal convergence has been selective on migration issues. In the period between the ratification of the Amsterdam and Lisbon treaties, legal migration remained a member state competence. As such, coordination over a common policy in line with the goals outlined in the Tampere Conclusions was difficult to achieve. The coming into force of the Lisbon Treaty is expected to deal with some of these difficulties, as it has altered the institutional setting that led to member states' selective convergence. Work is being carried out on the establishment of a comprehensive legal migration framework at EU level. An example is the EU Blue Card Directive, a special work permit for highly qualified migrants (DG Home Affairs 2011). In addition, the 2010 Stockholm Action Plan emphasizes a stronger role for European institutions with competences on these matters (European Commission 2010a). Nonetheless, it is too early to assess how these initiatives will be implemented, and the degree of further convergence they will entail. What has been more dominant so far is continued cooperation on control issues, for instance successful member state cooperation with FRONTEX (European Commission 2009), and the introduction of emergency measures to deal with migration flows following the Arab revolts of 2011 (European Commission 2011a).

The EU and the Mediterranean: dominant bilateralism

Similar to the Hague Programme, the 2005 Global Approach was conceived as a strategy for pursuing a comprehensive approach to migration at the external level. In its conceptualization, the Global Approach is a multilateral endeavour that brings together origin, destination and transit countries in order to manage migration flows. The implementation of this vision, however, is hindered by divisions between the Commission and the member states on the desirable approach and on the competencies each holds. Selective convergence at the internal level leads to an external dimension where bilateralism dominates, an observation that coincides with the cooperation pattern observed above for energy policy.

In addition to disagreeing on how to deal with migration priorities, European states differ in their views of the Mediterranean. Certain European states (France, Italy, Spain, Malta and Portugal) show greater interest in establishing closer relations with countries of the region. Member states that are geographically closer to the southern Mediterranean tend to emphasize the desirability of establishing stronger relations with MPCs. These divergences at EU level are evident in negotiations over a comprehensive approach to the Mediterranean on migration issues. How to achieve migration-related objectives repeatedly sparks intra-EU debates. Various European Council meetings have addressed the issue of whether to condition concessions in other policy areas on progress made in migration matters (see European Council 2002). Reflective of the thorny nature of migration, there was disagreement over what to include in the UfM framework. Member states are said to have explicitly left migration out of these discussions in order to secure progress on other issue-areas of interest (author's interviews, September–November 2009).

Convergence is observed in cooperation on restrictive migration policies, similar to patterns observed at internal EU level. Managing undocumented migration individually is costly and challenging, to say the least, and states seek to cooperate with external partners in order to tackle irregular migration movements. The Mediterranean is key in this sense; it is not only a region of origin but also one of transit of (mostly) sub-Saharan African migrants. The idea of establishing a buffer zone of sorts around the EU cannot be implemented without the concerted efforts of neighbouring third countries. At EU level, the Euro-Mediterranean Partnership was not conducive to joint, regional management and control of irregular migration. However, member states resorted to other multilateral venues to advance restrictive measures. The 5+5 Dialogue is a case in point; it brings together Mauritania, Morocco, Algeria, Tunisia, Libya, Portugal, Spain, Italy, France and Malta to discuss migration under the auspices of the International Organization for Migration (Lavenex 2006).

Member states' multilateral engagement with MPCs on other aspects of migration policy, such as migration for development and legal migration, is largely lacking. Rhetorically, member states have intermittently advocated targeting development aid to deal with the causes leading people to leave their countries of origin. However, this objective has not translated into actual multilateral policies. Funding for migration-related initiatives in the Mediterranean has been allocated and increased over time, but the content of programmes does not prioritize developmental aims. This is the case of the chapter on Migration, Social Integration, Justice and Security, also known as JAI, introduced at the 2005 Euro-Mediterranean Summit, which outlines the aims for better managing legal migration, offering more job opportunities in Europe, establishing linkages between development concerns and migration movements, and jointly controlling irregular migration (European Council 2005a). The EMP's JAI chapter has predominantly focused on endeavours that target research initiatives, data collection, information dissemination, and capacity-building and training (European Commission 2007a), and the kinds of programmes pursued are symbolic in that they have not institutionalized cooperation among partners (Abdelkhaliq 2010).

Limited member state engagement in multilateralism is also the case for legal migration. European governments are reticent about offering opportunities for legal migration into the EU, especially to Mediterranean partners due to security considerations. Legal migration opportunities are generally negotiated bilaterally between individual member states and third countries, and are limited in number. For instance, seasonal workers' recruitment is organized between Spain and Morocco, and France and other North African countries, but these programmes are not widespread (Ibid.).

The Commission, for its part, has participated in and supported meetings of member states who shape the EMP political agenda (Bicchi 2007). The increase in its competences post-Amsterdam has allowed the Commission's involvement in drawing up an external dimension of migration that aims at tackling all kinds of measures – legal, irregular, and development-related (European Council 2005b). The Commission has been quite active in developing the Global Approach framework, and in presenting proposals regarding common objectives and ways to achieve them. Examples of these efforts include Communications regarding cooperation with third countries on migration and asylum matters, a policy plan for legal migration, ensuring the coherence of a comprehensive approach, and complementary thematic lines for working with a range of organizations outside the frameworks for relations with partner governments (European Commission 2005, 2006a, 2006b, 2006c).

Being in charge of the Global Approach has given the Commission a direct role in negotiating with MPC within the EU's institutional framework. Therefore, within the EMP's JAI chapter, in bilateral relations, and in line with the ENP, the Commission has a role in implementing the Union's aims on migration. The Commission is indeed involved in managing and running JAI. It has also been given a mandate to negotiate readmission agreements with third countries. In its programmes in third countries, funding has been allocated to target developmental aims linked to migration, and there are operational initiatives to tackle migration control – such as the joint patrolling of borders, capacity-building, and cooperation with FRONTEX (Lavenex 2008).

A closer look at these initiatives, however, reveals limitations in the Commission's role and aspirations for promoting multilateral endeavours. Commission officials in charge of relations with the Mediterranean criticize member states for not granting more legal migration opportunities to MPCs, and for excessively stressing control measures. They instead support positions that could make multilateral cooperation more effective – such as offering more legal migration opportunities, or supporting the developmental goals of Mediterranean countries. These difficulties are directly linked to the internal level of multilateral cooperation. Imbalances at EU level constrain the Commission in its ability to negotiate with third countries, and in the kinds and volume of programmes it can implement there (author's interviews, September–November 2009).

Mediterranean countries are generally interested in more legal migration and development-related cooperation, rather than on the predominant focus on migration control. However, they have been reticent to cooperate as part of a multilateral framework, favouring instead their bilateral relations with the Union (Aghrout 2000; Collinson 1996; Gillespie 2006; Volpi 2004). As a consequence, relations with Mediterranean partners are more successful at the bilateral rather than at the multilateral level. The ENP framework is attractive for MPCs because of this reason; it allows for the differentiation of bilateral relations. Morocco is a case in point. It has been acknowledged to be one of the most active MPCs in advancing its bilateral relations with the EU on a number of policy areas, and as one of the most cooperative on migration issues (European Commission 2004).

The difficulties – between member states and with the Commission – are therefore reflected in the content of negotiations with third countries. The latter are inclined to endorse comprehensive goals that mix preventive and restrictive measures. Mediterranean governments have committed to the multilateral implementation of common policy objectives. In practice, however, the EU's focus on security-related restrictive objectives has rendered comprehensive, multilateral cooperation unsuccessful (author's interviews, September–November 2009). FRONTEX is perhaps an example of an initiative that has managed to bring together various actors to control irregular migration into the EU (Lavenex 2008). But again, it is reflective of the internal EU prioritization of restrictive measures and does not reflect the comprehensive approach endorsed in multilateral declarations.

International migration management and limited compliance

So far, the discussion has focused on how member states cooperate with one another and the Commission for dealing with migration internally and externally with the Mediterranean partner governments. But how does the EU relate to international organizations and NGOs whose work deals with, or touches on, migration issues? Unlike the case of energy policy, in the case of migration we can observe limited compliance in work done at international level. There are two underlying reasons for this: the EU's approach to the international scene and its relation to the international standards advocated by organizations whose remit covers migration issues, such as the IOM, and the UN and its pertinent agencies.

To begin with, it is important to note that there is no international migration management regime as such. However, a range of organizations have been engaged in discussions for decades on how such a regime could be created, which would allow for the integrated management of migratory movements at local, national and international levels (Ghosh 2000; Loescher 1989; Thouez and Channac 2006; Widgren 1989). The restrictive policies pursued by states in the 1980s and 1990s drove various organizations – the IOM, the International Labour Organization (ILO) and the UN, for instance – to discuss ways in which migration concerns could be tackled without sidelining developmental considerations (Olesen 2002). This approach would, in theory, in the long term target the reasons leading people to migrate: poverty, unemployment, political instability and so on, rather than adopting a short-term stance that seeks to stop migration.

Without directly participating in these international endeavours, the Commission has tried at various points to integrate these debates into Community initiatives (Butt Philip 1994; European Commission 1994). This comprehensive approach was adopted post-Tampere, both in the Hague Programme and in the Global Approach. In addition, the Commission relies on the norms and practices of international organizations when elaborating its programmes. According to various officials, the expertise and access provided by the IOM and UN is instrumental in the way migration policy is conceptualized and pursued (author's interviews, September–November 2009).

What is noteworthy, however, is that the EU employs international debates as a basis for its initiatives but creates its own frameworks for dealing with migration issues. Moreover, when it comes to international conventions that address migrants' issues, or touch upon migration, compliance is rather limited. Geddes (2008) argues that there are two reasons for this compliance gap. First, international (UN) standards are expansive in that they grant rights to people regardless of nationality (EU/non-EU) or status (legal/irregular migrant). Second, they are legally weak, especially in comparison with EU law. A case in point is the 1990 International Convention on the Protection of the Rights of All Migrant Workers and Members of their Families. The Commission invited member states to sign the Convention, but none has done so at the time of writing. The justification given is that the Convention does not make clear distinctions between legal and irregular migrants and may give the wrong message to migrants about how extensive the rights granted are (author's interviews, September–November 2009). Like this Convention, there are certain responsibilities states should adhere to as outlined by the ILO or the Council of Europe for ensuring the rights of migrants and their protection: however, compliance depends on the national context, as well as on the categories of migrants and their citizenship (Geddes 2008).

Other organizations and patchy cooperation

The relevance of international organizations for the EU's approach to migration is better observed at the external level, rather than in terms of internal compliance. Alongside its multilateral and bilateral endeavours, the EU supports a range of organizations to carry out work that is in line with its migration policy goals. These organizations allow for the pursuit of objectives that are difficult to channel at EU level. International and non-governmental organizations at the internal and external levels fill the void for comprehensive initiatives that are difficult to agree on multilaterally with partner countries and between EU actors. The result is that pursuing this avenue for implementing migration objectives results in patchy cooperation. In this regard, cooperation patterns are similar to the limited cooperation observed in the energy realm. For migration policy, patchy cooperation depends on whether funding is allocated and awarded, and on the expertise and access that relevant organizations have.

Since 2001, the Commission has resorted to thematic budget lines, such as B7-667, the AENEAS Programme and the Thematic Programme for Cooperation with third Countries in the Areas of Migration and Asylum (European Commission 2006c). These were created by the Commission to support cooperation with third countries on migration-related matters through a sectoral focus, in a way that is complementary to official frameworks for relations with governments. Thematic budget lines have become prominent over time and receive increasing amounts of funding.

Thematic frameworks allow the Commission to work with civil society, non-governmental and international organizations operating in the EU and the Mediterranean in projects that comply with the EU's migration policy goals. For instance, the IOM manages a number of initiatives across the Maghreb region on irregular migration management, capacity building, and assisting undocumented migrants to return to their countries of origin (European Commission 2004, 2007b; IOM 2010). NGOs also work within the thematic framework, focusing, for example, on initiatives related to human rights and civil society participation in migration matters, or providing services for stranded migrants (European Commission 2006a).

Thematic budget lines facilitate the implementation of initiatives without necessarily involving governments and are not liable to binding agreements (author's interview, November 2009). They are the most comprehensive of migration initiatives, despite not conforming to the conceptualization of multilateral cooperation within regional official frameworks. However, they often result in patchy cooperation because of their very nature of not always involving and operating on a project-by-project basis. Far from resulting in an international migration management regime, patchy cooperation highlights the difficulties of establishing one.

Conclusions

To what extent is the EU able to work multilaterally and effectively in energy and migration matters? To answer this general question it is useful to adopt a comparative perspective on EU-Mediterranean energy and migration cooperation. Both policy areas exhibit similarities in their resulting cooperation patterns for the different quadrants presented in the matrix we devised. For energy, internal dynamics between EU institutions and member states reveal convergence towards the creation of an integrated energy market. Migration policy is a case of selective convergence for this quadrant, as EU actors involved favour restrictive policies over preventive ones. Where EU actors engage with the Mediterranean, both energy and migration policy areas exhibit bilateralism as the dominant form of cooperation. When it comes to the internal level vis-à-vis other governmental and non-governmental actors, energy policy demonstrates compliance, whereas on migration policy internal dynamics are selectively compliant – again, depending on whether policies are restrictive or preventive. Finally, where the EU interacts at the external level with the Mediterranean and with other actors, energy policy reveals limited cooperation as opposed to patchy cooperation for the case of migration.

All in all, it is reasonable to claim that the EU does not live up to its multilateral rhetoric and potential in the Mediterranean. The reasons why this is the case have been discussed in this chapter. They range from existing national policies and preferences that clash with one another, to the limited articulation and inconsistent pursuit of common goals and rules in conjunction with other international and regional actors. Perhaps other policy areas would tell a different story about the EU's practice of 'effective multilateralism'. But we are inclined to think that they may well exhibit similar characteristics.

Notes

1 Nur Abdelkhaliq is a researcher based at the University of Edinburgh and Silvia Colombo is researcher in the Mediterranean and Middle East programme at Istituto Affari Internazionali (IAI) in Rome. Nur Abdelkhaliq has written the section on migration, while Silvia Colombo the one on energy. The other sections of the chapter have been drafted by both authors. The authors wish to thank Nathalie Tocci, Geoffrey Edwards, Julie Smith and John Peterson for their insightful comments on previous drafts of this piece. An extended version of the chapter was published as a working paper for the MERCURY Project.

2 We refer here to the so-called Arab Spring that has been sweeping across the Mediterranean and the Middle East since the beginning of 2011. Since then tremendous changes have taken place in the region, including the downfall of long-lasting authoritarian regimes such as those of Ben Ali in Tunisia, Mubarak in Egypt and Qaddafi in Libya. These developments have been triggered and accompanied by changes at the

societal level as well as in the relations with external partners, including the EU. On this last point see, for example, Tocci and Cassarino (2011).

3 The key actors to be dealt with in this chapter are the EU institutions and member states *in relation to* the Mediterranean Partner Countries (MPCs), some non-EU governmental and non-governmental actors, including Russia and the United States, and organizations such as NATO, the International Energy Agency (IEA) and the International Organization for Migration (IOM), as well as civil society and private companies. The analysis focuses on EU institutions and member states in their interaction with other actors to gauge EU multilateralism. We will not assess the role of other actors in multilateralism as such due to the limited scope of the chapter.

4 It is important to differentiate between 'external energy policy' from the perspective of individual member states and that of the EU. Viewed from the member states, external energy policy comprises energy relations with both member and non-members of the Union. From the EU's perspective, external energy policy addresses only third parties. Thus, only if the EU's internal relations are harmonized sufficiently through the creation of an internal energy market and solidarity mechanisms, can the EU and member states' external energy policies become one and the same. This does not mean that an integrated EU market is the precondition for addressing the external dimension of the EU's energy policy, but rather that internal and external policy dimensions are mutually dependent (Baumann and Simmerl 2011: 3).

5 See the EU-Egypt Action Plan at http://trade.ec.europa.eu/doclib/docs/2010/april/tradoc_146097.pdf (accessed on 13 August 2012) and the EU-Morocco Action Plan at http://trade.ec.europa.eu/doclib/docs/2006/march/tradoc_127912.pdf (accessed on 13 August 2012).

6 See the ENPI Libya Strategy Paper and National Indicative Programme 2011–2012. Online. Available: http://ec.europa.eu/world/enp/pdf/country/2011_enpi_csp_nip_libya_en.pdf (accessed on 13 August 2012) and the ENPI Algeria Strategy Paper 2007–2013 and the National Indicative Programme 2007–2010. Online. Available: http://ec.europa.eu/world/enp/pdf/country/enpi_csp_nip_algeria_en.pdf (accessed on 13 August 2012).

7 Author's interviews in Algeria and Morocco, December 2009 and October 2010.

8 See the Europe 2020 document at http://ec.europa.eu/eu2020/pdf/COMPLET%20EN%20BARROSO%20%20%20007%20-%20Europe%202020%20-%20EN%20version.pdf (accessed on 13 August 2012).

9 The IPCC has requested developed countries as a whole to reduce green house gas emissions by 80–95 per cent by 2050. See http://ipcc.ch/ (accessed on 13 August 2012).

10 See NATO's new Strategic Concept at http://www.nato.int/lisbon2010/strategic-concept-2010-eng.pdf (accessed 13 August 2012).

References

Abdelkhaliq, N. (2010) *Externalising Migration Policy: The European Union's 'Global' Approach*, MERCURY e-paper 4.

Aghrout, A. (2000) *From Preferential Status to Partnership*, Aldershot: Ashgate.

Baumann, F. and Simmerl, G. (2011) *Between Conflict and Convergence: The EU Member States and the Quest for a Common External Energy Policy*, CAP Discussion Paper.

Bicchi, F. (2007) *European Foreign Policy Making Towards the Mediterranean*, Basingstoke: Palgrave Macmillan.

Butt Philip, A. (1994) 'European Union Immigration Policy: Phantom, Fantasy or Fact?', in M. Baldwin-Edwards and M.A. Schain (eds) *The Politics of Immigration in Western Europe*, Ilford: Frank Cass.

Collinson, S. (1996) *Shore to Shore: The Politics of Migration in Euro-Maghreb Relations*, London: Royal Institute of International Affairs.

DG Home Affairs (2011) *Well-managed Labour Migration in all our Interest*. Online. Available http://ec.europa.eu/home-affairs/policies/immigration/immigration_work_en.htm (accessed 17 July 2011).

European Commission (1994) Communication from the Commission to the Council and the European Parliament: On Immigration and Asylum Policies, COM (94) 23 final of 23.02.1994, Brussels: European Commission.

European Commission (2004) European Neighbourhood Policy: Strategy Paper, COM (2004) 373 final of 12.5.2004, Brussels: European Commission.

European Commission (2005) Communication from the Commission: Policy Plan on Legal Migration, COM (2005) 669 final of 21.12.2005, Brussels: European Commission.

European Commission (2006a) Aeneas Programme: Programme for financial and technical assistance to third countries in the area of migration and asylum: Overview of projects funded 2004 – 2006, Brussels: European Commission.

European Commission (2006b) Communication from the Commission to the Council and the European Parliament: The Global Approach one year on: Towards a Comprehensive European Migration Policy, COM (2006) 735 final of 30.11.2006, Brussels: European Commission.

European Commission (2006c) Communication from the Commission to the Council and the European Parliament: Thematic Programme for the Cooperation with Third Countries in Areas of Migration and Asylum, COM (2006) 26 final of 25.1.2006, Brussels: European Commission.

European Commission (2006d) A European Strategy for Sustainable, Competitive, and Secure Energy, COM (2006) 105 final, Brussels: European Commission.

European Commission (2007a) Euro-Mediterranean Partnership: Regional Cooperation: Overview of Programmes and Projects, Brussels: European Commission.

European Commission (2007b) Communication from the Commission to the Council and European Parliament: An Energy Policy for Europe, COM (2007) 1 final, Brussels: European Commission.

European Commission (2009), Communication from the Commission to the Council, the European Parliament, the European Economic and Social Committee and the Committee of the Regions: Justice, Freedom and Security since 2005: An Evaluation of the Hague Programme and Action Plan, COM (2009) 263 final of 10.6.2009, Brussels: European Commission.

European Commission (2010a) Communication from the Commission to the European Parliament, the Council, the European Economic and Social Committee and the Committee of the Regions: Delivering an area of freedom, security and justice for Europe's Citizens – Action Plan Implementing the Stockholm Programme, Brussels: European Commission.

European Commission (2010b) Communication from the Commission to the European Parliament, the Council, the European Economic and Social Committee and the Committee of the Regions: Energy 2020: A Strategy for Competitive, Sustainable and Secure Energy, COM (2010) 639 final, Brussels: European Commission.

European Commission (2011a) Communication from the Commission to the European Parliament, the Council, the Economic and Social Committee and the Committee of the Regions: Communication on Migration, COM (2011) 248 final, Brussels: European Commission.

European Commission (2011b) Joint Communication to the European Council, the European Parliament, the Council, the European Economic and Social Committee and the Committee of the Region: A Partnership for Democracy and Shared Prosperity with the Southern Mediterranean, COM (2011) 200 final, Brussels: European Commission.

European Council (1999) Tampere European Council Conclusions, 15–16 October 1999.

European Council (2002) Seville European Council Presidency Conclusions, 21–22 June 2002.

European Council (2004) The Hague Programme: Strengthening freedom, security and justice in the European Union, 13 December 2004.

European Council (2005a) 10th Anniversary Euro-Mediterranean Summit: Five Year Work Programme. Barcelona, 27–28 November 2005.

European Council (2005b) Presidency Conclusions, Brussels 15–16 December 2005.

Geddes, A. (2008) *Immigration and European Integration: Beyond Fortress Europe?*, Manchester: Manchester University Press.

Ghosh, B. (2000) 'Introduction', in B. Ghosh (ed.) *Managing Migration: Time for a New International Regime?*, New York: Oxford University Press, 1–5.

Gillespie, R. (2006) Onward but not Upward: The Barcelona Conference of 2005, *Mediterranean Politics*, 11: 271–8.

IOM (2010) *Assisting Voluntary Return*, International Organisation for Migration.

Lavenex, S. (2006) 'Shifting Up and Out: The Foreign Policy of European Immigration Control', *West European Politics,* 29: 329–50.

Lavenex, S. (2008) 'A Governance Perspective on the European Neighbourhood Policy: Integration Beyond Conditionality?', *Journal of European Public Policy*, 15: 938–55.

Loescher, G. (1989) 'Introduction: Refugees Issues in International Relations', in G. Loescher and L. Monahan (eds) *Refugees and International Relations*, New York: Oxford University Press, 1–33.

Olesen, H. (2002) 'Migration, Return and Development: An Institutional Perspective', *International Migration* 40(5): 125–50.

Rosner, K. (2009) 'The European Union: On Energy, Disunity', in G. Luft and A. Korin (eds), *Energy Security Challenges for the 21st Century. A Reference Handbook*, ABC Clio Praeger Security International, 160–75.

Thouez, C. and Channac, F. (2006) 'Shaping International Migration Policy: The Role of Regional Consultative Processes', *West European Politics*, 29(2): 370–87.

Tocci, N. and Cassarino, J.-P. (2011) *Rethinking the EU's Mediterranean Policies Post-1/11*, Rome: Istituto Affari Internazionali, March 2011.

Volpi, F. (2004) 'Regional Community Building and the Transformation of International Relations: The Case of the Euro-Mediterranean Partnership', *Mediterranean Politics*, 9: 145–64.

Widgren, J. (1989) 'Europe and International Migration in the Future: The Necessity for Merging Migration, Refugee, and Development Policies', in G. Loescher and L. Monahan (eds) *Refugees and International Relations*, New York: Oxford University Press, 49–61.

8

MULTILATERALISM AS ENVISAGED?

Assessing European Union's engagement in conflict resolution in the neighbourhood

Tomáš Weiss, Nona Mikhelidze and Ivo Šlosarčík[1]

Introduction

This chapter examines the European Union's (EU) practice in conflict resolution. More specifically, it analyses whether and how the EU lives up to the principles of multilateralism declared in its key documents while intervening in regional conflicts. It focuses on the EU's performance in its neighbourhood. These local conflicts are especially important for the Union and the temptation to resort to other forms of engagement, such as uni- or bilateral action, may be greater as a result.

'The Union's aim is to promote peace' – that is the first among the European Union's objectives as defined by Article 3 of the Treaty on European Union (TEU). Having settled the disputes among its members through integration, the EU has turned to conflicts abroad and adopted conflict resolution as one of the core objectives of its external action. In its relations with the world the EU 'shall contribute to peace, security, [...] mutual respect among peoples, [...] and the protection of human rights' (Art. 3.5 TEU). The reasons are not only ethical, but also pragmatic. Regional conflicts are considered one of five key threats that the EU has to face. According to the European Security Strategy:

> Violent or frozen conflicts, which also persist on our borders, threaten regional stability. They destroy human lives and social and physical infrastructures; they threaten minorities, fundamental freedoms and human rights. Conflict can lead to extremism, terrorism and state failure; it provides opportunities for organized crime. Regional insecurity can fuel the demand for [Weapons of Mass Destruction]. The most practical way to tackle the often elusive new threats will sometimes be to deal with the older problems of regional conflict.
>
> *(European Council 2003: 4)*

In particular, the EU aspires to build security in the neighbourhood and to promote 'a ring of well governed countries to the East of the European Union and on the borders of the Mediterranean with whom we [i.e. the Union] can enjoy close and cooperative relations' (Ibid.: 8).

The stabilization of the European Union's space has been achieved through an internal system of law. By analogy, the EU has looked to a similar system at the international level with the United Nations (UN) at its core. It aims at contributing 'to the strict observance and the development of international law, including respect for the principles of the United Nations Charter' (Art. 3.5 TEU) and helping to create 'an international order based on effective multilateralism' (European Council 2003: 9). Such an order is to rely on other 'international organisations, regimes and treaties' (Ibid.: 9) to confront threats to international peace and security.

This chapter first reviews the concept of multilateralism in conflict resolution and the EU's tools and policies for resolving conflicts. Second, two case studies scrutinize the EU's recent performance in practice. The developments in Georgia and Bosnia and Herzegovina have represented prime examples of long-lasting conflicts within the EU's neighbourhood where the Union has been trying to contribute to a resolution. Although similar in many ways, not least their possible importance for the EU, the two conflicts are very different – especially in the involvement of other external powers. Comparing them may lead to a deeper understanding of the EU's engagement in the neighbourhood. The study concludes that the EU has been an effective multilateral player while supporting other actors, but much less so a leading partner of multilateral efforts.

Multilateralism in conflict resolution

An external intervention can occur during any phase of a conflict – pre-violent, armed conflict, ceasefire or post-agreement – that are usually recognized in academic literature (see Gilboa 2009; Diehl 2008: 18). For the purpose of this chapter, conflict resolution incorporates intervention in any of the four phases of a conflict. It is more ambitious than conflict management, which seeks simply to reduce the dangers of a crisis, and more durable than keeping the conflicting parties apart from each other. External actors may choose from various forms when contributing to conflict resolution. They may seek to mediate between the conflicting parties; they may take sides and impose sanctions on one of them; they may also use armed force to stop the fighting and impose negative peace.[2] In all cases, they may proceed unilaterally, bilaterally or multilaterally within the scope of the definition applied in this book (see Chapter 2).

There are always at least three actors present in conflict resolution – the conflict parties and the intervening actor. This chapter, however, focuses on the role of the external actor only. In this way, all forms of engagement are possible, which raises interesting questions. The external actor's contribution might be labelled as unilateral, for example, if its action reflects just its own objectives without any consultation with the parties to the conflict, e.g. intervention on humanitarian grounds. An activity with the consent of or in concert with the conflicting parties would then correspond with bilateralism, because the external actor would bilaterally cooperate with the local actors.[3] It could, for example, mediate a ceasefire between two warring states. Moreover, a peace enforcement operation against the will of warring states in cooperation with another external actor would also be labelled as bilateral, as there would be two actors cooperating on an activity with the local actors being restricted to objects. With the same logic, a multilateral conflict resolution would comprise cooperation with the parties of the conflict and one or more other external actors (or two or more external actors without the participation of the conflicting parties). By analogy, the more or less equal rules for all required by Peterson and Bouchard definition must be understood as more equal for all intervening parties and rather less equal for the conflict parties receiving external assistance.

The European Union's approach to conflict resolution

For its part, the European Union recognizes the four phases of conflict resolution outlined above, namely conflict prevention, crisis management, peacebuilding and reconstruction (Council of the EU 2005: Art. 2). It has declared itself ready to 'facilitate peaceful solution to disputes' and emphasizes the need to address the root-causes of conflicts (European Council 2001: para. 3). When violence breaks out, the EU has military and civilian crisis management tools at its disposal within the Common Security and Defence Policy (CSDP). The CSDP missions can contribute both during crisis management and peacebuilding phases of the conflict, being tasked with, *inter alia*, disarmament operations, peace-making or post-conflict stabilization (Art. 43.1 TEU; see also European Council 2004a; European Council 2004b). For the most part, the Union contributes to post-conflict reconstruction either in the framework of enlargement policy, European Neighbourhood Policy or development policy.

The EU aims at cooperating with external partners in conflict resolution. There are institutionalized ties to the United Nations and NATO, but the EU recognizes the role of many other organizations, such as the World Bank, the International Monetary Fund, the Organization for Security and Co-operation in Europe (OSCE) or the Organisation for Economic Co-operation and Development (European Commission 2001). In addition, the Union considers civil society to be an important actor in conflict resolution (Tocci 2008).

The EU is in principle thus able to cover the whole spectrum of conflict resolution and ready to cooperate with other international actors. It suffers, however, from incoherencies that follow from its specific institutional structure and allocation of competencies. The Commission is primarily responsible for reconstruction as well as trade and development tools of prevention. The Council, on the other hand, determines crisis management policy, insofar as member states' capabilities are used. Internal coordination has not always been very efficient (see, for example, Stewart 2008). Nor has external cooperation always been smooth. EU–NATO coordination has suffered from conflicts between member states and the efficiency of other organizations, such as the UN or OSCE, is curbed by veto powers. Yet, resolving conflicts in cooperation with other actors clearly belongs to the EU's vision of effective multilateralism.

EU and Georgia's territorial conflicts: effective non-multilateralism

The South Caucasus is currently the most conflict-plagued region in the post-Soviet space, where ancient hatreds and geopolitical rivalries are interwoven. Georgia's conflicts with the breakaway entities of Abkhazia and South Ossetia are an exemplification of both. In the early 1990s, the explosion of the Soviet Union's 'matrioshka' policy coupled with Georgian nationalism caused brutal wars between the metropolitan state and the two autonomous republics, which ended with the separation of Abkhazia and South Ossetia from the central government in Tbilisi. The ceasefire agreements of 1992/93 established a joint Georgian/Russian/Ossetian peacekeeping force plus a monitoring role of the OSCE in South Ossetia, and a Commonwealth of Independent States' peacekeeping force and a UN observer mission in Abkhazia. The wars caused some 9,000 deaths and more than 250,000 internally displaced persons (ICG 2006). Over the years, the conflicts were labelled as 'frozen'. Actually, what was frozen was the conflict resolution process that left a precarious security situation in the South Caucasus, which, ultimately, led to the military escalation between Georgia and Russia in August 2008 and the Russian recognition of the *de facto* republics. Thus, these unsolved conflicts have turned out to be the largest threat to the stability of the region, posing challenges also for the security of the EU's eastern neighbourhood.

The actors involved

Given the strategic location of the South Caucasus, major external powers have remained at loggerheads with each other, thus illustrating both the frozen and unfrozen natures of reconciliation and conflict dynamics respectively. The initial peace process was accompanied by the direct or indirect presence of single external states (Russia, the US and Turkey) and multilateral organizations (the EU, OSCE and UN). Those involved in the conflict considered the EU as the most neutral broker among these actors. Within the framework of its European Neighbourhood Policy, the EU–Georgia Action Plan of 2006 pledged 'strong EU commitment to support the settlement of Georgia's internal conflicts, drawing on the instruments at the EU's disposal, and in close consultation with the UN and OSCE'. Both parties also agreed that 'the issue of territorial integrity of Georgia' was to be included 'in EU–Russia political dialogue meetings' (EU–Georgia Action Plan 2006). Thus, by seeking to engage several actors in the region, the EU aimed at contributing to the peace process through multilateral diplomacy. This case study analyses whether the EU has been true to its rhetorical pledge to engage in conflict resolution through multilateral activities, as opposed to unilateral, bilateral or inaction. The study addresses the question by examining four phases in the conflict cycle, including conflict prevention, open violence, post-war reconstruction and long-term conflict resolution.[4]

The EU and the peace process: a bilateral actor at the margins of multilateralism

The EU's impact on the peace processes was not impressive, especially in the first phase of conflict resolution. First, the wars of 1992–3 were over by the time the EU decided to get involved in the region. Second, for years, the Union interpreted the conflicts as two-party games between the state of Georgia and the *de facto* republics, without acknowledging Russia's crucial role. Georgia's request to internationalize peacekeeping in the conflict zones in order to prevent escalation bore no fruit. Even in 2004, when Tbilisi called upon the EU to send an international monitoring mission after Russia had vetoed the extension of the OSCE border-monitoring mission in South Ossetia, Brussels turned down the invitation, thus avoiding direct confrontation with Russia.

Between 1998 and 2008 the EU's tendency was towards inaction. In the post-war phase of reconstruction and long-term conflict resolution, the Union tended to act bilaterally, engaging with the parties to the conflict, primarily with Georgia. The EU tried to induce peace in the region through aid as well as democracy promotion, state-building and support to civil society. The implicit aim was to raise the appeal of reintegration for the secessionist entities into Georgia. Additionally, during the entire period, the EU financed rehabilitation programmes for Georgia/Abkhazia.[5] In the implementation phase of these projects, the United Nations Development Programme and the United Nations Observer Mission in Georgia were also involved. It can therefore be argued that in the post-war phase, the EU's activities, while primarily bilateral in nature, were also marginally multilateral, particularly in the implementation of specific rehabilitation programmes.

In 2004, the EU began to fund civil society groups in Georgia through the European Instrument for Democracy and Human Rights. Between 1997 and 2001, it had also funded the Conflict Prevention Network in order to receive recommendations from international civil society actors on how to enhance its conflict resolution policies in Georgia. Notwithstanding the enormous analytical support provided by the network, the initiative was considered ineffective and was ultimately shut down. The Network had provided the possibility to create a multilateral forum for interaction between the EU, the Georgian government and civil society. However, the EU did not fully use the Network's potential and limited itself to being a donor at the bilateral level with civil society organizations in Georgia and the secessionist entities, separately. The EU's assistance to civil society organizations has been important in strengthening the third sector, but it has not had a visible effect on the peace process. This was because the EU's engagement with civil society organizations was a substitute rather than a complement to the EU's (limited) engagement with the official level involved in conflict resolution (Popescu 2010).

In 2003, the EU appointed an EU Special Representative (EUSR) to the South Caucasus. With the EUSR, the Union set out to engage in conflict settlement multilaterally, through collaboration with the UN and the OSCE (Council of the EU 2008). However, the EU specifically designated itself as a secondary actor in this process, in order not to irritate Russia substantially.[6] The EUSR was not authorized to act as a mediator between the parties at the bilateral or multilateral levels, but rather to engage in conflict resolution only in support of international organizations already engaged in mediation.

A final dimension of the EU's involvement in conflict resolution in the first post-war phase was through its financial support for the multilateral Joint Control Commission (JCC). The JCC, under the aegis of the OSCE, monitored the ceasefire in South Ossetia. In 2001–8, the Union acquired observer status in JCC meetings on demilitarization and economic projects. At first sight, the EU was thus involved in a multilateral framework, but the Georgian side considered the JCC bilateral, insofar as the OSCE and the EU rarely consulted the conflict parties (the Georgian government in particular). At the same time, the EU argued that the Georgian government claimed a veto right rather than seeking genuine collaboration.[7] Irrespective of the rights and wrongs of both sides, the JCC had clear limits and could be considered multilateral more in name than practice.

The August 2008 war marks the beginning of the second phase of the conflict. The EU played a primary role in reaching a ceasefire between Georgia and Russia. The mediation took place in Moscow and Tbilisi at the bilateral level; the United States supported the EU only behind the scenes (Asmus 2010). In view of Russia's rejection of US involvement in Caucasian affairs, the EU's bilateral approach with Russia was seen as preferable to a multilateral one, be this a trilateral approach involving also Washington or one including Georgia.

Likewise, in the aftermath of the August 2008 war, when the OSCE called for the establishment of a mediation forum in Geneva aimed at security and stability in the South Caucasus, the EU's role was mostly supportive rather than that of a leading player. The initiative goes back to the 'Six-Point Ceasefire Plan', reached by French (then EU) President Nicolas Sarkozy and his Russian counterpart Dmitry Medvedev, which brought the military confrontation between Moscow and Tbilisi to an end. The agreement, together with its follow-up document of 8 September 2008, envisaged the creation of a new multilateral platform involving the EU, the OSCE, the UN and the United States, as well as Georgia and Russia (see Civil Georgia 2008). At Russia's request, officials from Abkhazia and South Ossetia were also included in the talks. Moscow's demand coincided with that of the EU and OSCE, the latter also considering that the talks should be all-inclusive. To date, the main achievement of this forum has been Russia's decision to withdraw its military troops from Perevi, a small Georgian village beyond the South

Ossetian administrative border. Its main failure has been the inability to prevent Russia from vetoing the extension of the UN and OSCE missions to Georgia's breakaway regions, thus hindering a further multilateralisation of the peace process (Mikhelidze 2010). In any case, the Geneva forum is the first multilateral forum in which the EU has participated and collaborated with other players as a direct conflict mediator. However, according to some authors, the Geneva forum seems to be aimed at crisis management (preventing another confrontation between Georgia and Russia) rather than conflict settlement and resolution (Whitman and Wolff 2010). Despite all their limits, the negotiations do offer some potential to reverse the conflict dynamics. First and related to the format, the process may contribute to breaking out the deadlock. The Geneva talks represent the only forum in which all conflict parties meet (albeit separately at times) around a negotiating table. It also offers to the external powers, and especially to the EU, the opportunity to play a constructive peacebuilding role, moving away from the current geopolitical 'zero-sum game' in which the EU, but in particular the US, have been embroiled without being able to develop a coherent diplomatic strategy towards the region. Although the EU, the OSCE and the UN have neither the resources nor the power to press Russia to make concessions, the existence of the Geneva forum internationalizes mediation efforts and generates institutional and political incentives among the external actors to elaborate concrete positions. Furthermore establishing a 'direct line' between Georgia, Abkhazia and South Ossetia with the help of the EU and other international actors is of the essence. The Geneva forum is one context in which this goal can be advanced.

Beyond the Geneva forum, the EU continues to influence the resolution of the conflict by indirect means, for example within the framework of the Eastern Partnership (EaP), launched in 2009. The initiative concentrates on four policy dimensions: bi- and multilateral relations, governance and financial assistance. The EaP emphasizes 'the need for their earliest peaceful settlement on the basis of principles and norms of international law' (Council of the EU 2009) and considers that conflict resolution in the South Caucasus is possible only through long-term goals related to democracy and development. Indeed, the activities that the EU promotes in the framework of the Eastern Partnership are centred on the promotion of good governance and financial assistance as well as regional trade and energy cooperation. Thus the Eastern Partnership reconfirms the EU's preference for economic and political assistance in post-war situations rather than direct conflict resolution activities (Mikhelidze 2010).

Factors impeding multilateralism

All actors, the EU included, in the region have tried to engage with the conflicts at the bilateral rather than multilateral level. This was especially true in the first period of the conflicts, up until the re-eruption of war in 2008. The motivations for its reluctance to create an effective multilateral forum for conflict prevention and resolution could be explained by the circumstances in which solutions have been sought. The EU, in principle, has represented an *encompassing institution*, able to gain trust and enjoy legitimacy among all parties involved. As noted by Bertram (1995) this represents a crucial component of successful multilateral diplomacy. Notwithstanding, a number of competing factors have impaired the EU's potential to act as an effective multilateral actor in conflict resolution in Georgia. Several factors impeded the EU's effective multilateral approach, which were particularly evident in the first phase (1990s–2008), although they have persisted to some extent in the second, post-2008, phase of the conflicts too.

First, there was a *lack of knowledge*. The EU did not engage with or seek to understand the causes and origins of the conflict when they first erupted (Coppieters 2007). Indeed, the EU was largely absent when the conflicts first broke out. By contrast, in the post-2008 phase, the EU rectified the problem by commissioning the 'Tagliavini report',[8] which provided a historical and legal assessment of the eruption and conduct of the war in August 2008. But the initial lack of knowledge hindered an accurate identification of the dynamics between the conflict parties. Georgia has always stressed the geopolitical aspect of the conflict, downplaying the Abkhaz and South Ossetian positions, portraying it as a confrontation with Russia. The EU meanwhile viewed the conflict exclusively as a confrontation between the metropolitan state and the *de facto* republics, and refused (at least officially) to acknowledge Russia's role in the conflict. Even when the August War revealed Russia's direct involvement in the conflict, the EU initially continued to regard the conflict as a two-party game (i.e. conflict between metropolitan and *de facto* states).[9] Both the Georgian and the EU's positions had partial truths in them, but both were also inaccurate. To some extent, this inaccuracy in the EU's position was rectified after the war. However, in other respects, the EU's original conceptualization of the conflict persists. The Union has in fact exerted little pressure on Russia to fulfil the Medvedev–Sarkozy six-point agreement or to reach a new Russian unilateral declaration on the non-use of force (in response to a similar initiative by Georgian President Mikheil Saakashvili).

Second, the EU's choice to focus only on two parties of the conflict rather than engage effectively with all parties in a multilateral setting can in part be explained by a *perceived lack of leverage* (Bertram 1995). Well aware of its dependence on Russian energy resources and underestimating the interdependence between the EU and Russia, the Union has come to lose its leverage over the Russia over the South Caucasus. The EU only directly engaged the Kremlin during the hot phase of war in 2008. Then, EU policy was exclusively aimed at ending the military confrontation and reaching a ceasefire agreement. Neither before 2008 nor since has the EU purposively engaged Russia through multilateral talks, alongside Georgia and the breakaway entities, to push forward the peace process.

Third and relatedly, the EU has displayed a *lack of sense of urgency* deriving partially from a *lack of clarity of purpose* (Bertram 1995). In the Georgian conflicts, the actors involved in the peace process, especially the EU and Russia, have, paradoxically perhaps, shared the same goal of supporting the *status quo* (in Russia's case, this was at least true until Kosovo's declaration of independence in 2008), while diverging in their policies to achieve it. The EU has aimed not to jeopardize its bilateral relations with Russia. The Kremlin has sought to maintain and manipulate the condition of stable instability in the region in order to keep its hold on the South Caucasus. Beyond the goal of preventing further destabilization, however, there has been little intra-EU agreement on what policy to pursue in the Caucasus. The internal division between member states pressing for further engagement in the Mediterranean versus the Eastern neighbourhood often prevented the parties from acting under a shared policy scheme. Besides, within the Union, there was no member state compliancy pushing for the South Caucasus' inclusion on the EU foreign policy agenda before the 2004 EU enlargement.[10] Therefore, the EU generally contented itself with acting in a complementary fashion to the OSCE and UN, mostly concentrating on humanitarian and development efforts. Its effective multilateral intervention was limited to August 2008, when the war challenged European security directly.

The Caucasus is a region in which any form of external action – uni-, bi-, multilateral or even inaction – is determined by Western actors' bilateral relations with Russia. These dynamics hinder the EU's effective multilateralism in conflict resolution. As noted by Klein *et al.* (2010), the preferences of the EU for a particular diplomatic approach 'depend primarily on the issue in question, the external partner concerned and/or the inter-institutional competition'. The Georgian conflicts highlight how the EU's institutional limits, its inability to formulate a common position/strategy towards the South Caucasus as well as 'paralysis of the EU decision-making' (Ibid.) have led to passive multilateralism.

This is not to say that the EU has always been marked by passivity. When its security interests have been directly threatened, as in the 2008 war, the Union has acted. Yet, such action reveals the EU's tendency to act in the framework of '*ad hoc* meetings and short-term arrangements to solve particular problem' (see Chapter 2), an approach which cannot be considered as multilateralism. Thus the EU's approach towards conflict resolution in Georgia was and continues to be pragmatic and reactive. In the past, its policy was driven mainly by maintaining the *status quo* rather than solving the conflicts. In this respect, there was little reason to engage Russia, which, paradoxically, acted to pursue the same goal.

The EU and the crisis in BiH: from successful multilateralism to failing unilateralism

Since the beginning of the civil war in Bosnia and Herzegovina (hereafter BiH or Bosnia) in the 1990s, BiH has turned into a laboratory that has tested the reaction of the international community to a post-Cold War conflict settlement and the post-conflict consolidation and reconstruction processes.[11] BiH has also been a country where the transition from NATO-led to EU-led military operation took place for the first time. And last but not least, BiH is the country of the Western Balkans where the conditionality of the EU association and membership has faced serious challenges in recent years.

The first phase of the conflict in BiH was an element of a broader fragmentation of the former Yugoslavia, which started at the beginning of the 1990s. The first inter-community clashes between Bosnian Muslims (Bosniaks), Serbs and Croats rapidly deteriorated into a full-scale civil war, with the heavy involvement of Bosnian neighbours – Serbia and Croatia. The first phase of the conflict lasted between April 1992 and December 1995 and resulted in the most devastating conflict in Europe since 1945, with some 100,000 persons killed and over two million displaced. Due to the ineffectiveness of international involvement led by the UN, the open internal military conflict in BiH stopped effectively only after the NATO operation *Deliberate Force* in August and September 1995. Consequently, the key elements of the constitutional framework for the Republic of BiH were set by the Dayton Accords (officially 'the General Framework Agreement for Peace in Bosnia and Herzegovina') signed by representatives of Yugoslavia/Serbia, Croatia and the president of BiH, and co-signed by France, the US, the UK, Germany and Russia in December 1995. The Dayton Agreement has also been a basis for the presence of the international community in Bosnia that has lasted ever since.

The actors involved

The abilities of international actors to tackle a post-Cold War conflict were tested in Bosnia, sometimes with very unimpressive results. The different international actors in BiH all cooperated or competed with each other in a very complex environment (see Penksa 2006: 12). The global and regional institutions involved primarily the UN, NATO, OSCE, the European Union and the Council of Europe. The regional and local actors included institutions connected directly or indirectly to the Dayton Accords, such as the Peace Implementation Council, the High Representative for Bosnia and Herzegovina (HR for BiH) or the International Criminal Tribunal for Former Yugoslavia among others. To this list should also be added state actors, such as those that sponsored the Dayton Accords and two others that co-signed it beside Bosnians.

The United Nations has provided the general legal framework for international involvement in BiH, both in the pre-Dayton and post-Dayton period. The UN's reputation in BiH was weakened significantly by its inability to end the atrocities in Bosnia in the first half of the 1990s; the Dayton Accords nonetheless explicitly envisaged a role for the UN Security Council in the country. The UN led the first post-Dayton police mission in BiH, the UN International Police Force (IPTF), and a UN Security Council resolution also established the post of the HR for BiH in 1995. NATO's role increased significantly after 1995 when the NATO-led operations IFOR and SFOR were vested with key responsibility for the military aspects of the implementation of the Dayton Agreement. NATO's presence in BiH was reduced again in 2004 when the SFOR operation was replaced by the EU-led operation EUFOR Althea. However, even after 2004, NATO was present in BiH via its Headquarters in Sarajevo and by fulfilling some operational tasks linked to the search for those indicted by the International Criminal Tribunal for Former Yugoslavia. The OSCE first assisted in the organizing of – and later monitoring of – elections and the election process in BiH. The potential of the OSCE, however, was much broader. It was even considered as a candidate to replace the post-Dayton UN police mission in 2003 (Penksa 2006: 5).

The Peace Implementation Council (PIC) has been the key multilateral platform for political and strategic decisions in the post-Dayton process, involving 55 actors – both states and key international organizations and agents. Within the PIC, a narrower Steering Group (composed of Canada, France, Germany, Italy, Japan, Russia, United Kingdom, United States, the European Union, and Turkey representing the Organisation of the Islamic Conference) serves as a forum for more frequent meetings and more intensive discussions. The PIC acts as a consultation body for the HR for BiH and can also (in a limited way) review his/her decisions. The Council also provides a framework for long-term strategic decisions about BiH, for instance regarding the financial assistance from the international community. The ambassadors of the members of the PIC and/or the Steering Group frequently comment on many issues of internal BiH politics.

However, the most visible external actors have been the High Representative for BiH and the Office of the High Representative (OHR for BiH) who has been vested with controlling civilian aspects of the Dayton implementation. The HR for BiH was given an impressive catalogue of competencies within the Bosnian constitutional structure, including the power of dismissing Bosnians (whether elected or non-elected) from their office if they are deemed to be obstructing the implementation of the Dayton Agreement (the so-called 'Bonn powers').[12] As an informal rule, the HR is a citizen of an EU country while their deputy has US citizenship. The time frame of the activity of the HR and his/her team was not defined in the Dayton Agreement. As a consequence, the possible closure of the Office of the HR for BiH has been discussed on several occasions.

The EU in Bosnia and Herzegovina

The European Union has been present in BiH, directly or indirectly, since the split of Yugoslavia, but the intensity and format of the EU's involvement has varied significantly. In general, three phases of the EU's involvement in BiH can be identified: the pre-Dayton period (1991–5); the period between the adoption of the Dayton Accords and the establishment of the EU Special Representative for Bosnia (1995–2002); and the period after the establishment of the EU Special Representative and the launch of EU-led police and military missions (2004–present). The EU is represented by three major European actors in BiH: the EU Special Representative for BiH, the EU military mission EUFOR Althea, and the EU Delegation in Bosnia (the Delegation of the European Commission in the pre-Lisbon period). This institutional trio is supplemented by the EU Police Mission (EUPM), which succeeded the UN-led International Police Task Force in 2003. Moreover, the majority of the

Union's member states are represented in Bosnia and coordinate their policies at the Heads of Missions (HoMs) meetings.

Relations between the EU and BiH have developed within a more general framework of the EU's relations with the Western Balkans. The cornerstone of this framework is a set of bilateral Stabilisation and Association Agreements between the EU and the individual states of the Western Balkans (see Gordon 2009; Fagan 2010). The structure and content of these separate agreements, however, are in many aspects similar to each other, including the perspective of EU membership, a regular evaluation process, and organization of joint summits between the EU and the participating states. As a result, the EU has combined multilateral and bilateral approaches to the states of the Western Balkans within this broader strategy. Nevertheless, the impact of the EU's multilateral approach to the Western Balkans should not be overestimated in the BiH case. The scope of the international presence in BiH and the intensity of the international involvement in the post-conflict reconstruction have been unique in comparison to neighbouring countries. For these reasons, this study focuses on the BiH case and pays a relatively limited attention to the general EU strategy for the Western Balkans.

The EU's multilateralism

In the period before the Dayton Agreement and its immediate follow-up, the EU seemed to live up to its declarations to engage multilaterally. The European Community/European Union was involved in several platforms that sought a solution to the conflict that followed the break-up of Yugoslavia, such as the Peace Conference on the former Yugoslavia and its Arbitration Commission, and co-authored several (unsuccessful) peace plans. However, the EU became increasingly marginalized in the practical handling of the conflict. It was represented at the peace conference by a special envoy, but it was not a formal signatory of the Dayton Agreement.

The major platforms for EU involvement in BiH were the Peace Implementation Council and its Steering Board. The EU's adaptation to the multilateral patterns of behaviour in BiH was strengthened by the format of the EU's involvement in the PIC. Within it, the EU was represented simultaneously by the Commission Delegation, the rotating EU presidency, and, indirectly, by several member states that were permanent members of the PIC such as the UK, France or Germany, whose positions in the PIC were not necessarily always in full harmony.

Within the complex international presence in BiH, the EU focused on financing elements of the BiH transformation, leaving political transition, elections and the secure environment agenda to other international actors. When it acted in these latter areas, it was only indirectly via the PIC. The fact that the EU lacked independent military capacity together with the informal agreement that the HR for BiH would be a diplomat from an EU state, made it easier for the EU to accept this limited role within the multilateral environment of the post-Dayton BiH.

In later periods, the EU's approach developed into what could be described as 'EU-led' or 'EU-dominated' multilateralism. The Union aspired to occupy a leading position within the multilateral framework through new institutions (such as the EU Special Representative) and autonomous operations (EUPM and EUFOR Althea) and take the actual responsibility for the development in BiH. Instead of backing the international efforts, the international community should back the EU's activity in BiH. The EU still declares its support for the multilateral format of the international engagement. In practice, however, when 'EU-dominated' multilateralism failed to be accepted by other international actors in BiH or to deliver the expected results, the EU has tended to choose other strategies, both bilateral and unilateral. At the same time, there is no unity among the EU members. Some EU states, in particular the UK, have not allowed the EU to abandon the multilateral environment completely and have tended to shift decision-making from HoMs to PIC consistently.[13]

The EU's bilateralism

The turning point of the EU's presence in BiH was the year 2002. Firstly, the Union created the post of EU Special Representative for Bosnia and Herzegovina in 2002. Subsequently, the EU launched its first foreign police mission/operation (2003) and the large-scale military operation EUFOR Althea (2004) in BiH. This shift in the BiH-tailored EU's approach was only strengthened by more general development of the EU's policy towards the Western Balkans, which materialized primarily in the Union's plan to conclude Stabilisation and Association Agreements.

This period also seems to be the starting point of EU bilateralism in BiH. Alternatively, the format of the EU's involvement can be described as European bilateralism under the umbrella of multilateralism. In all cases of the EU bilateral involvement, the EU actor was 'shielded' by resolution(s) of the UN Security Council and approved by the PIC. In several policy areas, the EU in BiH replaced another international actor which dominated in the earlier phases of the international involvement in the BiH. Two important examples have been the police operation EUPM and the military operation EUFOR Althea. In both situations, the transfer of responsibility was not a 'hostile takeover' by the Union. The international predecessor agreed with the new EU role. NATO, for example, has even remained present in BiH, both through the Althea operation conducted under Berlin Plus format,[14] and through officers seconded to the BiH defence ministry. However, the transfer of responsibility has been much less debated and welcomed by some internal actors in BiH. In particular, the EU's involvement in police reform in BiH received a particularly cold reception (Penksa 2006: 5).

The most complicated and confusing situation resulted from the EU's bilateral policy towards the HR for BiH. The post of the EUSR for BiH was established in 2002. From the very beginning, there was, by political decision, a 'personal union' between the holders of the EUSR post and the post of HR for BiH under the Dayton Agreement. However, the formal mandates as well as the staffs of the EUSR and the HR differed even though they shared the premises (Grevi 2007: 85). In particular, the Bonn powers were exercised by the double-hatted HR/ EUSR in his capacity of the HR only. The merger between the EUSR and the HR was therefore primarily based on a bilateral agreement between the EU and the HR. In 2011, the EU decided to terminate this practice and appointed a new EUSR, this time double-hatted with the Head of the EU Delegation.

The EUSR is vested with an extensive catalogue of tasks. They include: towards the EU's institutions, to 'provide the High Representative and the European Commission with advice' regarding the rule of law in BiH; towards other EU structures in BiH, to 'provide EUFOR commander with local political advice', 'provide head of mission of the EUPM with local political guidance' and 'contribute to reinforcement of internal EU coordination and coherence in BiH'; towards institutions of BiH, to 'offer advice and facilitation in the political process' and 'provide political advice and facilitation in the process of constitutional reform'; and towards the general public, to 'ensure consistency and coherence of EU action'.

In contrast to the 'hard' competencies of the HR (demonstrated in particular in the Bonn powers), the EUSR is vested primarily with 'soft' powers, such as advice or facilitation. The HR/EUSR's double-hatting seemed to provide a framework for the gradual increase of the EU presence in BiH. The EU attempted to attract the coordination role for the international activity in BiH after a potential phasing-out of the HR and his/her Office from Bosnia. At the same time, the HR/ EUSR's double-hatted format could provide the EU with a change to benefit from higher visibility and profile of an already well-established international actor in BiH. However, this strategy has not worked out as it may have been anticipated.

First, the 'EU hat' of the HR/EUSR has been significantly obscured by the activities undertaken by the HR, in particular the exercise of the Bonn powers. The EUSR's role suffered from a lack of visibility and it was the European Commission/ EU Delegation and not the EUSR that was understood, by stakeholders, as the representative of the EU in BiH.[15] Second, the EU failed in its policy aimed at decreasing the use of the Bonn powers by the HR. The EU hoped that with a 'membership perspective', the carrot of accession to the EU would bring about a decline in the need to use the HR's powers. Other primarily non-EU actors, such as the United States or Turkey, however, pushed for further use of HR's Bonn powers as the transformative tool in BiH. This created almost schizophrenia in the EUSR/HR's position. While there was a temporary reduction in the use of Bonn powers under the 'hands off' approach of HR/EUSR Schwarz-Schilling, his successors, HRs/EUSRs Lajčák and Inzko, have found it necessary to use them once again.[16]

Third, the phasing-out of the HR and the OHR has not continued as quickly as expected at the beginning of the 2000s. Despite a gradual reduction in the size of the OHR, the institution continues to exist. Moreover, due to pressure in the PIC from the US and Turkey, which still want the OHR to remain engaged in BiH, it 'survived' an attempt to close it down in 2009 (Vogel 2009). Debates were ongoing over the location of the OHR, including over the possibility of moving the Office physically outside the BiH. However, at the time of writing, no such step has been taken.[17]

The EU as a unilateral actor

As a reaction to this failure of strategy, the EU seemed to adhere to more unilateral steps in 2010–11. Besides merging the EUSR with the position of the EU delegation head, the Union seemed to aspire to a more leading role in the HoMs meetings, on the basis of the enhanced powers of the EU in foreign policy after the Lisbon Treaty and the new structural role of the European External Action Service.[18] Delays in implementing these ideas were caused primarily by the vacancy in the post of the head of the EU delegation in BiH and not by any debate about the EU's strategy. The new EUSR should benefit both from the enlarged team of the EU delegation, primarily by personnel with expertise in policy and governance agenda, and from a special tool box to influence the political situation and guarantee the transformation pace in BiH.[19] As of April 2011, the content of this 'EU tool box' had yet to be made public, but it is likely to include some instruments analogous to the present Bonn powers of the HR – with a difference that they could be used unilaterally by the Union and would be explicitly embedded in the constitutional order of BiH.

Another element of a more unilateral EU policy towards the BiH is implicit in the process of the association to and potential membership of BiH in the EU. The European Council confirmed a membership perspective for Bosnia in 2005 and the EU–BiH Stabilisation and Association Agreement was signed in 2008. However, the BiH, in contrast to Croatia and Macedonia, has yet to acquire a candidate country status. It has also failed to experience the same progression as Serbia and Montenegro towards this status. Another step, with both practical and symbolic value, was the EU's decision to facilitate (2008) and to partially liberalize (2010) its visa regime for the citizens of BiH. Regardless of the frequently expressed hopes for improved dialogue between the Union and the associated/candidate state and its entities within the EU association and accession process, the very fact of the conditionality applied towards the BiH turns the Union's policy towards this country into an essentially unilateral one. In contrast, the multilateral element of the EU strategy for the Western Balkans, including (for example) support of mutual cooperation of the states of the region, seems surprisingly invisible in the case of BiH.

The mismatch of tools and aspirations

The post-Dayton regime gave rise to a moderate optimism about the efficiency of the international intervention in BiH. Hostilities were brought to an end, state functions were re-established, and many practical barriers between the Bosniak–Croat Federation and the Republika Srpska were removed. More recent developments in

BiH, such as the failure of constitutional reform, the critique of the Dayton-based power-sharing regime by the European Court for Human Rights, or the secessionist steps by Republika Srpska, have produced sceptical comments on Bosnia's future.[20]

What have been the major reasons for this (alleged) failure? The EU was able to operate efficiently within the multilateral framework in the BiH as long as it was not the leader of the process. However, the dramatic increase in the EU's presence in BiH after 2002 sent several consecutive and partially colliding signals which, eventually, hampered the efficiency of the EU's role. The first message was about the need to phase out the directly controlling and micro-intervening role of the international community in BiH (a 'job done' type of message) which took the form, among others, of the EU's critique of the use of Bonn powers by the HR for BiH. This message was not received well by several other international actors in BiH. The second message sent by the EU was about the new role of the association process and the perspective of EU membership as a new, and potentially more efficient, tool for the international community in BiH. Again, the inherent element of this message was the dominant role of the EU within the more general context of multilateral international involvement in BiH and a potential marginalization of the role of other international actors. However, this message was not complemented, on the side of the EU, by a real and reliable 'European vision' for BiH as the whole integration process of the Western Balkans has been delayed in recent years. As a result, it is primarily the EU's aspiration for a leading role in the international community in BiH, in combination with the lack of efficient conditionality tools at the EU's disposal, which have contributed to a situation in which the EU in BiH has shifted from relatively successful multilateral cooperation to primarily ineffective unilateralism.

Conclusion

This chapter has analysed the EU's involvement in conflict resolution in its neighbourhood, in Georgia and in Bosnia. In both cases, the EU has sought to play a major role in helping the countries to resolve their conflicts during all stages. Neither of them can be regarded as yet resolved. The 2008 Russia–Georgia war showed that the long-term absence of violence may reverse rapidly if a sense of 'positive peace' is not achieved. In Bosnia, no such spectacular events could be observed, but the massive presence of international organizations in the country and the key constitutional role of the High Representative suggest that the country still needs external assistance.

The EU was not fully constituted as an international actor at the beginning of the 1990s during the first phases of the conflicts. It has, however, increasingly raised its profile, but also tended to engage rather slowly. Both in Bosnia and in Georgia, it took a long time before the EU started playing an independent role. In the first phases, it instead supported other already active external actors and only recently has it taken over or substituted itself for them. In both cases, the EU has been able to establish itself as a legitimate and active player, a status acknowledged both by the conflict parties and the international community.

There is, however, a significant difference in terms of impact. Whereas the EU has been pushing for a more rapid pace of reform in Bosnia, which should contribute to long-term conflict resolution, it has not yet been able to make a significant difference in Georgia. Context has played an important role in shaping these differences (see Klein *et al*. 2010). Although the same actors are involved in both regions, their engagement varies. The viability of most EU actions depends heavily, too, on external actors. It has not been easy for the EU to engage with Russia. Clearly, Moscow is less interested in acting multilaterally with the EU than keeping relations at the bilateral level with particular member states. Similarly, if a potential partner's activity is curtailed by domestic politics (US low-profile reaction to the Georgian crisis in 2008) or internal disputes (the end of the OSCE mission in Georgia), there is very limited room for cooperation in a multilateral format. At the same time, the EU's partners' strong opinions also make a multilateral cooperation difficult, as it is more challenging to reach a common position.

Unsurprisingly, the EU's multilateral effectiveness is always reduced when there are internal disagreements. The case of Bosnia clearly shows that as long as the member states are able to follow a common line, the EU's influence is enhanced. In recent years, however, in the face of the seeming intractability of the problems in BiH, the consensus has apparently disappeared. Member states have started acting on their own and against each other in other fora (such as the PIC) and the EU's ability to lead the conflict resolution process in Bosnia has declined.

A common approach is necessary, not least because the EU is hardly ever represented in a unitary way. In Bosnia, the EU Delegation and several member states have all been members of the Peace Implementation Council. Moreover, the EU has launched a number of European (Common) Security and Defence operations in Bosnia, which often have been only loosely connected and coordinated. Similarly, besides the EU presence in Georgia, the member states have also been members of the OSCE, the most active external actor in the conflict.

Indeed, if we searched for a single word capturing the EU's involvement in both conflicts, it would be 'plurality'. The EU has been using various types of engagement. It has acted on a uni-, bi-, and multilateral basis as well as remained inactive. Inaction was the dominant EU approach in the first phases of the conflicts, when the Union was not fully constituted and the member states were not able to agree on a sustained single position – a phenomenon painfully visible in the case of Bosnia in the early 1990s. Since its first involvement, the EU has acted multilaterally, participating in various councils that aimed at coordinating external actors. A tendency to remain in the background can be seen in efforts to support the activity of other organizations (for example, the EU's support to the Joint Control Commission in Georgia).

Bilateralism, unlike the other forms of involvement, seems to have been circumstantial rather than a matter of choice. The most evident example was the Russian–Georgian war in 2008, when the EU negotiated the ceasefire, because there was nobody else available. The US was preoccupied with the upcoming presidential elections and both the UN and the OCSE were disabled by the fact that Russia was one of the warring parties. A slightly different development with the same result can be observed in Bosnia, where other external actors were ready to disengage with the rising EU presence in some phases of the process.

However, unilateralism is an ever-present factor of EU activity in the neighbourhood. The EU has been unilaterally pushing its own ideals and concepts on both Bosnia and Georgia. It has done so through the association/enlargement conditionality common to the whole of the Western Balkans in the case of the former and through financial assistance to both the state and civil society in the case of the latter.

A striking similarity can be found in the reasons for the EU's underperformance in both Georgia and Bosnia. The most pressing problems have revolved around the EU's misunderstanding of the situation. In Georgia, the EU did not see the real nature of the conflict in the beginning and underestimated its urgency. Similarly in Bosnia, the EU judged the state of affairs wrongly in the mid-2000s. In terms of the problems on the ground, it has underestimated the strength of nationalism and the vested interests of all entities. In terms of the positions of other external actors, it has underestimated their willingness to remain engaged actively in Bosnia and has failed to consult them on an equal basis. As a result, it has not been able to play the leading role it expected to play and instead has resorted to a frustrated and ineffective unilateralism.

To conclude, the European Union uses all forms of engagement in conflict resolution in the neighbourhood. Diplomatic non-action was restricted to the first phases of the conflicts when the EU lacked the structure and experience needed as prerequisites for acting together. Whereas bilateralism is circumstantial and does not seem to be a preferred mode of EU activity in the conflicts, both uni- and multilateralism became favoured EU choices. Yet, both approaches were used with a varying degree of effectiveness. What our analysis suggests is that the EU has been effective in supporting multilateral activities of other organizations, but has been much less so as a leading partner of such endeavours.

Notes

1 The authors would like to thank Geoffrey Edwards and John Peterson for their comments on the previous drafts of the text.
2 The term 'negative peace' labels a ceasefire when the conflicting parties stop using force, but maintain their conflict of interest. The term 'positive peace', in contrast, describes a situation when the conflict is eliminated altogether.
3 Even though there always are at least two conflicting parties, this type of intervention may still be considered bilateral for the purpose of this research, which is not interested in how the conflicts are resolved, but in how the external actor intervenes in the process. At the same time, the intervening actor may have a different approach to each of the parties, thus combining a unilateral and bilateral approach, which might be labelled as 'selective bilateralism'.
4 In the case of Georgia, these phases have not been linear and can be divided in two periods: the first period including violence of 1992–3, immediate de-escalation (1993), post-war reconstruction (1993–6), accompanied by long-term peacebuilding (1996–); and the second period encompassing escalation leading to violence in 2008, de-escalation (2008), post-war reconstruction, and long-term peacebuilding (2008–).

5 For the past sixteen years the European Union has been funding programmes in Georgia/
   Abkhazia/South Ossetia. More than 100 projects are currently being implemented (cf.
   EU Delegation to Georgia 2012).
6 Other factors for the EU's law profile engagement with the conflict resolution in Georgia
   are described below in the sections: Factors impeding multilateralism.
7 Interviews with Georgian official and EU diplomat, Tbilisi, December 2010.
8 An independent international fact-finding mission on the conflict in Georgia.
9 Interview with EU diplomat, Tbilisi, December 2010.
10 Interview with Georgian official, Tbilisi, December 2010.
11 A number of civilian and military operations have been conducted in Bosnia so far and
   many of them are mentioned in this chapter. The UN-led International Police Force and
   the EU Police Missions have played an important role in the re-building and transformation of the law enforcement authorities. The military operations led by NATO (IFOR,
   SFOR) and the EU (EURFOR Althea) have been tasked with the military aspects of
   the conflict resolution process, including the establishment of a secure environment.
12 The Bonn powers were not included in the original version of the Dayton Accords but
   added only later. They have been controversial and subject to critique by the Council of
   Europe (see Venneri 2007: 27).
13 Interview with a Czech embassy official, Sarajevo, April 2011.
14 Berlin Plus is a label for an EU–NATO agreement of 2002/3 which allows the EU to
   use NATO assets in its crisis management operations.
15 Interviews with foreign diplomats and local community representatives, Sarajevo, April
   2011; also cf. Penksa 2006: 13. In contrast, the EU element of the holder of the HR/
   EUSR post was described as crucial for the establishment of European integration
   department within the ministry of foreign affairs of BiH (Grevi 2007: 83).
16 The holders of the HR's office (and their nationality) have been the following: Carl Bildt
   (1995–7; Sweden), Carlos Westendorp (1997–9; Spain), Wolfgang Petritsch (1999–2002;
   Austria), Lord Paddy Ashdown (2002–6; the United Kingdom), Christian Schwarz-
   Schilling (2006–7; Germany), Miroslav Lajčák (2007–9; Slovakia) and Valentin Inzko
   (since 2009; Austria).
17 Interview with Czech embassy and OHR officials, Sarajevo, April 2011.
18 Interview with an EU delegation official, Sarajevo, April 2011.
19 Interview with an EU delegation official, Sarajevo, April 2011.
20 For example, Lord Ashdown, a former High Representative, stated in April 2011 that
   the international community in BiH 'foolishly allowed itself to believe that the job was
   done and, distracted by Iraq and Afghanistan, shifted attention elsewhere' (*The Economist*
   2011).

References

Asmus, R.D. (2010) *A Little War that Shook the World: Georgia, Russia and the Future of the West*,
   New York: Palgrave Macmillan.
Bertram, C. (1995) 'Multilateral Diplomacy and Conflict Resolution', *Survival* 37(4): 65–82.
Civil Georgia (2008) 'Six-Point Ceasefire Plan', Tbilisi, 20 August 2008. Online. Available
   HTTP: <http://www.civil.ge/eng/article.php?id=19478&search=Six-Point%20
   Ceasefire%20Plan> (accessed 20 May 2011).
'Consolidated Version of the Treaty on European Union' (TEU). OJ C 83, 30.3.2010,
   p. 13–45.
Coppieters, B. (2007) *The EU and Georgia: Time perspectives in Conflict Resolution*, Occasional
   Paper no. 70, Paris: EU ISS.

Council of the European Union (2005) 'Council Common Position 2005/304/CFSP of 12 April 2005 concerning conflict prevention, management and resolution in Africa and repealing Common Position 2004/85/CFSP', OJ L 97, 15.4.2005, p. 57–62.

Council of the European Union (2008) 'Council Joint Action 2008/132/CFSP of 18 February 2008 amending and extending the mandate of the European Union Special Representative for the South Caucasus', OJ L 43, 19.2.2008, p. 30–3.

Council of the European Union (2009) Joint Declarations of the Prague Eastern Partnership Summit, Prague, 7 May 2009, doc. 8435/09.

Diehl, P.F. (2008) *Peace Operations*, Cambridge: Polity Press.

The Economist (2011) 'Two Visions for Bosnia', Eastern Approaches Blog, 13 April 2011. Online. Available HTTP: <http://www.economist.com/blogs/eastern-approaches> (accessed 20 May 2011).

EU Delegation to Georgia (2012) 'List of projects'. Online. Available HTTP: <http://eeas. europa.eu/delegations/georgia/projects/list_of_projects/projects_en.htm> (accessed 16 January 2012).

'EU–Georgia Action Plan', Brussels, 14 November 2006.

European Commission (2001) 'Communication from the Commission on Conflict Prevention', doc. COM(2001)211 final.

European Council (2001) 'EU Programme for the Prevention of Violent Conflicts', doc. 9537/1/01REV 1.

European Council (2003) 'A Secure Europe in a Better World. European Security Strategy', Brussels, 12 December 2003.

European Council (2004a) 'Headline Goal 2010', Brussels, 25–26 June 2004.

European Council (2004b) 'Civilian Headline Goal 2008', Brussels, 16–17 December 2004.

Fagan, A. (2010) *Europe's Balkan Dilemma: Paths to Civil Society or State-Building?*, London: I.B.Tauris.

Gilboa, E. (2009) 'Media and Conflict Resolution: A Framework for Analysis', *Marquette Law Review* 93(1): 87–111.

Gordon, C. (2009) 'The Stabilization and Association Process in the Western Balkans: An Effective Instrument of Post-conflict Management?', *Ethnopolitics* 8(3/4): 325–40.

Grevi, G. (2007) *Pioneering foreign policy: The EU Special Representatives*, Chaillot Paper no.106, Paris: EU ISS.

ICG (International Crisis Group) (2006) 'Abkhazia Today', Europe Report no. 176, 15 September 2006.

Klein, N., Reiners, W., Chen, Z., Jian, J. and Šlosarčík, I. (2010) 'Diplomatic Strategies of Major Powers: Competing Patterns of International Relations? The Cases of the United States of America, China and the European Union', MERCURY E-paper no. 2. Online. Available HTTP: <http://www.europa.ed.ac.uk/global_europa/external_relations/mercury> (accessed 19 May 2011).

Mikhelidze, N. (2010) *The Geneva Talks over Georgia's Territorial Conflicts: Achievements and Challenges*, Documenti IAI no. 1025, Rome: IAI. Online. Available HTTP: <http://www.iai.it/pdf/DocIAI/iai1025.pdf> (accessed 20 May 2011).

Penksa, S. (2006) *Policing Bosnia and Herzegovina 2003–05. Issues and Mandates and Management in ESDP Mission*, CEPS Working Document no. 255. Brussels: CEPS.

Popescu, N. (2010) 'The EU and Civil Society in the Georgian-Abkhaz Conflict', MICROCON Policy Working Paper no. 15, Brighton: MICROCON. Online. Available HTTP: <http://www.microconflict.eu/publications/PWP15_NP.pdf> (accessed 20 May 2011).

Stewart, E.J. (2008) 'Capabilities and Coherence? The Evolution of European Union Conflict Prevention', *European Foreign Affairs Review* 13(2): 229–53.

Tocci, N. (2008) 'The European Union, Conflict Transformation and Civil Society: A Conceptual Framework', MICROCON Policy Working Paper no. 1. Brighton: MICROCON. Online. Available HTTP: <http://www.microconflict.eu/publications/PWP1_NT.pdf> (accessed 20 May 2011).

Venneri, G. (2007) *Modelling States from Brussels? A Critical Assessment of the EU-Driven State Building of Bosnia and Herzegovina*, Nicosia: Cyprus Centre of European and International Affairs.

Vogel, T. (2009) 'Cypriot Threats Could Affect Role of Top Envoy in Bosnia', *European Voice*, 9 July 2009. Online. Available HTTP: <http://www.europeanvoice.com/article/imported/Cypriot-threats could-affect-role-of-top-envoy-in-bosnia/65434.aspx> (accessed 20 May 2011).

Whitman, R.G. and Wolff, S. (2010) 'The EU as a Conflict Manager: The Case of Georgia and its Implications'. *International Affairs* 86: 87–107.

9

THE EUROPEAN UNION DEVELOPMENT STRATEGY IN AFRICA

The economic partnership agreements as a case of 'aggressive' multilateralism?

Lorenzo Fioramonti

Introduction[1]

Since the end of World War II, unprecedented development policies have been implemented throughout the world. Yet, poverty is rampant in most countries and the economic gap between rich countries and the poorest regions of the globe is still increasing today, which results in further global polarization. Interestingly, inequalities have not only grown at the international level, but also within countries, where increasing numbers of citizens live in poverty vis-à-vis pockets of concentrated wealth. This trend was aggravated during the 1980s and 1990s, which have often been described as the 'lost decades' of the developing world, through free-market policies and liberalization reforms forced onto poor countries by international financial institutions and international donors subscribing to the neo-liberal paradigm (the so-called Washington Consensus). Within developing countries, the adverse effects of globalization have been most visible as countries have been coerced into liberalizing their markets as a condition of debt rescheduling, in the hope of attracting new foreign direct investment.

For several decades, Europe entertained a preferential relationship with its former colonies in Africa, the Caribbean and the Pacific (the so-called ACP group). This relation was largely influenced by a principle derived from the process of regional integration in Europe, according to which both aid and trade constituted the cornerstones of a successful development policy. This approach translated into a set of preferences granted to the ACP: these countries' primary resources and goods were granted tariff-free access to the European market; European companies would enjoy a special treatment when investing in these underdeveloped economies; and development aid would be largely unconditional. Due to a number of factors, including the mismanagement of trade preferences, competition among Member States and corruption in poor countries, this approach to development did not achieve its intended (official) results but mainly served the purpose of reinforcing pre-existing linkages between the former colonizers (mainly Belgium, France, the Netherlands and the UK) and their ex-colonies. In a nutshell, the European traditional development philosophy proved a tool of hegemony, strengthening the influence of the 'old continent' especially in its sub-Saharan African backyard, which accounts for more than 60 per cent of the ACP membership. During the 1990s, with the progressive erosion of trade barriers and the diffusion of market liberalization, such a preferential relationship began to be called into question. The establishment of the World Trade Organization (WTO) in 1995 and the expansion of multilateral trade meant that the European approach to development (especially in sub-Saharan Africa) had to be reformed, at least in so far as its trade component was to become compatible with the non-preferential treatment promoted by the WTO.

These evolutions partly contributed towards a general change of attitude in the EU–Africa relationship. As Cosgrove-Sacks highlights, '[s]ince the end of the Cold War, many political and ideological motivations for cooperation between Europe and Africa have evaporated' (Cosgrove-Sacks 2001: 274). For the EU, the political and financial challenge of integrating the countries of Central and Eastern Europe caused Africa to slip to a lower level of importance, with policy towards African countries somewhat hardening. Political conditionalities regarding good governance and democratic performance became more important than before, while previously 'the vagaries of African leaders were politely overlooked' (Babarinde and Wright 2010: 6). From a rhetorical point of view, the new context of EU–Africa relations was couched in terms of 'partnerships' and 'mutual respect', but the reality stayed much the same: African states were in an inferior position, and often ended up accepting whatever they were offered by the EU (Olivier 2011).

This chapter analyses how the 'multilateralization' of development (as opposed to traditional bilateralism) has influenced the EU approach in the past few years, culminating with the adoption of the Economic Partnership Agreements (EPAs) with sub-Saharan African countries. It endorses the definition of multilateralism proposed by Bouchard and Peterson, which highlights the importance of 'voluntary' and 'institutionalized' cooperation 'governed by norms and principles' applying to all parties involved (Bouchard and Peterson 2011: 10). In this study, the parties involved are the European Union (EU) and its sub-Saharan African counterparts (as the most important subset of ACP countries involved in the EPA process). But the 'multilateralization' process also refers more broadly to the context within which the EPAs were designed and implemented, which was characterized by a growing international emphasis on shared development strategies, complementarity and coordination among all development actors. On the one hand, this multilateral evolution called for a more integrated approach to development policy, underlining that development does not occur in a vacuum and, therefore, there must be more coherence between the long-term objectives of aid policies and, importantly, other key policy sectors such as trade. On the other hand, it ended up conflating the development-trade nexus into a new set of hybrid regimes fundamentally influenced by the tenets of market liberalization. In this process, therefore, the strive for coherence and consistency (a positive and much needed objective in principle) had the unintended effect of shrinking the development side of the equation to the advantage of trade. In turn, it resulted in a new approach to development that was dominated by commercial elements at a time in which multilateral trade meant, by and large, free trade.

The chapter is based on a thorough analysis of official documents, negotiation reports, newspaper articles and a set of face-to-face interviews with African specialists and policy makers conducted at the headquarters of the African Union in Addis Ababa, Ethiopia, during September 2011. In the next sections the chapter discusses, first of all, the recent evolution of multilateral policies in the field of development. It then discusses how the EU policies in this field have evolved, with a particular emphasis on the development-trade nexus. The central sections analyse the controversies and tensions spurred by the EPA negotiations with sub-Saharan Africa and describe the EU-led process as a case of 'aggressive' multilateralism, thus indicating a dynamic dominated by a stronger and better-resourced partner at the expense of many (and fragmented) weaker counterparts. Albeit within an overall framework characterized by accepted norms and legitimacy, the EPA process was largely monopolized by the EU and ultimately presented to Africa as a 'take it or leave it' deal, thereby triggering resentment, opt-outs or unwilling acquiescence. Finally, the concluding section reflects on what the EPA case means for our analysis of multilateral processes against the backdrop of a 'new scramble' for Africa that sees the rising influence of emerging powers.

The multilateralization of development

In spite of over five decades of international aid policies (at least from the end of colonization), it is generally recognized that results have fallen short of expectations. Most so-called developing countries have been 'on the way' to development for a protracted period of time, often caught into vicious circles of endemic poverty and instability. At the same time, international donors have been competing for influence, generally through uncoordinated bilateral programmes, thereby producing redundancies and resource mismanagement.

In order to develop a common global agenda for development and increase coordination among a myriad of public and private aid providers, the United Nations (UN) promulgated the Millennium Development Goals (MDGs) in 2000, highlighting the need to bolster cooperation between donor and recipient countries as well as trace the impact of development policies in achieving eight key targets, from the eradication of poverty to the promotion of primary education and gender equality, within a global partnership for development.

Although the underlying principle of all goals was the definition of a multilateral strategy to achieve enduring development across the world, the call for the establishment of a global partnership very much laid the groundwork for a long-term and comprehensive multilateral strategy. It indeed aimed at establishing an open rule-based, predictable and non-discriminatory trading and financial system, explicitly recognizing that durable development cannot be achieved without taking a holistic approach to other key areas of global economic governance, which have traditionally seen poorer countries excluded from the decision room and often victimized by infamous structural adjustment policies. In part, this effort built on the original call made by the United Nations Conference on Trade and Development (UNCTAD) in 1968, which recommended the creation of a 'Generalized System of Preferences' (GSP) under which industrialized countries would grant non-discriminatory trade preferences to 'all' developing countries, successively incorporated into the General Agreement on Tariffs and Trade and the WTO.

The same approach permeated the 2002 UN Conference on Financing for Development that took place in Monterrey, Mexico. The so-called Monterrey Consensus, which has ever since become a reference point in the global debate on development aid, highlighted the urgent need to increase financial resources for development (including the well-known target of 0.7 per cent of gross national income (GNI)), mobilize foreign direct investment and other private flows, give priority to international trade as an engine for development, increase technical cooperation, resolve the issue of external debt, and address systemic multilateral problems, such as the inconsistency of the global financial, monetary and trading systems (UN 2003). A few years later, when the progress towards the MDGs was already showing some signs of faltering,[2] the issue of aid effectiveness prompted a major multilateral conference held in Paris, gathering together all main international donors (OECD 2005). Trying to tackle the structural deficiencies that aid policies had encountered for several decades, the donor countries and the most important non-governmental actors pledged to revamp their approach in order to guarantee: more ownership by recipient countries and beneficiaries, subscribing to the principle that development projects should be locally designed and driven; better alignment between donors' programmes and the priorities set out by recipient countries' governments, thereby stimulating a steadier flow of development funds into the national budget laws; more harmonization within the development sector in order to coordinate policies among donors and achieve complementarity (rather than competition and redundancy as had been the case in the past); a stronger focus on measurable results rather than generic qualitative achievements; and, finally, a new emphasis on mutual accountability, whereby donors and recipients would become mutually responsible for their development impacts (or lack thereof). In 2008, this new approach was further strengthened by the Accra Agenda for Action, which called for more predictability in the provision of international aid funds, so as to allow governments to plan ahead in their national policies (OECD 2008). It also established that recipient country systems would take precedence over donor country systems to allocate funding and that conditionalities on type and timing of expenditure would be removed. Finally, it invited donors to 'untie' aid, that is, relax those restrictions that prevented developing countries from buying the goods and services they needed from whomever and wherever they could get the best quality at the lowest price. Until then, most international donors had forced recipient governments to use development funding to purchase services and goods from companies based in the donor countries, thereby reabsorbing the money that was 'officially' spent on aiding the poor. The same year, the Doha Declaration on Financing for Development sent out two additional messages to the aid sector: development funds would continue aiming for the official targets despite the global economic crunch and more work should be put into analysing the developmental impacts of the financial crisis (UN 2008).

An important byproduct of this multilateralization process was a shift in the official language: development countries would no longer be referred to as 'recipients', but – due to the new emphasis on ownership and mutual responsibility – their role would be officially upgraded to that of 'partners'.

The EU and the trade development nexus

The EU and its Member States have played a rather proactive role in all above-mentioned multilateral fora. As key members of the Organisation for Economic Co-operation and Development (OECD), most European countries have also led the rest of the world in terms of overall aid commitment. In 2010, the United Kingdom, France and Germany were among the largest donors of official development assistance (ODA) (OECD 2010). In the same year, the EU members of the OECD Development Assistance Committee (DAC) provided a combined USD 70.2 billion, representing 54 per cent of the total aid disbursed by OECD donors (OECD 2010). Since the adoption of the Monterrey Consensus, the European Commission has been tracking the EU's performance on an annual basis: its data shows that aid levels increased by more than 30 per cent from 2004 to 2005, and the provisional target of reaching 0.39 per cent of GNI in 2006 was exceeded with a record USD 47.7 billion in official development assistance. After a temporary decline in 2007 (0.37 per cent of GNI), EU aid increased again to over 0.40 per cent in 2008 (European Commission 2010). In 2009, aid volumes were slowed down by the eruption of the financial crisis, although the EU remained the most generous global donor mobilizing more than half of global development assistance: the overall European aid (EU institutions plus the Member States) totalled 0.42 per cent of their combined GNI (European Commission 2010).

At the same time, the EU has not been able to meet its collective intermediate target of 0.56 per cent ODA/GNI by 2010, although five of the six countries that have already exceeded the UN final target of 0.7 per cent of GNI devoted to development aid are EU Member States: Belgium, Denmark, Luxembourg, the Netherlands and Sweden (European Commission 2010). In order to bridge the gap between more and less 'virtuous' European donors, the Commission has proposed that all Member States establish annual action plans for reaching individual targets by 2015 (European Commission 2010). Although the EU and its Member States have fully subscribed to the growing multilateralization of the development sector and often played a leading role in this process, their policies have only gradually evolved from a tradition of bilateral and preferential treatments, which have by and large generated replications, overlaps and ineffectiveness. To this, one must add the inevitable bureaucratic machinery that appears to be endemic of Brussels politics and that, over the course of time, has led to duplicate offices, sectoral conflicts and institutional competition.

The European development policy is as old as the very idea of a united Europe. The Treaties of Rome, which in 1957 formally established the then European Economic Communities, also provided for the creation of the European Development Fund (EDF), an instrument originally designed to support European colonies in Africa, the Caribbean and the Pacific (ACP) as well as the so-called overseas countries and territories (OCT) falling under European control. Ever since 1959, there have been ten partnership agreements (also known as convention cycles) that have governed the EDF life, the latest of which is the current 2008–13 EDF totalling EUR 22,682 billion. Even though a heading has been reserved for the EDF in the Community budget since 1993 (following a request by the European Parliament aimed at simplifying the institutional complexity of the system), the Fund has not yet come under the Community's general budget. It is, therefore, funded directly by the Member States and is subject to its own financial rules and specific management committee. By contrast, what falls under the EU budget is development aid that the Commission administers on its own and that is currently managed by one single office, EuropeAid Development and Cooperation. This recently established unit (it was inaugurated in early 2011) brings together the former Development and Europeaid Directorates General and is expected to simplify programming and communication in the development field while acting as a single contact point for the brand-new External Action Service. Previously, the Commission's development policies were managed by a variety of different offices depending on their geographical reach and thematic nature (e.g. democracy aid, cooperation with non-state actors, reconstruction in the Balkans and the former Soviet Union, etc.), making it quite complicated to draw a coherent and unitary assessment of their efficacy. To this overall complexity, of course, one could add the bilateral development policies that all EU Member States have been implementing in developing countries, especially those which used to belong to the previous colonial empires and have, ever since, remained within Europe's sphere of influence.

Since the European focus on development cooperation historically originated out of the 'privileged' relationship between Europe and its colonies, it is not surprising that such an imprinting is still driving EU aid policies nowadays. After the two Yaoundé Conventions (1964–75) and the four Lomé Conventions (1975–2000), the Cotonou Agreement has been governing the relationship between the EU and the countries of the ACP group since 2000 (and, in its revised form, since 2008). To these macro-conventions one should also add the Everything But Arms (EBA) initiative, a special trade scheme that allows least-developed countries (LDCs) a duty-free access to the European market (for all goods except arms and ammunitions), without any quantitative restrictions (with the only exception of bananas, sugar and rice).

Since 2000, the EU's development assistance underwent a phase of reforms and re-planning, which was also based on an overall evaluation of aid policies highlighting how the links across the various actors, particularly the Community and the Member States, had to be strengthened in order to maximize the impact of overall EU development aid (Holland 2002). Having had different philosophies and priorities in the field of development aid, the EU attempted to achieve some clarity in 2005, with the promulgation of the widely heralded European Consensus on Development. As admitted by the EU itself, 'for the first time in fifty years of cooperation, the Union was to give itself a framework of common principles within which the EU and its Member States would each implement their development policies in a spirit of complementarity' (EU 2005). Thus, better complementarity and coordination in terms of division of work (also with other donors) were underlined as necessary ingredients of a more effective development strategy. More importantly, the focus was put on 'consistency' across different policy sectors so as to ensure that development objectives would also be taken into account in the conduct of other common policies. This final call for a holistic philosophy capable of promoting a more development-friendly approach to the overall set of EU's external policies pointed out an essential relation: the crucial link between trade and development.

In the Consensus, the EU reiterated its commitment to a more coherent approach to development targets and, against the backdrop of a multidimensional understanding of poverty eradication (which includes promoting human rights and equitable access to public services, sustainable management of natural resources, pro-poor economic growth, trade, migration, and social cohesion), it stated the following:

> The EU is fully committed to taking action to advance Policy Coherence for Development in a number of areas. It is important that *non-development policies* assist developing countries' efforts in achieving the MDGs. The EU shall take account of the objectives of development cooperation in *all policies* that it implements which are likely to affect developing countries. To make this commitment a reality, the EU will strengthen policy coherence for development procedures, instruments and mechanisms *at all levels*, and secure adequate resources and share best practice to further these aims.
>
> *(EU 2005, emphasis added)*

Since the adoption of the Consensus, the Commission has admittedly focused on the contribution that policies beyond development – such as trade, agriculture, environment, security and migration – can make to achieve the MDGs and has recognized that development goals must be backed up by other policies to have a major impact. As it declared, the 'EU's aim is to maximize the positive effect of its policies while minimizing their negative impact on developing countries' (European Commission 2007b). Notwithstanding the stress on development-friendly policies at all levels, though, the EU's approach to trade with developing countries has remained largely based on the key tenets of market liberalization. Some lofty guarantees were made that the EU would 'maintain its work for properly sequenced market opening, especially on products of export interest for developing countries, underpinned by an open, fair, equitable, rules-based multilateral trading system'. But very little was achieved in practice, particularly against the background of a failing Doha Round at the WTO.[3]

Given the historical relationship linking Europe and Africa, it is surprising that until 2007 there was no overall cooperation framework between the EU and the overall African continent, let alone a coherent development policy. Africa has been traditionally approached in a piecemeal fashion, with the northern countries included in the Barcelona Process and then Neighbourhood Policy and the sub-Saharan countries conflated into the ACP group. The adoption of the Africa–EU Joint Strategy in 2007 partly addressed this deficiency although it is not yet clear what the tangible developmental effects of this new cooperation scheme will be. In principle, such a framework should allow both parties to broaden development cooperation by also addressing mutual political issues and move beyond a strategy that is focused exclusively on African concerns to also address European and global problems in multilateral fora. Perhaps, though, the most interesting shift is at the level of language. Mirroring the evolution described above with regard to the multilateralization of development, the new strategy speaks of the EU and Africa as 'equal partners', ushering in a phase in which the parties involved should be able to interact on equal grounds in order to benefit each other. In 2009, the former EU Development Commissioner Louis Michel maintained that it was 'in the economic and political interests of Europe' to invest in Africa, given that the latter has the economic and human potential 'to play a greater role in this emerging new world order' (Michel 2009: 2).

Thus a historic relationship of asymmetry and dependence has been rhetorically re-framed as a 'strategic partnership', which intimately links development, trade and other allegedly 'mutual' concerns such as migration and security (Olivier 2011: 62–3). Needless to say, though, there is significant scepticism in most African countries regarding the equal nature of this partnership, as will be further illustrated in the section below.

As a consequence, while the official EU discourse has outlined a gradual revolution in the way in which trade has been re-designed to support sustainable development, in practice the main emphasis has remained on pushing developing countries to introduce liberalization reforms, remove trade barriers and espouse free market of goods and services, the very same issues that most emerging and poor economies have been fighting against in the multilateral context of the WTO negotiations. The Economic Partnership Agreements negotiated in 2007–8, which were to reform the preferential arrangements of the Cotonou Agreement in order to make it compatible with the multilateral trade regime forged by the WTO, fully reflected this contradiction. Officially presented as a development-friendly trade scheme, they were ultimately opposed by most African countries as aggressive neo-liberal impositions.

The economic partnership agreements: 'aggressive' multilateralism

The original text of the Cotonou Agreement (also known as Partnership Agreement) envisaged the creation of reciprocal trade agreements between the EU and regional blocks of ACP countries by 2008, with preliminary negotiations to formally begin in 2002 (EU 2000, Article 37.1). The Agreement also specified that all 'necessary measures' would be taken into account in order to ensure that the negotiations were concluded within the indicated period and, quite importantly, the preparatory period should be actively used for 'capacity-building in the public and private sectors of ACP countries, including measures to enhance competitiveness, strengthen regional organizations and support regional trade integration initiatives' (EU 2000, Article 37.2/3).

As discussed above, the rationale behind the introduction of the EPAs related to the new multilateral trade framework sponsored by the WTO, which was a catalyst of the whole reform process. While the various Yaoundé and Lomé conventions had historically offered the ACP a comparative advantage (that is, preferential market access) vis-à-vis other (also developing) countries, this type of 'privileged' relationship would no longer be tolerated under the new reciprocity philosophy endorsed at the global level. Since non-discrimination is a fundamental tenet of multilateral trade, and countries that had traditionally suffered the consequences of the EU's development policy became increasingly willing to bring legal challenges before the WTO, the EU was faced with only two options: offer the same preferences in a non-discriminatory way to all developing countries or negotiate a free trade agreement with the ACP after the expiry of the waiver in 2007. Concerned about the negative implications that an all-round preferential access to its market would have had for the European economy, the EU opted for the 'safer' alternative, that is, the establishment of a free trade area, sugar-coated through the apparently neutral label of economic partnership.

The conditions under which the WTO allows for positive discrimination in favour of certain partner countries are covered by Article XXIV of the General Agreement on Tariffs and Trade (GATT). More specifically, the WTO permits members that are creating a free trade area to discriminate in favour of their partners (and against outsiders) provided that two key requirements are met: 1) the liberalization must regard 'substantially all' trade between the ACP and the EU; 2) and the liberalization process must be completed within 'a reasonable length of time'.[4] Since the meaning of both these requisites ('substantially all' and 'reasonable length of time') is not clearly defined, there is considerable leeway for a multilateral engagement able to take the various needs of the contracting parties into account while preserving the WTO legitimacy. Yet, in the EPA negotiations the EU unilaterally fixed the coverage at a minimum of 90 per cent of tariff elimination and the transition period to obtain this at a maximum of 15 years for all ACP countries irrespective of their 'different needs and levels of development' as required by the Cotonou Agreement (Article 35.3). While some ACP countries, notably in the Caribbean group (CARIFORUM), complied with the EU's demands and timeframe, most African counterparts argued for a different interpretation of the WTO rules and called for a more development-friendly revision of Article XXIV (AU 2006).

Moreover, while the WTO regulations only covered trade in goods, the EPAs ended up also including trade in services, intellectual property rights and the so-called Singapore issues.[5] Historically, the ACP had been reluctant to embark on negotiations dealing with these more sophisticated commercial sectors (also known as WTO-plus issues) because of potential disadvantages, the uncertainty about medium- to long-term implications and the lack of capacity to identify offensive and defensive interests. They preferred dealing with such issues on an autonomous basis first, at the national or regional level, a prerogative also supported by the Cotonou Agreement that explicitly stated that service-related liberalization would only be negotiated after the ACP countries had 'acquired some experience' in dealing with the key aspects of the general agreement on trade in services (Article 41.4). In response to growing criticisms, the EU Council acknowledged 'the right of all ACP States and regions to determine the best policies for their development' but it reiterated that it would like the EPAs to also include 'trade in services, investment and other trade-related areas' (EU Council 2007).

Although negotiations formally began in 2002, the first three years passed without significant progress. As already observed, the parties could not agree on basic principles and interpretations, which were made even more complicated by differing stances regarding EPAs' developmental impacts. The development component of EPAs was (and still is) hotly contested. From the Commission's point of view, the reciprocal character of EPAs and the inclusion of binding regulations addressing issues such as competition, investment and government procurement policies rendered them development-friendly (Meyn 2008). African countries, by contrast, emphasized the need to link aid-for-trade to the EPAs as well as secure long-term financial resources for their implementation. While they aimed to tie liberalization commitments to development aid arguing, that guaranteed access to long-term funds was crucial to overcoming supply-side constraints and diversifying the production base, the EU insisted that EPA negotiations and talks on development finance were two separate issues. Whereas the EU pledged that specific funds to implement the EPAs would be made available under the 10th EDF, its African counterparts found it unacceptable to limit guaranteed funding to the year 2013, given that the implementation process would extend beyond this date and the full effects of major liberalization and regulatory reforms would only be felt thereafter (AU 2007).

In 2006, the African Union (AU) Conference of Ministers of Trade issued an alarming message to its European counterpart reiterating that the EPAs should, first and foremost, 'be tools for the economic development of Africa':

> We express our profound disappointment at the stance taken by negotiators of the European Commission in so far as it does not adequately address the

development concerns that must be the basis of relations with Africa. [T]rade liberalization together with the accompanying liberal policies, may not by itself deliver economic development.

(AU 2006)

The EU had little to offer to address these concerns. On the one hand, it insisted that ACP countries take binding decisions that would lock them in for 15 to 25 years. On the other hand, it was neither able to prove that these reforms would bring about development, nor willing to guarantee that EPA costs would be met with additional development aid. According to some estimates, compliance costs would amount to at least € 9 billion, the bulk of which would be borne by African countries (Milner 2006). In addition to these costs, during the first stage of liberalization alone, African nations are expected to lose US$ 359 million per year due to tariff elimination (Bilal and Stevens 2009).

Two additional issues impacted directly on the multilateral essence of the EPA negotiation. The first concerns regional integration in Africa, one of the alleged top priorities of the EU's involvement in the continent. Although presented as a free trade agreement among 'regions', the EPAs were widely criticized for being potentially disruptive of indigenous regionalism in Africa. In so far as they forced African countries into specific groupings that were not coterminous with pre-existing formations, they inevitably exerted an additional strain on an already complicated web of overlapping regional economic communities (RECs) and customs unions, which African leaders have been trying to reconcile with the overall integration project of the AU (Trade Law Centre for Southern Africa 2010a, 2010b).[6] In the specific case of Southern Africa, the impact of an EPA on regional integration was further compounded by the existence of a free trade agreement between South Africa, the regional powerhouse, and the EU. This agreement, also known as the Trade, Development and Cooperation Agreement (TDCA), was imposed by the EU in the late 1990s in order to prevent the too-competitive post-apartheid South African economy from enjoying preferential treatment under the Lomé convention, and has ever since complicated internal relations within the two key organizations insisting on the region: the Southern African Development Community (SADC) and the Southern African Customs Union (Olivier 2006). While the SADC group was not able to sign an EPA in 2007, they *initialled* an interim Economic Partnership Agreement (iEPA) but only four countries actually signed it in 2009. These were Botswana, Lesotho, Swaziland and Mozambique, which had broken ranks with South Africa and Namibia (the other two members) for fear of losing market access for their exports to Europe (Trade Law Centre for Southern Africa 2010b). These events followed a prior division within the region, when other members such as Mauritius, Malawi, Zambia and Zimbabwe decided to quit SADC and join the East Africa EPA grouping, at a time when SADC was in the process of establishing a trade protocol to liberalize all internal trade.

According to Kornegay and Olivier, the EPAs posited the threat of 'an economic recolonization' of Africa through a new 'divide and rule' rendition of 'an already complicated regional integration terrain' (Kornegay and Olivier 2011: 7–8). For trade specialist Peter Draper, the most enduring legacy of the EPA process is likely to be the potentially fatal blow they have dealt to feeble regional economic integration efforts in sub-Saharan Africa. According to his analysis, the 'well-intentioned' differentiation made by the EU between LDCs and non-LDCs (and the presence within all groupings of both categories of countries) results in the anomaly that some countries are obliged to open their markets to EU exports whilst others are not, 'rendering internal policing of EU-sourced goods probably a chimerical task in the face of chronic institutional weaknesses in trade administrations across the sub-continent' (Draper 2008: 1–2).

Also the AU pointed out the serious risk that the EPAs might undermine the lengthy process of regional cohesion and cooperation, at a time when Africa was 'taking significant measures to enhance regional integration and address the question of rationalization of the RECs':

> The EC should fully recognize and respect these measures, and work within them. The EPAs should be supportive of this process and should not be seen to undermine it, including, among others, in the areas of trade liberalization [...]. Reinforcement of regional integration is a pre-requisite for the African countries being able to benefit from the EPAs. In this regard, regional integration should always be given primacy over EPAs, which should support and strengthen it.
>
> *(AU 2007)*

In December 2007, at the eve of the Africa–EU Lisbon summit signalling the expiry of the WTO waiver, EU negotiators exercised enormous pressure on African states to sign all EPAs eliciting a poignant response from their counterparts, who accused the EU of 'mercantilist interests' that 'have taken precedence over the ACPs developmental and regional integration interests' (ACP Council of Ministers 2007).

The second issue impacting on the multilateral essence of the EPAs regards the link with the global trade and development negotiations of the so-called Doha Round. As underlined by African institutions, the suspension of the Doha Round was 'likely to have serious implications on the progress and content of the EPA negotiations and on the final agreed EPA texts' (AU 2007). African policy makers believed that it 'would be premature to finalize and conclude EPAs before the conclusion of the WTO negotiations' and that, in any case, it was of paramount importance that '[i]ssues that have been rejected in the WTO by Africa should not now be introduced in the EPAs (AU 2007, emphasis added).

Therefore, the EPA negotiations were also influenced by the growing rift between developed economies and developing markets concerning the overall multilateral reforms proposed at the WTO. In 2007, at the peak of the EPA process, the Doha Round had already revealed fundamental tensions, especially between the EU/US bloc and the leading emerging markets, such as China, India and Brazil.

Most sub-Saharan African countries aligned with the emerging markets' positions thereby augmenting their relative strength, which would have not been possible outside of a multilateral framework. Thus, the re-introduction via the EPAs of the very same themes – such as trade in services and the Singapore Issues – that had already been disqualified at Doha appeared not only anachronistic but also duplicitous on the part of the EU.

In general, the negotiating strategy of the EU, which brought about regional divisions and attempted to bypass Doha through a last-minute approval of the EPAs, was widely criticized by observers and local policy makers. According to some, the EU has 'repartitioned' the sub-Saharan African region in order to preserve its leading role and historical leverage (Lee 2009; Goodison 2007a, 2007b, 2007c). For others, the EPAs have been an attempt at re-colonizing Africa by 'maximizing trade dominance' with the region (Stoneman and Thompson 2007: 112). According to Arndt Hopfmann, regional director for Africa at the Berlin-based Centre for International Dialogue Cooperation, some of the clauses included in EPA agreements 'are designed to prevent growing influence from China, Brazil and other emerging nations',[7] while other local analysts are of the opinion that Africa would reap greater rewards trading within its borders, rather than breaking ranks with fellow regional members to accept a 'forced trade' with the EU.[8]

The Namibian trade minister, Hage Geingob, was particularly vociferous in criticizing the negotiating approach of the EU representatives, especially the EU Trade Commissioner Karel de Gucht, whose attitude was defined as 'condescending'. Speaking about the treatment his country received when it pulled out of the initialled interim SADC EPA, he lamented that 'we cannot sign an agreement just for the sake of giving in to the demands of the other side':

> Is this perhaps part of the tactics of divide-and-rule and playing us off against our fellow African countries? Bulldozing a member and so-called partner? Surely we should not condone this.
>
> *(Geingob 2010)*

According to Rob Davies, the South African Minister of Trade and Industry, the European Commission adopted a 'threatening' strategy characterized by a 'take-it-or-leave-it' approach: 'This led to a situation where a country that was unwilling to sign on did so under huge duress and with little enthusiasm' (Cronin 2007). In April 2010, the South African President, Jacob Zuma, hinted at the divisive impact that the EPA negotiation was having on Southern Africa, underlining that the future of the local customs union was 'undoubtedly in question' if African countries were not given a chance to 'pursue the unfinished business of the Economic Partnership Agreement negotiations as a united group' (van der Merwe 2010).

The underlying imbalance between the parties was not only evident in the EU's negotiating attitude towards resilient African countries, but also in the technical resources available to those partners that showed a more conciliatory predisposition.

Due to the complexity of the issues under discussion and their long-term impact, it appears that a number of African delegations did not have the capacity to conduct their own independent impact evaluations and heavily relied on assessments provided by European counterparts. More recently, this asymmetry was also evident in the negotiation of the EU–Africa energy partnership, when the European Commission created the Partnership Dialogue Facility (PDF), an institution funded by and headquartered in European countries to support developing countries in their negotiations with their European counterparts. Although the PDF allegedly served the purpose of building negotiating capacities in Africa, it inevitably revealed deeply entrenched conflicts of interest.[9]

After the 2007 debacle, when most African countries refused to sign EPAs and the WTO waiver was let expire, the only way ahead for many ACP states was to sign interim agreements with the EU. To date, partial EPAs were agreed upon with Cameroon in Central Africa and Botswana, Lesotho, Swaziland and Mozambique in Southern Africa; individual agreements with Ivory Coast and Ghana in West Africa; a regional agreement with Comoros, Madagascar, Mauritius, Seychelles, Zambia, Zimbabwe (but with individual market access schedules), and a regional agreement with the East African Community.

By the end of 2010, three years after the deadline of the WTO waiver, the AU Commission in cooperation with the RECs drafted a position paper on the EPAs, which was then adopted by the Ministers of Trade in Kigali, Rwanda. In this declaration, African states reaffirm their commitment to respecting the 'objectives agreed by the international community at the multilateral level' and call on the EU to 'show greater appreciation' and 'display more sense of understanding' so that the EPAs 'can achieve the development objectives, including the maintenance of adequate policy space, the need to sustain and deepen regional integration and the non-acceptance of WTO-plus commitments' (AU 2010).

It is not yet clear whether the African signatories of the interim EPAs will have the capacity to implement these agreements and for how long these temporary schemes will be in force. As these countries open their markets to EU exports, they are likely to experience competition, concomitant trade disruption and possibly trade diversion. Countries that depend on import taxes to sustain their public finances may also experience declining revenues and, possibly worst of all, a process of 'de-industrialisation as what little industry there is in African economies may disappear' (Draper 2008).

Conclusion

For decades, the relations between Africa and Europe have been driven primarily by interests, in spite of overtones of altruism and benevolence. Bilateralism has prevailed since the end of colonization and for most of the twentieth century. Privileged agreements, preferential treatments and other ad-hoc mechanisms guaranteed the enduring grip of European interests in the continent, while preserving

African governments' access to conditionality-free development aid. The new multilateral framework of the twenty-first century, epitomized by the global trade reforms promoted by the WTO, partly challenged this state of affairs by introducing principles such as reciprocity and non-discrimination. At the same time, though, it also presented Europe with new avenues for reaffirming its leadership in Africa through the overall reform of the two continents' trade and development relationship guaranteed by the EPAs.

To the surprise of European policy makers, though, the EPA process was a bumpy ride. Amid tensions, misunderstandings and fears of hidden agendas, the 2007 deadline was approached with no significant achievements between Europe and its African counterparts. Quite ironically, this stalemate coincided with the widely heralded EU–Africa summit promulgating the strategic partnership between Africa and Europe. Contrary to the EU's rhetoric, though, this new relationship has not been marked by a 'partnership of equals' but rather by Europe's increasing negligence of Africa's development concerns. At the same time, the attitude of African countries towards the EU has also changed. Nowadays, Europe has become a less attractive market for African exports, especially due to increasingly stringent safety standards, subsidies and other non-tariff trade barriers imposed by the EU. As maintained by a scholar, '[t]he drama being played out over EPAs is providing an example of what happens if an external power tries to force the pace of change in other countries' (Stevens 2006: 449).

For all intents and purposes, the EPA negotiation was an eminently multilateral process. Not only was it conducted within the WTO framework, but also aimed at guaranteeing non-discrimination towards third parties and involved a variety of regional groupings, each composed by various countries. Nevertheless, the asymmetry of power and resources *de facto* turned it into a quasi-unilateral negotiation, in which dissenting counterparts were only given the 'loyalty' option with little or no 'voice' (Hirschman 1970). As a consequence, many of them chose to 'exit'. Rather than ushering the two continents into a new developmental trajectory, the EPAs became a catalyst of tensions and will probably be remembered as the 'most aggressive regional trade agreements ever witnessed in the history of the trade relations between the EU, the world's biggest economic bloc, and the world's poorest countries'.[10] Throughout the protracted negotiation phase (over eight years), local analysts also highlighted additional distorting factors such as the EU's substantial leverage as the leading donor in the region, with a penchant for orchestrating 'puppet' mechanisms on the African side to do the EU's bidding (Vickers 2011: 190).

As an extension of what is depicted as a 'distributive strategy' based on this leverage (Kornegay and Olivier 2011), it was also pointed out how the EU orchestrated African business support for its negotiating agenda, which included DG Trade's deliberate decision to create 'an EU-African corporate consensus on EPAs to back up its own agenda' and to push 'the European employers' federation, BusinessEurope, to take a more extreme position on the negotiations'.[11] For some, Europe's economic woes may be lending an added sense of urgency to the EPA project to, in effect, arrive at a post-colonial re-integration of Europe and Africa in a manner that locks in

Africa's subordinate status within a rapidly changing global political economy and in the process, reinforcing the continent's fragmentation (Kornegay and Olivier 2011).

Obviously, the EPA case raises a number of questions regarding the effectual nature of multilateral processes. Undoubtedly the EU exploited the multilateral nature of the EPAs (i.e. conformity with WTO requirements, mainstream approach to development through free trade and parallel negotiations with a variety of developing countries) to push its own agenda. Through the leadership it exerted in terms of trade volumes, technical expertise and political leverage, it could easily marginalize the most resilient counterparts (including emerging economies such as South Africa) and induce poorer countries to break away from their regional alliances and sign on separate agreements. On the other hand, African countries did not always manage to prioritize common as well as regional interests and ceded to the temptation of joining whatever grouping that appeared to secure the best short-term returns, largely at the expense of regional cohesion and integration.

The EPA negotiations took place against the backdrop of fundamental changes impacting the developmental trajectory of Africa. For the past decade, sub-Saharan Africa has become a fertile ground for the ambitions of emerging powers, from China to India and Brazil. The growth of such 'South–South' economic cooperation has largely occurred at the detriment of traditional European markets, which have lost about 50 per cent of their share over the last few years (Roxburgh *et al.* 2010). For better or worse, African countries have now more commercial partners than ever before and can more freely negotiate the deals that suit them best. As remarked by LSE's Africa specialist, Chris Alden, the continent is 'once again the object of Great Power interest':

> The West […] seeks to tie its prevailing commercial dominance to an ambitious agenda of structural change for the continent. By way of contrast China has entered Africa simply to satisfy the insatiable [needs] of its own infant market economy, and has little interest in Africa's internal problems or politics. The result has been a new scramble for African resources, […] pitting two visions of foreign partnership with Africa against one another.
>
> *(Alden 2007: 93)*

As early as 2007, looking at the increasing relevance of non-European interests in Africa, the Commission already sent out the alarm that the EU might be losing ground in its post-colonial backyard. Rightly, it identified the need for a rejuvenated relationship capable of reinventing itself in potentially radical ways:

> Africa is now at the heart of international politics, but what is genuinely new is that Africa […] is emerging, not as a development issue, but as a political actor in its own right. […] This means that if the EU wants to remain a privileged partner and make the most of its relations with Africa, it must be willing to reinforce, and in some areas reinvent, the current relationship.
>
> *(European Commission 2007a)*

In fact, the EPA debacle shows that the EU has not yet been able to rethink this relationship beyond the classical categories of dependence and dominium, hidden under the benevolent image of 'partnership'. Yet, a genuine multilateral process should start from focusing on the profound meaning of this term. What does it mean for Africa and Europe to be equal partners? What are the underlying structural deficiencies that need to be addressed for this to become more than a self-serving rhetorical label? How should not only the interests at stake and the various preferences be redefined, but also the ultimate goals of this alleged partnership?

In this regard, it is perhaps worth citing again the Namibian Minister of Trade:

> I call on our friends in Europe not to abandon us and to work with us towards a lasting solution. After all, the EPA is about partnership towards the shared goals of poverty alleviation and economic development. Let's not use bully tactics or old colonial arrogance. Let's be partners who are equal in sovereignty.
>
> *(Geingob 2010)*

Notes

1 The author wishes to thank Alida Kok for her precious research assistance.
2 Most observers and policy makers have indeed concluded that the MDGs will most probably not be achieved by 2015.
3 Ever since 2008, the Doha Round has been stalled over a number of controversies involving different expectations and demands by the European Union, the United States, and most emerging and developing economies.
4 Article XXIV is available online: http://www.wto.org/english/docs_e/legal_e/gatt47_02_e.htm (accessed on 13 August 2012).
5 The Singapore Issues include: transparency in government procurement, trade facilitation (customs issues), trade and investment, and trade and competition. Deriving their name from the WTO working groups that gathered in Singapore to discuss them in 1996, they have since been opposed by most developing countries within the Doha Round.
6 'EU's "divisive" trade deal comes under fire at SADC conference', *Business Day*, 25 June 2010.
7 'EU as a hidden agenda in EPA, says expert', *East African Business Week*, 30 November 2010.
8 'SADC uniform EPA negotiation no mean feat', *Informanté*, 21 January 2011.
9 This case was mentioned during one of our interviews at the EU delegation in Addis Ababa, Ethiopia, in September 2011.
10 'EU as a hidden agenda in EPA, says expert', *East African Business Week*, 30 November 2010.
11 'EU Commission manufactured African business support for EPAs', Corporate Europe Observatory, 23 March 2009. Available online: http://www.corporateeurope.org/global-europe/news/2009/03/23/commission-orchestrated-support-epas (accessed 13 August 2012).

References

ACP Council of Ministers (2007) Declaration at the 86th session expressing serious concern on the status of the negotiations on the economic partnership agreements. ACP Secretariat document ACP/25/013/07. Online. Available HTTP: <http://www.acpsec.org/en/com/86/ACP2501307_declaration_e.pdf> (accessed 31 December 2011).

Alden, C. (2007) *China in Africa*. Claremont, London and New York: David Phillip and Zed Books.

AU (2006) Nairobi Declaration on Economic Partnership Agreements, AU Conference of Ministers of Trade, 12–14 April 2006, Nairobi, Kenya. Online. Available HTTP: <http://www.africa-union.org/root/au/Conferences/Past/2006/April/TI/Nairobi%20Declaration%20on%20EPAs.pdf> (accessed 31 December 2011).

AU (2007) Short Background Brief on Economic Partnership Agreements, AU Conference of Ministers of Trade, 15–16 January 2007, Addis Ababa, Ethiopia. Online. Available HTTP: <http://www.acp-eu-trade.org/library/files/AU_EN_15-170107_AU_Trade-Ministers-meeting-background-note.pdf> (accessed 31 December 2011).

AU (2010) Kigali Declaration on the Economic Partnership Agreements Negotiations, 29 October–2 November 2010, Kigali, Rwanda. Online. Available HTTP: <http://www.acp-eu-trade.org/library/files/AU_EN_15112010_AU_Kigali%20declaration%20EPAs.pdf> (accessed 31 December 2011).

Babarinde, O. and Wright, S. (2010) 'The Millennium Development Goals: A New EU-Africa Strategic Partnership?', Paper presented at the 40th annual UACES conference, Exchanging Ideas on Europe: Europe at a Crossroads, College of Europe, Bruges, Belgium, 6–8 September 2010. Online. Available HTTP: <http://www.uaces.org/pdf/papers/1001/babarinde.pdf> (accessed 31 December 2011).

Bilal, S. and Stevens, C. (eds) (2009) 'The Interim Economic Partnership Agreements between the EU and African States: Contents, challenges and prospects', Policy Management Report 17, Maastricht: ECDPM-ODI. Online. Available HTTP: <http://www.ecdpm.org/Web_ECDPM/Web/Content/Download.nsf/0/B6CB574AC6DA08AAC125760400322BDE/$FILE/pmr17-def.pdf> (accessed 31 December 2011).

Bouchard, C. and Peterson, J. (2011) 'Conceptualising Multilateralism: Can We All Just Get Along?', Mercury E-Paper 1, January 2011. Online. Available HTTP: <http://www.europa.ed.ac.uk/global_europa/external_relations/mercury> (accessed 31 December 2011).

Cosgrove-Sacks, C. (ed.) (2001) *Europe, Diplomacy and Development: New Issues in EU Relations with Developing Countries*, Palgrave: Houndmills.

Cronin, D. (2007) 'EPA Signed "Under Duress", Says South Africa', IPS 21 December 2007. Online. Available HTTP: <http://ipsnews.net/news.asp?idnews=40567> (accessed 31 December 2011).

Draper, P. (2008) 'Africa-EU Trade Relations: Round number two!', VOX: research-based policy analysis, 29 January 2008. Online. Available HTTP: <http://www.voxeu.org/index.php?q=node/896> (accessed 31 December 2011).

EU (2000) Partnership Agreement between the members of the African, Caribbean and Pacific Group of States, of the one part, and the European Community and its Member States, of the other part, Brussels: European Commission.

EU (2005) European Consensus on Development, 2006/C46/01. Online. Available HTTP: <http://ec.europa.eu/development/icenter/repository/european_consensus_2005_en.pdf> (accessed 31 December 2011).

EU Council (2007) Conclusions of the Council and the Representatives of the Governments of the Member States meeting within the Council, 15 May 2007. Online. Available HTTP:

<http://register.consilium.europa.eu/pdf/en/07/st09/st09560.en07.pdf> (accessed 31 December 2011).

European Commission (2007a) Communication from the Commission to the European Parliament: From Cairo to Lisbon, the EU-Africa Strategic Partnership, Brussels, 27 June 2007. Online. Available HTTP: <http://eur-lex.europa.eu/smartapi/cgi/sga_doc?smar tapi!celexplus!prod!DocNumber&lg=en&type_doc=COM final&an_doc=2007&nu_ doc=357> (accessed 31 December 2011).

European Commission (2007b) Annual Report 2007 on the European Community's Development Policy and the Implementation of External Assistance in 2006, COM (2007) 349 final.

European Commission (2010) Financing for Development. Annual Progress Report 2010: Getting Bank on Track to Reach the EU 2015 Target on ODA Spending, SEC (2010) 420 final. Online. Available HTTP: <http://ec.europa.eu/development/icenter/reposi-tory/SEC_2010_0420_COM_2010_0159_EN.PDF> (accessed 31 December 2011).

Geingob, H. (2010) 'An update on the EPA negotiations', official statement. Online. Available HTTP: <http://www.namibiahc.org.uk/resources/content/Ministerial%20 Statement%20-%20An%20update%20on%20the%20EPA%20Negotiations.pdf> (accessed 31 December 2011).

Goodison, P. (2007a) 'The Future of Africa's Trade with Europe: "New" EU Trade Policy', *Review of African Political Economy*, 34 (111): 139–51.

Goodison, P. (2007b) 'What is the Future for EU-Africa Agricultural Trade after CAP Reform?', *Review of African Political Economy*, 34 (112): 279–95.

Goodison, P. (2007c) 'EU Trade Policy and the Future of Africa's Trade Relationship with the EU', *Review of African Political Economy*, 34 (112): 247–66.

Hirschman, A. (1970) *Exit, Voice and Loyalty: Responses to Decline in Firms, Organizations and States*, Cambridge: Harvard University Press.

Holland, M. (2002) *The European Union and the Third World*, Basingstoke and NY: Palgrave.

Kornegay, F. and Olivier, G. (2011) 'The European Union and Africa's Regional Economic Communities: Asymmetrical Versus Developmental Multilateralism', MERCURY Working Paper, April 2011.

Lee, M.C. (2009) 'Trade Relations between the European Union and Sub-Saharan Africa under the Cotonou Agreement: Repartitioning and Economically Recolonising the Continent?', in R. Southall and H. Melber (eds), *A New Scramble for Africa? Imperialism, Investment and Development*, Pietermarizburg: University of KwaZulu-Natal Press.

Meyn, M. (2008) 'Economic Partnership Agreements: A 'Historic Step' Towards a 'Partnership of Equals'?,' ODI Working Paper 288. Online. Available HTTP: <http://www.odi.org. uk/resources/download/1088.pdf> (accessed 31 December 2011).

Michel, L. (2009) 'Investing in Africa: A European Commission's Perspective', speech delivered at the conference 'Outlook Africa: Investing in Africa's Growth and Health', Brussels 29 April 2009 (Speech/09/209).

Milner, C. (2006) *An Assessment of the Overall Implementation and Adjustment Costs for the ACP Countries of Economic Partnership Agreements with the EU*, Report to the Commonwealth Secretariat. Online. Available HTTP: <http://www.acp-eu-trade.org/library/files/ Milner_EN_011005_Commonwealth-Sec_Assessment-of-impl-and-adj-costs-of-EPAs. pdf> (accessed 31 December 2011).

OECD (2005) *The Paris Declaration on Aid Effectiveness*, Paris: OECD. Online. Available HTTP: <http://www.oecd.org/dataoecd/11/41/34428351.pdf> (accessed 31 December 2011).

OECD (2008) *The Accra Agenda for Action*, Paris: OECD. Online. Available HTTP: <http://www.oecd.org/dataoecd/11/41/34428351.pdf> (accessed 31 December 2011).

OECD (2010) 'Development Aid Rose in 2009 and Most Donors will Meet 2010 Aid Targets'. Online. Available HTTP: <http://www.oecd.org/document/0,3746,en_2649_34447_44981579_1_1_1_1,00.html> (accessed 31 December 2011).

Olivier, G. (2006) *South Africa and the European Union-Ideology, Self-interest and Altruism*, Protea Book House: Pretoria.

Olivier, G. (2011) 'Africa and Europe: from colonialism to partnership?', *The International Spectator*, 46 (1): 45–57.

Roxburgh, C. *et al.* (2010) *Lions on the Move: The Progress and Potential of African Economies*, Washington: McKinsey Global Institute.

Stevens, C. (2006) 'The EU, Africa and Economic Partnership Agreements: Unintended Consequences of Policy Leverage', *Journal of Modern African Studies*, 44 (3): 441–58.

Stoneman, C. and Thompson, C. (2007) 'Trade Partners or Trading Deals: the EU & US in Southern Africa', *Review of African Political Economy*, 34 (111): 227–45.

Trade Law Centre for Southern Africa (2010a) 'Botswana in Fragile Balancing Act at EPA Talks', 21 June 2010. Online. Available HTTP: <http://www.tralac.org/cgi-bin/giga.cgi?cmd=cause_dir_news_item&cause_id=1694&news_id=88707&cat_id=1052> (accessed 31 December 2011).

Trade Law Centre for Southern Africa (2010b) 'SADC-EU Trade Pact in Place Before Year End', 23 June 2010. Online. Available HTTP: <http://www.tralac.org/cgi-bin/giga.cgi?cmd=cause_dir_news_item&cause_id=1694&news_id=88823&cat_id=1052> (accessed 30 April 2011).

UN (2003) *Monterrey Consensus on Financing for Development*, New York: United Nations. Online. Available HTTP: <http://www.un.org/esa/ffd/monterrey/MonterreyConsensus.pdf> (accessed 31 December 2011).

UN (2008) *Doha Declaration on Financing for Development*, Doha, Qatar: United Nations. Online. Available HTTP: <http://daccess-dds-ny.un.org/doc/UNDOC/LTD/N08/630/55/PDF/N0863055.pdf?OpenElement> (accessed 31 December 2011).

Van der Merwe, C. (2010) 'Zuma Urges SACU to Tackle EPA Negotiations as a United Front', *Engineering News South Africa*, 23 April 2010. Online. Available HTTP: <http://www.bilaterals.org/spip.php?article17195&lang=en> (accessed 31 December 2011).

Vickers, B. (2011) 'Between a Rock and a Hard Place: Small States in the EU-SADC EPA Negotiations', *The Round Table: The Commonwealth Journal of International Affairs*, 100 (413): 183–97.

10

THE EU'S ENGAGEMENT WITH CHINA IN GLOBAL CLIMATE GOVERNANCE

Bo Yan, Giulia C. Romano and Chen Zhimin

Global climate change poses one of the most serious threats to the international community. In order to cope with this threat, an international climate change regime was established in the 1990s. It is still under construction after several rounds of international negotiations.

This multilateral endeavour could arguably be conceived as a form of crystallizing multilateralism, with new international rules and organizations in the process of being established (Bouchard and Peterson 2011: 20–1). It is a well-established fact that 'from 1990 until 2008 the EU has positioned itself, and was conceived, as the lead actor in global climate governance' (Keukeleire and Bruyninckx 2011: 360). In particular, the EU succeeded in establishing the Kyoto regime, even without the support of the sole remaining superpower, the United States. However, in the process of building a post-Kyoto regime, the EU found itself less influential than in the past. The return of the US and the more assertive role played by the emerging countries complicated the situation at the Copenhagen summit in 2009.

The European Union and China are two key players in climate change politics, in terms of their huge contributions to, and their significant influence in, solving the problem. While the EU has been a crucial actor in the climate change regime-building for over a decade, China's rising role only fully emerged at the 2009 Copenhagen Climate Change Conference, where supported by the other BASIC countries (India, Brazil and South Africa), China cut a modest deal with the US. This agreement, known as the 'Copenhagen Accord', became the only reachable outcome from the high-profile and long-awaited conference. The Accord, seen by the European countries as a minimalist one, was finalized without European participation, but European countries had to endorse it, albeit reluctantly.

The Copenhagen experience indicates that the EU's claim of being a 'leader' on the climate change issue has been confronted with the visions that third actors hold on this subject, and which clash with the predominant European vision. Among these third actors, China is surely one of the most challenging, given its weight in world affairs as well as its strong stance during the climate change negotiations, calling into question the EU's capacity to play a leading role on this issue and of being followed by other actors.

This chapter will analyse the EU's efforts to engage with new rising players, particularly China, as it sought to build a post-Kyoto multilateral climate regime. First, it will trace the development of the EU's engagement with China before the Copenhagen Conference. Second, it will analyse the EU-China interactions during and after the Copenhagen Conference, highlighting how they failed to build on their bilateral collaborations to produce a global pact that the EU had desired. Lastly, the chapter will look at the adjustment of the EU's climate change negotiation approach, and its more pragmatic bilateral engagement with China, which contributed to the more substantial results coming out of the Cancun Conference in 2010 and Durban Conference in 2011. In the conclusion, we will offer a few suggestions for the EU if it seeks to play a more effective role in moving the multilateral climate change negotiation forward in the future.

The EU's pre-Copenhagen engagement with China in global climate governance

With the multilateral process of global governance of climate change involving 194 countries, the EU attaches growing importance to China's role in international negotiations. Their relations on climate change have evolved accordingly.

China as an insignificant partner (1991–2000)

In the period from February 1991 to May 1992, during which the international community negotiated and adopted the United Nations Framework Convention on Climate Change (UNFCCC), international negotiations of climate change proceeded on a broadly triangular basis among the (then) European Community (EC), the US and developing countries (Dasgupta 1994: 139; Djoghlaf 1994:97).

The divergences during international climate negotiations arose above all between two main camps. On one side the developed countries, tended to ignore, or at least to de-emphasize, the link between the historical responsibility of developed countries in their contribution to climate change and the collective responsibility of all countries to take corrective action. On the other side were the developing countries, arguing that developed countries should take the lead in addressing climate change because of their historical responsibility of being the first polluters (Dasgupta 1994: 134). While the developed countries pressed the developing countries to accept commitments on carbon reduction, developing countries emphasized that eliminating poverty and improving people's lives were their priorities. In this context, China fully participated in the work of Group 77[1] while simultaneously maintaining its independent status. The Group 77 plus China as a negotiating force took common positions on some proposals and arrived at a consensus on other issues. However, during this period China was not yet an important player.

Due to the clear opposition of the US on binding targets and on a timetable of stabilization of emissions, and due to its share of emissions, the largest worldwide, most of the EC's efforts were put on formulating consensus with other industrialized countries such as Japan and Australia, and directed towards trying to change the US's position. At the same time, China tended neither to oppose, nor over-emphasize, the binding target for developed countries to limit greenhouse gases proposed by the EC to be included in the convention, while firmly rejecting any specific target of limiting greenhouse gas (GHG) for developing countries. After the finalization of a common US–EC formulation of their commitments regarding emissions, the Convention was close to being reached (Dasgupta 1994: 143).

The adoption of the UNFCCC implied that the main negotiators, including the EU, the US and developing countries, achieved consensus on climate change at a multilateral level, while putting aside divergences. As parties to UNFCCC, they are all committed to the stabilization of greenhouse gas concentrations in the atmosphere at a level which would prevent dangerous anthropogenic climate interference with the climate system, and in accordance with their common but differentiated responsibilities and respective capabilities. For the EC, the Framework Convention 'made a large contribution towards the establishment of key principles of the international fight against climate change' but it fell short in that it did 'not contain commitments in figures, detailed on a country by country basis, in terms of reducing greenhouse gas emissions'.[2]

However, between 1995 and 1997, the international efforts were directed towards an advancement of the climate regime and especially towards reaching a binding protocol to strengthen the commitments made in the UNFCCC. In that period, China enjoyed enhanced national power in terms of economic growth and political influence, while also observing an increase in its emissions. The EU, as an important proponent of international climate change governance, reiterated its position in COP3,[3] favouring a consideration of new commitments for developing countries, China included. Although maintaining a low profile, the EU joined the US in exerting pressure upon China to accept the items favouring their own positions (Liu 1998), namely new commitments for developing countries, which were immediately refused by China. The G-77 plus China said 'it is not the time to address developing country commitments, but to strengthen developed country commitments' (IISD 1997: 2). Moreover, China raised the issue of the poor performance of Annex I Parties[4] in meeting existing commitments and made explicit that 'it is impossible' for the country 'to fulfill the duty of reducing greenhouse gases' before it 'becomes a medium-developed country' (IISD 1997: 2).

However, despite the divergences among major players, the Kyoto Protocol was finally adopted on 12 December 1997. The key feature of this treaty is that it commits developed countries to reduce greenhouse gases within the timeframe of 2008 to 2012, one of the EU's biggest objectives for the Kyoto Conference. In this occasion the EU joined once more the US in exerting subtle pressure on China, even if it still regarded the country as just another developing state rather than a player in its own right. But differently from the US, which argued that developing countries should accept targets or limitations during the Kyoto Protocol's first commitment period, the EU took a more conciliatory approach. Thus, right after the Kyoto Conference, the Chinese leadership believed that the biggest pressure in the short term would come from the US rather than the EU, although it had the general sense that the developed countries would have exerted further pressure on China later (Liu 1998). In particular, it realized that in the following rounds of negotiations developed countries would have urged China to take on more commitments of reducing emissions, a request going well beyond its capacities at that time.

China's growing importance (2001–7)

Following Kyoto, two external factors pushed the EU to regard China as a more important player amid China's rapid growth in both emissions and national power. The first was the collapse, in 2000, of the Hague Conference (Conference of the Parties (COP) 6), due to the irreconcilable divergence between the US and the EU on the issue of carbon sinks.[5] The second was the withdrawal of the US from the Kyoto Protocol in March 2001 after President George W. Bush came to power. In this context, the EU and other developing countries including China collaborated closely in international climate change negotiations and jointly contributed to the adoption of the Marrakesh Accords in COP7 in November 2001 which include detailed rules for the implementation of the Kyoto Protocol. The EU established and solidified its leading role in this process by actively engaging other players and setting a good example in climate change policy.[6]

Since the coming into force of the Kyoto Protocol, and the beginning of the post-Kyoto in 2005, the relations between the EU and China on climate change have greatly been enhanced. Especially at the multilateral level, the EU as a leader and China as an important player, started to share common positions in the approach and framework of a post-Kyoto process. They both ratified the Kyoto Protocol and contributed to its entry into force. Moreover, the two sides reaffirmed their commitments to both the UNFCCC and the Kyoto Protocol. They also committed to moving forward in the UN-led talks on a post-Kyoto process and called on all parties to participate actively and constructively in the UNFCCC conferences. Specifically, they both held that developed countries should commit to a binding scheme in the post-Kyoto process (Council of the European Union PRESSE [279] 2007). Therefore, the EU and China, as well as others, met in December 2005 in Montreal and adopted the Montreal Action Plan, an agreement to 'extend the life of the Kyoto Protocol beyond its 2012 expiration date and negotiate deeper cuts in greenhouse-gas emissions' (IISD 2005). The two sides also shared common positions in the Bali Conference in December 2007 and welcomed the adoption of the Bali Road Map, a two-year process designed to finalize a post-Kyoto climate regime at the 2009 Copenhagen Conference.[7]

Beyond multilateral action, the EU also decided to strengthen cooperation with China (and other partners) on climate change on a bilateral basis. Indeed, since 2005, the EU has developed climate change partnerships and dialogues with important emerging economies, including Brazil, India, South Korea, South Africa and China, aimed at 'involving and committing all large emitters' by the realization of 'specific projects or programmes to improve energy efficiency or to promote low-carbon technologies as well as more comprehensive policies' (European Commission COM 2005: 8). Moreover, behind these bilateral initiatives there was a precise multilateral purpose, clearly made explicit by the European Commission (Romano 2010: 5). The EU–China Partnership on climate change is one of these initiatives. Hailed as one of the major outcomes of the 2005 China–EU Summit, the Partnership is committed to strengthening cooperation and dialogue on climate change and energy between the EU and China and, in theory, provides for a robust follow-up process, which includes a regular review of progress in the context of annual EU–China Summits.[8] The initiative has been praised as 'an important step forward towards bridging the North-South Divide' (Dai and Diao 2011: 262), contrary to the confrontational approach the US adopted towards China during the negotiations. The EU indeed decided to establish this partnership with the purpose of understanding China's point of view on climate change and encouraging the country to step up its ambitions in the fight against it. At the Tenth China–EU Summit, held on 28 November 2007, the two sides agreed to increase their efforts to further enhance bilateral cooperation, including their cooperation on technology development and transfer (Council of the European Union PRESSE [279] 2007). Although it is a variant of a bilateral cooperation partnership, it underlines both the EU and China's adherence and commitments to working within the UN framework.

Once the common positions between the EU and China were established, and with their cooperation steadily deepening, the Union paid more attention to the status of China in the discussions of a post-2012 multilateral climate change regime. For example, the European Parliament's Temporary Committee on Climate Change dispatched an official delegation to China in November 2007, just before the Bali Conference. The delegation met with key officials, politicians and experts in order to facilitate cooperation with China in Bali (European Parliament 2007). The EU Commission President, José Manuel Barroso, said at the time that China was a trustworthy partner for the EU on the issue of climate change and that the two partners should take common but differentiated responsibilities (Wu and Yang 2007: A7).

Deepening collaboration as well as divergence (2008–9)

Since 2007, China has become the world's largest emitter of GHGs (IEA 2009). This development pushed the issue of emissions by developing countries onto the centre stage of international negotiations on climate change (Foot and Walter

2011: 182–6). In the period leading to the 2009 Copenhagen Conference, the EU managed to deepen its bilateral collaboration on climate change with China, while the negotiation positions of the two sides in multilateral fora witnessed a growing divergence.

At the bilateral level, China and the EU continued to consult on institutional guarantees, funding arrangements, technical cooperation and other issues for enhancing capacities to address climate change (Wen 2009). The two sides deepened 'The EC–China Energy Dialogue' and conducted concrete cooperation in the fields of renewable energy, clean coal, bio-fuel and energy efficiency. In 2008, President Barroso, led a delegation of nine commissioners to visit Beijing and discuss climate change (among other issues). On that occasion, the EU and China agreed to enhance and strengthen their cooperation on energy saving, emission reduction, environmental protection, climate change and technological innovation (Embassy of the PRC in the USA 2008). Moreover, in January 2009, the European Commission and the Chinese Government signed a financing agreement to fund a joint EU–China Clean Energy Centre in Beijing, with the aim of providing a comprehensive approach (including technological but also political and regulatory tools) to develop clean energy technologies and to support Chinese efforts to switch to a low carbon economy. In addition, in the Joint Statement of the 12th EU–China Summit held on 30 November 2009, 'the two sides recognized the comprehensive cooperation in the field of climate change between the EU and China, and agreed to enhance coordination and cooperation to further implement the EU–China Joint Declaration on Climate Change', and 'to upgrade the current Partnership on Climate Change' (Council of the European Union PRESSE [353] 2009).

The EU and China also tried to coordinate their positions on a bilateral basis before the Copenhagen Conference (COP15). At the 11th EU–China Summit, Barroso said there would have been a huge area opened for the EU and China to cooperate in Copenhagen, based on their partnership on climate change, while the Chinese Premier Wen Jiabao declared that China was willing to contribute to a positive outcome together with the EU.[9] Furthermore, in the Joint Statement of the 12th EU–China Summit, the two sides stated that they would work together with other parties 'for a comprehensive, fair and ambitious outcome at the UN Climate Change Conference in December 2009 in Copenhagen' (Ibid.). At the same time, both the EU and China gave a positive evaluation of the role the other side was playing in addressing climate change. In addition, the EU sent a delegation to China on 13 July 2009 and held talks with Chinese officials to seek more cooperation, including speeding up international negotiations on climate change prior to the Copenhagen Conference (Li 2009).

But despite these bilateral efforts, in practice, divergences between the EU and China's positions at the multilateral level tended to be more apparent and related to the essential structure and principles of a global regime on climate change (Bo 2010: 19). First, they diverged on the role of the Kyoto Protocol. With the clear signal that the US would not come back to Kyoto, and the ambitious target of having both China and the US taking on commitments under one treaty, the EU called for 'a global and comprehensive agreement in Copenhagen that builds on and broadens the architecture of the Kyoto Protocol' in COP14, held in 2008 (IISD 2008). But China stressed that 'any attempts to deviate from, breach or re-define the Convention, or to deny the Kyoto Protocol, or to merge the Convention process with the Kyoto Protocol process, will be detrimental, and will ultimately lead to a fruitless Copenhagen Conference' (Xie 2008).

Second, the EU and China diverged on the sharing of responsibility and commitments for emission reductions between developed and developing countries. In this period, the EU highlighted common responsibilities, while playing down differentiated ones and exerted more pressure on major emerging countries and especially China, provoking its opposition. In COP14, the EU required at least a 50 per cent reduction at global level by 2050 compared with 1990 levels, and for developing countries to deviate from business-as-usual by 15–30 per cent by 2020. By contrast, China emphasized historical responsibility and outlined criteria involving cumulative emissions and said developed countries should cut their emissions significantly in order to allow developing countries the space to develop (IISD 2008).

EU and China in the Copenhagen Climate Change Conference

The Copenhagen Climate Change Conference would witness a far a more conflictual relationship between the EU and China on climate change, a situation which persisted in their post-conference reflections.

EU–China collision in Copenhagen Conference

Relations between the EU and China in the Copenhagen Conference can be divided into two phases. In the first half of the conference, the EU, together with the US, imposed direct pressure on China to take on more commitments, which provoked an intense counterattack. Indeed, despite their friendly bilateral contacts, the EU and China in practice did not settle their disputes on core issues of international climate change negotiations such as numerical targets. When the Copenhagen Conference's curtain rose, the EU adopted the strategy of imposing pressure on China and intentionally linked negotiations to the trilateral relationship among the US, China and the EU. Since the US already committed itself to quantitative targets of emissions under UNFCCC, the EU believed that Washington would not have taken on more commitments without developing countries on board – especially China. Besides, there was no hope for the US to come back to the Kyoto Protocol. Therefore, with the help of the US, the EU attempted to urge developing countries to take on more commitments and, in return, expected to gain greater commitments from the US.

The divergences and confrontation between China and the EU created the following situations. First, while the EU tended to merge the UNFCCC process with the Kyoto Protocol process, China insisted on the dual-track negotiating mechanism of the Convention and its Kyoto Protocol. The EU called for an inclusive agreement, encompassing non-Annex I parties, and urged that the agreement should be translated into a universal, legally binding document in Copenhagen, or by a specified time in 2010 (IISD 2009). The EU and the US also opposed references to the second commitment period of the Kyoto Protocol. Meanwhile China, together with other developing countries, opposed a new protocol, and stressed that negotiations should result in separate agreements under the Kyoto Protocol and the UNFCCC (IISD 2009).

Second, the EU and China were not satisfied with each other's numerical targets. China announced before the conference that it would reduce the intensity of carbon emissions per unit of its GDP by 40–45 per cent from the 2005 level by 2020. The EU considered this target not ambitious enough (Zhang B. and Zhang F. 2009: A6) and wanted China to make more commitments. The EU negotiator also suggested to compare China's numerical target with that of the EU's, provoking strong reaction from China's Chief Negotiator, Su Wei: 'the EU is unkind in comparing the two kinds of targets which are incomparable' (Yan and Xu 2009). Fighting back, he argued that the EU target (a voluntary reduction of 20 per cent from 1990 levels and a 30 per cent if others' commitments to reductions were comparable) was 'far from being enough' (*China Daily* 2009). Indeed 'with a figure of 20 per cent, the EU's annual target of reduction is only 1.05 per cent which does not reach (even) the half level of its commitments in the first commitment period of Kyoto Protocol' (*People's Daily* 2009). Furthermore, the EU's policy on financial aid to developing countries was problematic in China's eyes. The EU promised to offer a 'fast-start' fund of €2.4 billion annually for the years 2010 to 2012 for 'adaptation, mitigation, research and capacity building in developing countries', take into consideration the pledges of other developed countries, and assume a 'reasonable share'. China complained that though developed countries had made some pledges, the aid was too small to address the problem and there was no long-term, stable and predictable fund-raising mechanism (Xie 2009).

In the second half of the conference, the EU continued to urge both China and the US to make more commitments. For example, Barroso called on both the US and China 'to contribute further to a successful outcome to the conference'.[10] But, the EU's strategy of urging both China and the US to alter their stance did not succeed. On the contrary it led to a degree of convergence between the US and China and other BASIC countries. As an emerging country eager to show itself as a responsible power, China wanted a successful outcome from the conference. At the same time, it claimed that it was still a developing country with low per capita GDP, and therefore tried hard to avoid binding and 'unreasonable' commitments of reducing emissions in the present period. Moreover, China's engagement in the coordination of positions with other BASIC countries enhanced China's status in multilateral climate change negotiations as well as in China–EU relations on climate change. On the US side, President Obama wished to break the deadlock of the negotiations and drive the conference to an agreement with a view to fulfilling his promise when running for the presidency of letting the US play its leading role in addressing climate change. However, he soon adopted a practical attitude to the conference, preferring to have a political agreement to a binding international protocol (Bo and Chen 2011: 112). Though President Obama expected China, India and other emerging economies to make pledges on emissions reduction, he needed all parties to compromise to achieve a final achievement. In this context, when the 'mini-summit of the 25'[11] took place on 18 December, the EU leaders were determined to secure commitments from China and India on the issue of the goal of a 50 per cent reduction in global CO_2 emissions by 2050 and continued to urge them to accept the target. But they soon met with direct opposition (Rapp *et al.* 2010). At this crucial moment, President Obama intervened. Although he also intended reaching an agreement in the conference and securing a commitment from China and India, he was more pragmatic about the final outcome both because of the difficult situation of the conference and of the domestic constraints he was facing. Therefore, he told his European counterparts that it would be better to shelve the concrete reduction targets for the time being and claimed that 'China still is as desirous of an agreement' as the US were (Rapp *et al.* 2010). Later on, the US and BASIC countries held a joint meeting to reach an agreement. The EU was left out of the meeting. As a result, the points that were most important to the Europeans were removed from the draft agreement, in particular the concrete emissions reduction targets. China had gone beyond its previous choice of sticking closely to negotiating only within the G-77 plus China, and the EU's leadership in climate change governance was seriously weakened (Bo and Chen 2011: 99).

Reflections on the Copenhagen outcomes

The EU and China have different assessments of the Copenhagen conference. Even if the conference made 'significant progress' in areas such as financing, deforestation and adaptation, on the whole, the EU expressed its strong disappointment with the outcomes. European leaders criticized the final accord as lacking in ambition, because it did not reach the form of a binding agreement, but rather of a non-binding political pledge. On this point the President of the European Commission stated that he was disappointed 'regarding the ambition in terms of the binding nature or non-binding nature of the future agreement', saying that the text agreed fell far short of the EU expectations.[12] Andreas Carlgren, Sweden's (at the time holding the rotating EU presidency) environment minister, said that the summit meeting had been a 'great failure' partly because other nations had rejected targets and a timetable for the rest of the world to sign on to binding emissions reductions (Kanter 2009).

On the other side, China evaluated the Copenhagen Conference and its outcome in a very positive way from the very beginning. The Chinese leadership firmly believed that the Copenhagen Conference was a significant and successful event. The Chinese Foreign Minister Yang Jiechi, who accompanied the Chinese

Premier Wen Jiabao to the conference, pointed out that Copenhagen provided an important opportunity for international cooperation in addressing climate change and 'fully demonstrated the great attention that the international community pays to the issue of climate change and the strong political will that it embraces to rise up to the challenge through closer cooperation' (The Central People's Government of the People's Republic of China 2009). Chinese leaders also thought that the Copenhagen Accord was the only possible outcome of the conference, and an important and positive result in that it upholds the principle of 'common but differentiated responsibilities' and the dual-track negotiating mechanism of the UNFCCC and its Kyoto Protocol (The Central People's Government of the People's Republic of China 2009; Xie 2009).

Apart from the assessment on the outcomes of the conference, some European leaders and media pointedly blamed China for the perceived failure. Reports in the European press depicted China as the main culprit. In an article in the *Guardian*, Mark Lynas argued that China 'wrecked the talks, [...] and insisted on an awful 'deal' so Western leaders' would walk away carrying the blame (Lynas 2009). Sharing this opinion was also the British Secretary of State on Energy and Climate Change at the time, and now Labour Party leader, Ed Miliband, who accused China, together with Sudan and Bolivia, of having tried to hijack the conference in order to prevent the reaching of a comprehensive accord (Vidal 2009). He added that the impossibility of reaching an agreement on the pledge to move to a 50 per cent reduction in global emissions by 2050, and an 80 per cent reduction for developed countries, was due to China's veto, 'despite the support of a coalition of developed and the vast majority of developing countries' (Miliband 2009). China was also accused of lacking real commitment by the attendance of its Deputy Foreign Minister instead of the Premier in the 'mini-summit of the 25' attended by the heads of other countries. This was regarded as a diplomatic offence and a display of arrogant behaviour.

Chinese leaders rejected the Western accusation of their being the 'wreckers' of the conference. Chinese Foreign Ministry spokeswoman Jiang Yu harshly criticized those remarks made by 'an individual British politician', containing 'obvious political attempts' to 'shirk the obligations of developed countries to their developing counterparts and foment discord among developing countries, but the attempt was doomed to fail'. On the whole, China's leaders considered they played a positive and useful role. The Chinese Premier, Wen Jiabao, deemed that China 'played an important and constructive role in pushing the Copenhagen climate talks to earn the current results, and demonstrated its utmost sincerity and made its best efforts' (Wen 2009). Chinese negotiators also took a flexible and constructive attitude to the two degrees Celsius issue and international consultation and analysis (Yu 2010). But they also believed, they believed that a 50 per cent reduction in global emissions by 2050 and an 80 per cent reduction for developed countries included in the agreement (as demanded by European leaders) would have implicitly meant long-term binding commitments for developing countries, hence seriously constraining their future development space (He 2010: A23). Therefore, they firmly rejected the proposals.

However, despite their different assessments and mutual criticisms, the two sides still shared some common positions. First, they both held that international climate change negotiations in the post-Copenhagen process should move forward in the UN forum, and called on all parties to actively and constructively participate in UN conferences on climate change. Second, with the EU coming to acknowledge that the Copenhagen Agreement made a big stride towards concluding a legally binding global agreement on fighting climate change (European Commission 2010; Council of the European Union 2010), both the EU and China emphasized that it should provide political guidance for further international climate change negotiations. Third, they shared the long-term objective of keeping the rise of the global average temperature below two degrees Celsius compared to pre-industrial levels. Fourth, they shared the general idea that an agreement could be reached first on more consensual issues such as finance, technology, adaptation, capacity building and forestry while the time frame of reaching a binding agreement could be postponed until the Durban Conference in 2011. These elements were thus signs of their more pragmatic and productive cooperation that would follow.

From Cancun to Durban: new steps forward

Since Copenhagen, the EU has adopted a different strategy for its engagement with China. This led to more constructive relations on climate change between the two partners and contributed to new developments in global climate negotiations. Indeed, despite the disillusioned atmospheres preceding the Cancun and Durban conferences, the outcomes showed some results in terms of progressing towards a new post-Kyoto climate change regime. And this would not surely have been possible without the contributions of both the EU and China.

A new EU strategy and a new EU-China partnership

Following Copenhagen, the European Commission reiterated that 'the EU should continue to pursue a robust and effective international agreement and a legally binding' one 'under the UNFCCC' (European Commission COM 2010: 4). But given the current difficulties in reaching a new agreement with specific emission reduction pledges, the EU responded by renewing its negotiating strategy including scaling down its ambitions for the Cancun Conference. Taking note of the increasing centrality of the US's and China's responses and attitudes in the negotiations, the EU started to consider the opportunity of converting its self-proclaimed 'climate leadership' role into that of a role of 'bridge builder' and redirect the negotiations towards transforming the voluntary pledges of the Copenhagen Agreement into an internationally binding agreement (Ibid.: 2). Furthermore, the EU sought to make Cancun the platform to address a series of unresolved questions remaining from Copenhagen, such as forestry emissions, surpluses in emission budgets from the 2008–12 Kyoto Treaty period (the so-called 'Russian hot air'[13]), the design of a 'robust and transparent' framework for emissions and performance accounting, and a fast-start funding and long-term finance to help mitigation and adaptation measures in developing countries. Moreover, the EU drew attention to the need to 'establish a global policy framework for reducing emissions from international aviation and maritime transport' (European Union MEMO/10/627 2010: 4). This pragmatic change in its negotiating strategy was due to the recognition that, in the presence of the ongoing divergences between the negotiating parties, the goal of reaching a comprehensive agreement in Cancun was unattainable. The EU's expectations for Cancun were to produce 'a balanced package of decisions', capable of capturing 'the progress achieved in the negotiations so far and of establishing the elements for the future global climate regime' (European Union IP 2010: 2). There was no mention of specific targets for developed or developing countries in either the post-Copenhagen Communication or in the Council conclusions prepared for the Cancun Conference, and the objective of a more inclusive agreement was deferred to the 2011 Durban Conference. Therefore, the EU's objectives for Cancun were limited to delivering a common agreement on specific and sectoral issues, in order to restore confidence in the international community on the possibility of brokering a more far-reaching agreement in the period following Cancun.

Nevertheless, far from receding from its leadership or at least pusher role, the EU continued to pursue its efforts by trying to convince third countries of the importance of taking more ambitious steps towards defining the future climate change regime. In fact, in the European Commission's Communication following Copenhagen, there is a specific recognition of the need to intensify bilateral and multilateral discussions outside the UN framework in order to better understand the EU's partners' positions, concerns and expectations and, at the same time, better explain the ambitions of the EU for the future climate change regime (European Commission COM 2010: 4–5). Thus, given the different points of view and interests among the negotiating parties, an important element of the EU's strategy was to obtain the support of other actors and 'facilitate convergence on action-oriented decisions to be agreed in Cancun' (Ibid.: 5). Among its negotiating partners, China is surely one of the most important.

In the run-up to the Cancun Conference, the EU and China decided to re-establish their bilateral cooperation and dialogue on the issue of climate change. On the occasion of a high-level EU delegation visit to China, on 29 April 2010, the Chinese chief negotiator in Copenhagen and Vice-president of the National Development and Reform Commission (NDRC), Xie Zhenhua, and the EU Climate Action Commissioner, Connie Hedegaard, released a joint statement explaining the objectives of this renewed initiative. The new partnership established a new regular dialogue mechanism at ministerial level, whose aim was to produce positive outcomes at the Mexican climate summit through deepened understanding, practical cooperation and an exchange of views (Hedegaard and Xie 2010). The ministerial-level dialogue was also reinforced by a Climate Change Hotline at the chief negotiators' level, facilitating a rapid 'exchange of views and sharing of information on new developments', and complemented by a senior officials' dialogue and meetings at a working level (Ibid.). Moreover, during the 13th EU-China summit of October 2010, the Chinese and European leaders restated their commitment to continue participating in the climate change negotiations, following the Bali Action Plan, and to promote 'a positive, comprehensive and balanced outcome at the Cancun Conference'. This should be pursued by a further enhancement of 'policy dialogue and practical cooperation' within the framework of their bilateral partnership on climate change (Council of the European Union PRESSE [267] 2010: 2). Nevertheless, despite these positive intentions, the renewed partnership showed that its fruits are still unripe. On this point, the EU Energy Commissioner, Günther Oettinger, underlined that even if the two partners have closer contacts, and despite their already 'long' experience of cooperation on the climate change issue, they are only 'at the beginning of a real partnership' (Fu and Zhang 2010). The rounds of negotiations preceding the 16th Conference of the Parties clearly showed that this was the case. The Tianjin talks, held in October 2010, were characterized by the continuing standoff between China and the US, confirming the secondary role of the EU.[14] The two countries were both accused of hindering progress during negotiations, and even if technical and forestry emissions questions were moved forward by negotiators, any extension or substitution of the Kyoto Protocol, as desired by the EU, was postponed to future negotiations (Watts 2010). Despite the EU's and other countries' (least developed countries, island states, Brazil and South Africa) willingness to make progress in the negotiations and to make further compromises on the legal form of the agreement and the measures for verification, the stubbornness of the 'G2', i.e. China and the US, ensured that any new deal would have been deferred at least until the 2011 Durban summit. On the road to Cancun, world leaders were already aware that the new agreement would have lacked ambition, and even decided not to participate in the conference, leaving their environment ministers to attend.[15]

One step forward in Cancun and the 'half-miracle' of Durban

Despite the disillusioned atmosphere preceding the Cancun Conference, the Cancun Agreement was finally reached. It includes which includes specific points concerning: finance to developing countries (the so-called 'Green Climate Fund', plus two finance bodies, the Transitional Committee, mentioned to design the Fund, and the Standing Committee, charged with the supervision and coordination of finance flows); a framework to develop a mechanism to reduce emissions from deforestation (the so-called REDD+ – Reducing Emissions from Deforestation and Forest Degradation); a new technology mechanism, aimed at sharing green technology; and an accord on the development of measurement, report and verification (MRV), and international consultation and analysis (ICA) (see Gupta 2010).

Moreover, the agreement made the two degrees Celsius objective legally binding and anchored the emission pledges made by developed and developing countries after Copenhagen to a formal COP decision. Nevertheless, it is still the 'lowest common denominator' agreed upon by the parties, with uncertainties even on the points settled by the agreement. For example, it left uncertain how the annual $100 billion for the Green Climate Fund will be raised. On technology cooperation, the accord also lacks details on how to facilitate the absorption of green technologies by developing countries (Doyle and Wynn 2010; Gupta 2010). More important, it leaves open the question of defining a long-term global emission reduction goal. Although many of the sensitive questions like technology transfer and finance at the root of the North–South divide were addressed, the crucial point of the negotiations (on how to establish a new post-Kyoto climate regime) still remained intractable. Japan, Russia and Canada said no to a second period for the Kyoto Protocol without the participation of the US and China (Morales and Biggs 2010). As for the EU, accused of trying to scrap the Protocol, it clearly stated that it was ready to commit itself for a second period, provided that the main emitters also joined in. For these reasons, as most negotiators and the Mexican host wanted to produce an outcome from the conference at all costs, the question of renewing Kyoto was deferred to December 2011. But despite the lacunae, the EU and China both felt that the final agreement moved forward on some specific and controversial issues and kept open the negotiation process within the UNFCCC. The Chinese affirmed that the conference restored full confidence in the multilateral mechanism and in the future South African conference (Liu and Wang 2010). On the EU side, Cancun was seen as making new steps after Copenhagen, even if the journey to 'a legally binding global climate deal' was still 'long and challenging' (European Commission MEMO/10/673 2010).

Yet there were points on which both partners were left unsatisfied. China was not happy with the fact that questions such as a second commitment period for the Kyoto Protocol, the clarity of sources and sizes of the fund for developing countries, and new ambitious mitigation efforts from developed countries remained absent (The Climate Group 2011: 10). And if Cancun was able to provide a balanced and substantive package of decisions, the EU recognized that there were still be unresolved issues, such as 'the legal form of the agreement and how to provide long-term finance' (Hedegaard 2010).

As for the role played by the two actors during the conference, this time China was depicted by the international press as willing to make compromises. Deploying a new strategy based on flexibility and transparency, it tried to demonstrate that the low ambition of the Copenhagen Accord was not due to its deliberate action, but rather to a lack of consensus among the main actors in the negotiations. To avoid new accusations in Cancun, it adopted a more pragmatic strategy, demonstrating its willingness to deliver at least lowest common denominator results and to build consensus for more significant steps in the future. The new attitude towards transparency and flexibility was confirmed by a dramatic change of its stance on the issue of measurement, reporting and verification (MRV), showing its capacity of facilitating a common international agreement and of removing one of the major points of disagreement it had with Western countries. Indeed, China agreed to accept the International Consultation and Analysis (ICA) mechanism, which measures the efforts of developing countries while respecting the principle of common but differentiated responsibilities and the sovereignty of states during its application (a matter of primary importance for China). Moreover, in Cancun, it adopted a publicity strategy aiming at demonstrating past and current action in dealing with climate change,[16] finally managing to significantly restore its international image.

For its part, the EU tried to play the role of a 'bridge builder' in Cancun, helping to find solutions to the disputes over a second Kyoto Protocol period. The EU representatives indeed stated that the Union not only 'worked tirelessly to be a bridge-builder' and was transparent on its process of mobilization of the €7.2 billion of fast-start funding, but also that it was able to negotiate as a unitary actor, the Achilles' heel for the EU in the Copenhagen Conference (European Union IP 2010; European Commission MEMO/10/673 2010). However these claims were controversial and disputed. During the conference, the EU was accused 'of taking unfair advantage of poor countries' by insisting that providing loans to reduce emissions is better than providing grants. Indeed, the Union started talking about giving part of its pledged funds in the form of loans, an outrageous proposal for many NGOs, fearing that they will add another burden to countries already fighting for development (Willis 2010). Seeking to counter this accusation, the EU's chief climate negotiator, Dr Artur Runge-Metzger, asserted that 'loans are often made on highly concessional terms', including a 'major grant element of up to 75%', and do not concern countries unable to repay them (cited in Vidal 2010). But one anonymous negotiator from a developing country affirmed that EU member states' methods of accounting for climate pledges are all different, making it all 'a complete mess'. Furthermore, according to environmental activist and former US Vice President Al Gore, the EU used 'creative accounting to cover up their shortfalls', giving the impression to developing countries that developed countries use these tactics in order to avoid meeting their commitments (cited in Vidal 2010). Moreover, NGOs also highlighted that developed countries' pledges were not new and additional funds as established in Copenhagen, but rather recycled money, increasing distrust among developing countries on the seriousness of developed countries' engagements. On this point, the European Environmental Bureau's (EEB) assessment of the Belgian Presidency was positive, confirming that in 2010 the EU actually mobilized €2.35 billion of its promised €7.2 billion for the 2010–12 period of 'fast start finance' and that the money assumed the form of grants and not of loans. However, the assessment also highlighted the uncertainty on how the money for the $100 billion annual green climate fund would have been raised, as well as the EU's share of contribution (European Environmental Bureau 2010).

On the role played by the EU during the negotiations, while there was a general consensus on the EU's ability to speak with one voice, opinions were divided over its capacity to play a leadership role. For CAN Europe (Climate Action Network Europe) and The Climate Group, one of the positive outcomes of the Cancun Conference was the ability of the EU to reassert itself as one of the key players in the negotiations (The Climate Group 2011: 11). Yet, other climate activists were surprised at the reticence of the European delegation to take a strong position.

For instance, the head of WWF Britain, Keith Allott, affirmed that the EU spent a lot of time 'licking its wounds' after Copenhagen and showed continuing internal divisions over the question of stepping up its commitment from 20 per cent to 30 per cent by 2020. The EU's offer of the unconditional 20 per cent and of 30 per cent if other countries make comparable commitments remained unchanged since Copenhagen. Even the verdict of the EEB was negative. Indeed, the indecision of moving to a 30 per cent emission reduction unilaterally made the EU lose the opportunity to 'set the right tone to the negotiations, that the EU is ready to do a larger part of its fair share' (European Environmental Bureau 2009: 4), an element capable of restoring its lost 'leadership by example' (Oberthür 2007: 8). However, it must be remembered that without a significant move from the American and the Chinese sides, Cancun could not deliver the expected results to save the planet. Moreover, given the disagreements between the main actors before the event, the EU was already conscious that a consensus on the most pressing issues, namely emission targets, was a remote prospect. Thus it preferred to secure an agreement on the objectives where a consensus could be found.

Yet the Cancun Conference left the international community with many issues still to be solved. And it made 2011 the decisive year for seeing the parties agree on specific commitments in order to save or to replace the expiring Kyoto Protocol. But the international context preceding the Durban Conference – the debt crisis of the Eurozone, the recovery efforts to exit from the 2008 economic crisis and the midterm elections in the US, that saw President Obama lose his majority in the House of Representatives and his ambitions to pass his climate change bill in Congress – weakened the hope for more elaborated action on the side of developed countries. Developing countries, especially newly emerging economies, despite their public commitments to reducing their emissions, continued to refuse binding international pledges by invoking the principle of common but differentiated responsibilities. This situation made the prospect of reaching a more decisive agreement in Durban very confusing and unlikely. However, surprisingly, the outcome of the Durban conference was not as unsatisfactory as expected. Indeed, for the first time, both the governments of developed and developing countries agreed on a 'platform' to draft and sign by 2015 an agreement on emissions reductions and to make it enter into force within five years (namely in 2020, when the Copenhagen–Cancun voluntary pledges will expire). However, there were no clear discussions about the speed and the quantities of emissions reductions. These questions were deferred to the following three years of negotiations (Harvey and Vidal: 2011b). But for the first time the conference saw all the parties agreeing on the discussion and development of a future climate protection arrangement that will have legal force. The main actors that made this possible were the EU, the proposer of the road map, and China, this time more ready to make concessions at an international level.

During the negotiations, the EU was the sole actor among developed countries to maintain its position on the extension of the Kyoto Protocol. Beyond preserving its support to a second commitment period under the Kyoto Protocol (considered as a transitional step towards a more comprehensive legally binding framework), the

EU knew that the Protocol remained dear to many developing countries, including China and India, and thus conditioned its adoption to the approval of its road map. This clearly meant that these countries committed themselves to reduce their emissions on the same legally binding base as developed countries, a fact that removes the historical distinction between developed and emerging economies, and recognizes the dramatic changes occurring since the signature of the Kyoto Protocol in 1997. This was the decisive point that made the US agree to join, as its 'battle' in the climate negotiations had always been conducted on this precise base (Harvey 2011). So, the partial success of Durban can be ascribed to the EU's strong capacity of gathering the other countries around its proposal, which makes sense in times of economic recession when governments are struggling to forecast their future involvement in a global climate change regime. The EU's 'guile', although unfulfilling for those expecting more ambitious action against climate change, had the capacity to restore confidence in the UN process and to make all the parties agree, for the first time, on a concrete project designing a future climate protection regime. Moreover, the same very fact that the US and China agreed to the platform can itself be considered a success, partially ascribed to the EU's capacities of getting them engaged in the process. On the last day of the Durban Conference only three countries remained vague on the EU's proposal, namely China, India and the US. With two members of BASIC countries supporting the European proposal, China was confronted with two possibilities: either be diplomatically isolated or stay in the rank of the emerging economies. As isolation would have been diplomatically painful (Harvey and Vidal 2011a), it opted for a cooperative although difficult choice. Moreover, the text was formulated in a way that permitted the approval of the more reticent countries (especially the US), and made possible its final adoption.[17]

However, in the Chinese case, the EU's and developing countries' engagement cannot solely explain the dramatic change in its international position. According to some Chinese experts, China would be able to pledge to binding commitments by 2020, based on its capacity to reach the status of a middle-income country.[18] This idea was confirmed by the Chinese Government itself when it gave leeway to its main negotiator, Xie Zhenhua, to compromise to support a legally binding agreement (Rosaspina 2011). This marked a significant change compared to the historical trend China had adopted in previous climate change negotiations. It is the first time that China made clear, in an international venue, its openness to commit to a legally binding document after 2020 (Hsu 2011). This change is probably in response to the US position, 'not open to any kind of legally-binding post-2020 agreement' unless other great players are on board (Ibid.), but also to the result of its internal changes and the progresses of an emerging country ranking at the top positions in the list of producers of renewable energies and submitting its economic growth plans to specific energy efficiency and emissions reduction targets.

As far as both China and the EU positions are concerned, China's propensity to agree to an international legally binding agreement was linked to some specific conditions including: 1) a second commitment period of the Kyoto Protocol; 2) the meeting of financial commitments by developed parties (in order to sustain mitigation and adaptation measures in developing countries); and 3) the definition of a post-2020 regime respectful of the principles of common but differentiated responsibilities and equity, of countries' respective capacities and of environmental integrity (Ibid.). This last condition in particular was largely shared by the EU's position, requiring a global framework engaging all parties, but respectful of the common but differentiated responsibilities principle, based on the countries' respective capabilities and environmental integrity (Council of the European Union 2011:7). This could be read as a sign of a progressive re-convergence of opinions between China and the EU.

Conclusion

As discussed above, past bilateral cooperation and dialogue between the EU and China have shown mixed impacts on the construction of a multilateral climate change regime. From the very beginning of their relations on the climate change issue, their contacts were characterized by a constant divergence on developing countries' responsibilities. Indeed, while the EU has always promoted a sharing of efforts between developed and developing countries (under the principle of common but differentiated responsibilities), China insisted on the historical responsibility of developed countries and on the right to growth of developing ones. Nevertheless, except in the Copenhagen Conference, these divergences have not hindered the EU and China in cooperating with each other in advancing the Kyoto regime, Bali Road Map, Cancun Agreement and Durban Platform. In fact, since the entry into force of the Kyoto Protocol in 2005, their relations have been significantly enhanced, especially with the establishment of the Partnership on Climate Change. This partnership enabled the two actors to improve their exchanges on the climate issue, and to institute concrete cooperation projects.

Nevertheless, bilateral activity does not always ensure that the two parties act as partners. While China and the EU continue to consult each other bilaterally, this may not be reflected at the multilateral level, as demonstrated by the bitter collision in Copenhagen. The reasons can be partly ascribed both to the EU's multiple weaknesses during the negotiations and to China's inflexible position. During the conference, the EU continued to urge China to take a pledge of international binding commitments, while it was already clear from the beginning that China would not have accepted them. At the same time, the EU's expectations of reaching a comprehensive agreement in Copenhagen were too high, given that the atmosphere preceding the event was already one of disillusionment and, because of the financial crisis, the attention of both developed and developing countries shifted to national economic issues. This particular conjuncture was also the basis of the dissent among EU member states, making them incapable of agreeing on an ambitious plan to reduce their GHG emissions and on aid for adaptation and mitigation for developing countries (Groen and Niemann 2010: 23).

After the disappointing experience in Copenhagen, in Cancun the EU demonstrated a much more pragmatic approach. Acknowledging that a comprehensive agreement on a 'Kyoto Protocol-style' was impossible to reach and that divergences among developed and developing countries were still sharp, the EU sensibly scaled down its ambitions, adopting a more 'sectoral approach', namely pushing on the issues that were not highly controversial among the parties and on which an agreement could be 'easily' reached. But it did not substantially change its basic position on its emissions reduction, nor has it been proven to have a serious approach on the financial issues. In our view, there are some elements that need improvement in order to enhance the EU's capacity to be one of the critical actors in the negotiations.

First, by lowering its ambitions, playing the role of a 'bridge builder' among the parties and pushing further on its commitments, the EU can still play a leadership role that has been demonstrated in Durban. If 'voluntary cooperation' is defined as a basic feature of multilateralism (Bouchard and Peterson 2011: 1), the EU has to find common ground with other key players. It is useful to remember that the EU is still one of the most committed parties in the negotiations and this can provide it with leverage to push the negotiation process forward. But in order to make this possible, the EU needs to strengthen its pledges, which are no longer credible; for example, by moving from the unconditional 20 per cent to an unconditional 30 per cent. It also needs to be clearer on the issue of financial assistance to developing countries, as the choice of loans instead of grants raises many doubts about the EU's willingness and capacity to finance adaptation and mitigation measures in vulnerable countries, especially after the global financial and the Eurozone crisis.

Second, the EU should make better use of its partnership with China. Despite six years of bilateral contacts on the climate change issue, the EU seems not yet to have understood what China wants or how to deal with it. However, what is clear is that putting excessive pressures on China could be counter-productive (even if the pressure it exerted on China in Durban partially helped the achievement of a common ground). It will not lead to a change of its negotiating position, but will, rather, entrench the country's position. It is perhaps better to continue involving China on issues in which the country could reasonably be expected to cooperate (for example, on technical cooperation), enhancing mutual understanding, and trying to find shared points to defend in international negotiations. The EU and China are only 'at the beginning of a real partnership' (Fu and Zhang 2010). If it is up to them to play a significant role in the negotiations, mutual comprehension should be reinforced, together with a renewed practical cooperation on the climate change issue.

Finally, we would suggest that if the EU's internal climate change policy succeeds in helping the European countries meet their emission targets while avoiding excessive costs for their economies and/or providing stimuli for their industrial sectors, China may be very interested in learning from the European example. Indeed, this would help the country in boosting its national measures to reduce its dependency from coal and, finally, to reduce its GHG emissions. But there will not be significant changes in China's international negotiating position unless the US also makes a concrete move. In China's eyes, notwithstanding its ranking as the first greatest world polluter, it is paradoxical that it is asked to make more efforts and to commit internationally when the second greatest polluter still occupies a free rider position and produces so-called 'luxury emissions' (whereas China's emissions can be considered 'developmental' or 'survival' ones). In other words, without the US on board, the Chinese will hardly make substantial concessions at the international level.

To conclude on an optimistic note, we feel that both China and the EU remain two crucial actors in the future negotiating process. Indeed, both the EU and China may prove central in the climate change negotiations by showing a more active approach and putting pressure on the US, still blocked in Congress on its climate bill. For its part, the EU should continue playing a role of bridge builder between developed, developing and emerging countries. On the other side, China could 'facilitate the reaching of a compromise' by easing its negotiating language on the commitments of non-Annex I countries (De Matteis 2010). In order to make this possible, the EU and China's renewed bilateral dialogue on climate change needs to go forward in reconciling their positions and defining a common strategy for the next round of negotiations. If this situation occurs in the near future, their bilateral cooperation may move beyond the purely rhetorical and engender significant progress in future negotiations. Indeed, something already has moved at the bilateral level. The example of the European bilateral partnerships for climate change with the emerging economies pushed the US to propose similar arrangements with China, trying to catch up with the Sino-European initiative (Dai and Diao 2011: 264). This is a positive signal from the American side, especially given that future climate change negotiations will run along the lines of a Sino-American 'entente'. As the two giants are also the two biggest greenhouse gases emitters, to which the whole international community is looking, and that they both observe each other's stance and take new steps on the climate change issue, a Sino-American dialogue and cooperation on these issues might increase the possibilities of reaching a future climate accord. This is mainly dependent on the concessions they will be able to make in order to reach an agreement. If the EU succeeds in treasuring this new resource by pushing on both the US and the Chinese sides, the prospect for a new international solution for the climate change issue will not be as bleak as they appeared after Copenhagen and may confirm the success attained in Durban.

Notes

1 The Group of 77 (G-77) is a loose intergovernmental organization grouping the developing countries in the United Nations. It was established on 15 June 1964 in the United Nations Conference on Trade and Development in Geneva. Its aim is to help developing countries 'to articulate and promote their collective economic interests and enhance their joint negotiating capacity on all major international economic issues within the United Nations system, and promote South–South cooperation for development'. See 'About the Group of 77'. Online. Available: http://www.g77.org/doc/ (accessed 13 August 2012).

2 'Kyoto Protocol on climate change', 14 June 2010. Online. Available: http://europa.eu/legislation_summaries/environment/tackling_climate_change/128060_en.htm (accessed 13 August 2012).

3 Since the UNFCCC entered into force, the parties have been meeting annually in Conferences of the Parties (COP) to assess progress in dealing with climate change, and beginning in the mid-1990s, to negotiate the Kyoto Protocol. From 2005 in which the Kyoto Protocol entered into force, the Conferences of the Parties have met in conjunction with Meetings of Parties of the Kyoto Protocol (MOP).

4 Parties to UNFCCC are classified as Annex I countries, Annex II countries and Non Annex I countries. There are 41 Annex I countries and the European Economic Community is also a member. These countries are classified as industrialized countries and countries in transition. They are Australia, Austria, Belarus, Belgium, Bulgaria, Canada, Croatia, Czech Republic, Denmark, Estonia, Finland, France, Germany, Greece, Hungary, Iceland, Ireland, Italy, Japan, Latvia, Liechtenstein, Lithuania, Luxembourg, Malta, Monaco, Netherlands, New Zealand, Norway, Poland, Portugal, Romania, Russian Federation, Slovakia, Slovenia, Spain, Sweden, Switzerland, Turkey, Ukraine, United Kingdom, United States of America. Annex II countries are a sub-group of the Annex I countries which shall provide new and additional financial resources to meet the agreed full costs incurred by developing country Parties in complying with their obligations under UNFCCC. Non Annex I countries are developing country parties.

5 A carbon sink is anything that absorbs more carbon that it releases. See 'What are carbon sinks?'. Online. Available: http://www.fern.org/campaign/carbon-trading/what-are-carbon-sinks (accessed 13 August 2012).

6 For example, in June 2000, the Commission launched the European Climate Change Programme (ECCP), which identified and developed all the necessary elements of an EU strategy to implement the Kyoto Protocol. See EU Commission (2001), European Climate Change Programme. Long Report, Brussels, June 2001. Online. Available: http://www.eu-greenlight.org/pdf/eccp_report_0106.pdf (accessed 13 August 2012).

7 The Bali Road Map includes the Bali Action Plan, which charts the course for a new negotiating process designed to tackle climate change along with a number of other decisions and resolutions. It comprises negotiations under the AWG-KP – Ad Hoc Working Group on Further Commitments for Annex I Parties under the Kyoto Protocol (AWG-KP) and the AWG-LCA – Ad hoc Working Group on Long-term Cooperative Action under the Convention (AWG-LCA). See 'Bali Road Map', Online. Available: http://unfccc.int/key_documents/bali_road_map/items/6447.php (accessed 13 August 2012).

8 'China-EU Partnership on Climate Change Rolling Work Plan', 19 October 2006. Online. Available: http://new.fmprc.gov.cn/eng/wjb/zzjg/tyfls/tfsxw/t283051.htm (accessed 13 August 2012).

9 'Wen Jiabao and EU leaders meeting with Journalist', 20 May 2009. Online. Available: http://www.gov.cn/ldhd/2009-05/21/content_1320555.htm (accessed 13 August 2012).

10 'Statement by EU Commission President Barroso at the UN High Level Segment COP 15 Copenhagen Climate Change Conference', 16 December 2009, Copenhagen. Online. Available: http://www.eu-un.europa.eu/articles/en/article_9343_en.htm (accessed 13 August 2012).

11 The meeting was held between 25 key nations of global climate change negotiations including the US, the EU, the UK, Germany, France, China, India, Brazil, South Africa and Mexico.

12 'Statement of EU Commission President Barroso on the Copenhagen Climate Accord', 21 December 2009, Copenhagen. Online. Available: http://europa.eu/rapid/pressReleasesAction.do?reference=SPEECH/09/588 (accessed 13 August 2012).

13 'Russian hot air' consists in the Assigned Amount Units (or more easily pollution credits) accumulated but not used by Russia, Ukraine and other former communist states of

Eastern Europe under the Kyoto Protocol. After the massive deindustrialization following the end of the communist regimes, many east European countries have accumulated these pollution credits. According to Stefan Singer, director of global energy policy at WWF, the amount of unused credits 'is more than the entire annual emissions of the EU 27 and may – if traded and sold – sink any environmental integrity of targets for developed countries'. See 'Russian "hot air" threatens UN climate deal', *Euractiv*, 22 October 2009. Online. Available: http://www.euractiv.com/en/climate-change/russian-hot-air-threatens-un-climate-deal/article-186633 (accessed 13 August 2012).

14 The Tianjin talks were the autumn preparatory meeting preceding the 16th Conference of the Parties (the Cancun Conference). It was the fourteenth meeting of the Ad-hoc working group on Further Commitments for Annex I Parties under the Kyoto Protocol (AWG-KP), and the twelfth session of the Ad hoc working group on Long-term Cooperative Action under the Convention (AWG-LCA), the two tracks of negotiations established with the Bali Action Plan in 2007, and in charge of reaching an agreed outcome to be presented to the Conferences of the Parties for its adoption. For more details see, 'Tianjin Climate Change Conference – October 2010', Online. Available: http://unfccc.int/meetings/tianjin_oct_2010/meeting/6277.php (accessed 13 August 2012).

15 On 1 December 2010, the Former Brazilian President, Luis Ignacio da Silva Lula, overtly declared that no great leader was participating in the conference, at the most Ministers of the environment were taking part. And as Ministers of Foreign Affairs were not even participating, there would not have been any progress. Lula eventually cancelled his flight to Cancun for the second week of negotiations (*Le Monde* 2010).

16 It distributed an NDRC Report recording the progresses of its climate change policy among the participants to the conference (Seligsohn 2010).

17 The text says that it launches 'a process in order to develop a legal framework applicable to all developed and developing countries', a sentence vague enough to avoid the words 'legally binding', thus to have the US on board. (Harvey and Vidal: 2011a).

18 Interviews conducted in Beijing, November 2010.

References

Bo, Y. (2010), 'The Trilateral Relations among China, the US and the EU on Climate Change', *Modern International Relations*, No.4, pp.15–20, Beijing

Bo, Y. and Chen, Z. (2011), 'EU's Weakening Leadership in Climate Change Governance', *China International Studies*, pp.99–117, January–February 2011, Beijing

Bouchard, C. and Peterson, J. (2011), *Conceptualising Multilateralism: Can We All Just Get Along?*, Mercury E-paper No. 1. Online. Available HTTP: <http://www.europa.ed.ac.uk/global_europa/external_relations/mercury> (accessed 23 July 2011)

The Central People's Government of the People's Republic of China (2009), 'Yang Jiechi's Comments on Premier Wen's Attendance to Copenhagen Conference', 20 December 2009. Online. Available HTTP: <http://www.gov.cn/jrzg/2009-12/20/content_1491905.htm> (accessed 10 March 2010)

China Daily (2009), 'US, EU Expected to do more on Emission Cuts: China', *Xinhua*, 9 December 2009. Online. Available HTTP: <http://www.chinadaily.com.cn/china/2009copenhagenclimate/2009-12/09/content_9144762.htm> (accessed 6 March 2011)

The Climate Group (2011), *Post-Cancun Analysis. Policy Briefing*, 17 January 2011. Online. Available HTTP: <www.theclimategroup.org/_assets/files/Post-Cancun-Analysis 1.pdf> (accessed 2 February 2011)

Council of the European Union (2007), PRESSE [279], *10th EU-China Summit Joint Statement – Beijing*, 28 November 2007, Brussels

Council of the European Union (2009), PRESSE [353], *Joint Statement of the 12th EU-China Summit – Nanjing*, 30 November 2009, Brussels

Council of the European Union (2010), PRESSE [267], *13th EU-China Summit Joint Press Communiqué*, 6 October 2010, Brussels

Council of the European Union (2011), PRESSE [359], Press Release – 3118th Council Meeting – Environment, 10 October 2011, Luxembourg

Dai, X. and Diao, Z. (2011), 'Towards a New World Order for Climate Change. China and the European Union's Leadership Ambition', in Wurzel, R.K.J. and Connelly, J. (eds), *The European Union as a Leader in International Climate Change Politics*, London: Routledge, pp.252–68

Dasgupta, C. (1994), 'The Climate Change Negotiations' in Mintzer, I.M. and Leonard, J.A. (eds), *Negotiating Climate Change: The Inside Story of the Rio Convention*, Cambridge: Cambridge University Press, pp.97–113

De Matteis, P. (2010), 'The "Post-Copenhagen Era" and Cancun: an Opportunity for the EU and China', 29 November 2010. Online. Available HTTP: <http://politicsinspires. org/2010/11/the-%E2%80%9Cpost-copenhagen-era%E2%80%9D-andcancun-an-opportunity-for-the-eu-and-china/> (accessed 6 December 2010)

Djoghlaf, A. (1994), 'The Beginning of an International Climate Law', in Mintzer, I.M. and Leonard, J.A. (eds), *Negotiating Climate Change: The Inside Story of the Rio Convention*, Cambridge: Cambridge University Press, pp.97–113

Doyle, A. and Wynn, G. (2010), 'Climate Talks End with Modest Steps but not Kyoto Deal', Reuters, 11 December 2010. Online. Available HTTP: <http://news.yahoo.com/s/ nm/20101211/wl_nm/us_climate> (accessed 12 December 2010)

Embassy of the People's Republic of China in the United States of America (2008), 'China, EU Start-up High Level Economic, Trade Dialogue', 25 April 2008. Online. Available HTTP: <http://www.china-embassy.org/eng/xw/t429082.htm> (accessed 10 September 2010)

European Commission, COM (2005), 35 final, *Winning the Battle Against Global Climate Change*, 9 February 2005, Brussels

European Commission, COM (2010), 86 final, *International Climate Policy Post-Copenhagen: Acting now to Reinvigorate Global Action on Climate Change*, 9 March 2010, Brussels

European Commission, MEMO/10/673 (2010), 'Statements by the President of the European Commission, José Manuel Barroso, and Connie Hedegaard, European Commissioner for Climate Action on the Cancún Agreement on Climate Change', 11 December 2010, Cancun

European Environmental Bureau (2009), *EEB's Assessment of the Environmental Results of the Swedish Presidency of the EU – July to December 2009*, 23 December 2009. Online. Available HTTP: <http://www.eeb.org/publication/2009/SE_ PresidencyFinalAssessment23Dec09.pdf> (accessed 14 July 2011)

European Environmental Bureau (2010), *EEB's Assessment of the Environmental Results of the Belgian Presidency of the EU – July to December 2010*, 20 December 2010. Online. Available HTTP: <http://www.eeb.org/index.cfm/news-events/news/belgian-eu-presidency-good-on-biodiversity-and-governance-bad-on-climate-and-finance/> (accessed 12 July 2011)

European Parliament (2007), 'China Committed to Fighting Climate Change, but not yet to Quantitative Targets, says EP delegation', 11 July 2007. Online. Available HTTP: <http:// www.europarl.europa.eu/news/expert/infopress_page/064-12738-309-11-45-911-20071107IPR12737-05-11-2007-2007-false/default_en.htm> (accessed 19 October 2010)

European Union, IP/10/1620 (2010), 'Climate change: Cancun Conference Must Mark Significant Step Towards Legally Binding Global Climate Framework', 29 November 2010, Brussels

European Union, MEMO/10/627 (2010), 'Climate change: Question and Answers on the UN Climate Conference in Cancun', 29 November 2010, Brussels

Foot, R. and Walter, A. (2011), *China, The United States and Global Order*, Cambridge: Cambridge University Press

Fu, J. and Zhang, H. (2010), 'Climate Change Mechanism Set Up', *China Daily*, 30 April 2010. Online. Available HTTP: <http://www.chinadaily.com.cn/china/2010-04/30/content_9794726.htm> (accessed 12 May 2011)

Groen, L. and Niemann, A. (2010), *EU Actorness under Political Pressure at the UNFCCC COP15 Climate Change Negotiations*, paper prepared for the UACES conference, Bruges, 6–8 September 2010. Online. Available HTPP: <http://www.uaces.org/pdf/papers/1001/niemann.pdf >(accessed 15 February 2011)

Gupta, J. (2010), 'Wishy-washy Agreement Saves Cancun', *Chinadialogue*,13 December 2010. Online. Available HTTP: <http://www.chinadialogue.net/weblogs/4/weblog_posts/219?utm_source=Chinadialogue+Update&utm_campaign=54a51f46c7-newsletter+13+Dec+2010&utm_medium=email->(accessed 20 December 2010)

Harvey, F. (2011), 'Durban Talks: how Connie Hedegaard got Countries to Agree on Climate Deal', *The Guardian*, 11 December 2011. Online. Available HTTP: <http://www.guardian.co.uk/environment/2011/dec/11/connie-hedegaard-durban-climate-talks?intcmp=239> (accessed 16 January 2012)

Harvey, F. and Vidal, J. (2011a), 'Durban COP 17: Connie Hedegaard Puts Pressure on China, US and India', *The Guardian*, 9 December 2011. Online. Available HTTP: <http://www.guardian.co.uk/environment/2011/dec/09/durban-climate-change-connie-hede-gaard> (accessed 16 January 2012)

Harvey, F. and Vidal, J. (2011b), 'Q&A: Why Durban is Different to Climate Change Agreements of the Past', *The Guardian*, 11 December 2011. Online. Available HTTP: <http://www.guardian.co.uk/environment/2011/dec/11/durban-questions-and-answers> (accessed 16 January 2012)

He, J. (2010), 'To Defame the Copenhagen Accord is to Deny the Climate Debt', *People's Daily*, 5 January 2010

Hedegaard, C. (2010), 'The Agreement in Cancun – a Victory for Europe', 17 December 2010. Online. Available HTTP: <http://ec.europa.eu/clima/news/articles/news_2010121701_en.htm> (accessed 20 December 2010)

Hedegaard, C. and Xie, Z. (2010), *Joint Statement on Dialogue and Cooperation on Climate Change*, 29 April 2010, Beijing. Online. Available HTTP: <http://ec.europa.eu/delega-tions/china/press_corner/all_news/news/2010/20100430_01_en.htm> (accessed 20 October 2010)

Hsu, A. (2011), 'Propelling the Durban Climate Talks. China Announces Willingness to Consider Legally Binding Commitments Post-2020', *World Resource Institute*, 6 December 2011, Online. Available HTTP: <http://www.chinafaqs.org/blog-posts/propelling-durban-climate-talks-china-announces-willingness-consider-legally-binding-comm> (accessed 18 January 2012)

IEA Statistics (2009), 'CO2 Emissions from Fuel Combustion', Highlights. Online. Available HTTP: <http://www.iea.org/co2highlights/co2highlights.pdf> (accessed 18 June 2011)

IISD (1997), 'Highlights from the third Conference of the Parties to the United Nations Framework Convention on Climate Change', *Earth Negotiations Bulletin*, 6 December

1997, Vol.12, No.72. Online. Available HTTP: <http://www.iisd.ca/vol12/enb1272e.html> (accessed 12 August 2011)

IISD (2005), 'Summary of the Eleventh Conference of the Parties to the UN Framework Convention on Climate Change and First Conference of the Parties serving as the Meeting of the Parties to the Kyoto Protocol 28 November–10 December 2005', *Earth Negotiation Bulletin*, 12 December 2005, Vol. 12, No. 291. Online. Available HTTP: <http://www.iisd.ca/download/pdf/enb12291e.pdf> (accessed12 July 2011)

IISD (2008), 'Poznan Highlights', *Earth Negotiation Bulletin*, 3 December 2008,Vol. 12, No. 387. Online. Available HTTP: <http://www.iisd.ca/vol12/enb12387e.html> (accessed 12 June 2011)

IISD (2009), 'Summary of the Copenhagen Climate Change Conference', *Earth Negotiation Bulletin*, 22 December 2009,Vol. 12, No. 459. Online. Available HTTP: <http://www.iisd.ca/vol12/enb12459e.html> (accessed 28 July 2011)

Kanter, J. (2009), 'E.U. Blames Others for "Great Failure" on Climate', *The New York Times*, 23 December 2009. Online. Available HTTP: <http://www.nytimes.com/2009/12/23/world/europe/23ihtclimate.html?_r=1> (accessed 19 April 2011)

Keukeleire, S. and Bruyninckx, H. (2011), 'The European Union, the BRICs and the Emerging New World Order', in Hill, C. and Smith, M. (eds), *International Relations and the European Union*, 2nd edition, Oxford: Oxford University Press, p.360

Le Monde (2010), 'La conférence de Cancun sur le climat 'ne va rien donner', estime Lula', 1 December 2010. Online. Available HTTP: <http://www.lemonde.fr/planete/article/2010/12/01/la-conference-de-cancun-sur-le-clim-at-ne-va-rien-donner-es-time-lula_1447688_3244.html> (accessed 7 December 2010)

Li, C. (2009), 'EU Calls for More Cooperation With China Against Climate Change', *Beijing Review*, 15 July 2009. Online. Available HTTP: <http://www.bjreview.com.cn/exclusive/txt/2009-07/15/content_207718.htm> (accessed 29 May 2011)

Liu, L. and Wang, Y. (2010), 'Cancun Conference a Success: Head of Chinese Delegation', *Xinhua*, 11 December 2010. Online. Available HTTP: <http://news.xinhuanet.com/english2010/china/2010-12/11/c_13645368.htm> (accessed 18 June 2011)

Liu, Z. (1998), 'Impact of Kyoto Protocol on China's Economy Development', 10 February 1998. Online. Available HTTP: <http://cssd.acca21.org.cn/clireporta.html> (accessed 1 April 2010)

Lynas, M. (2009), 'How do I know China Wrecked the Global Deal? I was in the Room', *The Guardian*, 22 December 2009. Online. Available HTTP: <http://www.guardian.co.uk/environment/2009/dec/22/copenhagen-climate-change-mark-lynas> (accessed 6 January 2010)

Miliband, E. (2009), 'The road from Copenhagen', *The Guardian*, 20 December 2009. Online. Available HTTP: <http://www.guardian.co.uk/commentisfree/2009/dec/20/copenhagen-climate-change-accord> (accessed 12 January 2010)

Morales, A. and Biggs, S. (2010), 'Japan Says 'No' to Kyoto Extension, Wants World Treaty', *Businessweek*, 1 December 2010. Online. Available HTTP: <http://www.businessweek.com/news/2010-12-01/japan-says-no-to-kyoto-extension-wants-world-treaty.html> (accessed 3 December 2010)

Oberthür, S. (2007), *EU Leadership on Climate Change: Living up to the Challenges*, Institute for European Studies, Vrije Universiteit Brussels, Brussels. Available HTTP: <http://ec.europa.eu/education/programmes/llp/jm/more/forum07/oberthur.pdf> (accessed 31 August 2011)

People's Daily (2009), 'Unfair Text Infuriates Developing Countries', 10 December 2009

Rapp, T., Schwägerl, C. and Traufetter, G. (2010), 'How China and India Sabotaged the UN Climate Summit', *Der Spiegel*, 5 May 2010. Online. Available HTTP: <http://www.spiegel.de/international/world/0,1518,692861,00.html> (accessed 28 December 2010)

Romano, G.C. (2010), *The EU-China Partnership on Climate Change: Bilateralism Begetting Multilateralism in Promoting a Climate Change Regime?*, Mercury E-paper No. 8. Online. Available HTTP: <http://www.europa.ed.ac.uk/global_europa/external_relations/mercury> (accessed 16 July 2011)

Rosaspina, E. (2011), 'Durban: la conferenza entra nel vivo. E la Cina fa il primo passo', *La Repubblica*, 5 December 2011. Online. Available HTTP: <http://www.corriere.it/ambiente/11_dicembre_05/cina-apre-durban-rosaspina_1dc4b74a-1f5b-11e1-befb-0d1b981db5e8.shtml?fr=correlati> (accessed 7 December 2011)

Seligsohn, D. (2010), 'Report from Cancun: China Emphasizes Energy Policy Progresses', *World Resource Institute*, 6 October 2010. Online. Available HTTP: <http://www.wri.org/stories/2010/12/report-cancun-china-emphasizes-energy-policy-progress> (accessed 12 January 2011)

Vidal, J. (2009), 'Ed Miliband: China tried to Hijack Copenhagen Climate Deal', *The Guardian*, 20 December. Online. Available HTTP: <http://www.guardian.co.uk/environment/2009/dec/20/ed-miliband-china-copenhagen-summit?intcmp=239> (accessed 5 January 2010)

Vidal, J. (2010), 'Cancun Climate Change Conference: Row over EU Loans Policy', *The Guardian*, 1 December 2010. Online. Available HTTP: <http://www.guardian.co.uk/environment/2010/dec/01/cancun-climate-change-conference-loans?CMP=twt_fd> (accessed 5 December 2010)

Watts, J. (2010), 'China and US Blamed as Climate Talks Stall', *The Guardian*, 8 October 2010. Online. Available HTTP: <http://www.guardian.co.uk/environment/2010/oct/08/china-us-blamed-talks-stall/print> (accessed 12 November 2010)

Wen, J. (2009), 'China's Role in Copenhagen Talks "Important and Constructive"', *Xinhua*, 21 December 2009, Online. Available HTTP: <http://news.xinhuanet.com/world/2009-12/21/content_12683488.htm> (accessed 19 June 2010).

Willis, A. (2010), 'EU funding offer sparks anger in Cancun', *EUobserver*, 2 December 2010. Online. Available HTTP: <http://euobserver.com/885/31404> (accessed 31 August 2011)

Wu, L. and Yang, A. (2007), 'China: Trustable Partner of the EU', *People's Daily*, 13 November 2007

Xie, Z. (2008), 'Statement by H.E. Mr. Xie Zhenhua, Minister and Vice-chairman of the National Development and Reform Commission of the People's Republic of China at the Joint High-Level Segment of COP14 and CMP4', 11 December 2008, Poznan. Online. Available HTTP: <http://www.ccchina.gov.cn/en/NewsInfo.asp?NewsId=19061> (accessed 19 August 2011)

Xie, Z. (2009), 'China made Important Contributions to the Achievement of Copenhagen Conference', 26 December 2009. Online. Available HTTP: <http://www.ipcc.cma.gov.cn/Website/index.php?ChannelID=11&NewsID=1134> (accessed 10 May 2011)

Yan, J. and Xu, L. (2009), 'China's Chief Negotiator: It is Unkind for the EU Delegate to Compare China and the EU', 9 December 2009. Online. Available HTTP: <http://www.gov.cn/jrzg/2009-12/09/content_1483593.htm> (accessed 28 May 2011)

Yu, Q. (2010), 'The Copenhagen Climate Change Conference and China's Positive Contribution', *Foreign Affairs Journal*, No.95, Spring 2010, Beijing. Online. Available HTTP: <http://www.cpifa.org/en/q/listQuarterlyArticle.do?pageNum=5&articleId=9&quarterlyPageNum=1> (accessed 23 June 2010)

Zhang, B. and Zhang, F. (2009), 'What are the Disputes Between You and Me?', *Review on Economy*, 14 December 2009

PART IV

The European Union in multilateral fora

11

THE EUROPEAN UNION AND THE REFORM OF THE UNITED NATIONS

Towards a more effective Security Council

Nicoletta Pirozzi, with Hubertus Jürgenliemk and Yolanda Spies[1]

Introduction

'Globalism' and 'regionalism' can be identified as the two driving approaches of the EU's presence on the international stage. The European Security Strategy (ESS) has reconciled these trends by declaring the EU's commitment to 'effective multilateralism' and placing the United Nations (UN) at the core of this concept. In the 2008 Report on the Implementation of the ESS, the EU pledged to campaign for the reform of the UN system, begun in 2005, and to support the crucial role of the UN Security Council (UNSC) in maintaining international peace and security.

Arguably, the EU's place as an international power depends more on its actions than on its status at the United Nations, in view of its lack of single representation within the UNSC (Gowan and Brantner 2010). Nevertheless, even in the realm of action, inaction has often appeared preferable, reinforced by a more widespread aversion to risk (Edwards 2011: 66; Coker 2009). This attitude has also inhibited the development of a single EU perspective on the UN Security Council's reform, which is still impeded by the divergent positions of the Union's member states. As such, while the EU can present itself as a role model for regionalism, it has not led by example on the thorny question of United Nations reform.

This said, the Lisbon Treaty offers additional opportunities for the EU to establish itself as a credible, reliable, responsible and accountable entity in the UN context. The Treaty gives the EU a legal personality, and in principle one voice internationally through the European Council President and the High Representative for Foreign Affairs and Security Policy supported by an External Action Service (EEAS). But are these institutional reforms sufficient to bolster significantly the EU's role at the UN?

Against this backdrop, this chapter aims at assessing the EU's contribution to the effectiveness of the UN through the analysis of its 'presence' and 'performance' in relation to reform of the Security Council. The Security Council is a crucial arena for the European Union. It is a 'legitimizer' of the EU's external actions in the field of peace and security, a 'legislator' by means of specific resolutions and the promotion of international norms, and an 'amplifier' of the EU's voice and power to influence the global agenda.

The EU's presence at the UNSC, which includes elements of both EU intergovernmentalism and supranationalism, will be evaluated both in terms of coordination among EU members which are also permanent and non-permanent members of the UNSC, and of the EU's representation at the UN as a single entity. Although speculations about a permanent EU seat may be sterile, emphasis on the opportunities that have emerged as a result of the Lisbon Treaty to reinforce EU practices as a single actor are not.

Consequently, the Union's performance at the UNSC will be assessed through the outcome that EU member states and institutions collectively achieve on a particular policy issue, namely UNSC reform. The reform of the UNSC remains one of the most contentious matters within the EU and a common position has not emerged or even been comprehensively discussed. The aim of this chapter is as well to identify points of convergence among the major EU member states, based on the recent evolution of their positions and partnerships at the UN. Looking ahead, it discusses the possible role that post-Lisbon institutions could play in brokering internal EU dialogue on UNSC reform.

Moreover, our assessment will consider the impact of recent EU campaigns conducted within the UN – i.e. the resolution for an enhanced observer role at the UN General Assembly – and of EU cooperation with other regional entities – i.e. the African Union (AU) – on the approach to regionalism within the UN context. The promotion of 'regional multilateralism' at the UN is investigated as a possible new path for the UNSC reform process. The final aim is to verify whether the post-Lisbon EU has been able to project effectively its own vision of 'effective multilateralism' in its diplomacy at the UN.

This chapter starts with an analysis of the 'regionalization' and 'globalization' tendencies in the EU's approach to effective multilateralism and explains how these tendencies influence its relations with the UN. Building on this assessment, the second and third sections review the Union's presence – through its member states and institutions – at the UN Security Council and its performance for the development of a unitary position on the issue of UNSC reform. The aim is to investigate how effectively the EU combines its efforts to consolidate its own identity vis-à-vis the United Nations (through its presence at the UNSC), and its goal of contributing to the reinforcement of the UN (through the UNSC reform). Finally, the last section analyses the prospects for regionalism within the UN, as a means to further UN reform and the EU's role in it in cooperation with other regional actors.

Globalism and regionalism in the EU's commitment to effective multilateralism

The milestone in the process of defining the European Union's approach to effective multilateralism was the 2003 Iraq crisis. It weakened both the UN and the EU by delegitimizing the role of the UN Security Council as a guarantor of international peace and security, and dividing EU member states. As a consequence, the EU decided to put a strong emphasis on supporting the UN, in an attempt to revitalize both multilateralism and its own actorness on the world stage (Van Langenhove *et al.* 2006).

This resulted in the adoption of two pivotal documents for EU–UN relations, both produced in the same year. The European Commission's Communication *The European Union and the United Nations: The choice of multilateralism* presented the EU's commitment to multilateralism as a defining principle of its external policy (European Commission 2003). The European Security Strategy (ESS) *A Secure Europe in a better world* defined the EU's vision of the international order based on 'effective multilateralism' and stated that 'strengthening the United Nations and equipping it to fulfil its responsibilities and to act effectively is a European priority' (European Union 2003: 9). This trend was confirmed in the *Report on the Implementation of the European Security Strategy*, adopted in December 2008, where EU leaders recognized once again that 'the UN stands at the apex of the international system' and affirmed that 'everything the EU has done in the field of security has been linked to UN objectives' (European Union 2008: 11).

In the EU's approach to 'effective multilateralism', globalization and regionalization are viewed as by and large complementary processes. On the one hand, the EU's strategy recognizes the UN as the main guarantor of international peace and security. On the other hand, the EU depicts itself as a regional player, which 'should be ready to share in the responsibility for global security and in building a better world' (European Union 2003: 1).

In fact, looking at the strategic priorities identified by the EU in the ESS, what emerges is the presumed coexistence between regionalism – 'building security in its neighbourhood' – and globalism – 'promoting effective multilateralism'. These two (potentially opposing) tendencies find their synthesis in the conception of a multi-layered system of global governance, which 'does not imply exclusive policy jurisdiction by one actor but rather a partnership among a variety of actors' (Weiss and Thakur 2010: 85). As underlined by the EU High Representative, Catherine Ashton, in her address at the UN Security Council, 'regional organizations are building blocks for global governance, with a dual responsibility. First, a responsibility to enhance security, development and human rights in their own region. And second, to support UN efforts to promote these goals around the world' (European Union 2011a).

Against this background, the EU's cooperation with the Security Council, which is described as the main referent of the EU 'both as a legitimising body and as the main peacekeeping implementer' (Tardy 2005), is crucial. The EU has always held an ambivalent position vis-à-vis the UNSC, which is evident in the Union's ad hoc-ism both in responding to the Security Council's requests for intervention and in seeking the UNSC's authorization to legitimize its own actions. In particular, the EU has not expressly declared itself to be a regional arrangement in the sense of Chapter VIII of the UN Charter (Articles 52 to 54), which regulates the relationship (by establishing a hierarchy) between the Security Council and regional organizations in the field of peace and security (White 2006: 94).

At the same time, the Lisbon Treaty assigns prime importance on the UN collective security system through a number of provisions. Respect for the principles of the UN Charter and international law is identified as one of the guiding elements of the EU's role in the world (Articles 3.5 and 21.1 TEU). In its action on the international scene, the Union is called to 'promote multilateral solutions to common problems, in particular in the framework of the United Nations' (Article 21.1 TEU) and 'preserve peace, prevent conflicts and strengthen international security, in accordance with the purposes and principles of the United Nations Charter [...]' (Article 21.2 TEU).

As argued by White, conformity with the principles of the UN Charter requires compliance with the rules governing the use of force (Article 2.4), an integral part of which is the UN Security Council's power to authorize states to use force under Chapter VII (Article 42) or regional arrangements under Chapter VIII (Article 53) (White 2006:92).[2]

This interpretation of the Lisbon Treaty is confirmed by the Treaty's provisions on the Common Security and Defence Policy (CSDP), which state that the EU may use civilian and military assets 'on missions outside the Union for peacekeeping, conflict prevention and strengthening international security in accordance with the principles of the United Nations Charter' (Article 42.1 TEU). This is complemented by the reference to the right of self-defence in the so-called 'mutual defence clause', introduced for the first time in the EU Treaties, which provides that 'if a Member State is the victim of armed aggression on its territory, the other Member States shall have towards it an obligation of aid and assistance by all the means in their power, in accordance with Article 51 of the United Nations Charter' (Article 42.7 TEU).

Moreover, the Lisbon Treaty specifically refers to the Security Council, elaborating procedural guidelines for the EU member states serving (permanently and non-permanently) in the SC and highlighting the prominence of their responsibilities under the UN Charter over those arising from the EU Treaties (Article 32 TEU). This is in line with Article 103 of the UN Charter, which determines that obligations under the Charter prevail in case of conflict with obligations under other international agreements – clearly including treaties establishing regional organizations (Drieskens 2010: 58).

Taken together, these provisions suggest a complementarity between globalism (embedded in the UN) over regionalism (the role of the EU) in the Union's understanding of its role in the world. In practice, however, the EU's behaviour has been fuzzier (i.e. through its CSDP missions or sanctions policy), oscillating between the imperatives of promoting its particular interests and values, and of abiding by UN rules and norms.

How much EU at the UN Security Council? Theory and practice

Europe as such usually has a significant presence at the UN Security Council, with two permanent members (France and the UK) and usually two or three non-permanent members (for example, Germany and Portugal were the European representatives in 2011–12) sitting at the UNSC at any point in time.[3] However, no formal EU representation is envisaged in this body.

There has always been a tension between 'intergovernmental' and 'integration' approaches among the EU member states regarding their role within the UN Security Council. This tension has impeded effective EU action regarding Security Council matters (Kissak 2010: 107–9). While the first approach entails the promotion of national actorness within the UN, the second favours the consolidation of an EU regional identity in the framework of the UN.

Both these approaches have manifested themselves in the context of the UNSC, although the EU Treaty and policy documents tend to favour the intergovernmental approach, focusing on the 'coordination' among EU member states rather than on the 'representation' of the Union as a single actor. EU member states have so far tended to prioritize their national UNSC seats over an EU common representation.

Concretely, what has changed in this respect with the entry into force of the Lisbon Treaty? The Lisbon Treaty replaces former Article 19 of the Treaty on European Union (TEU) with Article 34 TEU, but it does not introduce innovative elements in terms of coordination among EU member states. It simply extends the obligation to defend the position and interests of the Union to all EU members of the UN Security Council, but continues to prioritize their responsibilities as UN members over those derived from their EU membership. Moreover, Declarations 13 and 14 on the Common Foreign and Security Policy annexed to the Treaty expressly safeguard the responsibilities and powers of EU member states in the formulation and conduct of their foreign, security and defence policies, with a specific reference to their national representation within the UN Security Council.

One positive outcome of the Lisbon Treaty, however, is the new role assigned to the new EU Delegation to the UN – in the person of its Head or one of its officers – which now has the responsibility to chair the coordination meetings among EU member states in New York. This should ensure a higher degree of continuity and institutional memory than in the past, when this task was assigned to the rotating presidency.

Article 34 TEU also provides that 'when the Union has defined a position on a subject which is on the United Nations Security Council agenda, those Member States which sit on the Security Council shall request that the High Representative be invited to present the Union's position'. Since the entry into force of the

Lisbon Treaty, Lady Ashton has intervened twice at the UN Security Council, but EU statements (by the Head of the EU Delegation to the UN) have numbered nearly forty (European Union 2010; European Union 2011a). In addition, the EU members of the Security Council must keep the High Representative (HR) fully informed about discussions and negotiations, allowing the EU to develop over time the institutional knowledge about multilateral cooperation, necessary to influence UNSC debates. At the same time, the HR has gained leverage over EU member states as she can propose civilian and military CSDP operations and therefore could potentially negotiate with the United Nations and key Security Council members on behalf of the EU member states. However, recent EU performances at the Security Council (i.e. the vote on Libya, where two European members – France and the UK – actively pushed for an intervention, while Germany was reluctant to accept, siding in practice with China and Brazil) show that these innovations introduced by the Lisbon Treaty have failed, so far, to achieve policy coordination among its member states.

The concrete outcome of the new European diplomatic corps on UNSC matters cannot be fully judged at this initial stage of implementation, as it will depend largely on its final configuration and functioning. The EEAS was launched in December 2010, appointments for its management were mostly made in early to mid-2011, and key positions were filled in early 2012 (European Union Press Department 2011; European Union 2011b). However, as and when it becomes fully operational, the added value of the new European diplomatic corps in New York is that it can act as the unitary interface of the EU within the UN. European diplomats will not only represent the focal points for UN members when they want to consult and negotiate with the Union, but they will also ensure a direct liaison between the UN and the institutions in Brussels. A constant interaction with national capitals will also be established through the presence of national diplomats within the service and through the links between the EU Delegation in New York and EU Delegations in third states. The downside to this is the risk of the EU having to act through 27 plus-one diplomatic services. Opportunities for confusion rather than coherence remain legion (Edwards 2011).

Beyond coordination issues, pragmatic approaches to make the Union's representation within the UNSC more effective have been repeatedly fostered since the beginning of the 1990s. However, they have regularly failed to gain the consent of all EU member states, and particularly the support of the two European permanent members of the UNSC (Pirozzi 2009a: 63–71).[4] After the entry into force of the Lisbon Treaty, an attempt was made to associate a representative of the EU HR to Portugal's delegation during its stint at the UNSC in 2011–12, but it did not produce any concrete result.

Following the recognition of the EU's legal personality (Article 47 TEU) and the elimination of the pillar structure, the European Union has replaced the European Community at the UN, with all its rights and obligations. On the basis of these innovations, in 2010 EU member states tabled a draft resolution to the General Assembly for a 'reinforced observer status' to be accorded to the Union, and not solely to the European Community. The adoption of the resolution, which had the potential to open the Pandora's box of regional representation within the UN, was challenged internally by the UK, which opposed an extensive interpretation of the privileges to be accorded to the EU, and externally by a bloc of African, Pacific and Latin American countries led by Suriname on behalf of the Caribbean Community and Common Market (CARICOM) and supported by India and China. While many small member states fear a progressive regionalization of the GA, some major powers, including the BRICS countries, oppose any alteration in the internal balance of power of the Assembly (Grevi 2011: 2–3).

The text of the resolution, which the GA finally passed on 3 May 2011, offers fairly modest rights to the EU compared to the initial proposal (UN General Assembly 2011; UN General Assembly 2010). The EU can now speak among the representatives of the major groups, circulate its documents directly and without intermediaries, present proposals and amendments orally, and respond to questions regarding its positions. However, representatives of the EU are not entitled to be seated among member states, to vote, to co-sponsor resolutions or decisions, or to put forward candidates.

The reluctance of the General Assembly to grant additional rights to the EU shows the difficulties the EU still faces internationally, as a regional organization that goes beyond exclusive intergovernmentalism (Norheim-Martinsen 2010). It has not yet earned international recognition, which limits the prospects for its role at the UN. UN members will need to be assured that the EU is a responsible and cohesive actor they can deal with. Otherwise, they will continue to prefer talking to the major EU member states.

Nevertheless, this vote at the UNGA bears a crucial significance both for the EU, by recognizing its reinforced status within the UN, and for other regional organizations, insofar as it envisages extending similar rights of participation to other groups of states that have observer status at the GA, following an agreement among their members. In the following section, we explore the impact that these developments could have on the discussion about the reform of the UNSC.

The EU and the reform of the UN Security Council

All EU member states agree on the need to reform the UN Security Council, so as to give it more legitimacy in exercising its primary international responsibilities and make it more representative of the current membership of the United Nations, particularly in terms of its regional balance. However, EU member states have never been able to formulate a common EU position on the question of UNSC reform. On this issue, rivalries between national governments motivated by the need to preserve or upgrade their status within the Security Council have constantly trumped the consolidation of a common EU position.

The idea that emerged from the post-Cold War debate on the UNSC membership was the so-called 'quick fix', consisting in the simple creation of two new permanent seats for Germany and Japan, to be added to the P5. This proposal, which resulted in the establishment in 1993 of the open-ended General Assembly Working Group on how to proceed,[5] quickly generated Italian resentment of the German candidature (Hill 2005: 31).

During the 2005 process, Germany and Italy put forward opposing approaches to UNSC reform, enshrined respectively in the G4 and the Uniting for Consensus (UfC) platforms. The G4 members (Brazil, Germany, India and Japan) put themselves forward as the main candidates for new national permanent seats, together with an unspecified African country (General Assembly 2006). The UfC group instead (which is composed of about 40 small and mid-size states, including Italy and Spain among the most active), envisaged an enlargement (from ten to 20) in the number of non-permanent seats only (Uniting for Consensus 2005).

Since at least 1993, immediately after the Common Foreign and Security Policy (CFSP) was first introduced in the Maastricht Treaty, there has been a series of attempts to increase the presence of the EU and its foreign policy at the UNSC, possibly by creating a permanent EU seat. Both the European Parliament (EP) and the European Commission (EC) have supported this idea on various occasions. The former High Representative for CFSP, Javier Solana, alluded to this option in an interview in the German newspaper *Die Welt* in March 2003 (*Die Welt* 2003). The proposal has also received strong endorsement from the members of the UfC movement, particularly from Italy. The newly appointed High Representative for Foreign Affairs and Security Policy of the Union, Catherine Ashton, struck a discordant note in this choir during her hearing before the EP in January 2010, when, in a reply to a question by the Vice-President of the Parliament, Mario Mauro, she stated that she had no opinion about an eventual EU seat in the Security Council.

At the same time, the proposal to give the EU, as a single actor, a greater voice in the UNSC has been hampered by the opposition first of France and the United Kingdom – both of whom have always been reluctant to support any UNSC reform proposal that would diminish their privileges as permanent members – and then of Germany.

The strongest argument against a common seat at the UNSC is that the EU has often proved unable to forge a common position among its members on sensitive UNSC issues. Notable cases in point are the split over the Iraq war in 2003, the recognition of Kosovo's independence in 2008, and the intervention in Libya in 2011. Some have even claimed that the lack of a single voice is not necessarily negative, insofar as it is preferable to have a 'polyphony of voices' spreading the same, or at least not dramatically divergent, messages (Kissak 2010: 119; Verbeke 2006: 53).

In September 2008, with the GA Decision 62/557, UN member states agreed to move the 15-year-old deadlocked discussions on Security Council reform from the open-ended Working Group to intergovernmental negotiations. Most UN member states, including EU countries, confirmed the positions adopted during the 2005 process. Nevertheless, it is possible to identify some emerging elements of convergence and consensus among the main European stakeholders.

Germany is now less qualified than in the past to stake its claim to a permanent seat, especially if compared to the status of Brazil and India. It occupies a peculiar position in the G4 and is engaged in striking a delicate balance between its national aspirations and its European commitments. The official position of Germany reveals this ambiguity: while in the long term Germany would like to see a joint European seat at the Security Council, in the meantime it is ready to assume greater responsibility on a national basis as a permanent UNSC member (Federal Foreign Office 2010). As a result, Germany has demonstrated its openness to alternative intermediary agreements as long as they have a good chance of gaining the necessary two-thirds majority in the GA and are backed by the other two major European powers, France and the United Kingdom.

The members of the Uniting for Consensus (UfC) group have recently launched a new initiative, proposing to create a new category of longer-term non-permanent seats to be assigned to regional groups. One of these seats would be shared on a rotating basis between the Western European and Others Group and the Eastern European Group (United Nations 2010a). The members of these groups would be encouraged to designate an EU member state to occupy the seat and thus ensure that the Union has an indirect institutional presence at the UNSC. Other EU members, such as Portugal, Sweden and Poland, seem more inclined today to support this kind of solution than they were in the past.

On their side, France and the UK (P2) have presented a proposal that envisages an expansion in both the permanent and non-permanent categories of members. However, these two countries also back pragmatic intermediate solutions, which would entail the creation of a new category of seat with a longer mandate than that applicable to the currently elected non-permanent members. At the end of this period, these new seats would be converted into permanent seats (United Nations 2010b).

Some consensus has been reached on key issues, such as the need to improve the relationship between the UNSC and the General Assembly, and to reform the working methods of the Security Council so as to make them more transparent and inclusive. There are a number of proposals on the possible limitations of the right of veto in the UNSC and there is broad agreement that the size of an enlarged Security Council would be around the mid-20s, or almost double the current size of 15.

On the more controversial issue of the categories of new UNSC members, some elements contained in the latest positions adopted by the major EU member states could form a nucleus of convergence: (1) the creation of a new class of semi-permanent members without the right of veto who would serve renewable or longer terms than the current non-permanent members having a two-year mandate; (2) the institutionalization of mechanisms and criteria for the election/ re-election and rotation of the members of this new category within regional groupings; (3) the establishment of an interim period for the implementation of these changes, at the end of which a new decision would be taken on the composition of the UNSC.

To date, any discussion on the reform of the UNSC within the EU has been a prerogative of the member states, with some of them being on the front line. EU institutions have only played a secondary role in building of consensus on this crucial issue. Open discussions on UNSC reform have been avoided, both in Brussels and in New York, as this matter was considered too controversial.

However, the institutional innovations introduced by the Lisbon Treaty, together with the strengthened role of the European Parliament, have established the basis for more balanced and cooperative inter-institutional relations. The '*reductio ad unum*' of policies and structures governed by the Treaty, especially concerning the EU's relations with third countries and organizations, has no precedent in the history of the Union. In this new framework, EU institutions have acquired adequate instruments to trigger a fruitful consultation and negotiation process, both in Brussels and in New York. The consensus areas that have emerged during intergovernmental negotiations constitute a modest but concrete starting point to sketch out a compromise proposal.

Specifically, the EU as a single entity has committed more strongly to the principle of regional representation to reinforce its own identity and build its credibility at the UN. New campaigns on the role of regional arrangements and their contribution to the Security Council could be conducted with the support of other groupings and would expand the influence of the EU on the restructuring of the UN.

Overcoming the deadlock in the UN reform process: the role of regional organizations

Although the United Nations is based on state membership, regional groups are pervasive in its deliberations and actions (Weiss and Thakur 2010: 85). The last 20 years have witnessed a disappointing performance of the UNSC both as a legitimizer of military interventions and as an implementer of peace-enforcement and peacekeeping initiatives (i.e. over Kosovo, Iraq, and Syria to name a few cases). At the same time, regional organizations have acquired an enhanced role in international peace and security matters. The EU, as well as the African Union, are telling examples.

This has led some to question the vertical UN-led approach and the exclusive legitimacy of the Security Council with regard to intervention decisions (Buchanan and Keohane 2011: 52). Others have pointed out that 'an ideological regionalism that ignores wider multilateralism cannot address the link between conflicts within the region and wider global politics' (Hettne and Söderbaum 2006: 230). In the attempt to reconcile these two logics of globalism and regionalism, Hettne and Söderbaum have put forward the idea of 'regional multilateralism', built around regional entities such as the EU and the African Union, as opposed to the UN state-centric multilateralism (Hettne and Söderbaum 2006: 229–30). These authors focus on the need for 'complementarity' and 'shared responsibility' between global and regional agencies, to be encouraged 'through interregional arrangements that support the values and principles associated with the idea of multilateralism' (Hettne and Söderbaum 2006: 231).

How can this idea find its place in the debate over the reform of the UN Security Council and the role of the European Union in it? A 'representative' solution would be to have a reformed UNSC with seats assigned to delegates from the various regions of the world. However, this option encounters a series of legal and operational obstacles. As provided by its Charter, the membership of the UN is open to 'peace-loving states' only (Article 4) and the Security Council shall consist of 'fifteen Members' of the UN (Article 23). Every amendment of these provisions requires a hard-won two-thirds majority in the UN General Assembly, including the permanent members of the UNSC (Article 108).

Notwithstanding these legal hurdles, there are other options for introducing regional representation in a reformed UNSC, which could be passed without the need to amend the UN Charter:

- conferring an enhanced representation to regional organizations through UNSC non-permanent seats. Non-permanent seats would thus be assigned to countries that have been selected within different regional groupings, on the basis of these counties' ability both to represent the regional grouping and to contribute to the UN's machinery and peace and security operations. The idea behind this proposal is to make UNSC members more accountable to the regions they represent, especially by establishing election/re-election and rotation mechanisms within the regional groupings themselves. This would require the review of existing electoral groups – agreed on in GA Resolution 1991 (XVIII) of 17 December 1963, after UNSC membership increased by four non-permanent members – to better account for the current international configuration. For example, current EU members are dispersed over three electoral groupings: sixteen in the Western European and Others Group (WEOG), eight in the Eastern European Group (EEG) and one (Cyprus) in the Asian group. A need to reconsider the composition of these groups is imperative;
- increasing the presence of regional organizations in UNSC debates and deliberations. This proposal could be implemented in two ways: (1) through an expansion of the scope of Article 39 of the Provisional Rules of Procedure of the Security Council (UN Security Council 1982), which allows the UNSC to invite 'persons, whom it considers competent for the purpose, to supply it with information or to give other assistance in examining matters within its competence'. Representatives of regional organizations could thus be regularly invited to assist the discussions of the UNSC; (2) as a more ambitious – but also more controversial – alternative, the UNSC could decide to grant observer status to regional organizations that have achieved a substantive level of integration within the UNSC, building on the recent GA Resolution on the participation of the EU in the work of the UNGA (Pirozzi and Ronzitti 2011: 10).[6]

The EU can be considered as a *sui generis* actor in comparison with the other regional organizations that play a role in the UN framework, being more advanced in terms of its level of integration and supranational institutionalization. These characteristics confer on the EU the competence to contribute to the UNSC's deliberations, particularly in fields such as the fight against terrorism, disarmament and non-proliferation, the protection and promotion of human rights and international peacekeeping (Pirozzi and Ronzitti 2011: 9–10). As such, the EU is ideally placed to play a pivotal role in advocating a higher degree of regional representation at the UN Security Council.

At the same time, the Union cannot conduct such a campaign without liaising with other regional entities that are qualified to do so and willing to engage in an interregional effort of this scope. Among the regional organizations at the UN, the African Union deserves particular attention. The AU is not only one of the most representative regional organizations – its membership includes 54 out of the current 55 (after the declaration of independence by South Sudan) African countries. It also has a privileged relationship with the EU, both in terms of political dialogue – embedded in the Joint Africa–EU Strategy adopted in 2007 – and of cooperation in peace and security matters – especially through the EU's support for the development of the AU's capabilities through the African Peace Facility (APF) (Pirozzi 2009b).

As for AU–UNSC relations, it must be recalled that Africa has an obvious practical stake in deliberations on the Security Council's working methods. No other continent dominates the UNSC agenda as Africa does, consistently yielding more than 50 per cent of the issues the Security Council is mandated to address (UN Department of Peacekeeping 2011). As a result, most of the UN's humanitarian efforts and its largest, most numerous, peacekeeping missions are based in Africa. It stands to reason that the elusive search for peace and security in Africa calls for a more authoritative, permanent African contribution to the Security Council's deliberations.

The AU's increasing commitment to address conflicts on the African continent has raised new questions regarding its relationship as a regional organization (under Chapter VIII of the UN Charter) with the Security Council (Institute for Security Studies 2010: 7). An understanding on how to strengthen relations between the Security Council, as the entity bestowed with primary responsibility for the maintenance of international peace and security, and regional organizations such as the AU, is therefore of key importance to Africa – arguably more so than the identity of future permanent UNSC members.

On the question of UNSC reform, Africa is the only region that has, thus far, endorsed a consensus position, but it seems to exist only in rhetoric. In the so-called 'Ezulwini Consensus', formally endorsed in the July 2005 Sirte Declaration, African leaders demanded two veto-bearing permanent seats and five non-permanent seats allocated to the continent (African Union 2005). Since then, several African states have declared themselves duly representative and in a position to become permanent members: Senegal, Kenya, Libya, Egypt, Nigeria and South Africa are notable examples, although only the latter three have been widely touted to stand a realistic chance. Yet, this proposal is increasingly downplayed by major African players, realizing that its prescriptions for UNSC reform could be counterproductive.[7]

This analysis suggests that there is space for a reinforced region-to-region diplomacy between Europe and Africa on matters of peace and security in the context of the UN, with a view to forging a realistic AU position on regional representation (Pirozzi 2010). The continent-to-continent approach is one of the pillars of the Africa–EU Strategy and has spurred, both at the conceptual and operational level, the African Union to deepen regional integration and create regional structures to address peace and security matters. A reinvigorated partnership on these themes at the UN could provide an additional stimulus and a wider framework for this cooperation. This could also take the form of an EU–AU–UN triangular dialogue aimed at elaborating an innovative approach to regionalism within the Security Council. In this endeavour, the institutions created by the Lisbon Treaty have a crucial responsibility: the HR is central in building closer ties with the leading AU representatives, while the EEAS is ideally placed to reach out to African institutions (in New York, Brussels and Addis Ababa) and the capitals of relevant players on the continent.

Conclusion

Despite its declared commitment to pursuing coherent action at the United Nations, the EU has not been able to perform as a unitary entity in its relations with the world organization and within its most powerful body, the UNSC. To date, its presence at the UN has been highly fragmented, with a proliferation of actors: the EC Delegation to the UN, the EU Council Liaison Office in New York, the rotating presidencies, the High Representative, as well as the 27 Missions of the EU member states. This has generated confusion and discord in its interactions with UN stakeholders and external partners. As a consequence, the EU has often not 'communicated its vision of multilateralism to others in a politically compelling way' (Gowan and Brantner 2008: 3).

What are the prospects for the EU's presence and performance at the UN Security Council in the framework of the Lisbon Treaty? The frequency and scope of the interventions made by the High Representative and the Head of Delegation at the UN Security Council after the entry into force of the Lisbon Treaty lead us to believe that the EU is willing and able to gain more visibility in this organization. However, the achievement of a greater EU presence at the UN Security Council is subject to two conditions, which are yet to be realized: a more cohesive foreign policy conducted by EU member states on UNSC matters and an effective European External Action Service to support the High Representative and ensure a strong EU diplomatic action. If these prerequisites are not fulfilled in the near future, the Treaty risks becoming irrelevant to the enhancement of the EU's actorness at the Security Council.

A landmark step in this direction would be the elaboration of a common EU stance on UNSC reform. This could be achieved by a gradual coordination of national policies under the authority of the institutions created by the Lisbon Treaty. Although the success of such an initiative cannot be taken for granted, it nevertheless has the merit of reactivating the EU's internal discussions on this issue within a more cohesive institutional framework and gives an opportunity to the HR and the EEAS to engage directly in multilateral negotiations in New York.

Both the HR and the EEAS can be instrumental in engaging with other regional actors at the UN, most notably the African Union, and promoting a more dynamic approach to strengthen global governance in the realm of peace and security. This approach should be based on 'regional multilateralism', which confers institutional recognition to the enhanced role of regional players in these matters by placing them at the core of the security architecture of the UN and envisaging their greater representation within its most powerful body, the Security Council. Beyond the institutional aspects linked to UNSC reform, a reinforced interregional dialogue at the UN could address the quest for legitimate decision-making at the global level and at the same time boost the EU's bid to pursue effective multilateralism.

Notes

1   Nicoletta Pirozzi is Senior Fellow in European affairs at the Istituto Affari Internazionali (IAI) of Rome. The author wishes to thank Prof. Christopher Hill and Prof. Geoffrey Edwards from Cambridge University, United Kingdom, for their advice and constructive comments. Hubertus Jürgenliemk is PhD candidate at Cambridge University, United Kingdom. Yolanda Spies is Senior Lecturer in the Department of Political Sciences and Programme Director of the Master of Diplomatic Studies programme at the University of Pretoria, South Africa.
2   Whether the inaction of the Security Council allows regional bodies such as the EU to intervene in its stead is still a contentious issue. As noted by White, the European Security Strategy hints at such forms of intervention by stating that 'we [the EU] should be ready to act before a crisis occurs', tackling such threats not 'by purely military means'.
3   European non-permanent members of the UNSC are elected among the Western European and Others Group (WEOG) and the Eastern European Group. The African and the Asian Groups usually have three members each in the UNSC, while the Americas are represented by normally three, and occasionally four, states. This amounts to 25 per cent of the UNSC members, while EU member states only account for 14 per cent of UN members.
4   Recent examples include the so-called 'European laboratory' promoted by Germany and Spain in 2003–4: the proposal to offer a seat to the EU Presidency within their delegations during their two-year mandate at the UNSC was blocked by France and the UK. Similarly, in 2007–8, Italy suggested that an EU Council representative be permanently associated with its delegation at the UN Security Council, but its initiative met with firm opposition from France and the UK and a lukewarm response from Germany.
5   The Open-ended Working Group on the Question of Equitable Representation on and Increase in the Membership of the Security Council and Other Matters related to Security Council (OEWG) was tasked with producing reports and recommendations on Security Council reform to be submitted to the General Assembly.
6   As suggested by Natalino Ronzitti, 'a proposal could be to draft a SC resolution modelled on the resolution recently passed which confers to the EU an enhanced status at the GA,

allowing the EU to sit as a kind of observer within the SC. The EU might be: a) Allowed to be inscribed on the list of speakers in order to make interventions; b) Invited to participate in the debates of the SC dealing with matters falling under the EU competence; c) Permitted to have its communications relating to the sessions and work of the SC; d) Permitted to present proposals and amendments orally as agreed by the member states of the EU; such proposals and amendments shall be put to vote only at the request of a member state; and e) Allowed to exercise the right of reply regarding the positions of the European Union as decided by the state holding the SC presidency. It is understood that the representatives of the European Union shall not have the righ to vote, nor to co-sponsor resolutions or decisions, nor to put forward candidates.'

7   South Africa, one of the main African candidates for permanent membership of a reformed UNSC, is a case in point: during 2011, South Africa became the fifth member of the BRICS, a power-bloc that already boasts two P5 members (Russia and China), and two that have a very strong claim to permanent membership (India and Brazil as part of the G4 coalition).

Bibliography

African Union (2005) *The Common African Position on the Proposed Reform of the United Nations: 'The Ezulwini Consensus'*, Executive Council of the African Union, 7th Extraordinary Session, Ext/Ex.Cl/2 (VII), Addis Ababa, 7–8 March 2005. Online. Available HTTP: http://www.africa-union.org/News_Events/Calendar_of_%20Events/7th%20extra%20 ordinary%20session%20ECL/Ext%20EXCL2%20VII%20Report.pdf

Buchanan, A. and Keohane, R. O. (2011) 'Precommitment Regimes for Intervention: Supplementing the Security Council', in *Ethics & International Affairs*, Vol. 25, No. 1.

Buzan, B. and Waever, O. (2003) *Regions and Powers. The Structure of International Security*, Cambridge: Cambridge University Press.

Churruca, C. (2005) 'Criticizing the EU Security Strategy : the EU as a Regional Cooperative Security Provider', in *Revista Electrónica de Estudios Internacionales*, n. 10, diciembre 2005. Online. Available HTTP: http://www.reei.org/index.php/revista/num10/articulos/ criticizing-the-eu-security-strategy-the-eu-as-regional-cooperative-security-provider

Coker, C. (2009) *War in an Age of Risk*, Cambridge: Polity Press.

Council on Foreign Relations (2010) 'Forward by Richard Haass to K.C. McDonald and S.M. Patrick', in *UN Security Council Enlargement and US Interests*, Special report 59, December 2010. Online. Available HTTP: http://www.cfr.org/un/un-security-council-enlargement-us-interests/p23363

Die Welt (2003) *Interview mit dem Hohen Beauftragten für die europäische Außen- und Sicherheitspolitik, Javier Solana, 'Einheit Iraks muss erhalten bleiben'*, 24 March 2003. Online. Available HTTP: http://www.consilium.europa.eu/uedocs/cms_data/docs/pressdata/ DE/sghr_int/75180.pdf

Drieskens, E. (2010) 'Beyond Chapter VIII: Limits and Opportunities for Regional Representation at the UN Security Council', in *International Organizations Law Review*, Vol. 7, N. 1, pp. 149–69.

Edwards, G. (2011) 'The Pattern of the EU's Global Activity', in C. Hill and M. Smith (eds), *International Relations and the European Union*, Oxford: Oxford University Press (2nd edition).

European Commission (2003) *Communication from the Commission to the Council and to the European Parliament. The European Union and the United Nations: The Choice of Multilateralism*, COM (2003)526 final, Brussels, 9 September 2003. Online. Available HTTP: http://eur-lex.europa.eu/LexUriServ/LexUriServ.do?uri=COM:2003:0526:FIN:EN:PDF

European Union (2003) *European Security Strategy. A Secure Europe in a Better World*, Brussels, 12 December 2003. Online. Available HTTP: http://www.consilium.europa.eu/uedocs/cmsUpload/78367.pdf

European Union (2008) *Report on the Implementation of the European Security Strategy. Providing Security in a Changing World*, S407/08, Brussels, 11 December 2008. Online. Available HTTP: http://www.consilium.europa.eu/ueDocs/cms_Data/docs/pressdata/EN/reports/104630.pdf

European Union (2010) *Statement by High Representative Catherine Ashton at the UN Security Council*, New York, 4 May 2010, A70/10. Online. Available HTTP: http://www.consilium.europa.eu/uedocs/cms_data/docs/pressdata/EN/foraff/114179.pdf

European Union (2011a) *EU HR Ashton Addresses UN Security Council on Cooperation between the UN and Regional and Subregional Organizations*, New York, 8 February 2011. Online. Available HTTP: http://www.europa-eu-un.org/articles/en/article_10651_en.htm

European Union (2011b) *EU High Representative Catherine Ashton Appoints Three New Directors in the European External Action Service*, A/310/11, Brussels, 4 August 2011. Online. Available HTTP: http://consilium.europa.eu/uedocs/cms_data/docs/pressdata/EN/foraff/124167.pdf

European Union Press Department (2011) *EU High Representative/Vice President Catherine Ashton Appoints 25 New Heads of EU Delegations*, Brussels, 3 August 2011. Online. Available HTTP: http://europa.eu/rapid/pressReleasesAction.do?reference=IP/11/944&format=HTML&aged=0&language=EN&guiLanguage=en

Federal Foreign Office (2010), *Germany at the UN Security Council*. Online. Available HTTP: http://www.auswaertiges-amt.de/sid_488B68D2FE53B24D8E47701B09A460B7/EN/Aussenpolitik/Friedenspolitik/VereinteNationen/DEUimSicherheitsrat/101230-VorschauSRMitgliedschaft-node.html

General Assembly (2006) *Brazil, Germany and India: Draft Resolution*, A/60/L.46*, 9 January 2006. Online. Available HTTP: http://www.reformtheun.org/index.php?option=com_content&view=article&id=14&Itemid=36

Gowan, R. and Brantner, F. (2008) *A Global Force for Human Rights? An Audit of European Power at the UN*, Policy Paper, London, European Council on Foreign Relations, September 2008. Online. Available HTTP: http://www.ecfr.eu/page/-/documents/30b67f149cd7aaa888_3xm6bq7ff.pdf

Gowan, R. and Brantner, F. (2010) 'Navel-gazing Won't Help at the UN', in *European Voice.com*, 4 April 2010. Online. Available HTTP: http://www.europeanvoice.com/article/2010/10/navel-gazing-won-t-help-the-eu-at-the-un/69084.aspx

Grevi, G. (2011) *From Lisbon to New York: The EU at the UN General Assembly*, Policy Brief, No. 81, Brussels, Fride, July 2011. Online. Available HTTP: http://www.fride.org/publication/922/from-lisbon-to-new-york:-the-eu-at-the-un-general-assembly

Hettne, B. and Söderbaum, F. (2006) 'The UN and Regional Organizations in Global Security: Competing or Complementary Logics?', in *Global Governance*, Vol. 12, N. 3, pp. 227–32.

Hill, C. (2005) 'The European Dimension of the Debate on UN Security Council Membership', in *The International Spectator*, Vol. 40, No. 4. Online. Available HHTP: http://www.iai.it/pdf/articles/hill_2.pdf

Institute for Security Studies (2010) *South Africa's Second Term at the UN Security Council: Managing Expectations*, ISS Situation Report, 8 December 2010. Online. Available HTTP: http://www.iss.co.za/uploads/sitrep8dec.pdf

Kissak, R. (2010) *Pursuing Effective Multilateralism. The European Union, International Organizations and the Politics of Decision Making*, New York: Palgrave Macmillan.

Marchesi, D. (2010) 'The EU Common Foreign and Security Policy in the UN Security Council: Between Representation and Coordination', in *European Foreign Affairs Review*, Vol. 15, pp. 97–114.

Norheim-Martinsen, P. M. (2010) 'Beyond Intergovernmentalism: European Security and Defence Policy and the Governance Approach', in *Journal of Common Market Studies*, Vol. 48, Issues 5, November 2010, pp. 1351–65.

Pirozzi, N. (2009a) 'Italy's Mandate at the UN Security Council (2007–2008): a Missed Opportunity?', in J. Wouters, E. Drieskens and S. Biscop (eds), *Belgium in the UN Security Council: Perspectives on the 2007–2008 Membership*, Antwerp [etc.]: Intersentia, pp. 63–71.

Pirozzi, N. (2009b) *EU Support to African Security Architecture: Funding and Training Components*, Occasional paper No. 76, Paris, EU Institute for Security Studies, February 2009. Online. Available HTTP: http://www.iss.europa.eu/uploads/media/op76.pdf

Pirozzi, N. (2010) 'Towards a Real Africa-EU Partnership on Peace and Security: Rhetoric or Facts?', in *The International Spectator*, Vol. 45, No. 2, June 2010.

Pirozzi, N. and Ronzitti, N. (2011) *The European Union and the Reform of the UN Security Council: Toward a New Regionalism?*, IAI Working Papers, May 2011. Online. Available HTTP: http://www.iai.it/pdf/DocIAI/iaiwp1112.pdf

Rasch, M. B. (2008) *The European Union at the United Nations. The Functioning and Coherence of EU External Representation in a State-centric Environment*, Leiden and Boston: Martinus Nijhoff Publishers.

Tardy, T. (2005) 'EU-UN Cooperation in Peacekeeping: a Promising Relationship in a Constrained Environment', in M. Ortega (ed.), *The European Union and the United Nations – Partners in Effective Multilateralism*, Chaillot Paper No. 78, Paris, EU Institute for Security Studies, June 2005. Online. Available HTTP: http://www.iss.europa.eu/uploads/media/cp078.pdf

UN Department of Peacekeeping (2011) *Current Operations*. Online. Available HTTP: http://www.un.org/en/peacekeeping/currentops.shtml

UN General Assembly (2010) *Participation of the European Union in the Work of the United Nations*, (A/64/L.67), New York, 31 August 2010. Online. Available HTTP: http://daccess-dds-ny.un.org/doc/UNDOC/LTD/N10/500/71/PDF/N1050071.pdf?OpenElement

UN General Assembly (2011) *Participation of the European Union in the Work of the United Nations*, (A/RES/65/276), New York, 3 May 2011. Online. Available HTTP: http://daccess-ods.un.org/access.nsf/Get?Open&DS=A/RES/65/276&Lang=E

UN General Assembly/Security Council (2008) *Report of the African Union-United Nations Panel on Modalities for Support to African Union Peacekeeping Operations*, A/63/666–S/2008/813, New York, 31 December 2008. Online. Available HTTP: http://www.un.org/ga/search/view_doc.asp?symbol=A/63/666

UN General Assembly/Security Council (2010) *Support to African Union Peacekeeping Operations Authorized by the United Nations. Report of the Secretary General*, A/65/510–S/2010/514, New York, 14 October 2010. Online. Available HTTP: http://daccess-dds-ny.un.org/doc/UNDOC/GEN/N10/570/13/PDF/N1057013.pdf?OpenElement

UN High-level Panel on Threats, Challenges and Change (2004) *A More Secure World: Our Shared Responsibility*, A/59/565, 2 December 2004. Online. Available HTTP: http://www.un.org/secureworld/

UN Secretary General (2005) *In Larger Freedom. Towards Development, Security and Human Rights for All*, A/59/2005, 21 March 2005. Online. Available HTTP: http://www.un.org/largerfreedom/contents.htm

UN Secretary General (2008) *Report of the Secretary-General on the Relationship Between the United Nations and Regional Organizations, in particular the African Union, in the Maintenance of International Peace and Security*, S/2008/186, 7 April 2008. Online. Available HTTP: http://www.un.org/Depts/dpa/reports/S_2008_186.pdf

UN Security Council (1982) *Provisional Rules of Procedure of the Security Council*, (S/96/Rev.7), New York, 21 December 1982. Online. Available HTTP: http://www.un.org/Docs/sc/scrules.htm

United Nations (2010a) *UfC Platform on Security Council Reform*, A/64/CRP.1, 21 January 2010. Online. Available HTTP: http://www.italyun.esteri.it/NR/rdonlyres/3661BCE2-6BFC-49A2-81E8-F8FFBFB58FE8/0/20100210125245277.pdf

United Nations (2010b) *UK/French Position on the Reform of the Security Council*, 1 March 2010. Online. Available HTTP: http://www.reformtheun.org/index.php?option=com_docman&task=doc_download&gid=789&Itemid=248

United Nations (2011) *The Role of Regional and Sub-Regional Arrangements in Implementing the Responsibility to Protect. Report by the Secretary General*, A/65/877-S/2011/393, New York, 27 June 2011. Online. Available HTTP: http://www.un.org/ga/search/view_doc.asp?symbol=A/65/877&referer=http://www.unric.org/en/unric-library/26580&Lang=E

Uniting for Consensus (2005) *Proposal on Security Council Reform*, 26 July 2005. Online. Available HTTP: http://www.un.org/News/Press/docs/2005/ga10371.doc.htm

Van Langenhove, L., Torta, I. and Felicio, T. (2006) *The EU's Preferences for Multilateralism; a SWOT Analysis of EU/UN Relations*, UNU-CRIS Occasional Papers No. 0-2006/21, Brugge, United Nations University. Online. Available HTTP: http://www.cris.unu.edu/fileadmin/workingpapers/20060919114318.O-2006-21.pdf

Verbeke, J. (2006) 'EU Coordination on UN Security Council Matters', in J. Wouters, E. Hoffmeister and T. Ruys (eds), *The United Nations and the European Union: An Ever Closer Partnership*, The Hague: T.M.C. Asser Press.

Weiss, T. G. and Thakur, R. (2010) *Global Governance and the UN. An Unfinished Journey*, Bloomington and Indinapolis: Indiana University Press.

White, N. (2006) 'The Ties that Bind: the EU, the UN and International Law', in *Netherlands Yearbook of International Law*, Vol. 37, pp. 57–107.

12

ALL TOGETHER NOW?

The European Union's contribution to fiscal multilateralism in the G20

Charlotte Rommerskirchen

> If any good has come from the past 18 months of turbulence, it must surely
> be that the European Union and the multilateralism it embodies have proved
> themselves more necessary than perhaps at any period.
>
> *(Barroso 2009: 7)*

Introduction

In sharp contrast to the Great Depression, the Great Recession of 2008–10 saw an
unprecedented number of attempts to coordinate macroeconomic policies internationally. As the financial crisis turned into a deeper macroeconomic crisis in the fall
of 2008, the political dilemma posed by the post–Bretton Woods system – financial
integration without fiscal coordination – became apparent, thus highlighting the
'fiscal realities of financial integration' (Pauly 2009). In light of increased international policy interdependence, the need for international policy coordination has
been brought into bolder relief. This chapter seeks to investigate the European
Union's (EU) contribution to fiscal multilateralism in the G20 during and in the
aftermath of the economic and financial crisis.

Although the focus is upon the EU's leadership role with respect to fiscal policy,
the G20 with its growing list of agenda items and working groups[1] is addressing
many more issues. This being said, the broader themes and conclusions identified
should be applicable to other policy areas of international macroeconomic cooperation as well. Analysing the EU's role in this comparatively fledging multilateral
setting is a particularly interesting focus of investigation since the G20 at the head
of government level emerged as *the* 'premier forum for economic policy coordination' (G20 2009) and has been the central stage of what initially promised to be

a pivotal moment of international economic policy coordination. Moreover, the case-study of the G20 is empirically interesting, since here EU external representation resembles a halfway house; five of the EU member states hold their own seats, while the Commission and the Council jointly represent the collective EU interest. Further, the gatherings of the G20 constitute an analytically interesting interface of the domestic, the EU and the international level. In short, they take place on stages for so-called 'three-level games' (Patterson 1997).

The G20, although a new addition to the growing family of multilateral fora, is in many aspects a traditional set-up for policy cooperation and runs counter to the alleged trend of the 'new multilateralism' (Ikenberry 2003). That is, instead of being more demanding and necessitating more significant concessions on the part of its member states than the 'old multilateralism', the G20 can be seen as imposing only soft constraints on its member states. In so doing, it is distinctly non-threatening to states' sovereignty. Due to the soft nature of its agreements in the absence of sanctions or strong control mechanisms, the G20 is especially accommodating to those states who are either less impressed or less targeted by the time-honoured punishment peer pressure. This design of multilateralism in the G20 impacts not only on policy outcomes (fiscal multilateralism), but also influences the (inter)actions of its member states. One of the key questions will hence be how the EU shaped international fiscal policy coordination within this soft multilateral setting.

Analysing the EU's involvement in the G20, this research is based on qualitative analysis of primary and secondary documents and interviews with key officials working on the G20 in the International Monetary Fund (IMF), the European Commission, the European Council and Member States' Permanent Representations. Interviews were conducted in the spring of 2011 in Washington, DC and Brussels. This chapter proceeds as follows. The next section outlines how this study relates to wider debates in the political economy literature on leadership in the face of collective action. It presents two modes of leadership, one of structural and one of informational leadership. Building on this distinction, this chapter scrutinizes the EU's role in facilitating fiscal multilateralism in the G20, arguing that the Union's leadership has been much stronger on the 'structural leg' than on the 'informational leg'. The conclusion outlines some policy implications.

Analysing EU leadership

Young (1991: 281) argues that strong leadership is a 'critical determinant' of the success of international regimes. This research (in contrast to Hayward 2008), is primarily concerned with external leadership. Yet, to analyse the leadership dynamics of the European Union is by no means a clear-cut exercise that distinguishes between the inter- and extra-EU levels. Instead, both levels of policy contestation are intertwined. Three potential sources of EU leadership in the G20 emerge:

a)   the EU member states represented in the G20 (Germany, France, Italy, the UK, and to a lesser extent Spain[2]);
b)   the EU delegation as represented by the European Commission; and
c)   the EU delegation as represented by the European Council.[3]

Either EU leadership is exerted solely by the European Commission and the Council, or it takes the form of tandem leadership. The latter refers to joint leadership by one of the EU bodies together with one of the EU/G20 member states. The political economy literature on the modes of leadership can be divided into two strands; one highlighting the informational sources and one the structural roots of leadership (Ahlquist and Levi 2011). The first is concerned with agenda control and the potential to exert leadership as an 'architect of change'; the second identifies leadership as information transmission, that is, signalling via policy action.

The importance of information for group production has been famously studied by Arrow (1974), who claimed that information transmission affects the formation and modification of individual beliefs and the willingness of individuals to comply with leaders' demands. One can distinguish between two sub-types of informational leadership, one potentially costly and the other one inherently cheap. The latter, known as *cheap talk*, consists of verbal statements that are not backed up by credible threats or promises (Farrell and Rabin 1996). In other words, it refers to the use of signals that do not directly affect payoffs, and which are costless to make. With no legalization of G20 policy commitments, members of the G20 never reached legally enforceable agreements. This in turn makes cheap talk highly likely since the price of defection is low. The role of a leader in this context is to manipulate information about the nature of the provision and allocation function to render coordination more attractive.[4]

The second form of informational leadership addresses the other side of the coin: action. Leadership is said to be concerned with the transmission of information to followers and, by the nature of the received information, the manipulation of their action. Therefore leaders are compelled to convince followers that this information is correct. One central way of doing so is via *leading by example* (Hermalin 1998), an aspect that has been highlighted by various debates about power in EU studies (see for example Manners 2002).

Structural accounts of leadership have analysed how control of the agenda leads to control of the outcome. Arrow (1951) discussed how leaders who know how to set the institutional situation can manipulate outcomes to their own advantage or can influence the institutional design to their own benefits. Moreover, not only does the institutional design matter but what is also crucial is what is deliberated within the institution: in short, the agenda. Successful leadership can accordingly more likely be achieved if the leader holds agenda-setting power. Technically, agenda-setting concerns the hard and soft rules of how debates and proposals come up for deliberation. More specifically, agenda-setting decides how much attention is given to an issue. This is a matter of degree rather than a matter of kind (being 'on' or 'off' the agenda, see Tallberg 2003: 5). Especially in the context of the G20 – a multilateral forum with a growing sphere of potential influence – policy space is contested and the 'uploading' and framing of a specific issue can prove crucial.

An interesting sub-category of agenda-setting and leadership concerns the case of crises. According to Schofield (1978) political leaders emerge as 'architects of change' at critical moments in time. Pivotal moments, or 'constitutional quandaries'[5] occur when a traditionally upheld belief system is put into question. Political economists have put forward a 'crisis hypothesis' according to which a severe enough crisis will lead to major reform (see for example Drazen and Grilli 1993; Olson 1982). Similar to the 'window of change' argument, a crisis is said to alter perceptions of how the world works and therefore creates awareness of a need for change not previously perceived (Harberger 1993). Facilitating reform, leaders are said to play a key role: 'effective leaders take advantage of crises, weak leaders do not' (Drazen 2011). Arguably, the Great Recession provided just such a 'constitutional quandary' challenging the global economic system. Discussing leaders as 'architects of change' can here be taken literally looking at the changing architecture for international policy coordination with the re-creation of the G20 as well as, more metaphorically, the (re)construction and promotion of specific economic policy ideas.

The EU's role in the G20

One of the main lessons emerging from the Great Depression for those championing multilateralism was that 'the weak and often counterproductive policy response [...] was partly due to the lack of international cooperation and coordination on economic matters' (European Commission 2009). Given the EU's long-standing commitment to multilateralism, did it live up to its ambitions to contribute to effective fiscal multilateralism during the Great Recession? Fiscal multilateralism can hardly be cast as a success story. At first glance, it would seem that the numerous G20 agreements concerning the fiscal management of the Great Recession heralded a new height of fiscal policy coordination on an international level. Yet, upon closer evaluation, it appears that unilateral policy responses still prevailed and that the various agreements on fiscal policy coordination did not amount to much more than the strategic adoption of common rhetoric.[6] Still it is useful to identify instances where the EU exerted leadership, and in so doing facilitated multilateral agreements on fiscal policy, and where it failed to do so. The following section will analyse the role of the EU in the G20 along the two categories of structural and informational leadership.

Structural leadership

Without doubt, the largest contribution of the EU to fiscal multilateralism can be found in the Union's pivotal leadership in the reorganization of the G20. Similar to the IMF and the World Trade Organization (WTO), the original G20 is a phoenix

TABLE 12.1 G20 members

G20 members
Argentina
Australia
Brazil
Canada ⋆
China
France ⋆
Germany ⋆
India
Indonesia
Italy ⋆
Japan ⋆
Mexico
Russia
Saudi Arabia
South Africa
Republic of Korea
Turkey
United Kingdom ⋆
United States of America ⋆
European Union

Notes: Participation in G-20 meetings ex-officio: the Managing Director of the IMF, the President of the World Bank, the chairs of the International Monetary and Financial Committee and Development Committee of the IMF and World Bank.

⋆ also member of the G7

institution, with its cradle standing in the ashes of a global crisis. In September 1999, the finance ministers and central bank governors of the G7 (Canada, France, Germany, Italy, the United Kingdom, Japan, the United States, plus the EU) decided to set up a new international group to address challenges in the financial system that became apparent with the widening East Asian financial crisis in 1997. Since then, the G20 has consisted of 19 countries plus the EU (see Table 12.1). The Managing Director of the IMF and the President of the World Bank, along with the chairs of the International Monetary and Financial Committee (IMFC) and the Development Committee (DC), also participate in G20 meetings of finance ministers and central bank governors *ex officio*. The G20 is not equipped with a bureaucratic machinery of its own: the secretariats change with every presidency (once a year) and working groups are non-permanent. The latter prepare meetings in advance and sherpas and sous-sherpas often work on G20 issues a long time in advance of the (usually) annual meetings. Sharing with the G7 the absence of a charter, voting procedures or legally binding decisions, and favouring 'exclusive executive multilateralism' (Rittberger 2008), G20 members are at least in theory supposed to interact as equals.

In the wake of the Great Recession, in autumn 2008, the G20 reorganized as a forum for the head of states/governments to deal with the ramification of the financial and economic crisis. Notably, the new 'country leaders G20' did not replace the old G20; finance ministers and central bank governors continue to meet at G20 summits. The main impulse for the reform of the G20 came from the French President Nicolas Sarkozy who, in his role as rotating EU Council president, 'wanted to give his presidency an aura of global recognition'.[7] His original suggestion was to set up a G8 plus 5 summit (China, India, South Africa, Mexico and Brazil). Yet these five countries resented the 'guest status' that was attached to this kind of institutional reform. Crucially, the proposal to hold a crisis summit in the country constellation of the G20 appealed to emerging economies because this would a) give them at least formally equally standing to the traditional G8, and b) was a symbolic victory – 'if the G20 was good enough to deal with our crisis than it is also good enough for your crisis'.[8] The re-creation of the G20 with a shift towards the inclusion of emerging market powers injected a multilateral impulse into internationally coordinated crisis management. At least on paper, it contradicted Kahler's prediction (1992: 707) that in 'certain issue areas, such as monetary and economic policy coordination, it is likely that great power minilateralism will continue to dominate'.

Falling back to an old institutional configuration while 'upgrading' its participants (from finance minister and central bank governors to the head of states), despite having the advantage of being relatively time efficient and comparatively convenient, was nevertheless not unproblematic. The new G20 was considerably biased in favour of EU representation and no longer reflected actual global economic power constellations. Indeed one issue that flared up from the very beginning of the G20 was that of EU over-representation (see Eichengreen 2009). During the inaugural meeting in Washington, six EU countries were represented at the roundtable. Spain and the Netherlands had argued that they should be invited due to the size of their economies and participated as part of the French and the EU delegations respectively. Not only do EU leaders take up more than one-third of the summit chairs, most of the key international civil servants present at the international gatherings were also Europeans (Dominique Strauss-Kahn, then head of the IMF; Pascal Lamy, director-general of the WTO; Mario Draghi, then Chairman of the Financial Stability Board). Surprisingly, one of the most vocal advocates for abolishing EU seats is the US and not the emerging market countries. This strategy is likely to divert attention to the EU in order to 'make it the hegemonic villain'.[9]

Three main reasons enabled the EU to provide structural leadership at this critical juncture as an 'architect of change'. First, the financial and economic crisis cast a shadow on the reputation of the US government, which was seen by many as the main culprit for the destructive creation of unfettered capitalism. As the financial meltdown had put the model of Anglo-Saxon Capitalism into question, this crisis was considered to have 'been born in the USA, so it was natural to start dealing with its repercussions right there'.[10] The decision to hold the first G20 summit in

Washington hence had symbolic significance, referring to the place of the meeting as not only the geographical but the causal point of origin. During this 'constitutional quandary' of capitalism, EU leadership presented its growth model as a valid alternative. Second, the creation of the G20 took place during a leadership vacuum. Traditionally, the US has been in a position of leadership on international cooperation (McNamara and Meunier 2002: 850). But 'over the eight years of the Bush administration the US became increasingly willing to resort to unilateralism and disengaged from multilateral organizations when its interests were compromised' (Kissack 2010: 7). Moreover in autumn 2008, President Bush was considered a 'lame duck'[11] with the international community waiting for the president-elect. Against the backdrop of a US leadership vacuum, the leadership space was open for the EU. This changed, however, fundamentally with the strong presence of President Barack Obama in 2009. From Pittsburgh on, 'Obama was the real driving force taking ownership of the G20'.[12] Tellingly, it was not until September 2009 after the London Summit that the member states agreed to make the G20 the 'premier forum for economic policy coordination' (G20 2009). Third, the re-creation of the G20 was an instance of tandem leadership between the European Commission and an EU member state. France's strong involvement was further bolstered by holding the rotating chair of the Presidency of the Council of the EU. This triad of legitimacy sources gave the EU delegation led jointly by Sarkozy and the European Commission President, José Manuel Barroso, more credibility in their efforts to speak for the EU as a whole and rendered its leadership more credible. What is more, together they combined considerable expertise in summitry. Barroso's involvement in setting up the G20 was less visible than that of the French president.[13] Yet, that should not lead to an underestimation of the role the Commission President played. Indeed interviewees both within and from inside the Commission highlighted the *joint* role of Barroso and Sarkozy.

The Mutual Assessment Process

A further vital EU contribution concerning the architecture of the G20, with implications not only for fiscal but for monetary and other macroeconomic policies more broadly, is the creation of the Mutual Assessment Process (MAP). It constitutes the backbone of the initiative launched at the 2009 Pittsburgh summit: 'Framework for Strong Sustainable, and Balanced Growth'. 'The MAP is essentially an attempt to export the Open Method of Coordination onto the G20 level',[14] and represented a mode of economic policy coordination where the EU felt on 'home turf'.[15] The MAP is based on both elements of surveillance and peer review that is now common practice in the EU. It was backed by all five G20/EU member states.[16] Two problems, again not unfamiliar in the context of fiscal policy coordination in the EU, remain paramount. First of all, huge discrepancies concerning the quality and consistency of information provided by the G20 countries for the MAP remain. This is true both for the accuracy as well as the detail of its content.

The IMF officially stated that, when evaluating the national plans within the MAP, 'in keeping with the G20 ownership of the exercise, individual country policies were taken at face value and no judgments were made by IMF staff concerning their feasibility, timing, or effectiveness' (IMF 2010).Yet it quickly became apparent that some of the data provided was, if not outright wrong, then at least based on growth assumptions that were too optimistic (IMF 2011). Second, the surveillance of fiscal multilateralism is faced with a classical problem of collective action due to the absence of sanction mechanisms and the nature of the rather soft commitment to the G20 policy goals. Similar to the politicized nature of the Excessive Deficit Procedure (EDP) of the EU, the final recommendations of the MAP are highly contingent on political agreements between the states. Likewise, G20 members have to agree on a version of the country non-specific MAP to be published.There is little reason to believe that the G20 commitments on fiscal policy will trigger any better compliance than the EU laws governing fiscal policy coordination. Arguably, by replicating EU structures in the design of the MAP, European leadership paved the way for costless and ultimately futile commitments to multilateral action that were already distinctly non-threatening to states' fiscal sovereignty.

Informational leadership

The gist of informational leadership is that one's action contains information. As the EU vocally advocated fiscal policy coordination on the G20 level, one of the litmus tests for the credibility of its commitment to fiscal multilateralism would be the state of fiscal policy coordination *within* the EU. At the early stages of the G20 in 2008 and 2009, the EU and its common currency union were considered a unique role-model for managing economic interdependencies through increased policy cooperation at the supranational level.[17] Although the EU's system of economic governance was never perceived as flawless, it still represented a regime of policy coordination and transfer of, or at least concessions on, national macroeconomic sovereignty unprecedented at the international level. Therefore, the EU member states and the EU delegation saw themselves as a natural leader: 'Economic policy coordination? That's what we do on a day-to-day basis'.[18] Yet, the aura of experience faded due to persisting disagreements between EU member states and a patchy record of fiscal policy coordination even before the sovereign debt crisis of 2010–11 discredited its system of economic governance.

Speaking with one voice

One of the main challenges the EU faced was to present a united, consistent position. In so doing the Commission and the Council had a bifocal leadership aim: first, to establish their respective fields of competence for the contested external leadership of the Union and, second, to use the G20 as a means to bring EU member states policy agreements in line with one another. With the Lisbon Treaty in effect, EU representation in the G20 underwent an important change. It was agreed that the rotating Presidency should give up its seat for the newly created President of the European Council. Hence from the 2010 Seoul summit on, Herman Van Rompuy and Barroso jointly represented the EU. Officially, this delegation arrangement was presented as ensuring 'full coherence, complementarity and clarity [...] in reaching our objective that the EU should speak with one voice'.[19] But behind the scenes this decision was by no means reached without conflict. Barroso's cabinet, without much success, 'used all the tricks in the book'[20] to achieve single representation of the Community interest at the G20 by the Commission. At the end of the day, since legally only some of the policies discussed in the G20 fall into the sole responsibilities of the Commission, member states insisted on a shared seat.[21] Arguably, the growing competition between both Community bodies was even more pronounced at the internal level, notably when Commission and Council both 'wanted to be in the driver's seat of reforming economic governance'.[22] To avoid confusion at the G20 level, a flexible division of labour was constructed according to which only one of them would attend meetings and participate in the discussions, depending on the policy issue at stake as indicated by the legal framework of the EU. Fiscal policy was a matter delegated to Barroso. Yet, the Commission was not unconstrained as an agent of the member states. Its delegation had to coordinate closely with the Cabinet of Van Rompuy led by Franciskus van Daele to reach a joint position for all policy issues, notwithstanding who was to represent the EU.[23] What is more, with five of its principals sitting in the same room the scope for discretion was severely limited. Especially since the Commission was only bound by a 'gentlemen's agreement' on how to represent EU interest, the five EU/G20 states were keen to keep an eye on the Union's delegation.[24] In addition to the joint European Union position papers prepared in advance of the various summits in agreement with member states, the EU delegation also sought to consolidate the different positions of the Union's five country members by setting up regular meetings a few hours before the actual meetings of all G20 states in a 'vain attempt to chart the course'.[25] But 'at the end of the day these internal coordination efforts just added another layer of paper to put on old cracks'.[26] In fiscal matters the 'agreed language' was sufficiently vague to provide ample room for dissent. What is more, EU/G20 states felt only partially bound by the internal agreement since the Commission was there to represent the Community interest.[27]

McNamara and Meunier (2002: 850) blame the 'cacophony' of European voices in multilateral settings for the unchallenged 'pre-eminence of the United States in international monetary matters, as in other realms'. Pascal Lamy goes one step further and sees the main problem not in the dissonance of European voices but in the fact that there are numerous voices to begin with:

> If one European takes the floor on one topic, and then another European takes the floor on the same topic, nobody listens. Nobody listens because either it's the same thing and it gets boring, or it's not the same thing and it will not influence the result at the end of the day.

Therefore he suggests that the EU member states and officials should 'at least make sure that they speak with one mouth. Not one voice – one mouth – on each topic on the agenda'.[28]

The difficulties in presenting a unified front on fiscal policy issues is based on more than inter-institutional rivalry or national sovereignty concerns, but reveal deeper divisions within the EU both in terms of economic fundamentals and economic paradigms. Whereas the EU was relatively successful in leading on architectural matters of fiscal multilateralism, its ideational leadership, despite the EU's considerable summitry expertise and numerical advantage, was hampered by the heterogeneous positions of its member states when it came to the content of fiscal policy coordination. Indeed, it is here that informational and structural leadership interface, as the EU's compromised informational leadership can be seen as a direct cause of the failure to influence the content of the G20's agenda more markedly. This is illustrated by four key fiscal policy questions discussed in the G20.

Fiscal activism vs. fiscal austerity

The US delegation repeatedly called for more stimulus spending from EU countries during the G20 meetings, accusing EU countries of not doing enough to boost domestic demand.[29] In a similar vein, Olivier Blanchard, the IMF's chief economist, warned that 'if the circumstances require it, states must be ready to do more – 3 per cent or more if necessary',[30] thus going beyond the originally recommended 2 per cent of gross domestic product (GDP) stimulus. Accusations that some countries – notably Germany – were spending too little money to stimulate their economies could also be heard within Europe. The consensus of European commentaries was that 'the German government's reluctance to enact a big fiscal stimulus that could spill over to its neighbors is one reason why the fight against global recession is not yielding enough results'.[31] Yet, even more importantly, with the sizes and shapes of fiscal policy responses varying largely within the EU, one cannot truly speak of fiscal multilateralism. Most member states engaged in discretionary spending as they saw fit. Realizing the political tides in favour of state interventionism, the Commission came forward with the European Economic Recovery Plan (EERP) which 'merely rubber-stamped the policy initiatives that member states had already in their pipelines anyway'.[32] In short, when it came to fiscal policy coordination, the EU can hardly be seen to have led by example.

Despite the broad consensus to use fiscal policy measures to counter the recession, conflicts about economic policy paradigm quickly became apparent. The remark of the German finance minister, Peer Steinbrück, who called the UK's cut in VAT 'crass Keynesian',[33] was perhaps the most public example of dissent. The fact that the German government was not only one of the first G20 countries to announce a fiscal stimulus package, but also had the largest economic stimulus plan of the EU (both in real terms and as a percentage of GDP), is often unmentioned. This is in part due to the rhetoric of the German government. Concerned with their domestic image as European figurehead of stability culture, German Chancellor Angela Merkel's cabinet did not embrace Keynesian politics openly. The economy minister, for instance, called the German crisis response 'a tailored economic growth package, not a classic stimulus program'.[34] Arguably, it does not only matter politically whether fiscal crisis policies are in line with a policy agreement, but whether other G20 member perceived them to be so. This matters especially in the context of overcoming a collective action problem, where the incentives for defection rise with the perceived likelihood of other countries complying, hence the importance of informational leadership.

The role of automatic stabilizers

The issue of automatic stabilizers[35] sparked 'lengthy discussions'[36] among the G20 members. This disagreement within the G20 was primarily one between developed countries, especially between the US and Germany. Fuest *et al.* (2010) analyse the effectiveness of automatic stabilizers both in the US and in the EU. Although there is considerable heterogeneity within the Union, the authors confirm the view that automatic stabilizers in the EU played a considerably larger role in mitigating the Great Recession than it did in the US (for similar results, see Schelkle 2011). Paul Krugman attacked the allegedly inadequate size of European states' fiscal responses to the crisis perhaps most vocally, bemoaning the EU member states' 'failure to respond effectively to the financial crisis'.[37] Barroso's spokesperson reacted to the remarks by pointing out the crucial role of automatic stabilizers which were 'obviously in Europe [...] more important than elsewhere in the world' (Laitenberger 2009). Consistent support by the IMF helped to create acceptance within the G20 for the EU's member to have a smaller discretionary stimulus than notably the US.[38] The agreement on the EERP furthermore softened the tensions concerning the role of automatic stabilizers *within* the EU. As it was agreed to spend 1.5 percent of GDP *in addition* to automatic stabilizers there was little reason to further contest this non-discretionary spending item. Nevertheless, far from showing EU unity, at the April 2009 G20 London Summit, the UK joined the US in calling for larger stimulus packages, whereas Germany and France, pointing to the role of automatic stabilizers, declared existing stimulus programmes sufficient (Nanto 2009).

Exit strategies

It is no coincidence that the G20 addressed exit strategies at the same time as the EU did internally. The European Commission and Germany were committed to put fiscal consolidation on the G20 agenda.[39] Once more, the theme of tandem leadership emerges: the EU appears most successful in asserting leadership when the Commission is supported by at least one EU/G20 member state. During the Pittsburgh Summit (G20 2010a), high deficit countries committed themselves to 'undertake fiscal consolidation', while at the same time promising to 'avoid any premature withdrawal of stimulus', a statement that pleased both the fiscal activism and fiscal austerity camps. Yet, who belonged to the group of G20 members with 'sustained, significant external deficits' (Ibid.) was never specified as was the meaning of 'premature'. The vagueness of these commitments, leaving ample room for interpretative latitude, reflects the conflicts between the G20 nations on the speed of fiscal consolidation. One group, led by Germany, pointed to the dangers of debt sustainability and lobbied for a quick return to fiscal prudence. Another, led by the US, warned of the dangers of premature exit strategies for the global recovery. These differences can be found also in the time-preferences of the EU's EERP and the US's Geithner Plan. The EU officially advocated for a '3T approach', which is fiscal policy for the crisis that is 'timely, targeted and temporary'. In contrast, Lawrence Summer, Director of the White House National Economic Council, stated that 'while [he] had once advocated for stimulus that was timely, targeted, and temporary, our analysis of the situation the economy was facing indicated that stimulus needed to be speedy, substantial, and sustained'.[40] It was the distinction between *temporary* and *sustained* that caused concerns for the timeframe of fiscal multilateralism in the G20. Although, mirroring the positions of the fiscal activism vs. austerity camps, the main advocates of both policy prescriptions can be found in the US and Germany respectively, the same schism runs through the EU as well.[41]

Eventually, the G20 leaders of advanced economies agreed to 'at least halve' (G20 2010a) fiscal deficits by 2013 and to stabilize or reduce public debt by 2016 during the Toronto summit. The IMF (2011) was highly critical of some countries' performance in meeting these two objectives, as the medium-term consolidation plans rely on relatively optimistic growth assumptions and very few countries have thus far articulated credible plans underpinned by specific measures in key areas. If the speed of fiscal consolidation remained the same in 2012 as it was in 2011, all four eurozone G20 countries and the euro area as a whole would not meet the self-set deficit reduction target. However, according to one European official, in large part due to market pressures associated with the sovereign debt crisis, EU member states were consolidating their public finances much more quickly than they would have done via European agreements alone.[42] Whereas G20 countries, as well as EU member states were 'more or less in agreement about stimulating their economies in times of crisis, when it came to tightening the fiscal belt this consensus eroded'.[43] Given the lack of agreement in the G20, one EU official predicted that 'coordinated consolidation is now extremely unlikely'.[44]

Imbalances

Closely linked to the underlying notion of free-riding (be it on other countries' fiscal prudence or fiscal exuberance) is the issue of internal imbalances. The appearance of account balances on the G20 agenda was another Keynesian moment reminiscent of the Bretton Woods conference of July 1944. Keynes, representing Britain, warned of the risks posed by asymmetric adjustment between surplus and deficit countries, an alert that was principally directed at the US, then the dominant surplus country.[45] 'Parts of the observed divergence of current accounts and competitiveness are a source of potential concern to the extent that they reflect underlying macroeconomic imbalances, which increased the vulnerability [...] to the shocks of the crisis' (European Commission 2010: 5). Put differently, behind the resurfacing of growing interest surrounding global imbalances is the fact that they are in part responsible for aggravating the credit boom which led to the financial crisis. The debate within the G20 focused almost entirely on the two biggest surplus countries, dubbed 'Chermany' by the media; China, with a current account surplus of $291 billion in 2010 and Germany, with a surplus of $187 billion.[46] Yet essentially this was a conflict on two fronts. On the one hand, it represented tensions within the eurozone with, most vocally, French policy-makers calling on Germany to take action. On the other hand, it indicated the growing imbalances between China and the US. The US delegation sought to discuss imbalances first and foremost to put pressure on China to appreciate the renminbi faster.

> Originally the issue of imbalances was a way for the US to bash China within the G20, yet for political reasons the Obama administration did not want to single out China and therefore Germany got in the line of fire as well.[47]

The question of how to deal with imbalances has on the remedy side a clear fiscal component: fiscal policy as a means to curb domestic demand and contribute to a more balanced global economy. Such unlikely agreement would reflect a new step forward in the quest for fiscal multilateralism. Not only would G20 members design individual fiscal policy to bring about national economic recovery, but the consideration of imbalances in national macroeconomic policy-making would amount to a pledge to spend money for the sake of account deficit countries (Buiter 2010).

The first mention of imbalances in the official G20 Communiqué appeared in April 2010 when finance ministers and central bank governors stated that balanced growth should not 'generate persistent and destabilizing internal or external imbalances' (G20 2010b). Yet what policy action should be undertaken to mitigate this threat was not specified. Following a push from the US government, imbalances were one of the key points of the Seoul summit.[48] G20 leaders agreed that 'persistently large imbalances [...] warrant an assessment of their nature and the root causes of impediments to adjustment as part of the MAP, recognizing the need to take into account national or regional circumstances, including large commodity producers' (G20 2010c). Crucially EU negotiators, in tandem with Germany, achieved an agreement that the eurozone should be considered as a whole for monetary and fiscal issues. This was particularly important for German negotiators as it meant that the German account surplus would not be admonished on the G20 level since the eurozone is not in surplus. Although the issue of internal imbalances is still highly debated within the EU, at least on the G20 level the European Commission reached an important agreement when other member states agreed not to use the MAP as a means to rein in Germany's economically dominant position, since it promised an inter-EU process to address the issue of internal imbalances.[49] This agreement reflected Europe's underlying attitude towards the purpose and scope of the G20. As one EU official put it 'we don't need the G20 to deal with our own problems, we need the G20 so that the problems of other states don't *become* our own problems'.[50] Yet, ironically, with the eruption of the sovereign debt crisis, the G20 arguably became an instrument for policy-makers outside of the EU to chastise European policy-makers for their lack of efficient crisis management and finally in an October 2011 communication to set a deadline of eight days 'decisively [to] address the current challenges through a comprehensive plan' (G20 2011).

The sovereign debt crisis and informational leadership

In the eyes of many, the EU's Council of Ministers, the European Commission and the ECB 'failed to provide a timely and effective response' (Featherstone 2011: 193) to the sovereign debt crisis of 2010–11. This in turn had an impact on its informational leadership position: 'The EU can no longer dictate to less rich countries what to do, whilst being unable to get its own act together'.[51] What is more, involving the IMF in managing the sovereign debt crisis resulted in resentment on the part of many developing nations.[52] Arguably, the IMF had moderated its infamous position on fiscal consolidation that had led to fierce discussions about the appropriate policy mix for IMF programme countries and the standard fiscal austerity prescriptions by the Fund. Already in Davos, in January 2008, the former managing director of the IMF argued for a need to stimulate the economy, a call which according to the former Treasury Secretary Larry Summers was nothing short of a revolution: 'This is the first time in 25 years that the IMF managing director has called for an increase in fiscal deficits'.[53] At the G20 summit in London, the G20 agreed to triple the IMF's lending capacity to $750 billion and to expand its Special Drawing Rights Allocation by an additional $250 billion. Strauss-Kahn (2009) stated that 'the global crisis is hitting emerging market and poor countries hard. The G20 leaders have sent a powerful signal that the international community is committed to support these countries'. Yet, instead, the one country that benefitted the most from this new arrangement was Greece receiving the largest loan in the history of the fund (see Buiter and Rahbari 2010). Especially for former programme countries, such as Argentina, this led to the question of whether the IMF was giving more assistance under softer provisions to a eurozone government than it would have ever given to a developing country.[54] Not only was there a problem of communication,[55] which made other G20 countries feel left out, but the sovereign debt crisis also put the agreement to treat the eurozone as a single bloc into question: 'If we cannot maintain stability within our own monetary bloc, but need money from China and other IMF contributors, what does this mean for our line of argument?'[56] Given that the EU's sovereign debt crisis is still unsolved, and negotiations on the reform of its internal economic governance are ongoing, the EU's credibility as a model for economic coordination is severely put into question. If 'credibility is one of the key currencies in times of crisis',[57] the EU's money experienced a sharp devaluation over the past two years.

Conclusion

This chapter has explored the influence of the EU on facilitating fiscal policy coordination, arguing that while the Union found itself in a strong position to provide structural leadership, its informational leadership was unconvincing. Thus, its position was weakened in terms of championing fiscal multilateralism. For both modes of leadership, the EU has been most successful when acting in tandem with one of its G20 member states. There is a 'widespread assumption in the literature that if the EU agreed on common positions and speaks with one voice it will have influence' (Smith 2006). Concerning the first of the two conditions, this study has shown that this approach might in practice be less effective. EU member states agreed formally on a 'common position' prior to the G20 summits. Yet, this common position did not translate into a single voice. In the light of the increased need and challenges for international economic coordination, the ECB (2011) recently called for reform:

> To effectively influence the global debate [...], Europe is well advised to reinforce its efforts to speak with a single voice. This requires that EU member states, as a minimum, step up internal coordination processes and adhere to jointly agreed policy lines when the relevant issues are discussed in international fora.

The failure to produce a single voice in a system of mixed representation consisting of five EU member states, the Commission, the Council and (on a sub-level) the ECB, suggests a good reason to 'downsize' EU representation to a single seat. Such a change might furthermore help to improve relationships with emerging economies, whose resentment over the multiplicity of European seats can hardly improve the setting for collective action. If the G20 wants to remain the key forum for international economic policy cooperation, it seems unlikely that the current seat arrangement can stand up to the shifting realities of economic and political power. To agree on a single seat for the EU member states would, however, have much larger implications for the Union and its members going beyond the forging of a united position in a multilateral forum. Instead, this change would challenge its internal economic governance structure markedly. The limited influence of the EU in advancing international fiscal policy coordination can be attributed in many instances to the failure of economic policy coordination *within* the European Union. Internal economic governance is the *sine qua non* for the external economic governance of the EU.

Notes

1 'These working groups, they are like the heads of the hydra, you chop one off and you will get twice as many in return' (author interview, 11.4.2011).
2 Spain has secured a standing invitation to G20 summits giving it a de facto permanent EU seat.
3 Since the subject of this chapter is *fiscal* multilateralism, the leadership potential of the EU in the head of state configuration of the G20 is addressed. Therefore the role of the ECB delegation in the context of financial and monetary affairs during the G20 meetings of the central bank governors and finance ministers is not explored.
4 For example, a policy announcement by the EU pledging a stimulus programme of 1.5 per cent in the framework of the European Economic Recovery Plan (EERP) can be seen by other member states as a signal for a) the desirability of discretionary spending policy generally, b) an assurance that EU member states will not free ride on other states' stimulus plans and c) the probability that other states will follow suit.
5 These moments or quandaries are similar to 'critical junctions' (Collier and Collier 1991), 'tipping points' (Finnemore and Sikkink 1998) or 'socially constructed openings for change' (Widmaier *et al.* 2007: 747).
6 For a detailed discussion of the failure of fiscal multilateralism and the G20, see Rommerskirchen 2011.
7 Author interview, 12.04.2011.
8 Ibid.
9 Author interview, 12.4.2011.
10 Author interview, 18.05.2011.
11 Author interview, 12.4.2011.
12 Author interview, 25.05.2011.
13 For one thing, there is no corresponding official statement as found on the French government G20 website stating that the G20 was re-established 'at France's instigation'.
14 Author interview, 14.3.2011.
15 Ibid.
16 Author interview, 12.4.2011.
17 Author interview, 11.4.2011.
18 Author interview, 12.4.2011.
19 *EUobserver* 19.3.2010.
20 Author interview, 23.5.2011.
21 Author interview, 25.5.2011.
22 Author interview, 28.3.2011.
23 Author interview, 18.05.2011.
24 Author interview, 24.03.2011.
25 Author interview, 24.5.2011.
26 Ibid.
27 Author interview, 25.5.2011.
28 *Der Spiegel* 19.05.2010.
29 Author interview, 18.5.2011.
30 BBC 23.12.2008.
31 *Financial Times* 8.12.2008.
32 Author interview, 16.03.2011.
33 Newsweek 11.12.2008.
34 *New York Times* 5.10.2008.
35 Automatic stabilizers are features of the tax and spending system which react automatically to the economic cycle to reduce its fluctuations. In times of sluggish growth or recession tax revenues decrease and the share of national income spent by the government in benefits and on public services increases. Consequently, the budget stance in percentage of GDP is likely to improve in years of high growth and low unemployment

and to deteriorate during economic slowdowns. That is how the effect of automatic stabilization in the economy is created.

36 Author interview, 24.03.2011.
37 *New York Times* 16.3. 2009.
38 Author interview, 11.4.2011.
39 Author interview, 24.3.2011.
40 *Financial Times* 19.07.2009.
41 Author interview, 24.5.2011.
42 Author interview, 23.5.2011.
43 Author interview, 16.3.2011.
44 Author interview, 25.5.2011.
45 *Financial Times* 2.10.2010.
46 *Financial Times* 16.3.2010.
47 Author interview, 12.4.2011.
48 Ibid.
49 Author interview, 16.3.2011.
50 Author interview, 17.3.2011.
51 Author interview, 24.05.2011.
52 Author interview, 12.04.2011.
53 *Financial Times* 27.01.2008.
54 Author interview, 24.3.2011.
55 One interviewee described the reaction of the Chinese delegation to the decision to loan money to Portugal: 'the Chinese were furious. No one had told them in advance and they were under the impression that the Europeans considered the IMF to be *their* institutions which they could use in any way they wanted' (25.5.2011).
56 Author interview, 24.05.2011.
57 Ibid.

References

Ahlquist, J. and Levi, M. (2011) Leadership: What it Means, What it Does, and What we Want to Know About it. *Annual Review of Political Science*, 14, 1–24.

Arrow, K. J. (1951) *Social Choice and Individual Values*. New York: Wiley.

Arrow, K. J. (1974) Limited Knowledge and Economic Analysis. *American Economic Review*, 64, 1–10.

Barroso, J.M. (2009) State of the Union: Delivering a 'Europe of Results' in a Harsh Economic Climate. *Journal of Common Market Studies*, 47, 7–16.

Bouchard, C. and Peterson, J. (2009) *Conceptualising Multilateralism*. MERCURY Working Paper, prepared for the MERCURY Joint Workshop, Cologne, 9–10 July 2009.

Buiter, W. (2010) The Limits to Fiscal Stimulus. *Oxford Review of Economic Policy*, 26, 48–70.

Buiter, W. and Rahbari, E. (2010) Greece and the Fiscal Crisis in the Eurozone. *ECPR Policy Insight*.

Collier, R. and Collier, D. (1991) *Shaping the Political Arena: Critical Junctures, the Labour Movement, and Regime Dynamics in Latin America*. Princeton, NJ: Princeton University Press.

Drazen, A. (2011) Financial Market Crisis, Financial Market Reform: Why Hasn't Reform Followed Crisis? *ECFIN Economic Brief*, 6, 12–16.

Drazen, A. and Grilli, V. (1993) The Benefit of Crises for Economic-Reforms. *American Economic Review*, 83, 598–607.

ECB (2011) The External Representation of the EU and EMU. *ECB Monthly Bulletin May*.

Eichengreen, B. (2009) The G20 and the Crisis. *VoxEU*.

European Commission(2009) Economic Crisis in Europe: Causes, Consequences and Responses. *European Economy*, 7.

European Commission (2010) The Impact of the Global Crisis on Competitiveness and Current Account Divergences in the Euro Area, *Quarterly Report on the Euro Area*, Volume 9, No 1.

Farrell, J. and Rabin, M. (1996) Cheap Talk. *Journal of Economic Perspectives*, 10, 103–18.

Featherstone, K. (2011) The Greek Sovereign Debt Crisis and EMU: A Failing State in a Skewed Regime. *Journal of Common Market Studies*, 49(2), 193–217.

Finnemore, M. and Sikkink, K. (1998) International Norm Dynamics and Political Change. *International Organization*, 52, 887–99.

Fuest, C., Peichl, A. and Dolls, M. (2010) Wie wirken die automatischen Stabilisatoren in der Wirtschaftskrise? Deutschland im Vergleich zu anderen EU-Staaten und den USA. *Perspektiven der Wirtschaftspolitik*, 11, 132–45.

G20 (2009) The Leaders Statement: The Pittsburgh Summit, 25 September 2009.

G20 (2010a) G20 Toronto Summit Declaration, 26 June 2010.

G20 (2010b) Meeting of G20 Finance Ministers and Central Bank Governors, Communiqué, 23 April 2010.

G20 (2010c) G20 Seoul Summit Leaders' Declaration, 12 November 2010.

G20 (2011) Communiqué of Finance Ministers and Central Bank Governors of the G20, 15 October 2011

Harberger, A.C. (1993) The Search for Relevance in Economics. *American Economic Review*, 83, 1–16.

Hayward, J. (ed.) (2008) *Leaderless Europe*. Oxford: Oxford University Press.

Hermalin, B.E. (1998) Toward an Economic Theory of Leadership: Leading by Example. *American Economic Review*, 88, 1188–206.

Ikenberry, G. (2003) Is American Multilateralism in Decline? *Perspectives on Politics*, 1(3), 533–50.

IMF (2010) IMF Note on Global Economic Prospects and Policy Challenges. IMF Staff Note.

IMF (2011) Tensions from the Two-Speed Recovery Unemployment, Commodities, and Capital Flows. *World Economic Outlook*, April 2011.

Kahler, M. (1992) Multilateralism with Small and Large Numbers. *International Organization*, 46, 681–708.

Kissack, R. (2010) *Pursuing Effective Multilateralism : the EU, International Organizations, and the Politics of Decision Making*. Basingstoke: Palgrave Macmillan.

Laitenberger, J. (2009) Paul Krugman's Visit at the EC and View on Fiscal Stimulus (EC Midday): extracts from the EC Midday press briefing.

Manners, I. (2002) Normative Power Europe: A Contradiction in Terms? *Journal of Common Market Studies*, 40, 235–58.

McNamara, K. and Meunier, S. (2002) Between National Sovereignty and International Power: What External Voice for the Euro? *International Affairs*, 78, 849–51.

Nanto, D. (2009) *The Global Financial Crisis: Analysis and Policy Implications*. CRS Report for Congress.

Olson, M. (1982) *The Rise and Decline of Nations*. New Haven CT: Yale University Press.

Patterson, L. (1997) Agricultural Policy Reform in the European Community: A Three-Level Game Analysis. *International Organization*, 51, 135–42.

Pauly, L. 2009 The Old and the New Politics of International Financial Stability. *Journal of Common Market Studies*, 47, 955–75.

Rittberger, V. (2008) Global Governance: From 'Exclusive' Executive Multilateralism to Inclusive Multipartite Institutions. *Tübinger Arbeitspapiere zur Internationalen Politik und Friedensforschung*, 52.

Rommerskirchen, C. (2011) *Fiscal Multilateralism in Times of the Great Recession*, MERCURY E-paper no. 15, http://www.europa.ed.ac.uk/global_europa/external_relations/mercury

Schelkle, W. (2011) Good Governance in Crisis or a Good Crisis for Governance? A Comparison of the EU and the US. *Review of International Political Economy*, forthcoming.

Schofield, N. (1978) Instability of Simple Dynamic Games. *Review of Economics and Statistics*, 45, 575–94.

Smith, K. (2006) Speaking with One Voice? European Union Co-ordination on Human Rights Issues at the United Nations. *Journal of Common Market Studies*, 44, 113–37.

Strauss-Kahn, D. (2009) G20 Backs Big Boost to IMF's Financing. *IMF Survey Magazine* 2 April 2009.

Tallberg, J. (2003) The Agenda-Shaping Powers of the EU Council Presidency. *Journal of European Public Policy*, 10, 1–19.

Widmaier, W., Blyth, M. and Seabrooke, L. (2007) Exogenous Shocks or Endogenous Constructions? Meanings of Wars and Crisis. *International Studies Quarterly*, 51, 747–59.

Young, O.R. (1991) Political Leadership and Regime Formation. *International Organization*, 45, 281–300.

13

THE EU AND THE MIDDLE EAST QUARTET

A case of (in)effective multilateralism

Nathalie Tocci

Introduction

In the past, mediation of the protracted Arab-Israeli conflict was exclusively unilateral in character, being dominated by the United States. With the outbreak of the second intifada in 2000, time seemed to be ripe for a substantial reshuffle of Middle East mediation. In 2002, what became known as the 'Middle East Quartet' came into being, constituted by the European Union, Russia, the United Nations and the United States. In principle, this new format reflected the exigencies of effective mediation in a new geopolitical context. Over the course of the 1990s, in fact, the European Union (EU) had emerged as a principle donor to the occupied Palestinian territory (OPT) and the nascent Palestinian Authority (PA) (Le More, 2005). Russia not only remained a major power and UN Security Council (UNSC) permanent member, but also enjoyed historically close ties to the Arab world and, more recently, an organic bond to the large Russian community in Israel. The United Nations brought with it international legitimacy. And few doubted that the US continued to be a vital player, the only one with the clout to substantially alter the parties' negotiating stances.

A decade has passed since the establishment of the Quartet, making an assessment of its workings a timely undertaking. In this context, this chapter explores the Quartet as a case of crystallizing multilateralism focusing on two questions. First, can the Quartet be regarded as a case of effective multilateralism? Has it been genuinely multilateral? Has it been effective? Second, the Quartet came into being around the same time as the EU proclaimed, for the first time, the goal of 'effective multilateralism' in its 2003 Security Strategy (European Council, 2003). This was no coincidence.[1] In view of this, has the EU contributed to the Quartet becoming a case of effective multilateralism?

The Middle East Quartet as a case of crystallizing multilateralism

The Middle East Quartet emerged from a foreign ministers meeting in Madrid in April 2002. Present at the gathering were US Secretary of State Colin Powell, EU High Representative for the Common Foreign and Security Policy (CFSP) Javier Solana, Spanish Minister of Foreign Affairs Ana Palacio, UN Secretary General (UNSG) Kofi Annan and Russian Minister of Foreign Affairs Sergei Lavrov (Musu, 2007).

The birth of the Quartet reflected the exigencies of the early twenty-first century. At the time, the second Palestinian intifada was at its height, featuring widespread Israeli military incursions into the Occupied Palestinian Territories (OPT) and repeated Palestinian suicide bombings. The peace process was in tatters. Following the collapse of negotiations at Camp David II in the summer of 2000 and Taba in January 2001, successive attempts to break out of the cycle of violence and restore dialogue between the parties came to no avail. The 2000 Mitchell report recommendations and the 2001 Tenet security workplan remained on paper. Violence raged on the ground. In those tragic months of 2000–1, the EU Special Representative for the Middle East Peace Process, the Special Representative of the UNSG, and the Russian Ambassador to Israel frequently met in Tel Aviv to seek ways to respond jointly to the unfolding crisis.[2] Albeit reluctant at first, the US Ambassador to Israel ultimately came round, not only to seeing the urgency of re-sparking a political process, but also of doing so with the support of the US's international partners in the region. The establishment of the Quartet one year later – in April 2002 – was then almost accidental. In Madrid, Secretary of State Powell met with his EU, UN and Russian counterparts, who had been meeting regularly, at lower levels, for one year on the ground. Powell saw the benefits of broadening international support for US initiatives towards the conflict. The Quartet had officially come into being.

What became known as the Quartet thus included four actors: the US, the EU, Russia and the UN. Its goal was to create a multilateral framework aimed at an Israeli-Palestinian negotiated solution based on UN Security Council (UNSC) resolutions 242 (1967) and 338 (1973), alongside the 'land for peace' principle enshrined in the Oslo process. More concretely, the stated aim of the Quartet was to support the establishment of two states, Israel and Palestine, living side by side within secure and recognized borders, as affirmed by UNSC resolution 1397 and endorsed by US President George W. Bush. The Quartet also explicitly lent its political backing to the Saudi peace initiative – later accepted by the Arab League and now known as the Arab Peace Initiative – which foresaw a full normalization of Israel's relations with the Arab world alongside a comprehensive Arab–Israeli peace, including not only Israel-Palestine but also Syria and Lebanon. The Middle East Quartet, therefore, did not aim at supplanting the US-led Middle East peace process. Less still did it aim at reversing the principles of the Oslo peace process. It rather aimed at instilling new momentum in the moribund peace process by complementing American mediation with the support of three critical players: the EU, the UN and Russia.

Viewed from this angle, the Quartet had a watertight rationale. In the twenty-first century, the logic of a closed three-party game featuring the two conflict parties – Israel and the Palestinian Liberation Organization (PLO) – and one mediator – the US – seemed wanting. The US continued to bring with it the strategic leverage, not only over the Palestinians, but above all over Israel. But George W. Bush's first administration had little interest in the Israeli-Palestinian conflict, immersed, as it was, in its 'Global War on Terror' and in garnering momentum for its planned attack on Iraq. With the Clinton administration gone and the intifada in full swing, the days of American monopoly over the 'Middle East Peace Process' appeared over. The EU had become the most important donor to the Palestinian Authority (PA) over the course of the 1990s. But as tirelessly reminded by Palestinians, the EU was 'a payer but not a player'.[3] Indeed, in the early 2000s, the Union watched the unfolding drama in the Middle East with extreme concern and unending declarations. But it was well aware that it could do precious little to unblock the impasse on its own. The complementarities between the US and the EU in Middle East peacemaking thus seemed evident. Russia and the United Nations played a secondary, but nonetheless important, role. The UN, as the repository of international law, brought with it international legitimacy, adding weight to a peace process aimed at respecting at least three UNSC resolutions (i.e. 242, 338 and 1397) (Prendergast, 2006). Russia, while not the superpower it once was, had been a co-sponsor of the Madrid conference, was a UNSC permanent member and continued to enjoy close ties to the Arab world (and particularly to Syria, as highlighted in the unfolding Syrian crisis in 2011–12). Since the collapse of the Soviet Union, Russia had also strengthened its relations with Israel, not least due to the presence of over one million Russian citizens in the country. In view of this, the Quartet was applauded by many at the time as an effective multilateralization of Middle East mediation. In the dark days of 2002, the Quartet – its peculiarities notwithstanding – seemed to represent the ideal N-group to resolve the thorny Middle East conflict.

More precisely, the Quartet represents a case of 'crystallizing multilateralism' (see Chapter 2). Unlike international organizations, the Quartet has remained deliberately uninstitutionalized and flexible. Yet it is not an *ad hoc* gathering of actors. Since 2002, its representatives have met regularly focusing on a single issue, have issued a series of joint statements and have conducted a number of key initiatives. Furthermore, the Quartet is endorsed by the UN Security Council (UNSC resolution 1435, September 2002). The Quartet has also nominated high-level personalities of the likes of James Wolfensohn and Tony Blair to act on its behalf, and has developed an operational capability to support their missions. Comparable to other 'contact groups' or 'group of friends' active in conflict settings, the Quartet has thus crystallized as a multilateral endeavour, without transforming itself into an international organization or having any prospects of doing so.

Reviewing the Quartet's actions... and inactions

The Quartet thus emerged over a decade ago and, at the time, held the promise of an effective multilateralization of the Middle East peace process. Unsurprisingly, the EU, which in 2003 made clear its ambition to promote 'effective multilateralism', was a principal driver and advocate behind this endeavour. A decade later, what has the Quartet done and what role has the EU played in it?

Promoting Palestinian reform

Almost upon its inception, the Quartet immersed itself in the question of Palestinian reform (Middle East Quartet, 2002a). In its July 2002 joint statement, the Quartet declared:

> Consistent with President Bush's June 24 statement, the UN, EU and Russia express their strong support for the goal of achieving a final Israeli-Palestinian settlement, which, with intensive effort on security and reform by all, could be reached within three years from now.
>
> *(Middle East Quartet, 2002b)*

The Quartet took the cue from US President Bush's 24 June call for Palestinian reform, making it its own.

To do so, the Quartet based itself on the 100-day reform programme published by the PA in early 2002 and established an International Task Force on Palestinian Reform under its aegis. Beyond the Quartet's representatives, the Task Force included also other major donors to the PA, namely Canada, Japan, Norway, the International Monetary Fund and the World Bank. It also met regularly with representatives from Egypt, Jordan, Saudi Arabia, Lebanon and Syria. The Task Force established seven working groups on the multiple aspects of PA reform: financial accountability, civil society, local government, elections, judicial reform, administrative reform and the market economy.

Within this endeavour, the EU played a prime role. As and when President Bush started humming the tune of Palestinian reform, in a not-so-veiled attempt to oust President Yasser Arafat, the EU, rather than contradicting Washington head-on, endorsed its line, while concomitantly trying to modify it. The EU appropriated the aim of Palestinian reform, but recast it in a broader (and less personalized) language. Rather than pressing for regime change and the removal of Arafat, the EU focused on the broader *problematique* of Palestinian reform. The EU's aim in pursuing reform was both direct and indirect. On the one hand, the EU was directly interested in engaging the Quartet on Palestinian reform. Indeed, the Commission had been focusing on Palestinian reform before the widespread Israeli and American interest in the question. The first EU-sponsored attempt to highlight the deficiencies of the PA came in 1999, with the publication of the EU-supported Rocard-Siegman Report (Sayigh and Shikaki, 1999). By 2001, the EU had started conditioning its financial assistance to the PA on reform conditions. On the other hand, the EU hoped that by working on Palestinian reform, the Quartet would indirectly induce a re-launch of the peace process by reengaging the US (and thus Israel) in it. The EU's approach was largely endorsed by the Quartet. Rather than the US's single-minded focus on removing Arafat, the Quartet adopted the EU's more comprehensive understanding of Palestinian reform (Emerson and Tocci, 2002). The seven working groups established under the aegis of the Quartet were a reflection of this. The European Commission chaired, either alone or jointly with other donors, several working groups.

The Roadmap

Alongside the Quartet's technical work on Palestinian reform, the Quartet engaged in a major diplomatic endeavour between 2002 and 2004: the 'Roadmap'. Work on the Roadmap began in the summer of 2002, and a first version of the document was published in September of that year. After several iterations, the final version was published in April 2003, and was subsequently endorsed by UNSC resolution 1515 in November 2003.

The Roadmap and the work on Palestinian reform were intertwined. Insofar as the indirect aim of Palestinian reform was that of reigniting US mediation of the peace process, the Roadmap provided the diplomatic framework to achieve this (Emerson and Tocci, 2002). The Roadmap foresaw three phases of implementation aimed at establishing a Palestinian state in three years (Middle East Quartet, 2004). The principles of the Roadmap included reciprocal steps undertaken by Israelis and Palestinians that were intended to be 'performance-based', i.e. based on actual implementation. By inserting Palestinian reform in phase 1, and directly working on this task, the Quartet aimed at putting the Roadmap immediately in action by inducing Israel's reciprocal steps and thus re-launching the peace process.

As in the case of Palestinian reform, the EU was in the lead within the Quartet on the Roadmap (Douma, 2006). The first text of the Roadmap was drafted by the Danish Presidency of the EU in August 2002, inspired, in turn, by German Foreign Minister Joschka Fischer's April 2002 'seven point plan' to achieve a peace settlement (Asseburg, 2003). The idea was that of operationalizing President Bush's vision of two states, through a three-year process leading to the establishment of a Palestinian state in 2005. Once again, the concept and strategy was that of taking the cue from the United States, but moulding the US line according to the EU's own aims and logic. Indeed, the Roadmap endorsed some elements of Washington's strategy, epitomized by President Bush's 24 June 2002 speech, while ignoring others (Emerson and Tocci, 2002). Specifically, the Roadmap accepted the notion that Palestinian reform was a precondition for final status negotiations, but refused to focus on leadership change in the PA. The Roadmap also insisted on reciprocity/parallelism in the first phase. Hence, alongside Palestinian security reform, the Roadmap foresaw a parallel cessation of Israeli settlement activity and withdrawal to the pre-28 September 2000 positions. Finally, the Roadmap introduced the novel idea of a state with provisional borders.

Disengagement

Months and years passed, and the parties remained stuck on the first phase of the Roadmap. The Palestinians had made some steps forward on their reform commitments in the Roadmap. Yet Palestinian violence, Israeli settlement construction and Israeli military presence and incursions in the OPT continued. Pressure was mounting on Israel in particular. In response, the Sharon government seized the opportunity to kill two birds with one stone by proposing a unilateral disengagement from the Gaza Strip. On the one hand, the disengagement plan was premised on unilateralism (as opposed to a negotiated agreement) and relieved Israel of the costs of direct occupation of the Strip. Indeed, not only did Gaza not have the same degree of political and religious symbolism as the West Bank and East Jerusalem, but also the Israeli security establishment was fully mobilized to protect a mere 8,500 Jewish settlers amongst 1.5 million Palestinians crammed in a narrow 40 km strip. On the other hand, disengagement was presented as an important Israeli move towards peace, while distracting attention from Israel's ongoing construction of settlements and the separation barrier in the West Bank. No matter the details of the plan and the other actions that Israel pursued, it was difficult to condemn a home-grown Israeli drive to dismantle settlements in the OPT.

The Quartet endorsed Israel's disengagement plan in its 9 May 2005 statement (Middle East Quartet, 2005a). Just as the Quartet's initiatives on Palestinian reform and the Roadmap had taken the cue from Washington, the Quartet now reacted to an Israeli move. The logic was the same. Rather than contrasting the move *tout court*, the Quartet embraced it, while attempting to mould it to its liking. Precisely, the Quartet endorsed what it approved from the disengagement plan – i.e. the withdrawal of settlements from the Gaza Strip – but refuted (or rather ignored) what it did not – i.e. its unilateral character. The declared intention, as argued by a Commission official, was that of casting disengagement within the framework of the Roadmap.[4] Viewing disengagement as an opportunity to be seized, the Quartet appointed a 'Special Envoy for the Gaza Disengagement', James Wolfensohn. The former president of the World Bank and his team on the ground was mandated to work on the non-security related aspects of disengagement, namely the disposition of assets, passages between the West Bank and Gaza, access and trade to and from the Gaza Strip, and the revival of the Palestinian economy.

Unlike the cases of Palestinian reform and the Roadmap, however, on disengagement, the US was in the lead. The EU played an important role in casting disengagement within the framework of the Roadmap. But primarily the EU was an implementor rather than a formulator of the Quartet's policies on disengagement. The EU staffed and financed the Office of the Quartet Envoy and it played an important role as implementor of the 2005 Agreement on Movement and

Access (AMA) (Euro-Mediterranean Human Rights Network, 2009). Its decision to deploy the EUBAM Rafah mission on the border between Gaza and Egypt in 2006 was an integral part of the functioning of the agreement.

The Quartet's conditions on Hamas

All the Quartet initiatives reviewed above were reactions to US and Israeli impulses, aimed at steering these in directions which the Quartet (and in particular the EU) viewed as more conducive to peace. In some cases the Union led on the design of the Quartet's policies – i.e. in the case of Palestinian reform and the Roadmap. In other cases, the EU was the principal implementor of the Quartet's approach – i.e. disengagement. But in all cases the Quartet essentially reacted to unilateral policy moves by the United States.

In 2006, this changed. When it came to the international response to the January 2006 Palestinian legislative elections, the Quartet itself was in the lead, defining what became known as the Quartet's conditions on Hamas. The precursor to the Quartet's conditions were two statements, on 20 September and 28 December 2005 (Middle East Quartet, 2005a, 2005b). In its September statement, the Quartet did not prejudge participation in the Palestinian elections, but pointed out the incompatibility between participating in elections and possessing armed militias. More explicitly, in December, the Quartet, while welcoming the elections as a landmark in Palestinian democracy, called on all participants to 'renounce violence, recognize Israel's right to exist, and disarm', adding that the future PA should not 'contain members who are not committed to these principles' (Middle East Quartet, 2005b). Immediately after Hamas's electoral victory, on 30 January, the Quartet reaffirmed its position: 'It is the view of the Quartet that all members of a future Palestinian government must be committed to non-violence, recognition of Israel, and acceptance of previous agreement and obligations, including the Roadmap' (Middle East Quartet, 2006a). In addition, the Quartet introduced the notion of aid conditionality linked to these principles. In the same statement, it posited that it was 'inevitable that future assistance to a new government would be reviewed by donors against the government's commitment to the principles of non-violence, recognition of Israel, and acceptance of previous agreements and obligations' (Middle East Quartet, 2006a).

The Quartet did not stop here. Having set out the principles and presented the notion of conditionality, it also judged the PA's performance. A mere two days after the adoption of the new Palestinian government's programme on 28 March, the Quartet declared: 'there inevitably will be an effect on direct assistance to that government and its ministries' (Middle East Quartet, 2006b). The Quartet adjudicated on the need for negative conditionality, be this in the form of boycotts, sanctions or withdrawal of assistance to the PA. With the green light from the Quartet, three of the four Quartet members engaged in negative conditionality on the Hamas government. The EU, the US and the UN Secretariat (particularly after UN Secretary

General Kofi Annan's end of office in 2007) all boycotted the Hamas government, refusing contact with its representatives. In addition, the US, and, above all, the EU, opted for a maximalist interpretation of what no cooperation with Hamas meant, sanctioning the government by withdrawing its assistance to (and through) it (Tocci, 2007a).

Sanctions and boycotts sting. But when it comes to an occupied territory lacking a recognized and independent state, sanctions and boycotts are lethal. Indeed two months after the suspension of contacts with and aid to the Hamas government, the PA was on the brink (Office of the Special Envoy for Disengagement, 2006; United Nations, 2006; Oxfam, 2007). A collapse of the Authority was not in the interest of the Quartet, committed as it was to a two-state solution. Less still was it in the interest of Israel, which, as occupying power, would have had to reengage in the costly task of administering directly the OPT. Finding a way out was imperative. Here again, the Quartet took the lead. In its 9 May 2006 statement, it called for a Temporary International Mechanism (TIM) aimed at resuming direct assistance to the Palestinians, while by-passing the Hamas government. Beginning in August 2006, through the TIM, the international community provided social allowances to civil servants and pensioners, direct financial and material support to the health, education, water and social sectors, as well as funds to pay fuel bills (EMHRN, 2009).

This time, within the Quartet Washington rather than Brussels (Moscow or New York) was clearly in the lead (de Soto, 2007). The Bush administration was behind the Quartet's push for the principles and conditionality on Hamas. The EU followed and implemented the Quartet's line. Only in May 2006, when the PA, in which the Union had invested so much, was on the verge of collapse, did the EU mobilize within the Quartet to approve the TIM. It was also the EU, that upon the TIM's approval, managed and channelled the lion's share of international assistance to the Palestinians through it. Indeed, the TIM led to a surge in EU aid to the OPT. Commission and member state contributions rose from €500 million in 2005 to almost €700 million in 2006 and €1 billion in late 2007 (European Commission, 2008).

The West Bank first policy and the Office of the Quartet Representative

The Quartet's approach to Hamas has remained unchanged since 2006 (Middle East Quartet, 2007a, 2007b). Its assessment of the PA was negative in March 2007, when the rival Palestinian factions – Hamas and Fateh – under Saudi mediation, brokered a National Unity Government (NUG) (Tocci, 2007a). The NUG, facing persisting international isolation and sanctions, lasted a mere three months. It collapsed in June 2007, when intra-Palestinian violence culminated in the political separation of the West Bank from the Gaza Strip, with Fateh in control of the former and Hamas of the latter. Since then, the Quartet, ignoring the uneasy truth that the Fateh-led PA lacked democratic legitimacy and accountability, embraced the new Authority in the West Bank as 'the legitimate Palestinian Authority'. It continued to boycott and sanction the Hamas-led government in the Gaza Strip (Middle East Quartet 2010). This approach crystallized in what became known (but officially denied) as 'West Bank first': the idea that the international community should cast its attention to the West Bank, building institutions and making the West Bank a more decent place to live in. This should have induced Palestinians in the Gaza Strip to revolt against Hamas and reintegrate under the Fateh-led PA.

To accomplish this (unstated) objective, the Quartet appointed a new Representative: former British prime minister Tony Blair. Blair's mandate was that of mobilizing international assistance, securing international support for governance needs, and promoting economic development and capacity building in Palestine. In principle, Blair's mandate did not cover only the West Bank. In practice it mainly did, supporting Salam Fayyad's Reform and Development Plan. His activities that related to easing of movement restrictions, private sector development, East Jerusalem, the rule of law, tourism and PA financing essentially concerned the West Bank-based government rather than Gaza.

As in the case of disengagement and conditionality on Hamas, the EU, rather than being the driver and advocate of the West Bank first policy within the Quartet, was its principal implementor. The political push, again, came from Washington. The EU implemented this approach through its copious assistance to the PA (via its financial mechanism approved in the fall of 2007 – Pegase), its Common Security and Defence Policy (CSDP) mission EUPOL-COPPS, and by staffing and financing the Office of the Quartet Representative.

The Quartet as a case of (in)effective (uni)multilateralism?

Having reviewed the Quartet's initiatives over the last decade, let us turn to an assessment. To what extent can the Quartet's actions (and inactions) be viewed as truly multilateral and effective?

Multilateral in name, unilateral in practice

In the early twenty-first century, with the collapse of the Oslo process and the eruption of the 'Global War on Terror', the era of unilateral American mediation seemed over. A decade later, has the Quartet affirmed itself as a genuine multilateral endeavour to promote peace in the Middle East?

Formally, it has. The role between the four Quartet partners has not been equal, with the US and the EU adopting a more proactive role than the UN and Russia. But all actors have endorsed and engaged in the Quartet's initiatives. However, scratching beneath the surface, the extent to which mediation in the Middle East has become truly multilateral is highly questionable. As put unflatteringly by former Arab League Secretary General Amr Moussa, the Quartet ought to be understood as a 'Quartet *sans trio*' (Patten, 2006: 109).

Not only has the US been *primus inter pares* within the Quartet, but the Quartet's early activities entirely revolved around engaging Washington rather than multi-lateralizing Middle East mediation. In the early years of the George W. Bush administration, American interest in engaging in the Israeli-Palestinian peace process was close to nil. This was a time in which the 'ABC' ('anything but Clinton') mantra was trumpeted in Washington. The Quartet, and notably the EU within it, twisted and turned in order to reignite American interest in mediation. The Quartet's early efforts regarding Palestinian reform and the Roadmap were as much (if no more) aimed at Washington than at the conflict parties. The vagueness of many of the conditions of Palestinian reform and commitments in the Roadmap were testimony to the fact that the prime purpose of these initiatives was to 'baby-sit' the peace process, i.e. maintain the semblance of a diplomatic process while waiting for the principal mediator – the US – to reengage in the Israeli-Palestinian conflict. Yet for the US in those years, the Quartet was paradoxically a useful means simply to give the impression that it was engaging in the peace process without substantively committing to it.[5]

This changed with the second Bush administration, and, thereafter under the Obama administration without, however, altering the dynamics of the Quartet (de Soto, 2007). Since 2005–6, the US reengaged in the Israeli-Palestinian conflict. In so doing, its approach towards the Quartet changed, but not in a manner that supported a true multilateralization of mediation.

The US engaged more actively in the Quartet, but viewed it as a means to legitimize its unilateral efforts, while conveying the message that Washington was committed to multilateralism.[6] Rather than the Quartet moulding American policy, the US used the Quartet to legitimize its own preferences. To America, the Quartet provided the ideal international forum to share the responsibility for failure and for supporting any eventual success in peacemaking. In 2005, the Quartet's endorsement of Sharon's disengagement plan reflected the US's support for the plan.[7] In the best of interpretations, disengagement was a spectacular *fuite en avant*: Sharon's leapfrogging of the Roadmap to its second phase. The Quartet scrambled to set conditions that cast disengagement within the Roadmap. But despite Sharon's neglect of these conditions, the Quartet, pressed by the US, backed disengagement and established an apposite Office to support it. Wolfensohn was, in fact, initially meant to act as the US envoy on disengagement. It was only upon insistence by the UN Secretary General and the EU, that Secretary of State Condoleezza Rice accepted that he should be the Quartet's Envoy. Wolfensohn painfully cobbled together the November 2005 Agreement on Movement and Access. But not only did Secretary of State Rice step in at the eleventh hour, elbowing aside the Quartet Envoy, she also unilaterally brokered last-minute changes to the agreement as the Quartet watched on the sidelines. Even starker is the way in which the US persuaded the Quartet to endorse its unilateral preferences regarding Hamas. The Quartet could have followed a 'common but differentiated approach' towards the new Palestinian government, concomitantly exerting pressure on Hamas without cutting all ties to it (de Soto, 2007). But rather than pursuing this track, the US led the Quartet to toe its line, by relying both on persuasion as well as by threatening to review the US contribution to the UN budget lest the Quartet followed its approach (de Soto, 2007: 18). Finally, the appointment of Tony Blair as Quartet Representative in 2007 also highlighted the US's unilateral instincts. The former British prime minister may have been seen as a unilateral European victory. In fact, Blair, while close to the Bush administration, was viewed with scepticism in many European quarters in view of his role in Iraq. Russia was also deeply opposed to the former British leader, in view of the cooling of British–Russian relations after the November 2006 Litvinenko affair. Blair's appointment was, in fact, a unilateral American choice. The Bush administration proceeded without consultation with its Quartet partners. Contacts took place between London and Washington, highlighting as much a failure in transatlantic as in British–EU dialogue (Moller and Hanelt, 2007).

The Quartet also represented an ideally informal framework for the US, which provided multilateral legitimacy to the peace process, without casting it within the 'straightjacket' of international law. Two examples highlighting this function of the Quartet were in February 2011 and September 2011. In February, when the US vetoed a UNSC resolution condemning Israeli settlements in the OPT, it called for such condemnation by the Quartet instead. The Quartet was viewed as a convenient means to provide the impression of multilateral action, without the baggage of international law that comes with it.[8] In September 2011, the US's virulent opposition to the PLO's quest for recognition of Palestine's statehood at the UN was accompanied by Washington's push for the Quartet to restart negotiations between the parties. Here again, the Europeans happily took the bat from Washington. Unlike the US, Europeans were not wholly opposed to the UN's recognition of Palestinian statehood. In fact, the EU was characteristically divided on the question. But in view of Washington's adamant rejection of the PLO's UN bid and its stark preference for political negotiations over a legal recognition of a Palestinian state, the EU reunited over its convenient support for the 'peace process', aiming, but failing, to restart negotiations through the Quartet in the fall of 2011.

In fact, when mediation efforts have taken place since 2006, they have excluded the Quartet. In May 2007, the Quartet 'welcomed' the bilateral summits between Israeli Prime Minister Ehud Olmert and Palestinian President Mahmoud Abbas, but played no role in them. Quartet members were present at the November 2007 Annapolis conference. But neither did it play a role in bringing the conflict parties together in Annapolis, nor did it mediate between them in the negotiations that ensued. What became known as the Annapolis process – between November 2007 and the Israeli military offensive on the Gaza Strip in December 2008 – was an all-American show: a last ditch attempt by President Bush to deliver on the protracted Middle East conflict. The same can be said of the attempted resumption of Israeli–Palestinian negotiations between March and September 2010. The Quartet welcomed US President Barack Obama and his Special Envoy George Mitchell's efforts to re-launch negotiations in 2010, first through proximity talks and then through direct negotiations. But Washington was in the lead and never indicated its intention to broaden mediation to its fellow Quartet members.

Perhaps even more striking is the fact that other mediation activities in the Arab–Israeli conflict have been conducted unilaterally by non-Quartet members. Here we can cite the mediation effort by Saudi Arabia to broker a Palestinian National Unity Government in March 2007; the Egyptian-mediated ceasefire between Israel and Hamas between June and December 2008; Turkey's mediation efforts between Israel and Syria between March and December 2008; and post-Mubarak Egypt's mediation of a Palestinian national reconciliation in April 2011. In all these instances of Middle East mediation, the Quartet took note and welcomed, but was entirely absent from frontline developments.

An ineffective cure to Middle East mediation?

The Quartet may not have become a genuinely multilateral forum for the mediation of the Middle East conflict. But has it been effective? And effective with respect to what? The EU's goal to promote effective multilateralism has, embedded within it, a fundamental ambiguity. What precisely is supposed to be effective? Are the methods, procedures and lines of communication within the multilateral forum supposed to be effective, or should multilateralism be effective vis-à-vis the substantive policy goal it has set out for itself? In what follows we shall assess effectiveness with respect to the content of the policy goal itself, i.e. in this case, the contribution to promoting a two-state solution in Israel-Palestine.

Here again, the answer is unambiguously negative. Over the last decade, the Quartet's activism and paperwork has been impressive. Yet, as aptly put by former European Commissioner Chris Patten (2006), its work has been largely 'virtual'. With Israel's occupation deepening, violence following its internal logic of ups and downs, and the PA being kept alive by foreign funds, the Quartet's work has been theoretical. At worst, it has been counterproductive, widening the gap, already present during the Oslo years, between the international diplomatic process and facts on the ground.

As revealed over the 1990s, the PA's governance was wanting. Yet neither did the Quartet effectively respond to this problem, nor was Palestinian reform the most pressing challenge in the spiral of the second intifada. On the one hand, the Quartet's focus on reform failed to engender a genuine transformation of the PA. Under the Quartet's supervision, the PA consolidated its budget lines into a Single Treasury Account, created a Palestinian audit system, ratified the Law on the Independence of the Judiciary, passed a Basic law, established the post of Prime Minister, and conducted local elections. But on the whole, results were disappointing. Reforms on paper often failed to translate into changes on the ground (Tocci, 2007b). Precious little was done to induce reconciliation between the Palestinian factions, in retrospect ushering the way for the political split between the Hamas-led Gaza Strip and Fateh-led West Bank five years later (Tocci, 2007a). The Quartet may not have been able to prevent all these outcomes. But the strong political colouring of the Quartet's reform work in 2002–4 by President Bush's insistence on the removal of

Arafat impaired its ability to work effectively on this dossier. On the other hand, all the focus on Palestinian reform was excessive in the broader dynamics of the Israeli–Palestinian conflict. A well-functioning PA is no doubt a fundamental element of a Palestinian–Israeli agreement. But not only was (and is) such a settlement far from sight. In the dark days of 2002–3, the Quartet's single-minded focus on Palestinian reform was a distraction from the most pressing developments on the ground – the cycle of violence, the humanitarian crisis and the eroding prospect of a viable Palestinian state.

Similar critiques can be made of the Roadmap. The Roadmap had many of the necessary elements for progress towards a just solution of the conflict. However, the Roadmap never got off the ground (Nabulsi, 2004). The problem was, on the one hand, that the Roadmap's phases lacked clear conditions with measurable benchmarks, and on the other hand, that the Quartet failed to put in place adequate mechanisms to monitor progress and induce compliance. Alongside this, unlike the Palestinians, the Israelis accepted the Roadmap with 14 reservations, which eroded its key principles of parallelism, monitoring and a clear endgame. In turn, the Roadmap remained on paper as the parties never moved beyond its fateful first phase. As stated by former UN Secretary General Kofi Annan (2006):

> we must admit our own weaknesses, and we have been too hesitant in emphasizing those very elements that most distinguish the roadmap from the Oslo process – parallelism, monitoring, and clear end goals. It is no surprise that today we find ourselves once again deadlocked.

As the decade progressed, the ineffectiveness of the Quartet persisted. The persisting ineffectiveness of the Quartet was evident in its efforts regarding disengagement. Wolfensohn's mandate to revitalize the Palestinian economy through, *inter alia*, the implementation of the AMA remained unfilled. Following the Quartet policy towards Hamas, the Envoy resigned, well aware that the accomplishment of his mandate had been transformed from difficult to impossible. Ineffectiveness also characterized the Quartet's policy towards Hamas. The principles imposed by the Quartet failed to deliver. Neither did the Quartet induce Hamas's moderation through its formal renunciation of violence or disavowal of its Charter. Nor did it trigger Hamas's defeat. Years passed and Hamas remained in control first of the OPT and, after June 2007, of the Gaza Strip. The Quartet's tough line on Hamas did have an impact, however. It hindered Palestinian good governance and democracy. After May 2006, the rising levels of international assistance, beyond leading to a paralysed PA and a deepening humanitarian crisis, also entailed the de-development of Palestinian governance. The by-passing of official institutions with the exception of the Presidency led to a re-centralization of power in the hands of Abbas and generated an increasingly unaccountable and opaque management of available PA funds, despite progress made on both counts in the three previous years. The effects of de-development were starkest in Gaza, where Israel's increasing closures post-disengagement alongside the absence of a functioning PA, pushed the

Gaza Strip into chaos and lawlessness, with the emergence of mafia-style gangs and al-Qaeda-like cells, which flourished from 2006 up until the Hamas takeover in June 2007 (International Crisis Group 2007, 2008). The Quartet's stance on Hamas also harmed the prospects for intra-Palestinian reconciliation. It put the spanner in the works of the short-lived NUG in the spring of 2007 and of intra-Palestinian reconciliation since then. It is precisely an implicit admission of this failure that has underpinned the EU and the UN's cautiously favourable response to the intra-Palestinian agreement reached in April 2011, and again in February 2012.[9] It is also a recognition of this failure that has led the Office of the Quartet Representative's to interpret the Quartet's approach to Hamas as goals rather than preconditions to be met in practice by the future Palestinian government.[10]

Alongside a lack of effectiveness, the Quartet also began losing international credibility. The Quartet's stance towards Hamas, and consequently its approach towards the West Bank, culminating in the appointment of Tony Blair as the Quartet's Representative, marked the steady decline in the Quartet's international credibility. When the Quartet transformed its principles vis-à-vis Hamas into preconditions, which were almost designed to be rejected, its credibility foundered. Furthermore, had the Quartet insisted solely on the renunciation of violence – not only in words, but above all in deeds – its conditionality may have retained widespread international legitimacy. Unlike the condition on violence, the other two principles rested on far shakier political and legal grounds. Hamas was called on to recognize Israel, despite the fact that only states (or at most the PLO as the legal representative of the Palestinians, of which Hamas is not part, and which has recognized Israel) recognize other states and that the borders by which Israel would be recognized are undefined. Likewise, it is the PLO that has negotiated and signed previous agreements with Israel, and Hamas has accepted that it would be the PLO that would continue to perform this role. The situation worsened after 2007. The Quartet, having called for reconciliation between Fateh and Hamas, refused to alter its stance towards the PA following the NUG agreement in March 2007, despite Hamas's apparent readiness to moderate its positions.[11] Thereafter, the Quartet continued to display the somewhat paradoxical position of bemoaning the situation in the Gaza Strip, while doing little to reverse it. Blair's work increased the Quartet's credibility problem, both because of the West Bank first policy that he has pursued, and because of the image that Blair himself has in the Arab world (Moller and Hanelt, 2007). The ineffectiveness and lack of credibility of the Quartet was further reconfirmed in 2011–12, both with the failed attempt to restart negotiations after the PLO's statehood bid at the UN, and with the absence of the Quartet in the more successful attempts by Egypt and Qatar at securing intra-Palestinian reconciliation, an objective which the Quartet has openly professed but practically worked against.

Conclusions

In view of the above, former UNSG Representative Alvaro de Soto's overall assessment of the Quartet was scathing:

> The Quartet has become a sideshow: because it is as much about managing transatlantic relations as anything else, it is only partly about the Middle East, it isn't a very apt mechanism for solving the Israeli-Palestinian conflict, and other members don't necessarily use it for that purpose.
>
> *(de Soto, 2007)*

Despite its potential as the ideal N-group to multilateralize mediation of the protracted Arab–Israeli conflict, the Quartet has failed both to represent a genuine multilateral endeavour and to pursue effective policies in relation to the conflict.

Such a damning assessment of the Quartet as an effective multilateral mediation forum raises the question: should we be judging the Quartet according to different benchmarks? If not, do we risk throwing the baby out with the bathwater? Some have argued that rather than viewing the Quartet as a multilateral mediation forum, it should rather be seen as a 'multilateral control framework', a consultation mechanism, or as a 'forum for transatlantic coordination on the Middle East' (Moller and Hanelt, 2007; Musu, 2010). Furthermore, its effectiveness may be assessed not simply in terms of its contribution to a two-state solution, but also of its efforts at reengaging the US in the peace process, setting the record in reaction to developments on the ground, and establishing the contours of a solution. Indeed one can argue that without the Quartet, the parties' unilateral actions and the US's unilateral mediation would have lacked any form of multilateral control and consultation. The Quartet can certainly be viewed as a useful multilateral framework in which the EU and the US, alongside the UN and Russia can act, react and interact (rather than mediate) on the thorny Middle East dossier. This is certainly a worthy asset.

Yet this chapter has pointed out how, as it stands, the Quartet has gone beyond this. By engaging in policy-making, adopting political positions beyond those clearly enshrined in international law and acting as an alternative to international law, the Quartet's balance sheet has been negative: it has failed to engage in effective multilateral mediation, while providing a multilateral fig leaf for dynamics that have remained quintessentially unilateral (and at most bilateral) in character, and which have rarely served the goal of promoting peace in the Middle East. As argued by a former UN official, the Quartet could play a useful role as a 'contact group' on the Middle East peace process.[12] It could act as a forum to establish a renewed international consensus regarding the way forward in the Arab–Israeli conflict, a laboratory to test international positions that could ultimately find expression through the United Nations.[13] This would entail stepping back from policy formulation as such, and limiting itself to serving as a regular multilateral consultation mechanism to maximize synergies in the foreign policies of its members. In this respect and in the context of a gradual move away from *pax americana* in the Middle East, one could also see the value of extending the Quartet to others, such as Egypt, Saudi Arabia, Qatar and Turkey, which have played a role in the peace process. If the purpose of the Quartet is reviewed to render this forum genuinely multilateral and effective in promoting a solution to the protracted Arab–Israeli conflict, then its ideal N-group may well need to be rethought as well.

Notes

1 Conversation with senior EU official, May 2011.
2 Conversation with former senior UN official, May 2011.
3 A phrase often repeated by Palestinian officials, academics and civil society leaders in meetings in Jerusalem, Ramallah and Gaza City since 2002.
4 Conversation with the author, Brussels, November 2005.
5 Conversation with US-based analyst, June 2011.
6 Conversation with US-based analyst, June 2011.
7 The US's support for the disengagement plan was reflected in President Bush's 'letter of assurances' to Israeli Prime Minister Sharon in April 2004 suggesting that, in the framework of a final settlement, the US would be ready to accept concessions such as the annexation of key settlements in the West Bank and the denial of the right of return to Palestinian refugees, See http://www.mfa.gov.il/MFA/Peace+Process/Reference+Documents/Exchange+of+letters+Sharon-Bush+14-Apr-2004.htm (accessed 13 August 12).
8 Barak Ravid, 'U.S. pushing Palestinians to drop UN resolution on settlement construction', *Ha'aretz*, 17 February 2011.
9 'Europe More Open than US on Palestinian Reconciliation Deal', *al Jazeera*, 24 April 2011. Online. Available: http://www.aljazeerah.info/News/2011/April/29%20n/Europe%20More%20Open%20than%20US%20on%20Palestinian%20Reconciliation%20Deal.htm (accessed 13 August 2012).
10 Conversation with officials of the Office of the Quartet Representative Tony Blair, May 2011.
11 In particular by agreeing to 'respect' (rather than 'accept') previous agreements and publicly acknowledging the existence of the State of Israel and committing to the two-state solution on several occasions. See 'Text of Mecca Accord for Palestinian coalition government', *Haaretz*, 8 February 2007; and Conol Urquhard (2007) 'Hamas official accepts Israel but stops short of recognition', *Guardian*, 11 January; Orly Halpern (2007) 'Experts Question wisdom of boycotting Hamas', *Forward*, 9 February.
12 Conversation with the author, May 2011.
13 Conversation with US-based analyst, June 2011.

References

Annan, K. (2006) 'Report of the Secretary General on the Middle East', 11 December, S/2006956, http://daccess-dds-ny.un.org/doc/UNDOC/GEN/N06/651/88/PDF/N0665188.pdf?OpenElement
Asseburg, M. (2003) 'From Declarations to Implementation? The Three Dimensions of European Policy Towards the Conflict', in M. Ortega (ed.) *The EU and Crisis Management in the Middle East*, Chaillot Papers, No. 62, Paris, EUISS
De Soto, A. (2007) 'End of Mission Report', *The Guardian*, http://www.guardian.co.uk/frontpage/story/0,,2101676,00.html

Douma, W. (2006) 'Israel and the Palestinian Authority' in S. Blockmans and A. Lazowski (eds) *The European Union and its Neighbours A legal Appraisal of the EU's Policies of Stabilisation, Partnership and Integration*, The Hague, Asser Press, pp.437–9

Emerson, M. and Tocci, N. (2002) *The Rubik Cube of the Wider Middle East*, Brussels, CEPS.

Euro-Mediterranean Human Rights Network (2009) *Active but Acquiescent: EU Response to the Israeli Military Intervention in the Gaza Strip*, Copenhagen, EMHRN

European Commission (2008) European Neighbourhood Policy – The Occupied Palestinian Territory, MEMO/08/213, Brussels, 3 April 2008, http://europa.eu/rapid/pressReleasesAction.do?reference=MEMO/08/213&format=HTML&aged=0&language=EN&guiLanguage=en

European Council (2003) *A Secure Europe in a Better World. European Security Strategy*, Brussels. 12 December, http://ue.eu.int/pressdata/EN/reports/78367.pdf

International Crisis Group (2007) 'After Mecca: Engaging Hamas', February 2007, http://www.crisisgroup.org/home/index.cfm?id=1271&l=1

International Crisis Group (2008) 'After Gaza', August 2008, http://www.crisisgroup.org/home/index.cfm?id=1271&l=1

Le More, A. (2005) 'Killing with Kindness: Funding the Demise of the Palestinian State', *International Affairs*, Vol. 81, No. 5, pp. 981–99

Middle East Quartet (2002a) Joint Statement by the 'Quartet', 10 April 2002

Middle East Quartet (2002b) Joint Statement by the 'Quartet', 16 July 2002

Middle East Quartet (2004) Statement on Israeli-Palestinian Peace Process, 4 May 2004

Middle East Quartet (2005a) Statement by the Middle East Quartet, 9 May 2005

Middle East Quartet (2005b) Quartet statement on Palestinian Legislative Council Elections, 28 December 2005

Middle East Quartet (2006a) Quartet statement on Palestinian elections, 30 January 2006

Middle East Quartet (2006b) Quartet statement on the New Palestinian government, 30 March 2006

Middle East Quartet (2007a) Statement by Middle East Quartet, 21 March 2007

Middle East Quartet (2007b) Statement by Middle East Quartet, 27 June 2007

Middle East Quartet (2010) Statement by Middle East Quartet, 21 June 2010

Moller, A. and Hanelt, C. P. (2007) 'Tony Blair needs a Plan. Suggestions for the Working Agenda of the New Representative of the Middle East Quartet', *CAP Aktuell*, No. 10, July, Berlin, Bertelsmann

Musu, C. (2007) 'The Madrid Quartet: An Effective Instrument of Multilateralism?', ISA, 48th Annual Convention, Chicago, 28 February

Musu, C. (2010) 'The EU Strategy for the Middle East Peace Process in the Post-9/11 Era', in *European Union Policy towards the Arab-Israeli Peace Process: The Quicksands of Politics*, Basingstoke, Palgrave Macmillan, pp. 63–79

Nabulsi, K. (2004) 'The Peace Process and the Palestinians: A Road Map to Mars', *International Affairs*, Vol. 80, No. 2, pp. 221–31

Office of the Special Envoy for Disengagement (2006), *Periodic Report*, April

Oxfam (2007) 'Poverty in Palestine: the Human Cost of the Financial Boycott', *Briefing Note*, April, http://www.oxfam.org/en/files/bn070413_palestinian_aid_boycott.pdf/download

Patten, C. (2006) *Not Quite the Diplomat*, London, Penguin Books

Prendergast, K. (2006) 'Interview with Sir Kieran Prendergast, Former UN Under-Secretary-General for Political Affairs', *The Fletcher Forum of World Affairs*, Vol. 30, No. 1, pp. 61–74, http://fletcher.tufts.edu/forum/archives/pdfs/30-1pdfs/prendergast.pdf

Sayigh, Y. and Shikaki, K. (1999), *Strengthening Palestinian Public Institutions*, Task Force Report, Council of Foreign Relations, New York

Tocci, N. (2007a) 'What Went Wrong? The Impact of Western Policies towards Hamas & Hizbollah', *CEPS Policy Brief* No. 135, July 2007, Brussels, http://shop.ceps.eu/BookDetail.php?item_id=1523

Tocci, N. (2007b) 'The Widening Gap between Rhetoric and Reality in the Israeli-Palestinian Conflict', in *The EU and Conflict Resolution*, London, Routledge

United Nations (2006) *Assessment of the Future Humanitarian Risks in the Occupied Palestinian Territory*, 11 April

14

CONCLUSION

The EU and effective multilateralism

Caroline Bouchard, Nadia Klein, John Peterson and Wulf Reiners

A rich variety of perspectives on multilateralism in the twenty-first century, and the European quest to make it effective, have featured in this volume. If there is one point of agreement between them, it is that demand for multilateralism is rising in the twenty-first century, not least because it promises to help manage both shifts in geopolitical power as well as the externalities of globalisation. Rising demand is evident in the extension of multilateralism beyond the traditional policy areas of trade and security, with multilateral agreements emerging in the areas ranging from climate change, health, energy, migration, conflict resolution and fiscal policy coordination. The European Union (EU) has been a very active player in all of these areas. As Lazarou *et al.* argue in Chapter 3, 'the EU's explicit focus on promoting "effective multilateralism" in Europe and beyond designates it as the principal advocate of multilateralism in the 21st century'. But a central question – addressed by all contributors to this book – remains: does the EU *deliver* on its commitment to effective multilateralism, however 'effective' is defined?

This volume was conceived with two main objectives: first, to shed new light on twenty-first century multilateralism. Our contributors have sought to do so either by genuinely conceptualising it as a distinctive form of international cooperation or by generating empirical knowledge on the practice of multilateralism – in key policy areas, geographic regions and multilateral settings. Second, our authors have aimed to determine whether, how and to what extent the EU contributes to the promotion of effective multilateralism. To address these objectives, this volume has investigated five main questions:

1. How should we understand multilateralism and is there a specific 'European way' of multilateralism?
2. How should 'effectiveness' be defined?

3. Is the European Union well tailored to promote effective multilateralism, however that is defined?
4. Does the EU live up to its ambitions to contribute to effective multilateralism globally and in a variety of policy areas?
5. What policy lessons can be drawn from the EU's contribution to the promotion of effective multilateralism?

This chapter revisits these questions and reviews the main findings of the volume. It reflects on how and to what extent research generated in a comprehensive research programme on the EU's contribution to promoting effective multilateralism, such as the MERCURY project,[1] has elaborated and clarified forms of multilateralism, and developed specific theses about how and when the Union embraces multilateralism, or not. It considers how the EU has employed multilateral instruments to pursue its interests and objectives. It also explores the effects of the EU's commitment to effective multilateralism in its engagement with other regions and strategic partners, and the impact of its external relations on formal and informal forms of multilateral organisations. Finally, we suggest directions for future research.

Multifaceted multilateralism in the twenty-first century

One of this volume's main preoccupations has been to understand, elaborate and clarify forms of multilateralism. As a number of its chapters have highlighted, multilateralism is now an indispensable as well as an ineradicable part of international relations. Yet, it still lacks conceptual clarity. While the concept of multilateralism has evolved significantly since 1945, multilateralism continues to be mainly understood as what it is not: unilateralism or bilateralism. In fact, a number of cases explored in this book suggest that the European Union betrays its commitment to effective multilateralism when it resorts to unilateral or bilateral actions. Two questions thus arise. First, is the EU committed to a fundamentally ambiguous objective (which, because of such ambiguity, it finds it easy to embrace in principle)? Second, is its commitment to multilateralism only skin deep?

Conceptualising multilateralism

The problem of conceptual clarity has been confronted squarely. In Chapter 2, Peterson and Bouchard stress that – while no single, accepted definition of multilateralism exists – multilateralism is more than just a sub-set of international cooperation. It has several main dimensions that set it apart from other forms. They include:

*   the importance of rules;
*   inclusiveness in terms of the parties involved or affected; and
*   voluntary cooperation that is at least minimally institutionalised.

In many ways, multilateralism became a form of cooperation with more legitimacy than other forms in the twentieth century because of systemic changes. It was embraced both because it could be inclusive and have rules that could be applied differently to international actors with varying degrees of power. Yet, multilateralism was also shaped through history by changes at the sub-systemic level of domestic politics, thus raising questions about how much purely systemic theories of international relations can explain changes – sometimes dramatic ones – in how IR is conducted.

As Peterson and Bouchard show, aspirations to advance multilateralism exist in different forms, including in aspirant and crystallised varieties that are not fully formed, let alone fully institutionalised, thus sometimes pointing towards tomorrow's possible multilateralism more than today's existing multilateral cooperation. Various new forms of multilateralism have also been identified throughout this volume. They range from 'multilateralism 2.0' featuring a more diverse set of multilateral organisations, a stronger role for non-state actors, new linkages between policy domains, and more citizen involvement (see Van Langenhove 2010), to a form of cooperation that is more demanding in nature and necessitates more concessions on the part of states, including major powers (see Ikenberry 2003; 2006; 2009; 2011).

Multilateralism is also defined in different ways in different parts of the world. In the past, most of the EU's partners have applauded a more active role for the Union in international politics, even if only to balance the influence of the US. But, in the current international order, Europe's partners do not necessarily share the EU's understanding of 'effective multilateralism' as put forward in the European Security Strategy (ESS). Emerging powers have embraced different meanings of what multilateralism entails and how it should be operationalised. For example, China and Russia's support for multilateralism is strictly selective, based on strategic or purely pragmatic concerns. It also excludes any type of outside intervention in any state's domestic affairs. Even in the US, the most important partner in the EU's pursuit of effective multilateralism, multilateralism is viewed differently by different political tribes and its meaning can vary greatly between US administrations. Despite the lack of a common understanding of the concept, numerous contributors to this book argue that multilateralism remains an attractive option for international cooperation.

The virtues that the multilateral approach is claimed to possess inevitably have prompted debates on the goals that lead states to embrace multilateralism, as well as ones about the compatibility of multilateralism with other forms of ordered relations between states, including regionalism and 'mini-lateralism'. Can multilateralism be effective even if states have different goals for cooperation? Is multilateralism always preferable to other forms of cooperation, such as minilateralism, especially if alternative forms might be more effective? Is the pursuit of 'normative multilateralism' – inclusive, with common rules for all participants, voluntary and institutionalised – necessarily to be prioritised above the question of the effectiveness of multilateralism? Is the EU compromising its commitment to creating an effective multilateral system, when it adopts a bilateral or minilateral approach to protect its security and interests? Debates remain open on most of these questions. But this volume clearly demonstrates that deep tensions exist between the EU's commitment to multilateralism as a value and the effectiveness of this distinct form of international cooperation.

Effective multilateralism

The concept of 'effective multilateralism' was embraced by the EU as a 'strategic objective' because the 'development of a stronger international society, well-functioning international institutions and a rule-based international order' were – and are – widely viewed in Europe as desirable outcomes (ESS 2003: 10). Hill and Peterson argue in Chapter 4 that the EU's commitment to effective multilateralism reflects its status as the most successful regional organisation in that it is the most significant attempt ever made at the coordination of national diplomacies. Yet, as stressed repeatedly in this book, the concept of effective multilateralism to this day lacks clarity. While a clearer conceptualisation or formulation of the concept would directly impact (and arguably improve) its promotion and implementation, it appears that the EU has adopted as a primary objective of its external action a vision of IR that is fundamentally ambiguous.

All the chapters in this book, to various extents, have explored the question of effectiveness. Tocci, in Chapter 13 on the EU and the Middle East Quartet, assessed effectiveness with respect to the content of the policy goal itself; that is, in the case of the Quartet, to multilateralism's contribution to promoting a two-state solution in Israel-Palestine. Other authors including Klein *et al.* in Chapter 5 have focused on Laatikainen and Smith's (2006) assessment of effectiveness. Looking at the specific context of EU–UN relations, Laatikainen and Smith have suggested that the EU's effectiveness in multilateral contexts has four different dimensions.

A first dimension, *internal* effectiveness, relates to the willingness of the EU member states to act collectively and put forward clear EU 'output'. *External* effectiveness, a second element of the EU's effectiveness, relates to the Union's influence on other actors, but also to its role as a leader or 'frontrunner', and to other states' perception of the EU as a unitary and influential actor. A third dimension of effectiveness is linked to the EU's contribution to the effectiveness of international organisations and the Union's role in strengthening these organisations' capacity to act. The fourth dimensions considers the UN's own effectiveness and whether the UN truly influences international relations.

Based on the evidence presented in this book, it is clear that the EU has yet to develop specific criteria to evaluate its own contribution to the effectiveness of multilateralism. Thus, it will continue to struggle to identify areas where it can and must improve its commitment to building an effective multilateral system.

The European Union's experience of multilateralism

This volume's contributions have demonstrated that the EU's experience of multi-lateralism is not typical but also not unique in International Relations. As Lazarou *et al.* show in Chapter 3, multilateralism is a focal point for European foreign policy. It is often presented in official EU foreign policy discourse as a means towards the effective achievement of specific goals and the construction of a 'better world'. Lazarou *et al.* demonstrate that multilateralism constitutes a key feature of the EU's approach to various areas of external relations including security, trade, climate change, migration and development.

The effective multilateralism advocated by the EU is principles-based and is considered an essential tool for delivering on Europe's responsibility to work for a more peaceful, cooperative international order. Multilateralism can thus be seen as doctrine, an explicit set of principles that justify the pursuit of defined ends, using specific means for action. However, considering the complex nature of the EU, our authors acknowledge that the interpretation and implementation of the doctrine – which remains, in any case, vague – may vary among EU member states. This lack of consistency on principles and the practice of the doctrine may directly affect the effectiveness and, to a certain extent, the usefulness of multilateralism.

Hill and Peterson stress in Chapter 4 that multilateralism has two faces: one within a given group of states, and another facing outwards as a group engages with other groups and international organisations. In other words, in the case of the EU, before it starts acting vis-à-vis third parties in multilateral contexts, it has already done a significant part of its multilateral homework, namely by coordinating and adapting the positions of its 27 member states. It is important to keep in mind this two-faceted multilateralism – first within the Union, then outwards – when assessing the EU's contribution to effective multilateralism. An exclusive focus on the EU's external effectiveness in multilateral settings would ignore the preced-ing internal coordination process and its own contribution to a more cooperative international order.

This volume has also focused on the question of whether the EU's own expe-rience of multilateralism automatically makes it a stronger actor in multilateral settings. It has found that significant tensions exist between the Union's aspirations to be a multilateral actor and the proclivity of EU actors – European institutions and member states – who are using multilateral institutions to pursue their own agenda and defend their interests. The question thus remains whether the consti-tutional and institutional set-up of the Union, as well as its policy instruments, are well tailored to promote effective multilateralism in the first place.

A tool kit for Europe's 'multilateral mission'

Contributions in this book have focused on the institutional framework of the EU's multilateral mission in various fields of external action, including external trade, energy, development, migration, and foreign and security policy. They also have analysed how the Union organises itself to try to influence outcomes in multilateral settings including the UN and the G20. As shown in detail in different chapters, the actual relevance of institutional factors for the multilateral action of the EU – both in terms of policy-making and polity-shaping – varies significantly.

In his chapter, Damro characterises the Union as 'Market Power Europe', which is able to upload economic and social market-related policies and regulatory measures to the international level. Thereby, he highlights two important points of debate about the EU's contribution to multilateralism. The first refers to the goals of Europe's external action. The externalisation of market-related policies in multilateral settings often sees the Union acting successfully to defend its economic advantage but rarely defending, objectively and altruistically, its doctrinal commitment to multilateralism. This finding is supported by the analysis of the legal output of the EU in the field of external trade carried out by Klein *et al.* in Chapter 5. The authors find that protectionist anti-dumping duties are the most frequently cited instruments with a reference to a multilateral framework, namely the General Agreement on Tariffs and Trade and the World Trade Organization. Yet, the very use of these instruments is in stark contrast to the notion of free trade that lies at the heart of GATT/WTO.

The second point of debate underlined by Damro's conceptualisation of a Market Power Europe is about the style of policy-making (see Chapter 6). He argues that the EU can and does use not only persuasive but also coercive means to achieve its policy goals. Given the importance of the single market, third states find it difficult not to adapt to the Union's economic and social regulations. Such an exercise of power, which may occur as intentional or unintentional behaviour according to Damro, suggests the EU is more prone to wielding coercive means and tools than has been suggested by other conceptualisations of the EU as a power.

In particular, Damro's argument puts into question the explanatory power of the Normative Power Europe concept as developed by Ian Manners (2002). For him, the normative basis or identity of the EU mainly accounts for its behaviour at the international level. By contrast, Damro's contribution raises questions about the meaning of 'effective multilateralism' when the Union behaves internationally. On the one hand, the concept usually refers to synergy effects generated by (the EU's) cooperative behaviour vis-à-vis other international actors – for example, by cooperating with the United Nations or NATO in the field of security policy. This understanding of 'effective' fits well with various concepts of the EU as an international actor, including the Normative Power Europe concept. On the other hand, seen strictly from a European perspective, multilateralism can be regarded as effective when multilateral settings such as the WTO allow the EU effectively to push for its own policy goals and material interests. For Damro, these interests are defined mainly via competition between European interests.

Crucially, the impact of a Market Power Europe may not be limited to the field of economic and social regulations. By linking its international relations to its market power, the EU may even be able to expand its role in non-market areas, such as climate change. Yet, the translation of market power into (negotiation) power in other policy fields is by no means an automatic process, as illustrated by Bo *et al.* in their examination of the EU's unsteady relationship with China in global climate governance (see Chapter 10).

Klein *et al.* (in Chapter 5) also consider the EU's approach to multilateralism in terms of effectiveness and the style of policy-making. They use a concept of effective multilateralism that focuses on the EU's *institutional architecture* for multilateral action, as well as on the actual use of the treaty provisions, and thus offer a different perspective on the Union's attempts and ability to live up to its multilateral ambitions. Their analysis focuses on the EU's structural set-up for the internal coordination of the European position as well as the EU's external representation. It shows that the Union significantly facilitates common positions in the area of trade within multilateral forums such as the WTO. The central role of a single institutional actor – the European Commission – with an exclusive right of initiative, a leading role during negotiations, and the responsibility for dispute settlement actions on behalf of EU member states, allows for an extraordinary level of coherence. In contrast, when it comes to the Common Foreign and Security Policy, the Union is less well equipped to act multilaterally. The EU appears less unified and complements rather than substitutes for national policy-making. In the light of the pressing need for improvements, the Lisbon Treaty offers a full set of innovations for EU external action ranging from the modified position of the High Representative and the External Action Service to the full-time President of the European Council. These institutional innovations can also be expected to have an impact on the EU's institutional effectiveness, over time, in multilateral settings including, as argued by Pirozzi *et al.* in Chapter 11, on the process of reforming the UN Security Council.

In contrast to these rather optimistic expectations, Rommerskirchen identifies a 'growing competition' between EU institutions in the G20 context. She states that to date – including since the adoption of the Lisbon Treaty – inter-institutional rivalry has hampered the EU's ability to present 'a unified front on fiscal policy issues' (see Chapter 12). Furthermore, she argues that 'the EU has been most successful when acting in tandem with one of its G20 member states'. One might conclude that the Union as such, or representatives from different EU institutions, has been able to influence the set-up of the G20 or the negotiations on fiscal coordination only at the margins without the support of at least one dedicated EU member state.

Competition between EU actors in the form of clashing national policies and institutional preferences, and the limited articulation and inconsistent pursuit of common goals and rules are also visible in the fields of EU energy and migration and development policies. As Colombo and Abdelkhaliq demonstrate in Chapter 7, the EU's energy and migration policies in the Mediterranean area show that (potential) forms of multilateralism are often not institutionalised and bilateralism remains the dominant form of cooperation. As for the EU's development policy, Fioramonti (Chapter 9) reveals that, in the case of Africa, a divided and complex institutional set-up and the absence of a clear framework of common principles according to which the EU and its member states would each implement their policies, can be identified as major challenges to effectiveness in terms of (policy goal) multilateralism.

At this point, it is important to stress once more the methodological challenge involved in evaluating the relevance of institutional factors vis-à-vis other factors, such as EU member states' interests and external pressures from other great powers. In particular, there is a lack of data available in the literature on possible linkages between the structural set-up of the EU and its multilateral action. The MERCURY project has tried to address this lack. Thus, as the chapter by Klein *et al.* shows, the strongly diverging institutional set-ups of external trade policy, on the one hand, and foreign and security policy, on the other, are also reflected to a certain extent in the respective legal output linked to multilateral action. While more than 80 per cent of the legal acts analysed in the area of the Common Commercial Policy refer to a multilateral legal basis, the respective share for CFSP usually ranges between 71 and 80 per cent since the adoption of the Nice Treaty. By confirming the link between the structural capacity to act multilaterally and a higher level of actual multilateral legal output, Klein *et al.* underline the relevance of institutional factors for EU multilateralism. Overall, EU trade policy can be regarded as more multilateralised than the foreign and security policy. However, both cases illustrate that the EU shows impressive commitment to multilateralism at the conceptual level and that it is indeed capable of producing a high degree of multilateral legal output in different policy areas.

To summarise, the evidence presented in this book confirms that the EU combines various approaches to multilateralism. Hence, the desire for multilateralism might find different expressions in different policies with an external dimension. One general observation is that analyses of the Union in multilateral contexts can benefit from differentiation between the internal institutional set-up of the EU, on one hand, and the institutional design of the (EU-external) multilateral forum with which the Union interacts, on the other.

The contributions to this volume have clearly shown that there is no single, shared understanding of what Europe's global multilateralism objectives are or should be, neither among member states, nor among member states and EU institutions, nor among the Union's institutions, nor among different EU external policies. Yet, it is clear that there is a strong commitment to multilateralism and international institutions in the EU Treaties and it has been re-enforced with every major revision. Furthermore, the institutional set-up for European foreign policy-making has been rapidly built up and restructured, with the general aim of making the European Union more effective, coherent and better equipped to act multilaterally, regardless of what its objectives are or how 'effective' is defined.

The power argument

When it comes to the implementation of multilateral solutions, however, the picture is mixed. The de facto promotion and appreciation of multilateral solutions and institutions is not always in line with the Treaties' general imperative for multilateralism. As shown in the contributions by Damro and Fioramonti, the EU promotes multilateral forums such as the WTO if they can be employed in the EU's interest to push its own agenda. But the question remains whether asymmetrical power constellations, following the EU's economic/trade/market powers, can lead to the kind of multilateralism promoted in the Union's Treaties. If multilateral partners, for instance the EU and sub-Saharan African countries during the negotiations on Economic Partnership Agreements (EPA), are 'by and large' not equal, then we witness a *de facto* application of unilateralism under the guise of multilateralism. At the same time, several chapters have shown that the EU prefers bilateral means even if a multilateral framework is provided.

The institutionalist argument

As for the institutional dimension of the EU external multilateral setting, the Union clearly has more difficulty engaging with weakly institutionalised forums. A clear institutional set-up as exemplified by the WTO dispute settlement procedure allows the EU and its member states internally to adapt to the external environment and to set up adequate structures and procedures to be 'good at multilateralism'. In turn, if a multilateral forum is less institutionalised, and in flux such as the G20, the EU (as a whole) faces significant difficulties in seeking to make effective contributions and defining its internal set-up to contribute effectively.

It becomes apparent that the main reason for the promotion of more institutionalised forms of multilateralism by the EU is connected to challenges deriving from the Union's own internal multilateralism. If the external multilateral environment is in flux or multilateral negotiations are evolving quickly, the Union has difficulty showing the necessary flexibility to get its foot in the door and to have a strong impact. In contrast, if the external multilateral environment is stable and negotiations are following established procedures, the EU can equip itself adequately. Consequently, it does not come as a surprise that the European Union promotes multilateral set-ups at the international level that mirror its own deep and established 'internal' multilateralism.

When analysing the connectedness of the *external* environment that the EU confronts with the degree of institutionalisation of the Union's *internal* multilateralism, however, the time dimension has to be taken into account. When facing an external framework long established before the EU entered the arena, the stickiness of the set-up makes it difficult for the Union to become a full player, even if the external multilateralism is strongly institutionalised and the EU has had time to equip itself. In other words, the Union struggles to develop a strong position and representation in established multilateral forums which are usually tailor-made for nation states in terms of membership and voting rights. This observation is best exemplified by the United Nations system, where differing ideas of multilateralism and national interest among EU actors (institutions and member states) add further complexity to the picture as in the case of the debate on the reform of the Security Council. We clearly are not close to the point at which the British and French (let alone the German and Italian aspirants) would be willing to vacate their permanent (or aspirant) seats on the UN Security Council to allow the EU to occupy a collective, European seat. One interpretation of this state of affairs would highlight the limits of the European Union's commitment to effective multilateralism.

The balanced argument

Clearly, the EU is good at writing multilateralism into its Treaties. Equally, it is bad at implementing a shared vision of multilateralism externally. One important reason why is because external EU policies co-exist with the national policies of its member states, which can act at cross-purposes to or even undermine EU policies entirely.

However, the EU is good at employing 'one' multilateralism for its own purposes if backed by power asymmetry. That is, it embraces multilateralism when it wields disproportionate power over other participants within the system for cooperation that is created. Here, as Peterson and Bouchard argue in Chapter 2, is multilateralism that is effective because it advances the EU's interests. Yet, the path from asymmetric multilateralism to outright unilateralism is a short one, and sometimes the former can obscure European behaviour that smacks of the latter. Moreover, as much as Europeans claim that the EU's Strategic Partnerships are designed to coax other powers to embrace multilateralism, they illustrate that the Union is good at ignoring its own commitment to multilateralism if bilateralism serves its needs better.

Finally, the contributions to this volume have shed light on the conditions under which the EU finds itself able to deliver effective multilateralism, however that is defined. If the Union is bad at EU internal multilateralism in a given area, it is bad at external multilateralism, too. Rommerskirchen's focus on the EU in the G20 (Chapter 12) shows that internal divisions within Europe over how to respond to the Eurozone crisis made its stances in multilateral diplomacy to cope with the global economic crisis less than credible.

Equally, however, even if the EU is good at organising its own internal multilateralism, the Union can still be bad at building external multilateralism. External trade policy, as Hill and Peterson suggest (in Chapter 4) is a case in point. The EU's own, internal system for coming to common positions is, arguably, a well-oiled machine that works well most of the time. That, however, has not prevented it from engaging in behaviour that was – again, arguably – shameful in negotiating a Trade, Development and Cooperation Agreement with South Africa or pushing former Lomé Convention states towards embracing European-style multilateralism even when it was clearly not the preferred option for many of them. Thus, effective internal multilateralism seems a necessary condition for the EU being an effective purveyor of external multilateralism. It is, however, not a sufficient condition. Other factors such as power constellations and the degree of institutionalisation of multilateral forums are also decisive. As we have seen, all else being equal, the EU is far better at engaging with more institutionalised forms of multilateralism than with less institutionalised forms. Its ability to show leadership in prodding crystallising or aspirant multilateralism to proper, tangible, institutionalised multilateralism is thus limited.

Ambitions and delivery: engagements with other regions

Institutions and different degrees of institutionalisation clearly matter in the EU's quest for effective multilateralism. Relatedly, how effective is it in 'exporting' its own, (generally and comparatively) highly institutionalised internal multilateralism to other regions of the world? As Karen Smith (2008: 76) notes, '[f]ostering regional cooperation is the oldest of the foreign policy objectives' in the EU's policy arsenal.

This volume has examined the EU's relations with its own neighbourhood, Africa and Asia. All are critically important regions and (potential) partners in terms of both EU interests and global order more generally. What all of these cases seem to suggest is that Telò (2001) is right that – as Smith (2008: 11) paraphrases – '[t]he EU's promotion of regionalism can succeed if [only] it interacts with deeply structural trends – if members of other regional groupings are autonomously pushing towards regional cooperation'. Moreover, they suggest that other, more immediate European goals can trump or take priority over the building of regional multilateralism.

Two contributions have focused on states in Europe's neighbourhood: those in the Mediterranean region (Chapter 7), and Georgia and Bosnia (Chapter 8). Colombo and Abdelkhaliq present evidence based on EU energy and migration policy cooperation with the Mediterranean region. Both are crucial issues to the EU's more general strategy for incorporating internal European policy objectives into external multilateral frameworks. Broadly speaking, the EU can be viewed as a truly multilateral actor in the Mediterranean region. A variety of European stakeholders are actively engaged in seeking to realise the Union's agreed objectives in the region and their continued engagement may well determine whether those objectives are achieved. Yet, the Arab Spring exposed the EU's bias towards preserving the status quo in the region: the Union never pulled the policy strings it possessed that would have allowed it to punish Mubarak's Egypt or Ben Ali's Tunisia for human rights abuses. It also exposed the limits of EU internal multilateralism, especially its (still very) intergovernmental CFSP.

In Georgia and Bosnia, as Weiss *et al.* show (in Chapter 8), the EU can claim to have played a major role in helping both countries and affected parties to resolve their conflicts. However, there have been significant differences in terms of impact and the Union's engagement with both states has varied as other foreign policy issues have risen on Europe's agenda. Weiss *et al.* show that the EU's efforts to resolve conflicts through multilateral means have been hampered by internal European disagreements on tactics and strategy. European engagement, at various times, has been unilateral, bilateral and multilateral in nature. There have also been times when its attention has strayed and it has been almost entirely inactive in engaging with these states. In both cases, the EU has been far more active in supporting the multilateral activities of other organisations, but far less so in showing leadership of its own. That point extends to the question of showing leadership in promoting regional cooperation, in the Caucasus and Balkans as well in the Mediterranean.

Then there is EU external action in Africa and Asia. In Africa, the European preference for Economic Partnership Agreements (EPA) has the potential to result in new multilateral frameworks that are consistent with global trade reforms. As Fioramonti demonstrates (in Chapter 9), these circumstances give the EU a chance to reaffirm its leadership in Africa, and particularly to export European habits of cooperation to former European colonies. However, no significant achievements in building African regional cooperation have been realised. Europe stands accused of neglecting African development concerns in the process. The EU's pursuit of EPAs with African groupings could plausibly be viewed as revealing its inability to rethink its relationship with Africa beyond the classical categories of dependence and dominium, while Europe hides behind the benevolent image it seeks to project under the category of 'partnership'.

In the case of Asia, Bo *et al.* (in Chapter 10) focus on only one of many external policy issues – climate change – and just one of the EU's many Asian partners: China. As such, it must fall to others to offer a broad judgement about Europe's contribution to, and engagement with, what scholars of Asia have begun to term the region's 'new multilateralism' (Calder and Fukuyama 2008; Green and Gill 2009). Still, climate change forms a litmus test for both the EU and China. Without a major effort on the part of both towards a global agreement to curb emissions, there can be no solution to what is arguably the most pressing, urgent and difficult international problem. With other major players – such as the US, India or Russia – either unable or unwilling to offer leadership, Europe and China have the potential, at least, to set the agenda on climate change by narrowing their own differences on the key component issues of an overall multilateral agreement.

Bo and colleagues demonstrate that bilateral cooperation between the EU and China on such issues has been impressive, but has generally not been 'uploaded' to multilateral negotiations on climate change post-Kyoto. In particular, they show that Europe and China approached the 2009 Copenhagen Conference with different expectations and negotiating strategies that led to clashes between them both during and after the conference. The problem seems not only one of insufficient communication but also basic differences of view, especially on the question of what should be the responsibilities of developing countries in a global agreement. Moreover, the EU and China confront divergent, basic challenges to make themselves credible players on climate change. For Europe, the challenge is to show capacity for leadership towards a comprehensive agreement, a test it dismally failed at Copenhagen. Meanwhile, China remains on trial accused of being unable to be a responsible and active player on climate change.

More generally, Hill and Peterson (in Chapter 4) consider the EU's contribution to so-called 'third generation regionalism' as well as evidence that a multilateralism 2.0 is emerging, featuring multilateral regional groupings that see themselves 'as fully fledged actor[s] in the theatre of international relations' (Van Langenhove and Costea 2007: 81). They find the EU's contribution to a new multi-regional global order – which, in a sense, moves a step beyond even Ikenberry's (2006) 'new multilateralism' – to exist mostly in the aspirant urgings of those who, at one time anyway, foresaw a 'New European Century' unfolding (see Chapter 4). Similarly, multilateralism 2.0 seems an attractive normative proposition more than an emergent, empirical international order.

To be clear, in engaging with other regions, the European Union always wields its own demonstration effect. It has the potential to coax other states to mimic its own multilateral habits of cooperation and, more narrowly, to export its own internal policy agreements and expand their scope and scale in the form of broader multilateral cooperation. Yet, a prior condition appears to be step-level advances in the actorness of regional cooperation organisations, particularly on the part of the EU's regional counterparts but also on the part of the Union itself (Doidge 2011). Meanwhile, in the here and now of the twenty-first century's second decade, Allen and Smith (2012: 162) strongly suggest that 'the impact of the crisis within the Eurozone [has had a] corrosive effect on a broader range of EU external policy activities [and] has arguably become one of the key limiting factors on the EU's international role and status'. It seems that the Union has considerable work to do on its own internal multilateralism before it can lead and convince others to embrace a new, multiregional global order.

Ambitions and delivery: the EU in multilateral contexts

Several chapters in this volume have explored the EU's interaction with both formal and informal institutional settings, including the United Nations, the WTO, NATO, the G20 and the Middle East Quartet. On the one hand, as we have seen (in the second section), some authors – Damro, Klein *et al.*, Pirozzi *et al.*, Rommerskirchen – have examined the EU's internal institutional framework and how it influences the EU's behaviour in multilateral settings.

On the other hand, Pirozzi *et al.*, Bo *et al.*, Rommerskirchen, and Tocci (also, in some cases) have opted to focus specifically on the EU's impact on international organisations. This latter group of contributors have examined whether and how the Union creates an effective multilateral system by strengthening international law, reinforcing existing international organisations, and building new international institutions. Pirozzi *et al.* examine the impact of the EU on a formal organisation: the United Nations. They assess whether and how Europe promotes the consolidation of a collective security culture within the UN by examining the EU's contribution to the reform of its main body, the UN Security Council. Rommerskirchen, Tocci, and Bo *et al.* turn their attention to cases of crystallising forms of multilateralism – the

G20, the Middle East Quartet and the global climate change regime – in which international cooperation is not yet fully institutionalised. Their focus is on the EU's role in developing the emerging rules of these organisations.

All of these authors offer significant insights on the EU's role in building and strengthening international organisations. In general, they have found that while the Union is, in principle, committed to all the previously mentioned objectives, it also has an obligation to defend its own interests in multilateral settings. This balancing act remains a challenging one for the EU, especially as enlargement to a Union of 27 member states has made it more difficult to act coherently and tactically in multilateral contexts. It thus has struggled to have a significant impact on international organisations.

To assess the impact of the EU in multilateral contexts, most contributions to this volume have considered questions of the Union's leadership and persuasion roles, its function as a source of ideas, and its capacity to act. The EU's potential as a rallying point for other actors and even as a model for other regional organisations and the evolution of regionalism within the multilateral system have also been examined. Not surprisingly, this collection demonstrates that the EU's impact on multilateral organisations, both formal and informal, varies considerably. The Union's level of ambition in its contributions to cooperation with and within international organisations also fluctuates depending on the questions at stake. The EU has high ambitions in some policy areas; in others, its aspirations appear more subdued. Europe's impact on international relations and its contribution to multilateralism also appear intrinsically linked to questions of the EU's own effectiveness, both internal and external, in multilateral settings. Its actorness continues to vary between issue areas and international forums, thus raising issues of coordination, cohesiveness and representation, and leadership.

Coordination, representation and cohesiveness

The EU's contribution to effective multilateralism is directly affected by its ability to act as a cohesive and unified actor in multilateral settings: simply put, the Union is in a better position to promote effective multilateralism when it speaks with one voice or when different European voices deliver the same message. EU member states have largely agreed on the necessity of defining the underlying principles and general objectives of the EU's external action in a way that not only makes it clear to European citizens, but also to Europe's partners in multilateral settings. Agreeing these principles and objectives, it was thought, would facilitate the definition of common interests and an EU strategy to defend them. Yet, finding a common voice in an EU of 27 remains a difficult task. Numerous episodes in recent years have highlighted the Union's member states' struggles to present a united front.

The EU has responded to criticism of a lack of coherence and unity in the messages that it sends to other international actors by focusing on the question of representation. 'Who speaks for Europe' continues, to this day, to generate vigorous debates both within the EU and in multilateral settings. One of the aims of the

Lisbon Treaty was to enhance the Union's international profile and performance by increasing the visibility of its external representation. To achieve these goals, the Treaty replaced the rotating European Council Presidency with a permanent one. It also enhanced the role of High Representative of the Union for Foreign Affairs and Security Policy, and created a European External Action Service (EEAS). The implementation of the Lisbon Treaty is still in its early days at our time of writing: even though it was formally launched in January 2010, it was clearly still finding its feet by late 2012. Moreover, the cases of the joint EU representation of the Presidency and the European Commission in addition to five EU member states at the 2010 G20 Summit in Seoul, plus various representations of the European Union around the table at UN Security Council, illustrate that problems related to the cohesiveness of the EU's message, and its multiple representations, have the potential to linger. New institutions – whatever level of public administration at which they are created: national, international or sub-national – inevitably require time to carve out and assume their intended role.

As we have argued, in the second section (above), if the EU is to focus on the issue of representation, it must also improve its internal coordination on foreign policy issues. Better internal coordination will undoubtedly have positive effects on the Union's chances of delivering a coherent message. A single messenger – or 'mouth' as Lamy puts it (see Rommerskirchen's Chapter 12) – may increase Europe's visibility in international organisations. But it will not fully compensate for inconsistent messages coming from the EU.

This lack of a common message continues to generate confusion for the EU's partners in multilateral settings. This confusion affects not only their willingness to join forces with the EU in promoting multilateral solutions. It also directly influences the Union's ability to lead in multilateral settings and sway crucial international players in the direction of European positions. In fact, both in formal or informal organisations, the EU's leadership capacity appears to be directly linked to its internal effectiveness in terms of coordination, representation and cohesiveness.

Leader, bridge-builder, implementer

In their chapter (11), Pirozzi et al. show that, while EU member states have agreed on the need to reform the UN and supported rebalanced regional representation within the UN framework, they have never been able to champion a common European position on key issues on reform of the Security Council. In fact, EU member states have repeatedly failed to coordinate their national positions on the crucial questions of the reform of veto rights and the size of membership of the Security Council. As the most integrated regional organisation, the EU is considered by others to be in a prime position to advocate a greater representation for regional organisations in the UN Security Council. Pirozzi et al. suggest that the Union could potentially rally other regional organisations such as the African Union to promote an approach based on 'regional multilateralism' that would recognise the need for an enhanced role by regional players and put them at the centre of the collective security framework. This approach would encourage an interregional dialogue on security issues which could, in turn, strengthen the legitimacy of UN decision-making and thus contribute to the pursuit of effective multilateralism. However, as Pirozzi *et al.* demonstrate, the EU's current internal divisions on reform of the Security Council have prevented it from shaping the terms of negotiations and assuming leadership on the question of the role of regional organisations in the UN's main organ. Nevertheless, in the context of another UN body, the General Assembly, these authors appear more optimistic about the EU's contribution to the establishment of regionalism as a principle within a reformed UN system. Again, assuming the European Union can get its own internal act together in its external policy, Europe has the potential to show leadership towards a genuine 'multilateralism 2.0'.

Given the existing state of the EU, is Europe successful in exercising leadership in informal multilateral settings where rules and dynamics have yet to be settled and may be influenced more easily? Rommerskirchen (see Chapter 12) argues that, in the case of the G20, the EU attempted to exercise two types of leadership: structural and informational. She shows that the Union was much more successful in a structural leadership role than an informational one. The EU was able to convince other international actors to enlarge the G7/G8 structure, to shape the rules of conduct, to have some control over the agenda, and, in many ways, played the role of an 'architect of change' within the new organisation. However, it was far less successful in communicating key policy ideas and getting other actors to follow its lead on the issue of fiscal policy coordination. As we have seen, the EU's success in structural leadership was mostly due to its institutions, namely the European Commission, working in tandem with one of the Union's member states (France). In addition, efficient coordination between EU actors and the cohesiveness of the European message presented in G20 negotiations noticeably improved the EU's credibility as a structural leader. In contrast, the Union's failure to be an effective informational leader was largely due to disagreement among EU member states on fiscal issues and poor coordination of fiscal policy within the Union.

The cases of the Middle East Quartet and climate change offer other perspectives on the EU's leadership. In both cases, the EU struggled to assert a leadership role and, thus, to build a stronger, rules-based multilateral order. In fact, the EU has been mostly unsuccessful in transforming both the climate change regime post-Kyoto and the Middle East Quartet from crystallising forms into institutionalised forms of multilateralism.

Bo *et al.* (Chapter 10) argue that the EU failed to 'reinforce' the rules of the climate change regime. It was not only unsuccessful in influencing negotiations in Copenhagen, but was also completely left out of crucial meetings. According to Tocci (Chapter 13), the Middle East Quartet has yet to become a genuinely multilateral organisation or an effective mediation forum in the Arab–Israeli conflict. Despite the EU driving efforts to mould the Quartet and add a multilateral dimension to the organisation, the Quartet remains essentially unilateral (or bilateral) in character and has not been effective in pursuing progress towards the goal of a two-

298 C. Bouchard, N. Klein, J. Peterson and W. Reiners

state solution in the Middle East. Yet, as Tocci argues, despite not becoming a truly multilateral forum, the Middle East Quartet has fulfilled one of its objectives: it has maintained US involvement in the peace process.

The EU might not have been a successful 'front-runner' in many cases explored in this volume. But it has played other roles that may become significant in developing a stronger multilateral international order. Following the disastrous results in the climate change negotiations in Copenhagen, the EU decided to rebrand itself as a bridge-builder. This new role appears to have helped the Union's efforts to be perceived as a crucial actor in UN-led climate change that followed talks, and thus allowed it to regain a certain influence on this crucial issue. But, it remains to be seen whether (and how long) the EU will be satisfied with playing this role.

Tocci (in Chapter 13) also demonstrates that the EU's role in the Quartet can be described, at times, as an 'implementer': the Union has provided essential resources to support the forum's work in encouraging negotiations between the main players. With this crucial role in the Quartet, the EU has the potential to shape the future of this forum. The Quartet may not necessarily become an institutionalised form of multilateralism, but may rather become a consultation forum that effectively tests international positions that could, in due course, be productively discussed at the United Nations.

Based on the evidence presented in this volume, one last observation can be made on the EU's role in formal and informal organisations. The European Union unquestionably needs the support of other international actors to promote effective multilateralism successfully. As we have emphasised earlier, the EU must also recognise that different international actors may have different understandings of multilateralism and how it should be operationalised. Incorporating how other international actors, including its own member states, view multilateralism has to become a significant part of the EU's reflection when it seeks to have impact on international organisations. Understanding how its own member states, its closest international partners, as well as emerging powers understand multilateralism may be one of the most significant stepping stones in the EU's quest to revitalise multilateralism in the twenty-first century.

Conclusion

One of the most important recent contributions to scholarship on multilateralism, published just as MERCURY began, was Keohane et al.'s (2009) article in the leading IR journal *International Organization*. Its main focus was on the conditions under which multilateralism could promote democracy in states that participated in it. Its main claim was that it identified the empirical conditions under which multilateralism led to net gains in democratisation. More broadly, the authors urged that IR scholars should make multilateralism the focus for a research programme that was 'deeply empirical' and based on 'comparative institutional analysis' (Keohane et al. 2009: 28). MERCURY generally – and this volume specifically – have engaged in precisely such a research programme. By no means have we either answered all questions about multilateralism that need to be answered, and we consider what some of those unanswered questions are (below). But, insofar as Europe's contribution to 'effective' multilateralism is concerned, we hope the IR academy finds that significant new light has been shed.

For a start, we have offered and worked with a new, modernised definition of multilateralism (see Chapter 2). It acknowledges that modern multilateralism involves more than just states and that NGOs, philanthropic foundations, multinational companies, industry associations and IOs – not least the EU – are major players in it. It must be voluntary, governed by norms and principles, and minimally institutionalised. Rules must exist, even if they may overweight the representation of powerful players or end up being bent to achieve some kind of compromise result (see Chapter 4). Whether multilateralism is a distinctive form of international cooperation may still be subject to debate. But the contributors to this volume all (with nuances) take the position that it does. IR scholars need to know when they encounter a case of it, and when they do not. We hope and even trust that the definition that guided the research presented in this volume helps them to do so more than those developed in the literature in the 1990s.

Second, we find little clear evidence of a specifically European way of approaching and 'doing' multilateralism. Of course, the EU's own internal multilateralism is distinctive and now time-honoured, if also subject to new and profound doubts about how effective it is. But the Union has yet truly to define a doctrine of multilateralism – or a set of guiding principles that facilitate coordination and legitimisation – for its external policy (see Chapter 3). There are a myriad of reasons why, but two stand out as particularly powerful.

One is that there is no one, single understanding of multilateralism in Europe. Differences between EU member states sometimes are about ends. To illustrate, post-war German foreign policy has always sought to strengthen international law as an end in itself (see Rittberger 2001). Germany was one of the most vocal member states advocating a shift in the EU's aid and trade policies away from supporting former European colonies and towards assisting the world's poorest countries in the mid-1990s (see Young and Peterson 2013). In contrast, the UK has traditionally been more circumspect about international law, as seen in domestic controversy about the European Charter of Fundamental Rights and its implications for the treatment of suspected terrorists (see Jackson 1997). In aid and trade policy, London has drifted away from prioritising former British colonies to viewing both aid and trade as tools to help realise wider foreign policy objectives (see Morrisey 2005).

But differences between EU member states about multilateralism, equally, can be about means. In the face of domestic protests, Germany abstained in a UN vote to authorise military action against Gadaffi's Libya in 2011, provoking fury in London, Paris and (especially) Washington. But Berlin supported the multilateral action in other ways, including by sending further troops and AWACS surveillance planes to Afghanistan to free up resources for NATO to deploy in Libya (Gady 2011; Spiegel Online 2011). The point is that, for Berlin, any multilateral action must first exhaust all other options before using force. For France and the UK, a dogged insistence on such a stance is senseless when a humanitarian crisis looms.

A second and related reason why no clear European doctrine of multilateralism exists is that, while there may exist a *Common* EU Foreign and Security Policy, Europe lacks a *single* foreign policy. Much of the disappointment with the CFSP globally after it was unveiled by the Maastricht Treaty stemmed from the misunderstanding – which was widely shared internationally – that it had somehow replaced national European foreign policies (see Hill 1994, 1998). Their continued existence means that different understandings in different EU national capitals inevitably persist.

Here, it is worth highlighting a profitable direction for future research. We still lack systematic evidence about how multilateralism is understood in different ways within the EU as well as beyond the European continent. Such evidence as does exist is presented in Chapter 2 (see also Bouchard and Peterson 2011). But a programme of research is needed that goes further and systematically examines how multilateralism is understood by other major powers, including the BRICS countries and the US, probably through extensive analysis of official statements and media reports, as well as elite and public opinion surveys, with some form of discourse analysis employed.

One unanswered question that could logically be tackled by such a programme of research is what it really means for multilateralism to be effective. This volume has considered (centrally, again, in Chapter 2) different ways in which it might be considered to be effective in the eyes of European policy-makers. We suspect that one reason why it was possible to designate it as a 'strategic objective' in the European Security Strategy is that care was taken *not* to be too precise about what 'effective' actually meant. Equally, we find it difficult to deny that the most important pathway to multilateralism that is viewed globally as effective is to reform existing international institutions to give greater representation to emerging powers. An EU that clings to a meaning of effective as forms of multilateralism that simply advance European interests is one that destines it to increasing irrelevance in IR.

However 'effective' is defined, is the EU well-tailored to promote multilateralism globally? This volume has shown that, in a rich variety of ways, it is not. Again, a fundamentally intergovernmental CFSP, a trade policy that has become increasingly hard-nosed (see especially Chapters 4 and 6), and an aid policy that often works at cross-purposes to national European aid policies all limit the Union's capacity for collective action in promoting multilateralism, or anything else. And as we have noted in this chapter, the EU's own, recent, internal problems have had global consequences, with the Eurozone crisis both limiting the scope of its external ambitions and slowing global recovery from the Great Recession of the twenty-first century.

At the same time, the EU itself remains the apogee of multilateralism on a regional scale. There is plenty of evidence to suggest that the way out of the Great Recession – especially with the multilateral trade agenda stalled – is advances in regional economic cooperation. Throughout this volume, contributors have noted instances of genuine advances in regional cooperation in Africa, Asia and elsewhere. Another productive area for future research is to pinpoint, more precisely than existing research, the extent to which designers of multilateral agreements beyond European shores have taken lessons from the EU's experiences as well as how much Europe itself tangibly has encouraged such advances.

A final question concerns what policy lessons can be drawn from the EU's attempts to promote multilateralism both in other regions and globally. The question itself is so complex that, we would guess, no careful reader of this volume or even reviewer of all of the wider literature on the EU and multilateralism (especially, notably, Kissack 2010) could come up with a clear, unambiguous answer. Perhaps the best that we can do is to point to the virtues of an international order in which cooperation is institutionalised, there are clear rules that govern it (based on norms and principles), and all parties to it view it as legitimate. Multilateralism, as we have seen (above all in Chapter 4), is naturally unwieldy. The EU itself illustrates the point vividly. The end result of multilateral cooperation – with different levels of government or IOs working at duplicative or even at cross-purposes, with rules that are bent, with some policies giving with one hand while others take away with the other all matters of routine – is usually, ultimately, some kind of compromise. Usually, if not always, compromise in politics – perhaps especially IR – brings the greatest overall good to the greatest number of citizens. Or so it could be argued.

Note

1   See http://www.europa.ed.ac.uk/global_europa/external_relations/mercury

References

Allen, D. and Smith, M. (2012) 'Relations with the Rest of the World' in N. Copsey and T. Haughton (eds) *The JCMS Annual Review of the European Union in 2011*, vol. 50: 162–77.

Bouchard, C. and Peterson, J. (2011) 'Conceptualising Multilateralism: Can We All Get Along?', *MERCURY E-Paper*, 1, January, available from: http://www.europa.ed.ac.uk/global_europa/external_relations/mercury.

Calder, K. E. and Fukuyama, F. (2008) (eds) *East Asian Multilateralism: Prospects for Regional Stability*, Baltimore: Johns Hopkins University Press.

Doidge, M. (2011) *The European Union and Interregionalism: Patterns of Engagement*, Franham and Burlington VT: Ashgate.

ESS (2003) *A Secure Europe in a Better World: European Security Strategy*, Paris: European Union Institute for Security Studies, December 2003.

Gady, F.-S. (2011) 'Semantics and the German "Nein" in Libya', *Foreign Policy Journal*, 28 March, available from: http://www.foreignpolicyjournal.com/2011/03/28/semantics-and-the-german-nein-in-libya/ (accessed 25 November 2012).

Green, M. J. and Gill, B. (2009) (eds) *Asia's New Multilateralism: Cooperation, Competition, and the Search for Community*, New York: Columbia University Press.

Hill, C. (1994) 'The Capability-Expectations Gap, or Conceptualizing Europe's International Role' in S. Bulmer and A. Scott (eds) *Economic and Political Integration in the Europe: Internal Dynamics and Global Context*, Oxford and Cambridge MA: Blackwell, pp. 103–26

Hill, C. (1998) 'Closing the Capabilities-Expectations Gap?' in J. Peterson and H. Sjursen (eds) *A Common Foreign Policy for Europe? Competing Visions of the CFSP*, London and New York: Routledge.

Ikenberry, G. J. (2003) 'Is American Multilateralism in Decline?', *Perspectives on Politics*, 1 (3): 533–50.

Ikenberry, G. J. (2006) *Liberal Order and Imperial Ambition: Essays on American Power and World Politics*, Cambridge and Malden MA: Polity.

Ikenberry, G. J. (2009) 'Liberal Internationalism 3.0: America and the Dilemmas of Liberal World Order', *Perspectives on Politics*, 7 (1): 71–87.

Ikenberry, G. J. (2011) *Liberal Leviathan: the Origins, Crisis and Transformation of the American World Order*, Princeton and Oxford: Princeton University Press.

Jackson, D. W. (1997) *Britain Confronts the European Convention on Human Rights*, Gainesville FL: University Press of Florida.

Keohane, R. O., Macedo, S. and Moravcsik, A. (2009) 'Democracy-enhancing Multilateralism', *International Organization* 63 (Winter): 1–31.

Kissack, R. (2010) *Pursuing Effective Multilateralism: the European Union, International Organisations and the Politics of Decision-Making*, Basingstoke and New York: Palgrave.

Laatikainen, K.V. and Smith, K. E. (2006) 'Introduction – The European Union at the United Nations: Leader, Partner or Failure?', in K. V. Laatikainen and K. E. Smith (eds) *The European Union at the United Nations. Intersecting Multilateralisms*, Houndmills: Palgrave Macmillan: pp. 1–23.

Manners, I. (2002) 'Normative Power Europe: A Contradiction in Terms?', *Journal of Common Market Studies* 40(2): 235–58.

Morrisey, O. (2005) 'British Aid Policy During the "Short-Blair" Years' in P. Hoebink and O. Stokke (eds) *Perspectives on European Development Co-operation: Policy and Performance of Individual Donor Countries and the EU*, Abingdon and New York: Routledge.

Rittberger, V. (2001) (ed.) *German Foreign Policy Since Unification: Theories and Case Studies*, Manchester and New York: Manchester University Press.

Smith, K. E. (2008) *European Union Foreign Policy in a Changing World*, Cambridge and New York: Polity, 2nd edition.

Spiegel Online (2011) 'Merkel Cabinet Approves AWACS for Afghanistan', 23 March, available from: http://www.spiegel.de/international/world/germany-s-libya-contribution-merkel-cabinet-approves-awacs-for-afghanistan-a-752709.html

Telò, M. (2001) (ed.) *European Union and New Regionalism: Regional Actors and Global Governance in the Post-Hegemonic Era*, Aldershot and Burlington VT: Ashgate.

Van Langenhove, L. (2010) 'The Transformation of Multilateralism Mode 1.0 to Mode 2.0', *Global Policy*, 1 (3): 263–70.

Van Langenhove, L. and Costea, A.-C. (2007) 'The EU as a Global Actor and "Third Generation" Regionalism' in P. Foradori, P. Rosa and R. Cartezzini (eds) *Managing a Multilevel Foreign Policy*, Plymouth and Lexington MD: Lexington Books: pp. 63–86.

Young and Peterson (2013) '"We Care About You But…" the EU and the Developing World', *Cambridge Review of International Affairs*, (2) (June) forthcoming.

Index

Taylor & Francis

eBookstore

www.ebookstore.tandf.co.uk

Over 23,000 eBooks available for
individual purchase in Humanities,
Social Sciences, Behavioural Sciences
and Law from some of the world's
leading imprints.

*"An innovative
way of approaching electronic
books...Recommended."* – Choice

ALPSP Award for
BEST eBOOK
PUBLISHER
2009 Finalist
sponsored by

Taylor & Francis **eBooks**
Taylor & Francis Group

A flexible and dynamic resource for teaching, learning and research.

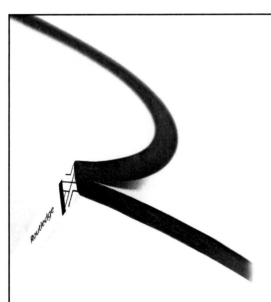

Routledge
Paperbacks Direct

Bringing you the cream of our hardback publishing at paperback prices

This exciting new initiative makes the best of our hardback publishing available in paperback format for authors and individual customers.

Routledge Paperbacks Direct is an ever-evolving programme with new titles being added regularly.

To take a look at the titles available, visit our website.

www.routledgepaperbacksdirect.com

 Routledge
Taylor & Francis Group

ROUTLEDGE PAPERBACKS DIRECT

ROUTLEDGE
Revivals

Are there some elusive titles you've been searching for but thought you'd never be able to find?

Well this may be the end of your quest. We now offer a fantastic opportunity to discover past brilliance and purchase previously out of print and unavailable titles by some of the greatest academic scholars of the last 120 years.

Routledge Revivals is an exciting new programme whereby key titles from the distinguished and extensive backlists of the many acclaimed imprints associated with Routledge are re-issued.

The programme draws upon the backlists of Kegan Paul, Trench & Trubner, Routledge & Kegan Paul, Methuen, Allen & Unwin and Routledge itself.

Routledge Revivals spans the whole of the Humanities and Social Sciences, and includes works by scholars such as Emile Durkheim, Max Weber, Simone Weil and Martin Buber.

FOR MORE INFORMATION

Please email us at **reference@routledge.com** or visit:
www.routledge.com/books/series/Routledge_Revivals

www.routledge.com

Routledge
Taylor & Francis Group